Translation: Sheldon Drzka

Lettering: Lys Blakeslee, Katie Blakeslee

LISELOTTE TO MAJO NO MORI Vol. 2 by Natsuki Takaya

First published in Japan in 2012 by HAKUSENSHA, INC., Tokyo.
English language translation rights in U.S.A., Canada and U.K. arranged with HAKUSENSHA, INC., Tokyo through Tuttle-Mori Agency, Inc., Tokyo.

Yen Press
1290 Avenue of the Americas
New York, NY 10104

Visit us at yenpress.com
facebook.com/yenpress
twitter.com/yenpress
yenpress.tumblr.com
instagram.com/yenpress

First Yen Press Edition: October 2016

Yen Press is an imprint of Yen Press, LLC.
The Yen Press name and logo are trademarks of Yen Press, LLC.

The publisher is not responsible for websites (or their content) that are not owned by the publisher.

Library of Congress Control Number: 2016936533

ISBN: 978-0-316-36022-7

10 9 8 7 6 5 4 3 2 1

BVG

Printed in the United States of America

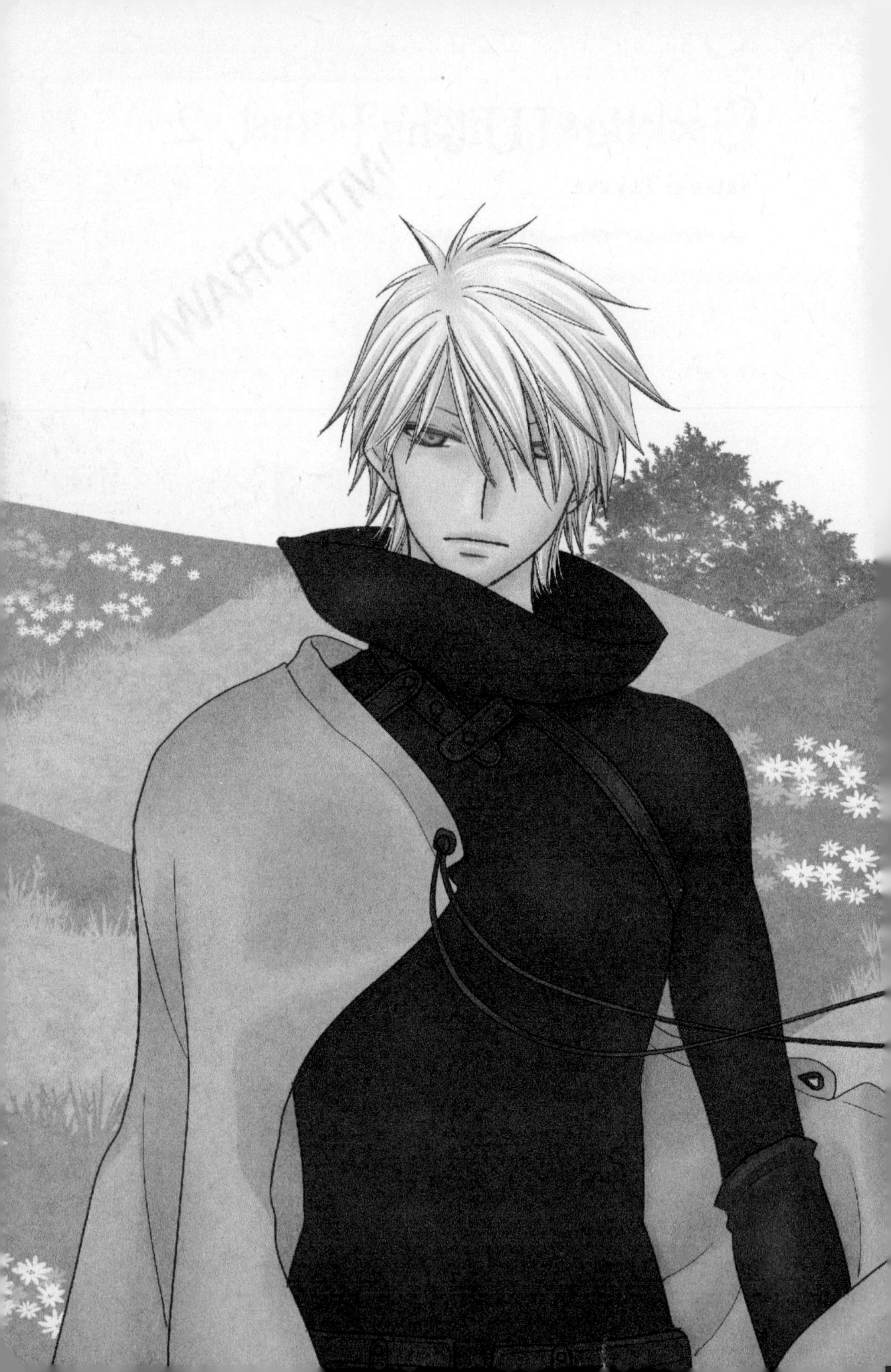

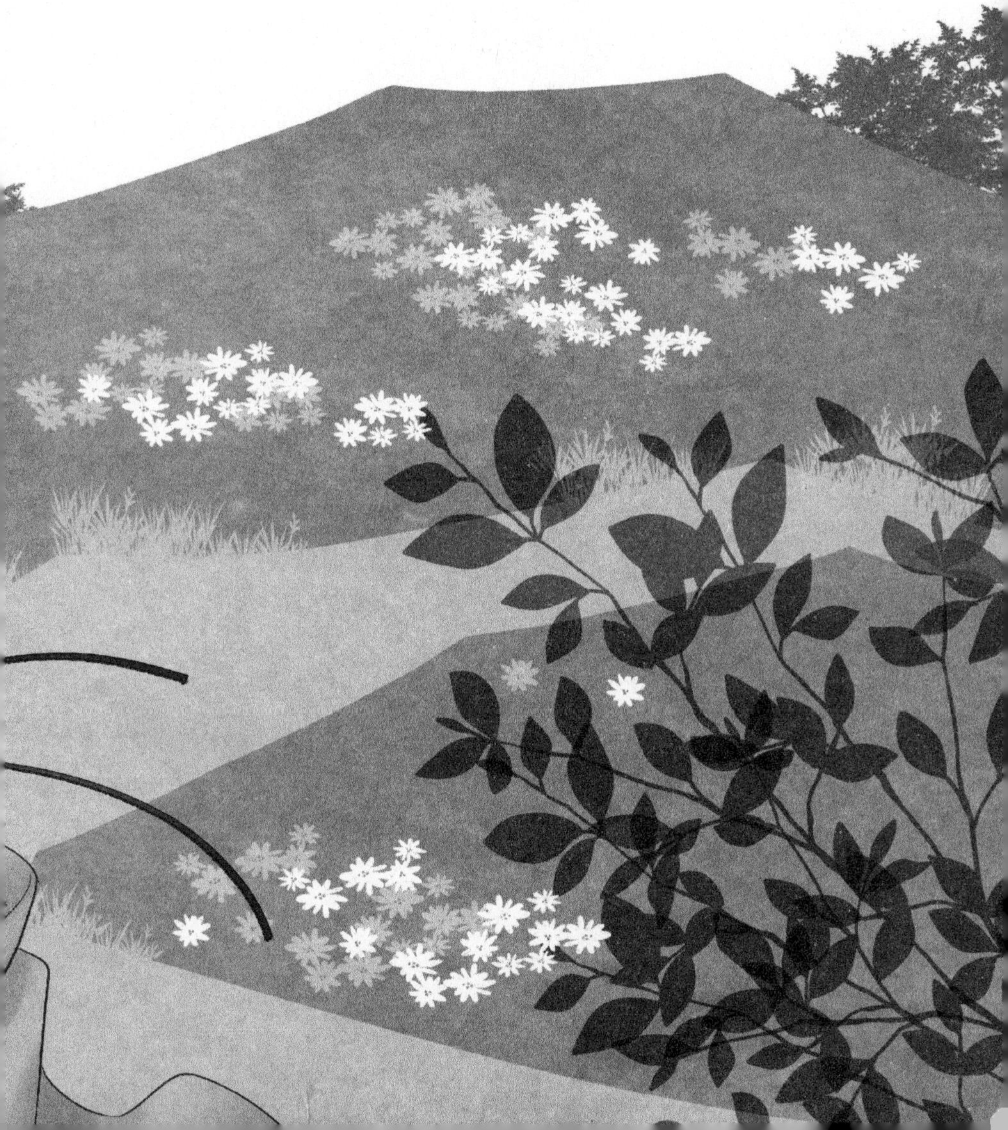

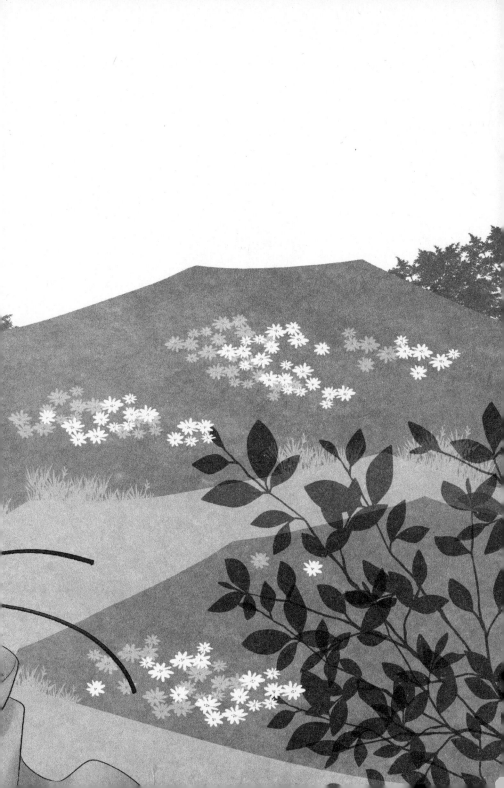

TRANSLATION NOTES

COMMON HONORIFICS

no honorific: Indicates familiarity or closeness; if used without permission or reason, addressing someone in this manner would constitute an insult.

-san: The Japanese equivalent of Mr./Mrs./Miss. If a situation calls for politeness, this is the fail-safe honorific.

-sama: Conveys great respect; may also indicate that the social status of the speaker is lower than that of the addressee.

-kun: Used most often when referring to boys, this indicates affection or familiarity. Occasionally used by older men among their peers, but it may also be used by anyone referring to a person of lower standing.

-chan: An affectionate honorific indicating familiarity used mostly in reference to girls; also used in reference to cute persons or animals of either gender.

Page 25
Ojou-san: *Ojou* is a formal word used for a proper young woman, usually wealthy or of high social standing. The term is also a respectful way to refer to another person's daughter as well as address her directly.

Page 54
Frikadeller: Danish flat, pan-fried minced meat dumplings.

Page 120
-dono: A very polite form of address, more formal than *-san*.

Page 182
The River Styx: The river in Greek mythology that forms the boundary between the living world and the underworld. Souls travel along it when passing into the afterlife.

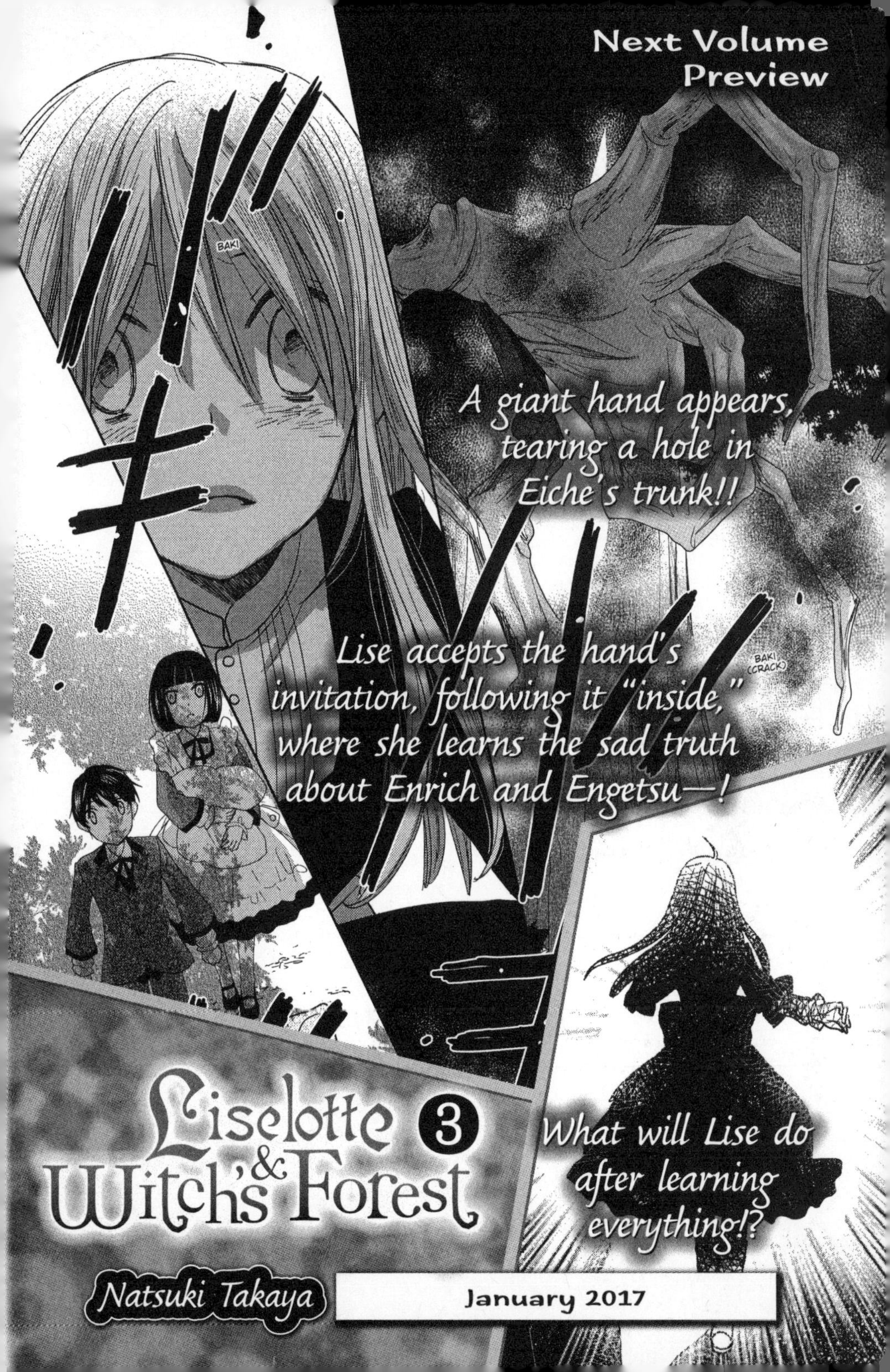
Next Volume Preview
A giant hand appears, tearing a hole in Eiche's trunk!!
BAKI
Lise accepts the hand's invitation, following it "inside," where she learns the sad truth about Enrich and Engetsu—!
BAKI (CRACK)
What will Lise do after learning everything!?
Liselotte & Witch's Forest 3
Natsuki Takaya
January 2017

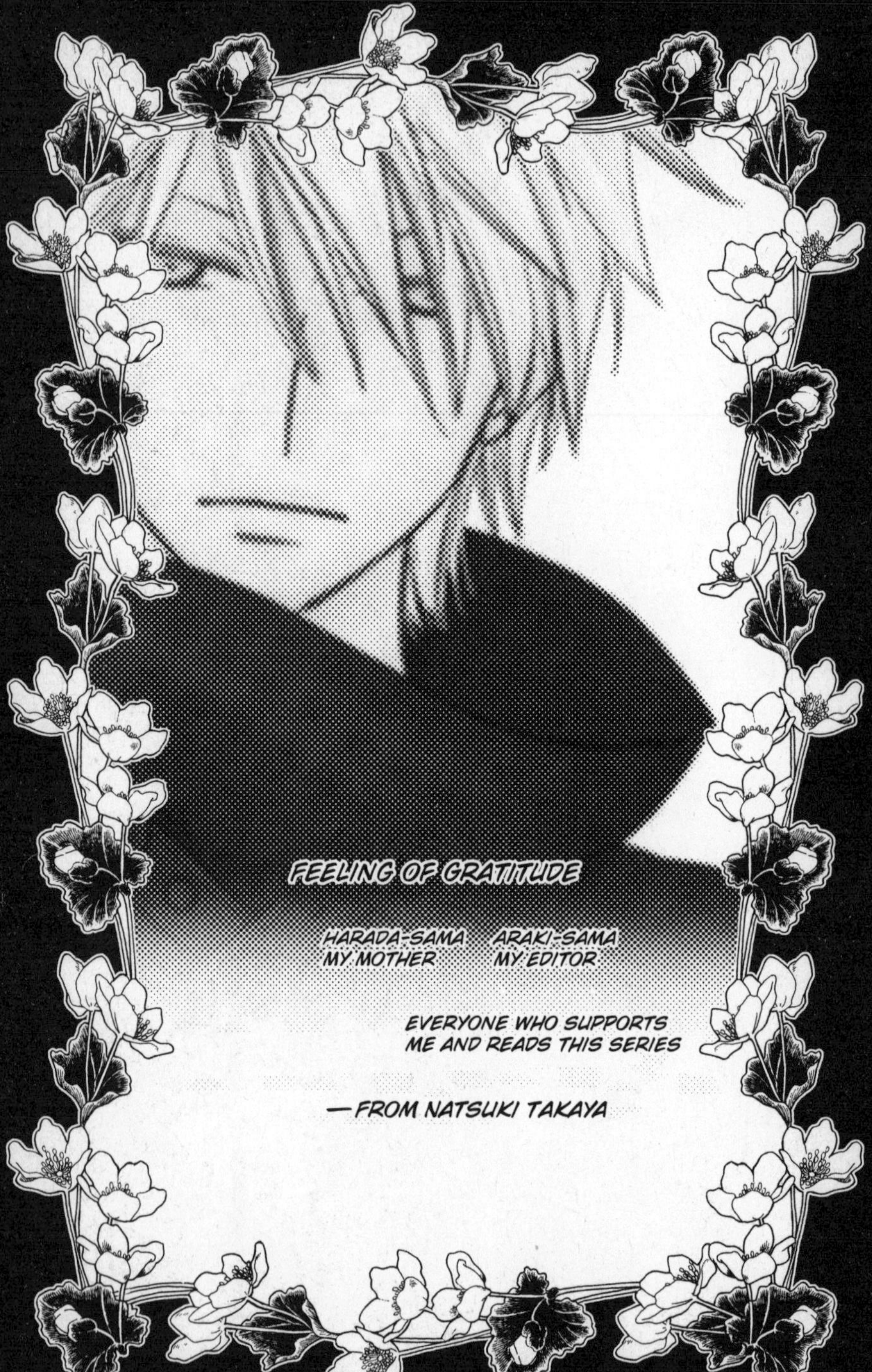
FEELING OF GRATITUDE
HARADA-SAMA
MY MOTHER
ARAKI-SAMA
MY EDITOR
EVERYONE WHO SUPPORTS ME AND READS THIS SERIES
—FROM NATSUKI TAKAYA

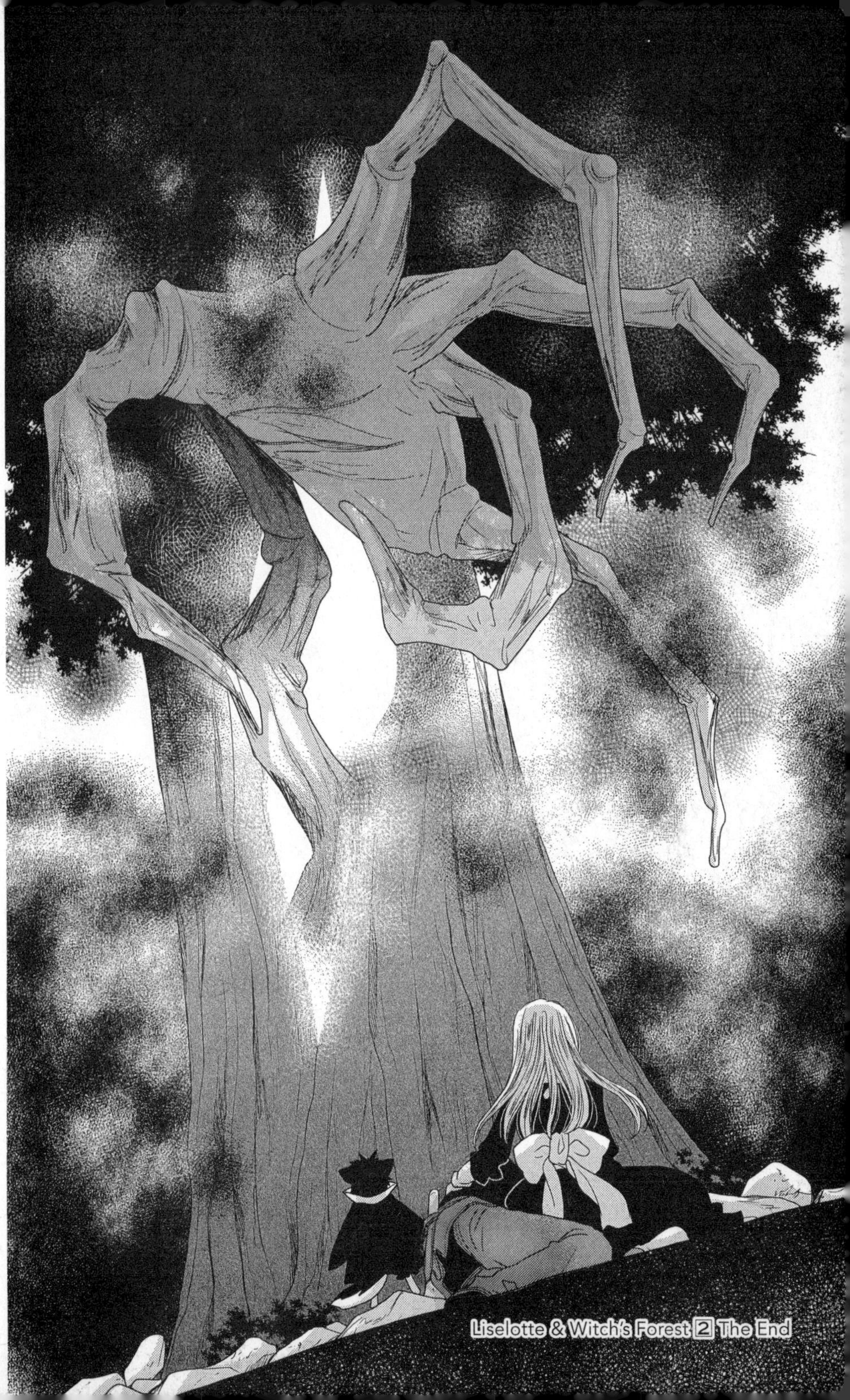
Liselotte & Witch's Forest 2 The End

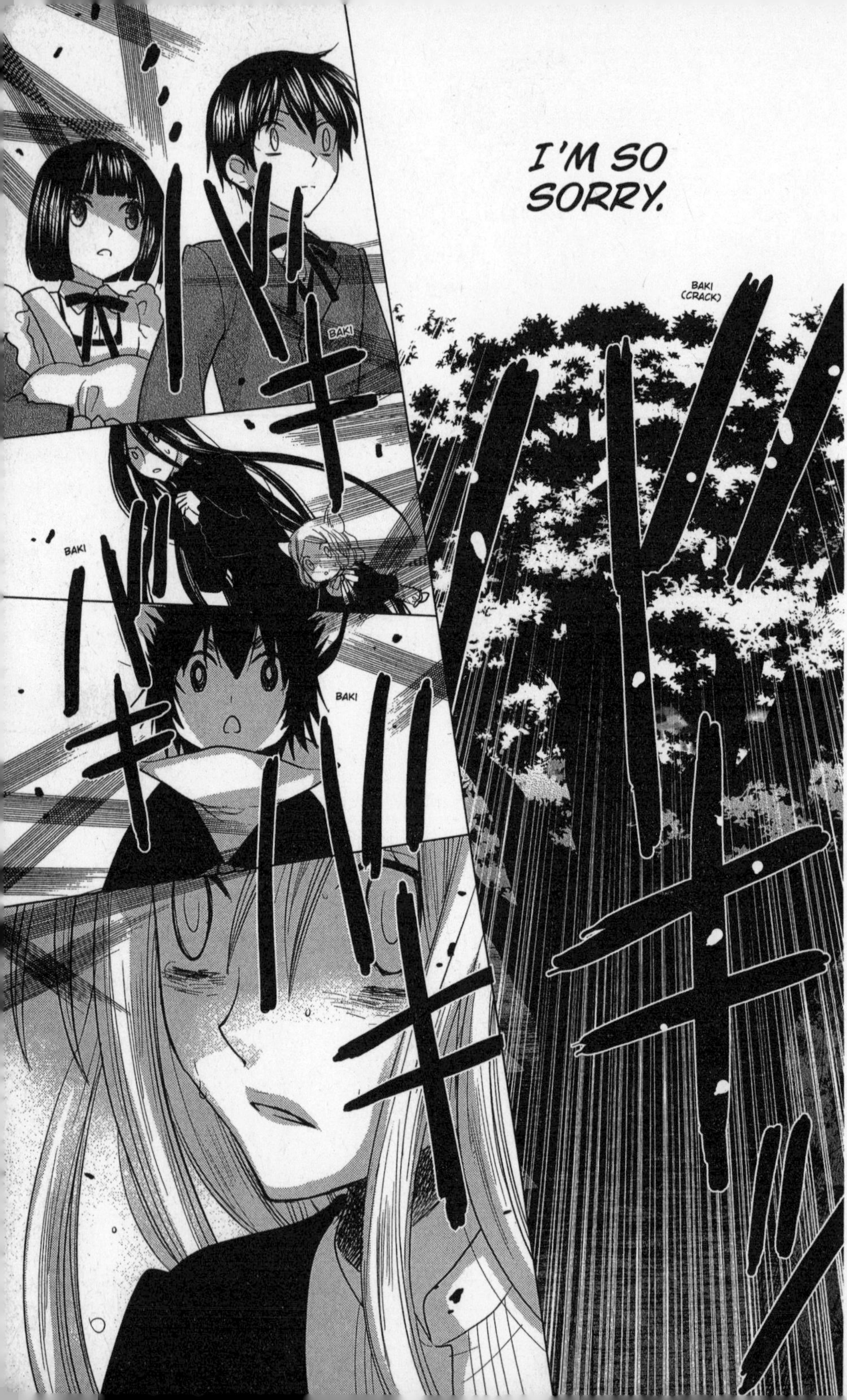
I'M SO SORRY.
BAKI (CRACK)
BAKI
BAKI
BAKI

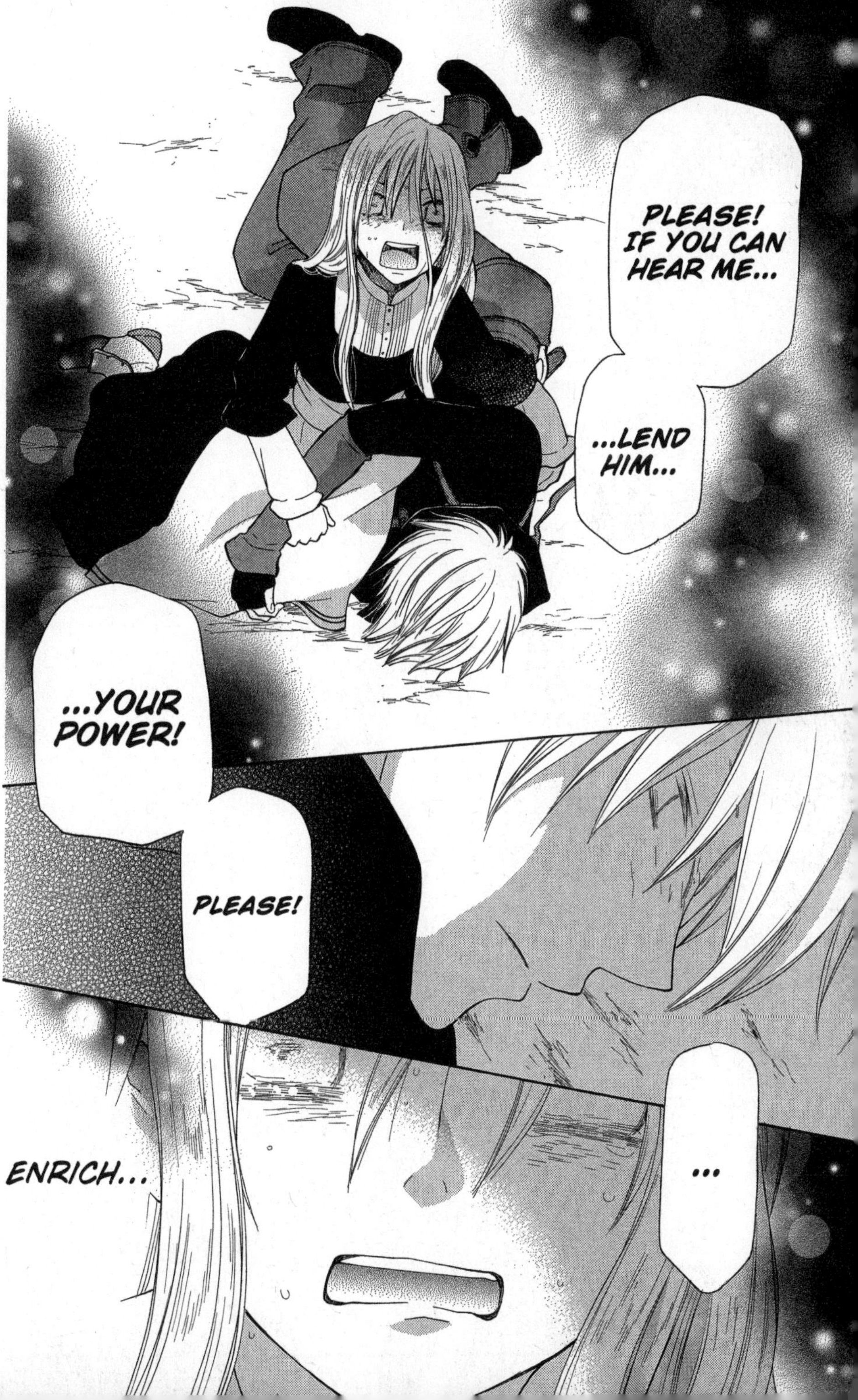
PLEASE! IF YOU CAN HEAR ME...
...LEND HIM...
...YOUR POWER!
PLEASE!
...
ENRICH...

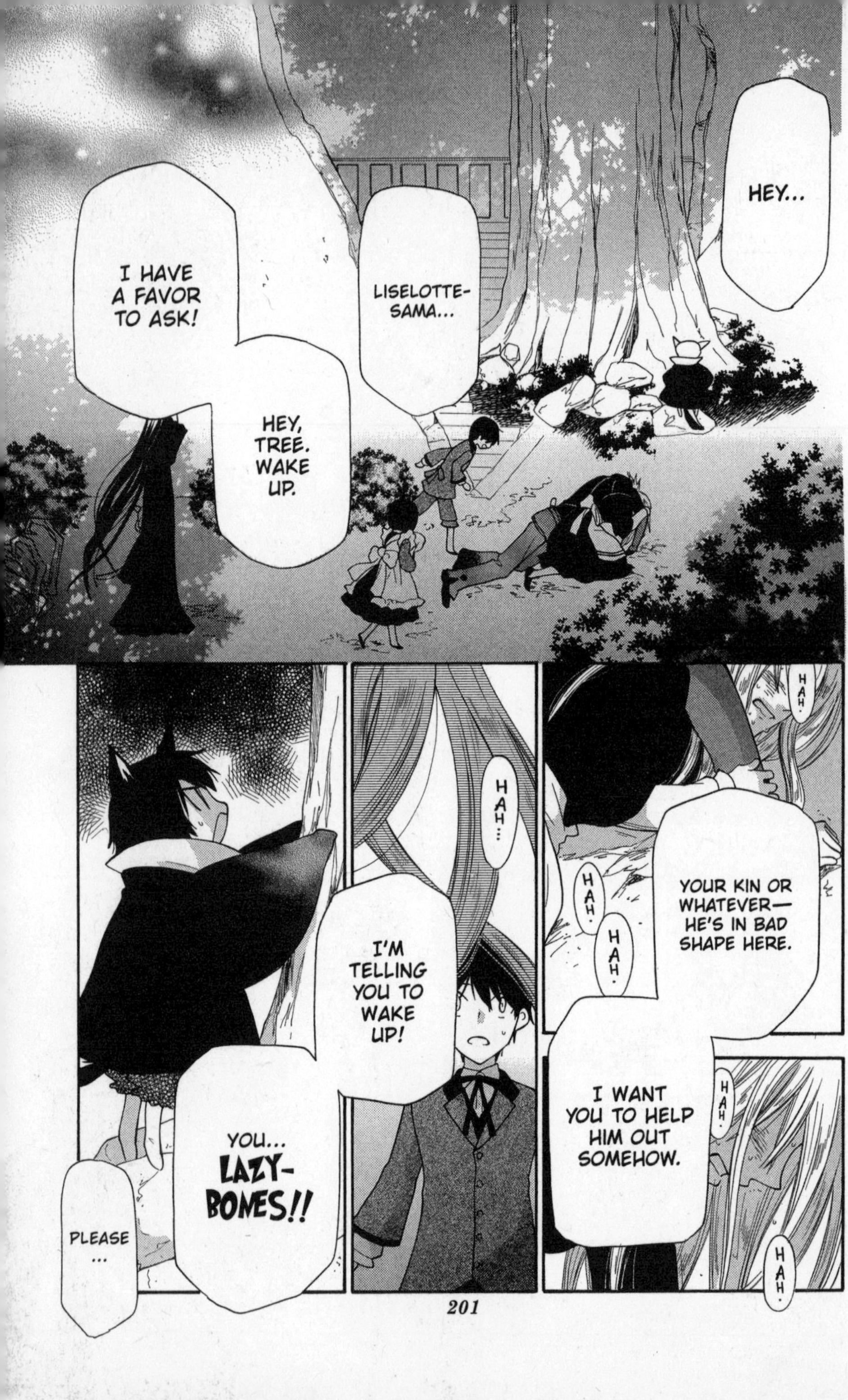
HEY...
LISELOTTE-SAMA...
I HAVE A FAVOR TO ASK!
HEY, TREE. WAKE UP.
HAH.
YOUR KIN OR WHATEVER—HE'S IN BAD SHAPE HERE.
HAH.
HAH.
I WANT YOU TO HELP HIM OUT SOMEHOW.
HAH.
HAH.
HAH...
I'M TELLING YOU TO WAKE UP!
YOU... **LAZY-BONES!!**
PLEASE...

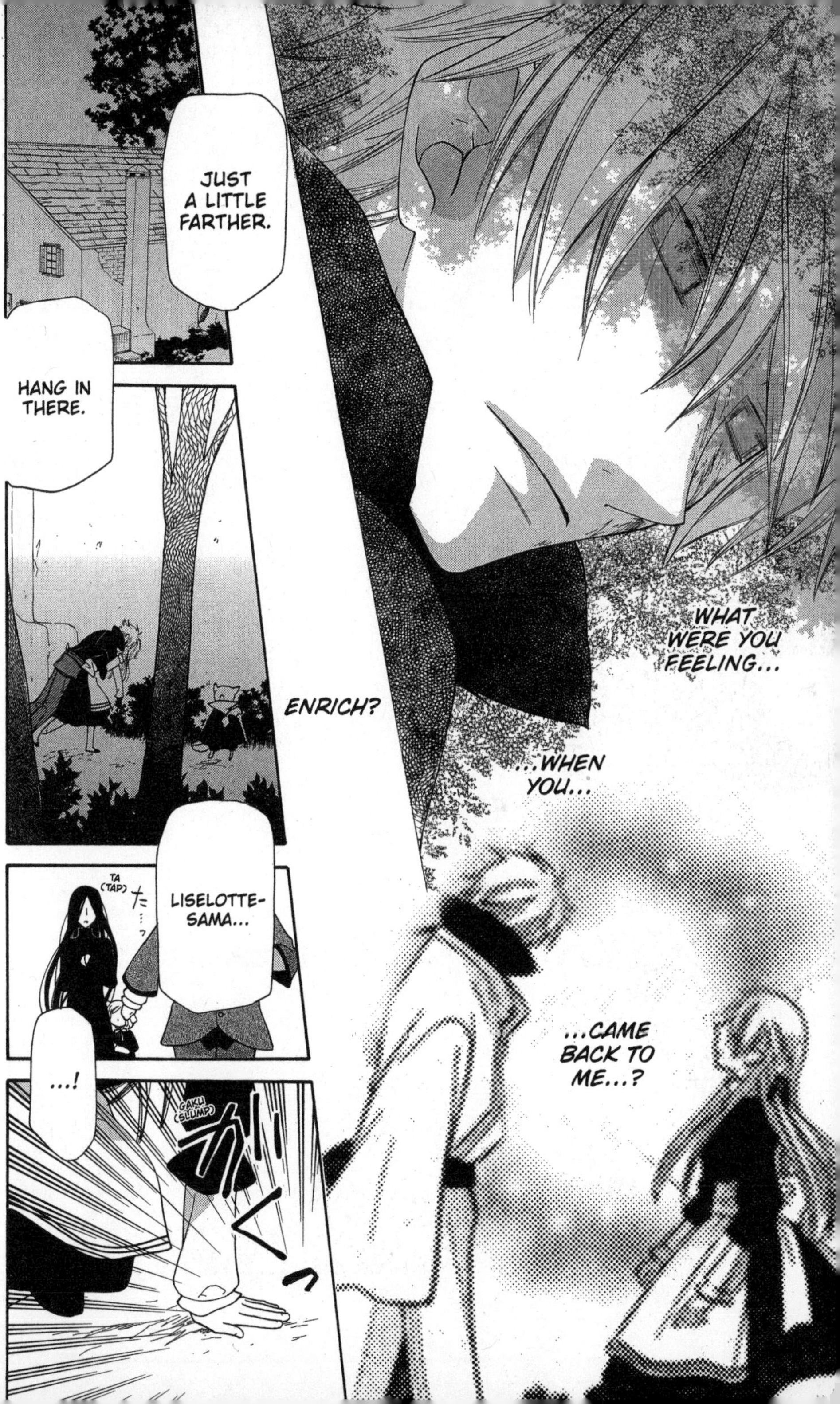
WHAT WERE YOU FEELING...
...WHEN YOU...
...CAME BACK TO ME...?
JUST A LITTLE FARTHER.
HANG IN THERE.
ENRICH?
TA (TAP)
LISELOTTE-SAMA...
...!
GAKU (SLUMP)

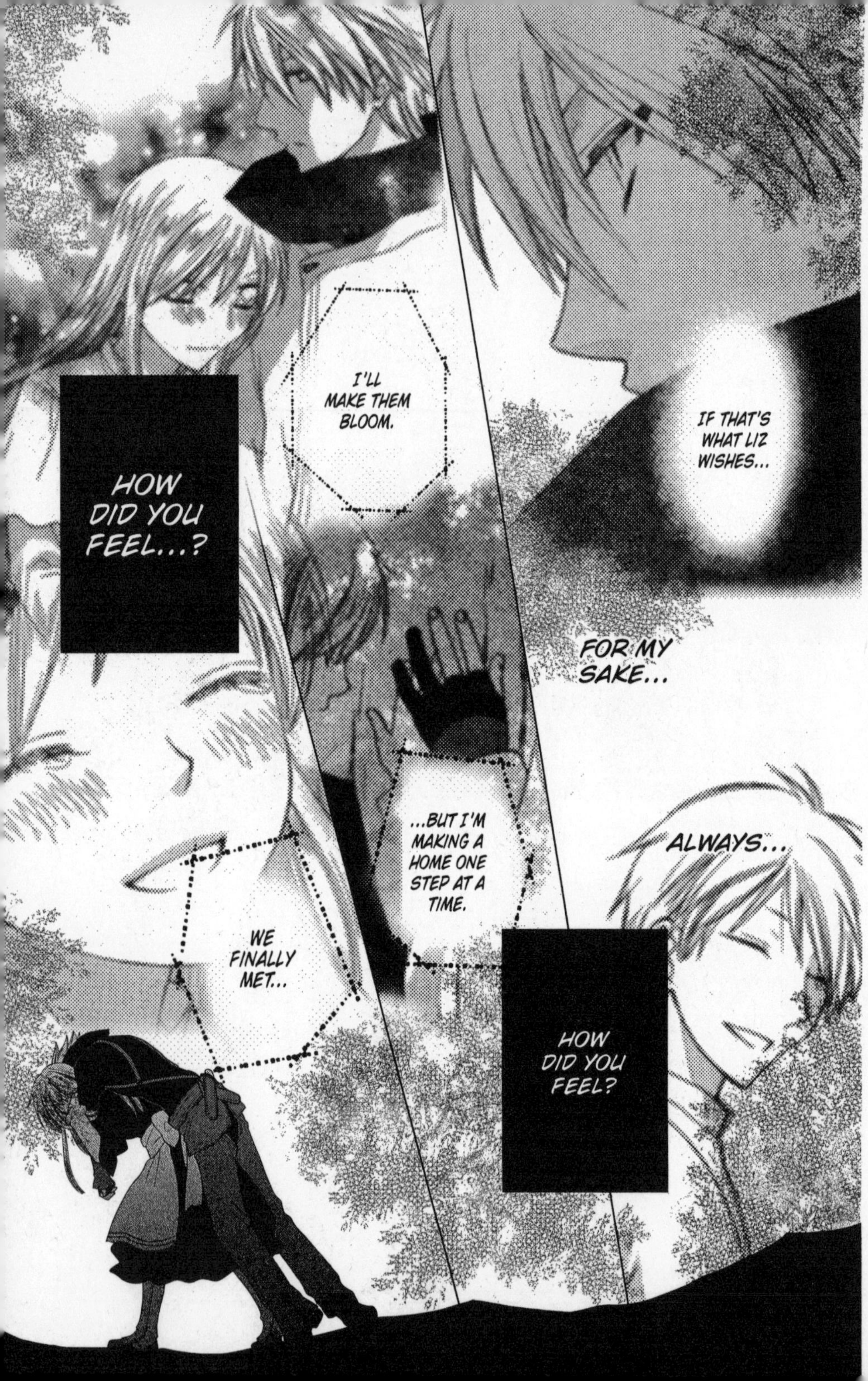

IF THAT'S WHAT LIZ WISHES...
FOR MY SAKE...
ALWAYS...
HOW DID YOU FEEL?
I'LL MAKE THEM BLOOM.
...BUT I'M MAKING A HOME ONE STEP AT A TIME.
HOW DID YOU FEEL...?
WE FINALLY MET...

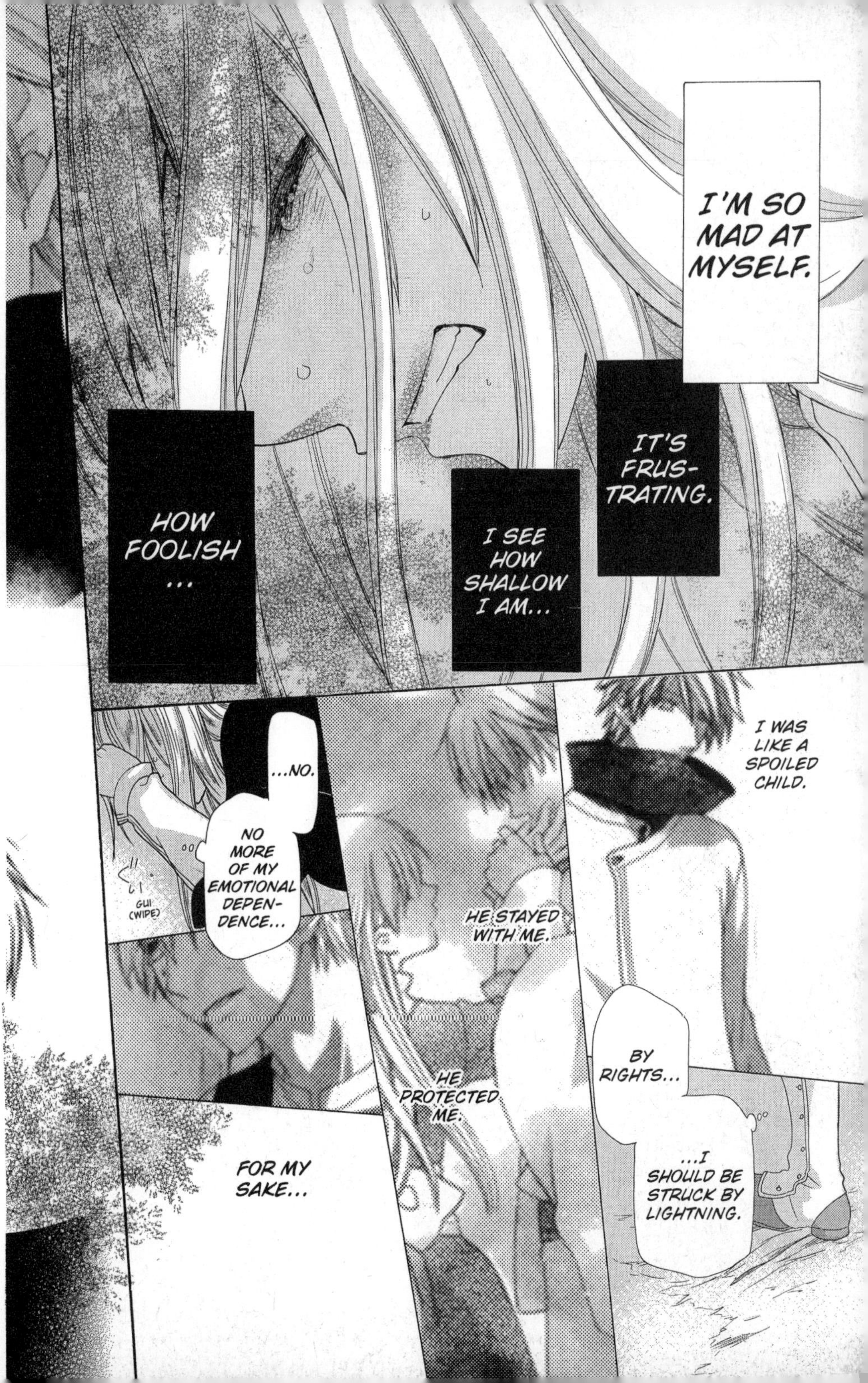
I'M SO MAD AT MYSELF.
IT'S FRUS-TRATING.
I SEE HOW SHALLOW I AM...
HOW FOOLISH ...
I WAS LIKE A SPOILED CHILD.
BY RIGHTS...
...I SHOULD BE STRUCK BY LIGHTNING.
HE STAYED WITH ME.
HE PROTECTED ME.
...NO.
NO MORE OF MY EMOTIONAL DEPEN-DENCE...
GUI (WIPE)
FOR MY SAKE...

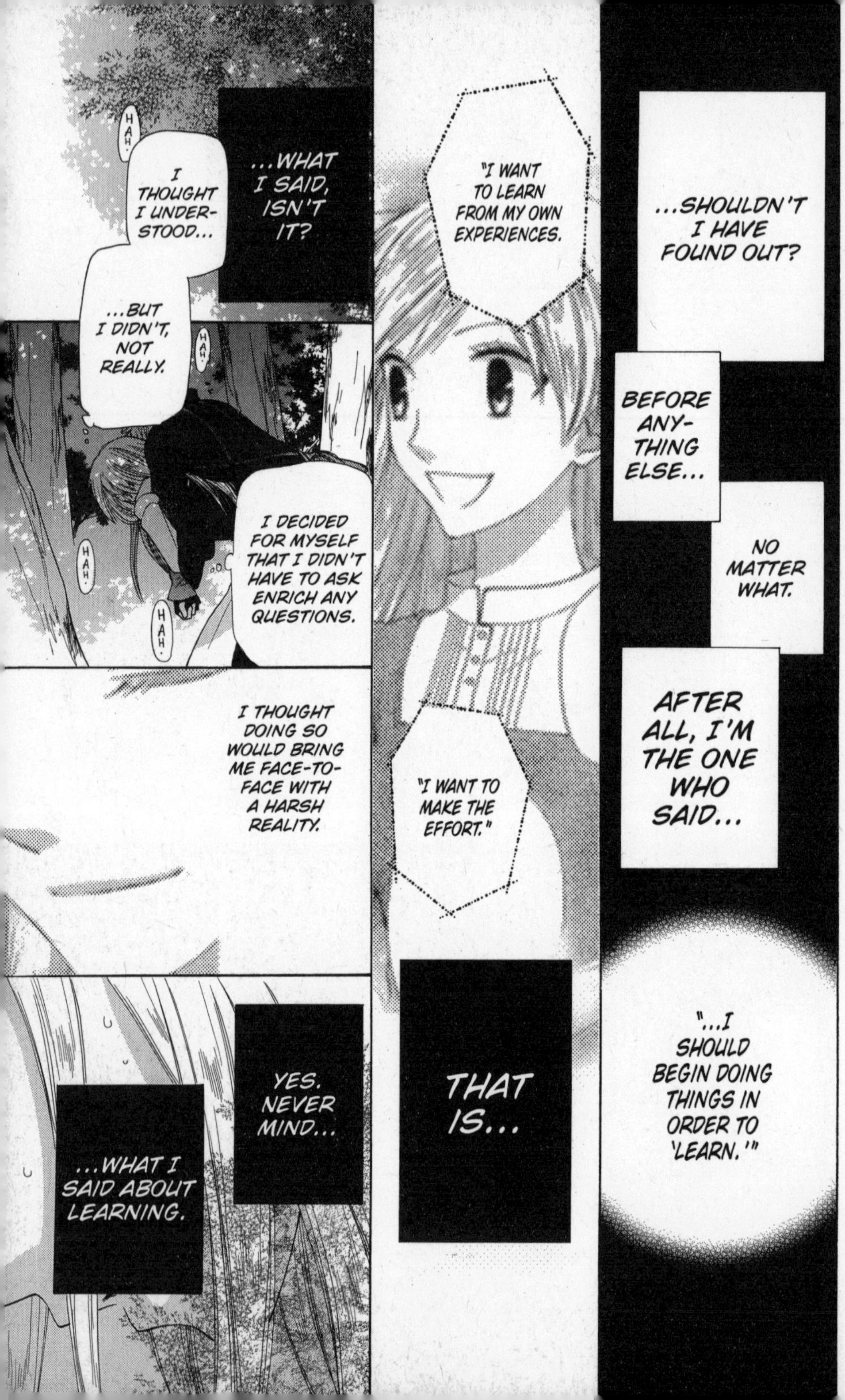
...SHOULDN'T I HAVE FOUND OUT?
BEFORE ANY-THING ELSE...
NO MATTER WHAT.
AFTER ALL, I'M THE ONE WHO SAID...
"...I SHOULD BEGIN DOING THINGS IN ORDER TO 'LEARN.'"
"I WANT TO LEARN FROM MY OWN EXPERIENCES.
"I WANT TO MAKE THE EFFORT."
THAT IS...
...WHAT I SAID, ISN'T IT?
HAH.
I THOUGHT I UNDER-STOOD...
...BUT I DIDN'T, NOT REALLY.
HAH.
I DECIDED FOR MYSELF THAT I DIDN'T HAVE TO ASK ENRICH ANY QUESTIONS.
HAH.
HAH.
I THOUGHT DOING SO WOULD BRING ME FACE-TO-FACE WITH A HARSH REALITY.
YES. NEVER MIND...
...WHAT I SAID ABOUT LEARNING.

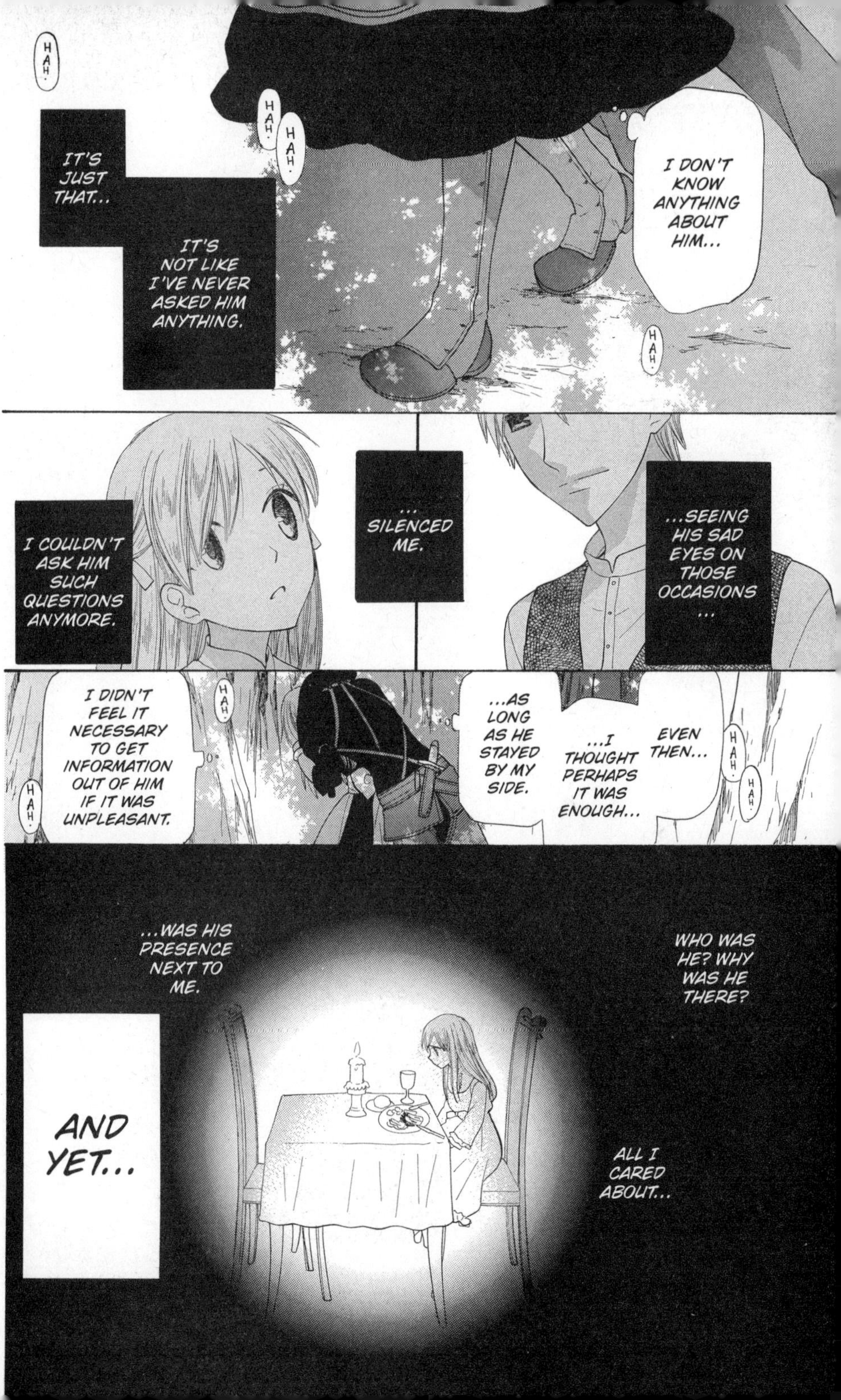
I DON'T KNOW ANYTHING ABOUT HIM...
HAH.
HAH.
HAH.
HAH.
IT'S JUST THAT...
IT'S NOT LIKE I'VE NEVER ASKED HIM ANYTHING.
...SEEING HIS SAD EYES ON THOSE OCCASIONS...
...SILENCED ME.
I COULDN'T ASK HIM SUCH QUESTIONS ANYMORE.
HAH.
HAH.
EVEN THEN...
...I THOUGHT PERHAPS IT WAS ENOUGH...
...AS LONG AS HE STAYED BY MY SIDE.
HAH.
I DIDN'T FEEL IT NECESSARY TO GET INFORMATION OUT OF HIM IF IT WAS UNPLEASANT.
HAH.
WHO WAS HE? WHY WAS HE THERE?
ALL I CARED ABOUT...
...WAS HIS PRESENCE NEXT TO ME.
AND YET...

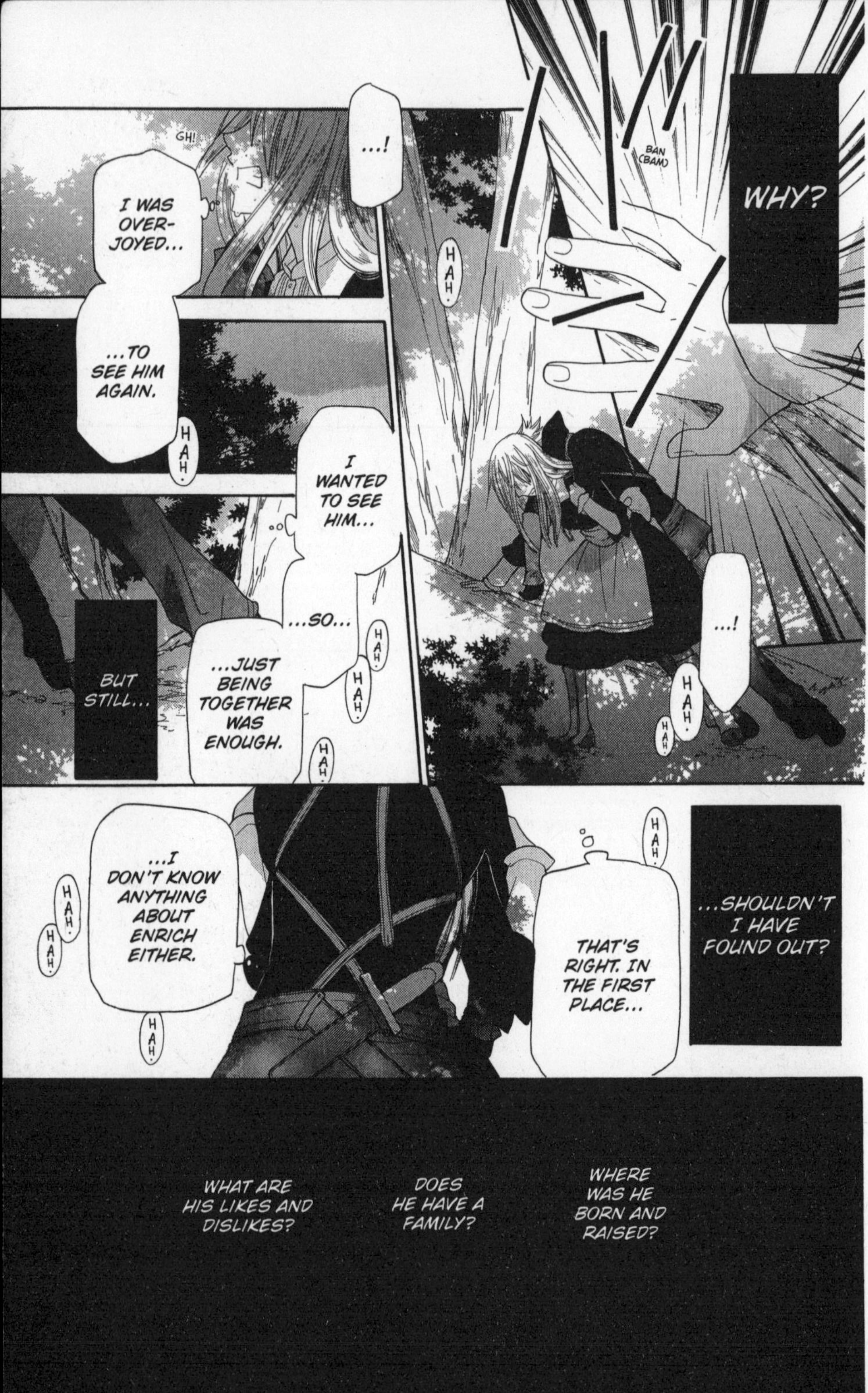
WHY?
BAN (BAM)
...!
GH!
I WAS OVER-JOYED...
...TO SEE HIM AGAIN.
HAH.
...!
HAH. HAH.
HAH.
I WANTED TO SEE HIM...
...SO...
HAH. HAH.
...JUST BEING TOGETHER WAS ENOUGH.
HAH.
BUT STILL...
...SHOULDN'T I HAVE FOUND OUT?
HAH.
THAT'S RIGHT. IN THE FIRST PLACE...
...I DON'T KNOW ANYTHING ABOUT ENRICH EITHER.
HAH. HAH.
HAH.
WHERE WAS HE BORN AND RAISED?
DOES HE HAVE A FAMILY?
WHAT ARE HIS LIKES AND DISLIKES?

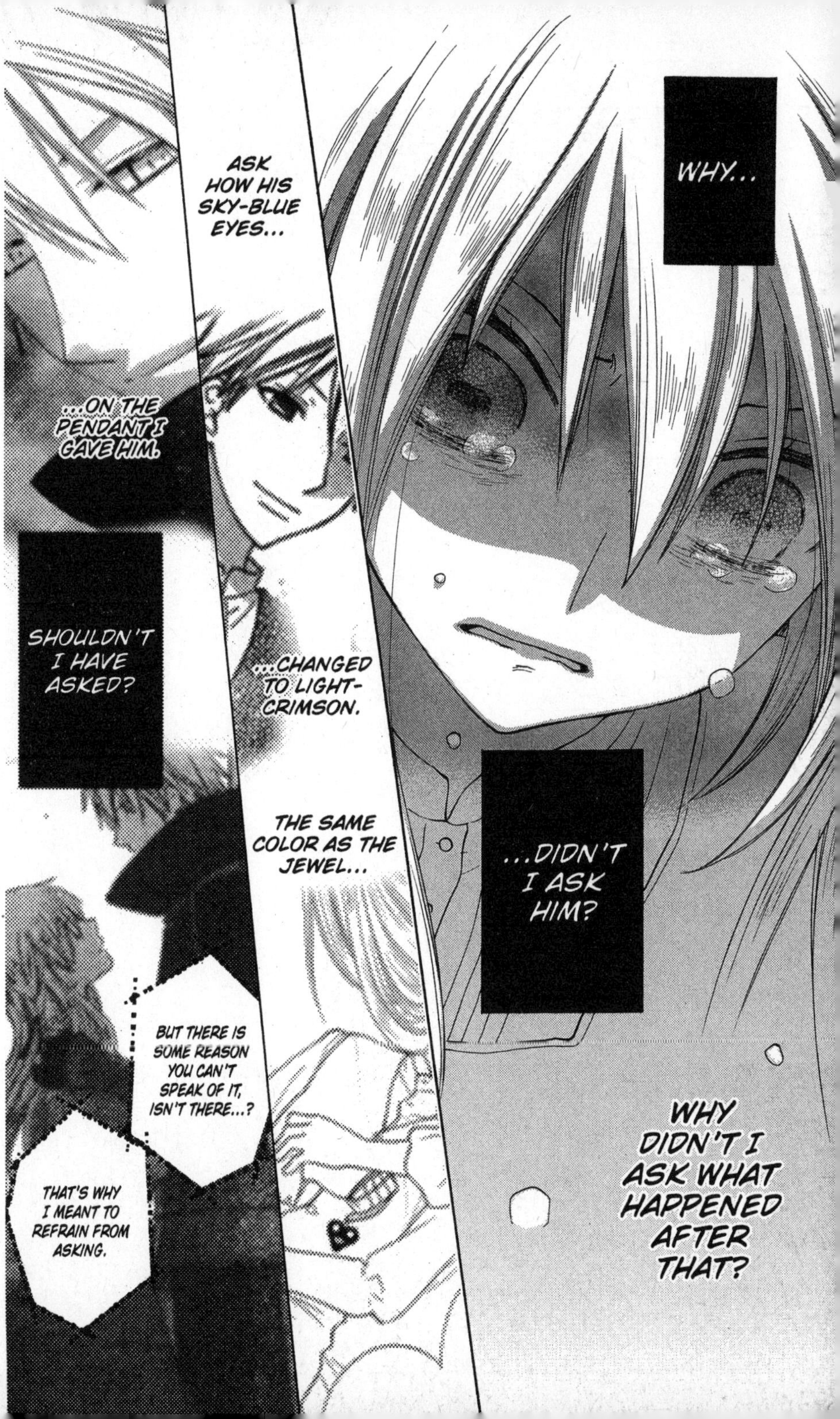
WHY...
...DIDN'T I ASK HIM?
WHY DIDN'T I ASK WHAT HAPPENED AFTER THAT?
ASK HOW HIS SKY-BLUE EYES...
...CHANGED TO LIGHT-CRIMSON.
THE SAME COLOR AS THE JEWEL...
...ON THE PENDANT I GAVE HIM.
SHOULDN'T I HAVE ASKED?
BUT THERE IS SOME REASON YOU CAN'T SPEAK OF IT, ISN'T THERE...?
THAT'S WHY I MEANT TO REFRAIN FROM ASKING.

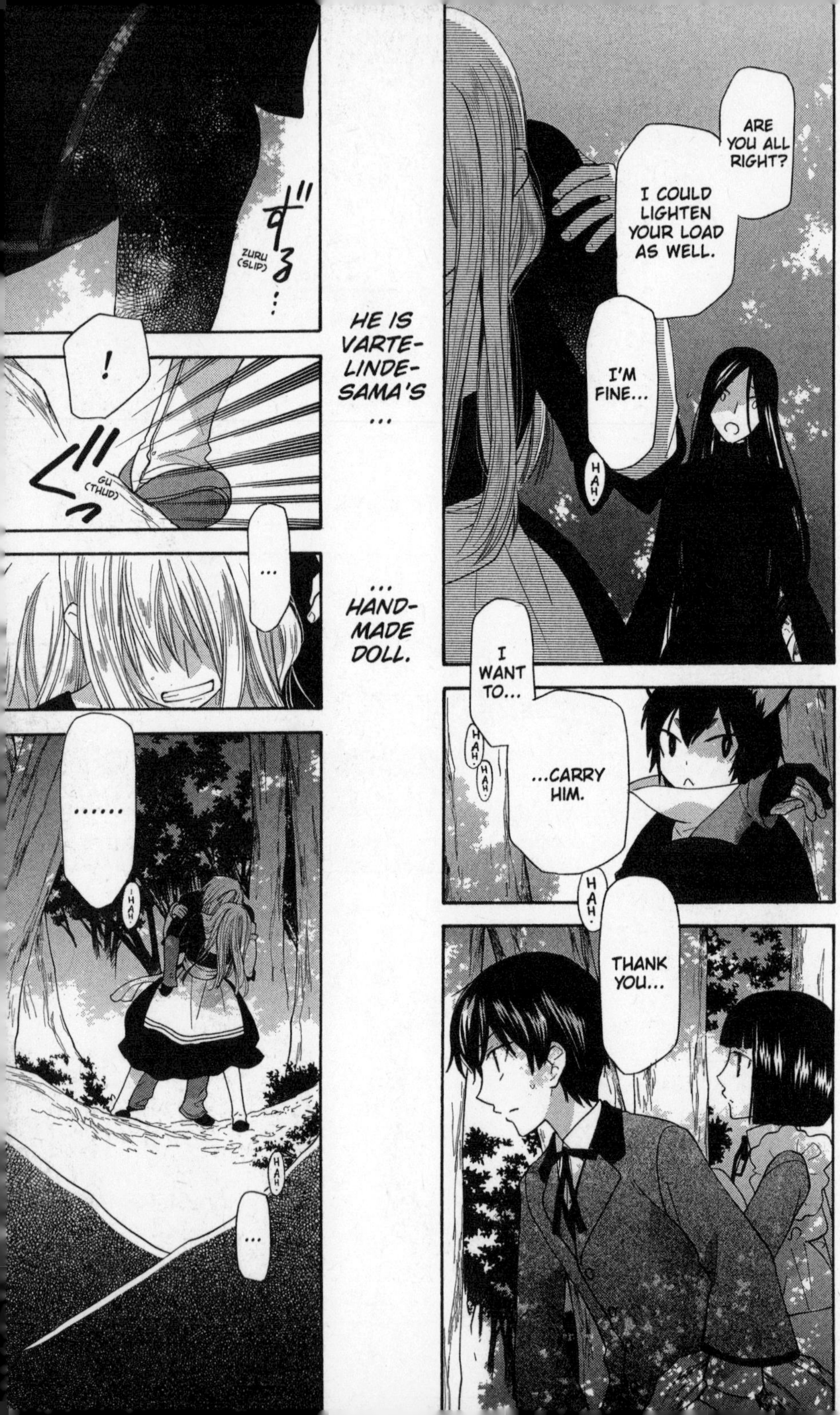
ARE YOU ALL RIGHT?
I COULD LIGHTEN YOUR LOAD AS WELL.
I'M FINE...
HAH.
I WANT TO...
HAH.
HAH.
...CARRY HIM.
HAH.
THANK YOU...
HE IS VARTE-LINDE-SAMA'S ...
... HAND-MADE DOLL.
ずる…
ZURU (SLIP)
!
ぐっ
GU (THUD)
...
....
HAH.
HAH.
...

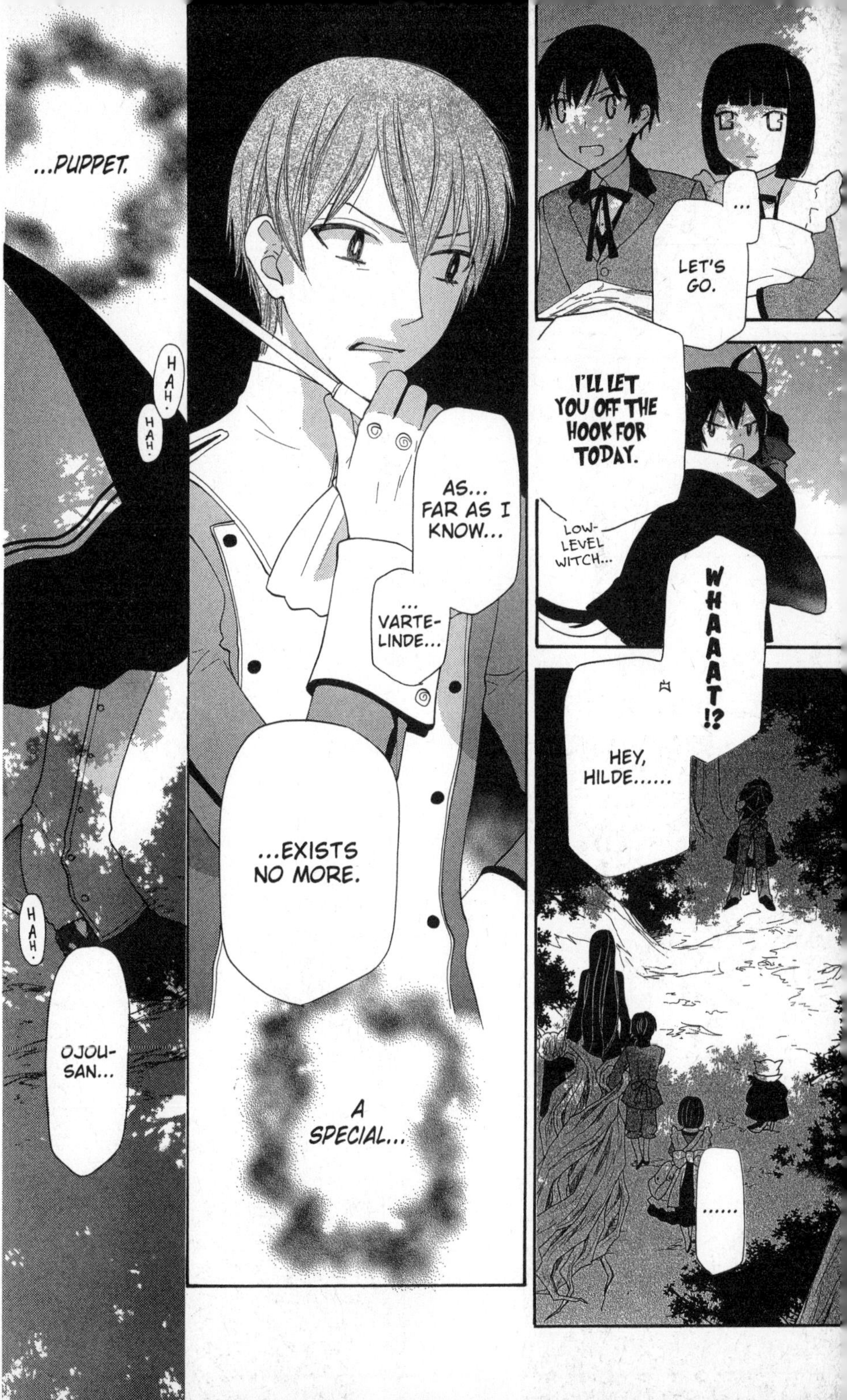
...
LET'S GO.
I'LL LET YOU OFF THE HOOK FOR TODAY.
LOW-LEVEL WITCH...
WHAAAAT!?
HEY, HILDE......
......
AS... FAR AS I KNOW...
...VARTE-LINDE...
...EXISTS NO MORE.
A SPECIAL...
...PUPPET.
HAH.
HAH.
HAH.
OJOU-SAN...

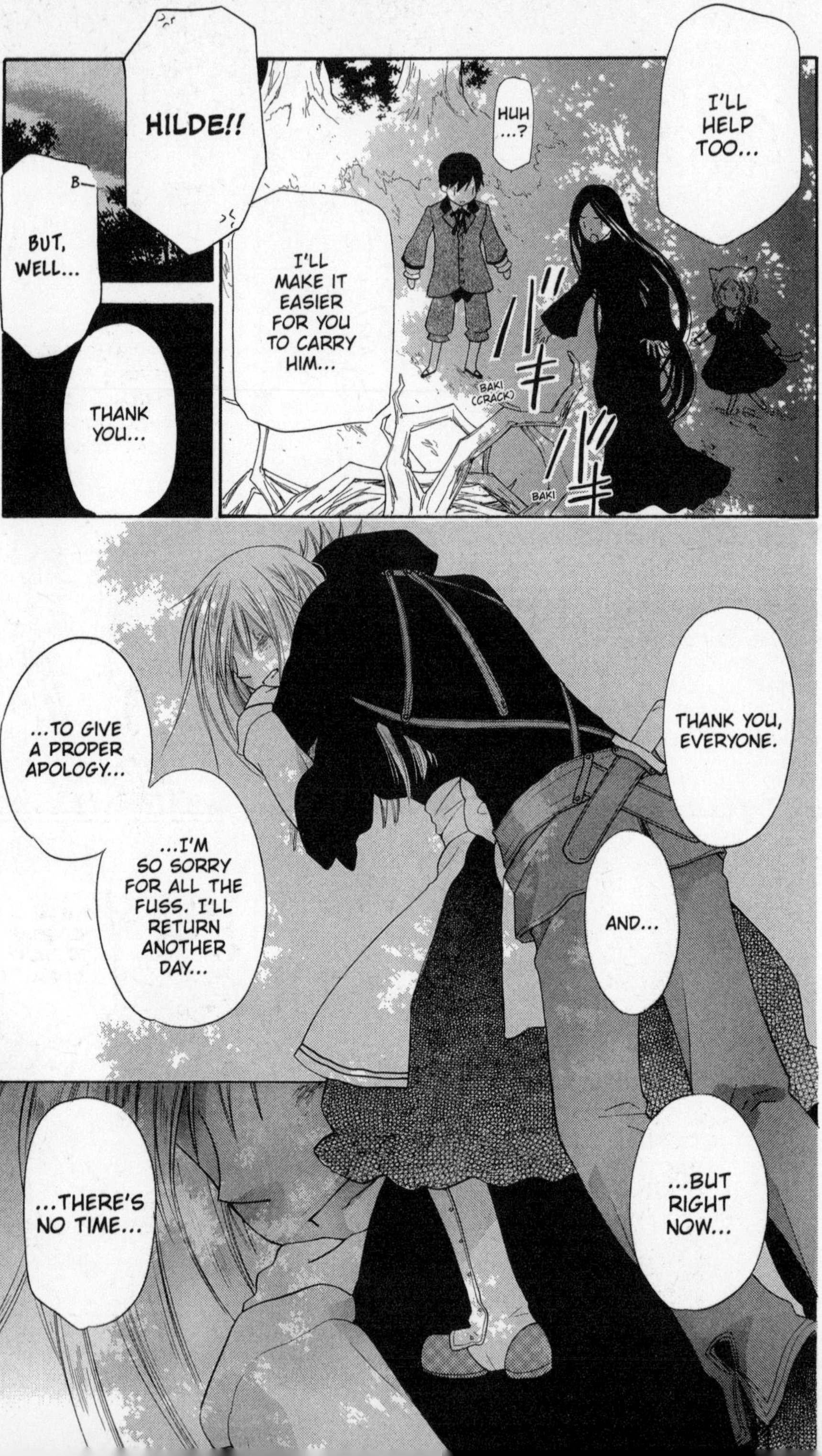
I'LL HELP TOO...
HUH ...?
HILDE!!
I'LL MAKE IT EASIER FOR YOU TO CARRY HIM...
バキ
BAKI (CRACK)
バキ
BAKI
B—
BUT, WELL...
THANK YOU...
THANK YOU, EVERYONE.
AND...
...TO GIVE A PROPER APOLOGY...
...I'M SO SORRY FOR ALL THE FUSS. I'LL RETURN ANOTHER DAY...
...BUT RIGHT NOW...
...THERE'S NO TIME...

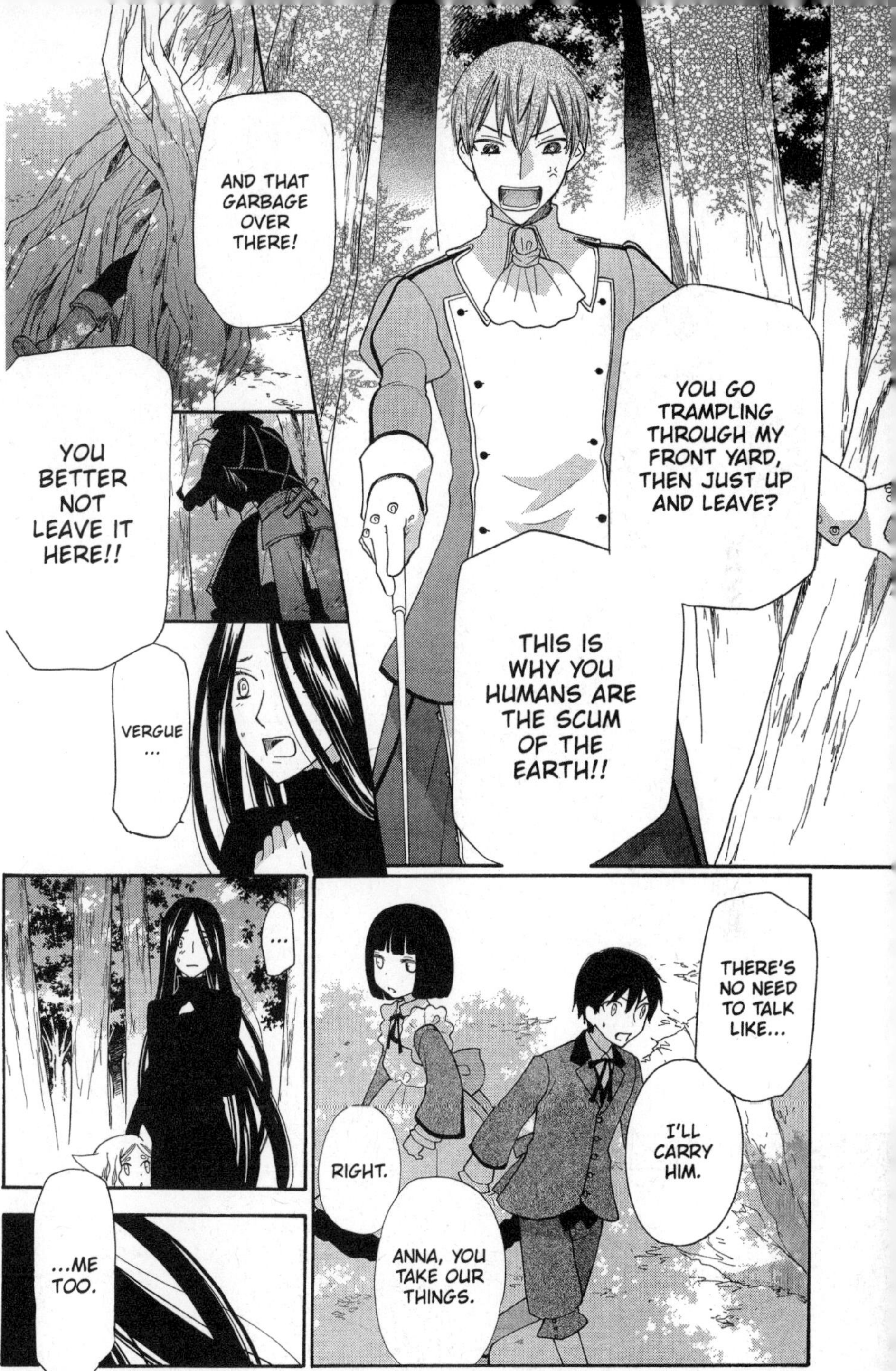
YOU GO TRAMPLING THROUGH MY FRONT YARD, THEN JUST UP AND LEAVE?
THIS IS WHY YOU HUMANS ARE THE SCUM OF THE EARTH!!
AND THAT GARBAGE OVER THERE!
YOU BETTER NOT LEAVE IT HERE!!
VERGUE...
THERE'S NO NEED TO TALK LIKE...
I'LL CARRY HIM.
ANNA, YOU TAKE OUR THINGS.
RIGHT.
...
...ME TOO.

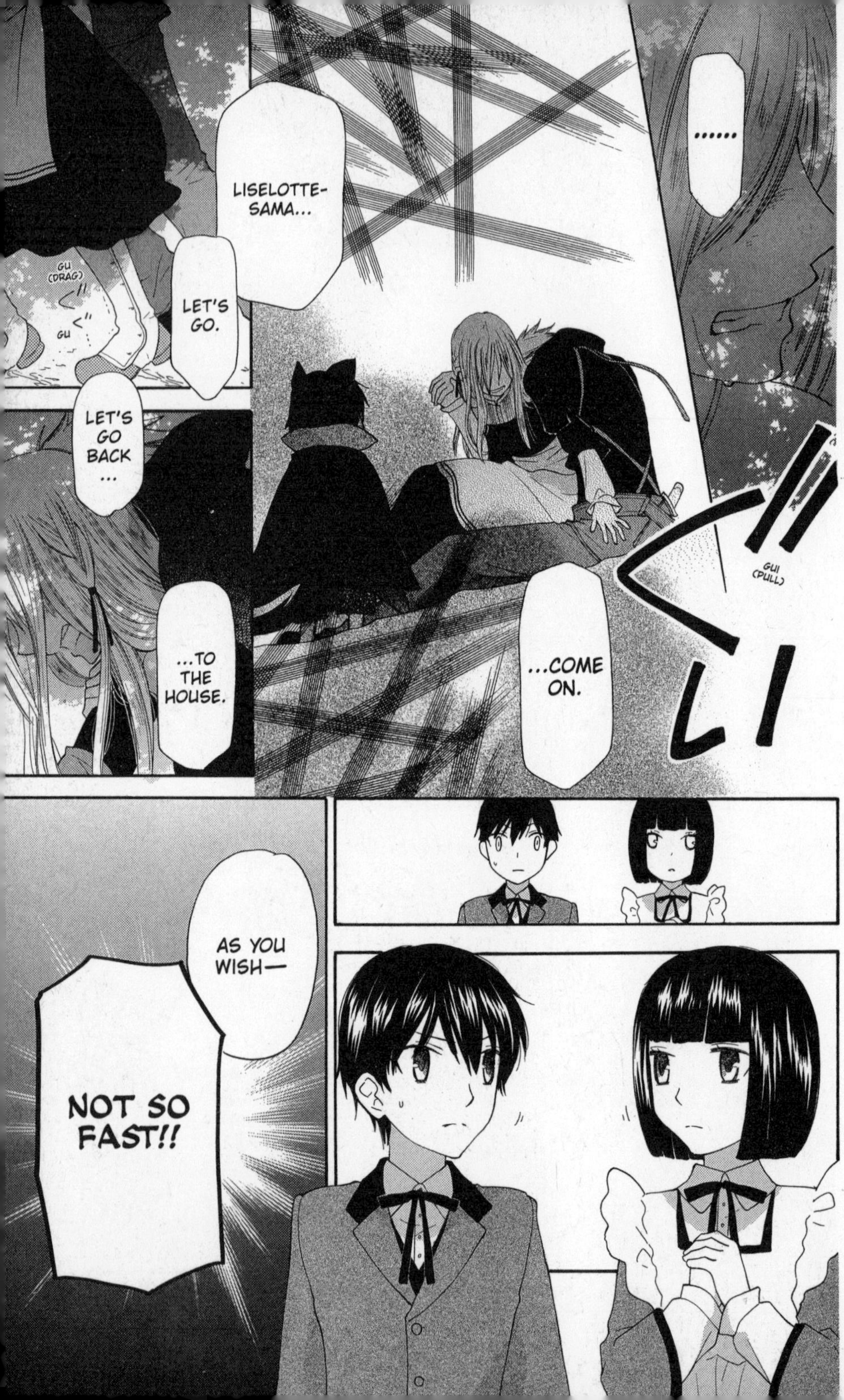
......
GUI (PULL)
...COME ON.
LISELOTTE-SAMA...
LET'S GO.
GU (DRAG) GU
LET'S GO BACK...
...TO THE HOUSE.
AS YOU WISH—
NOT SO FAST!!

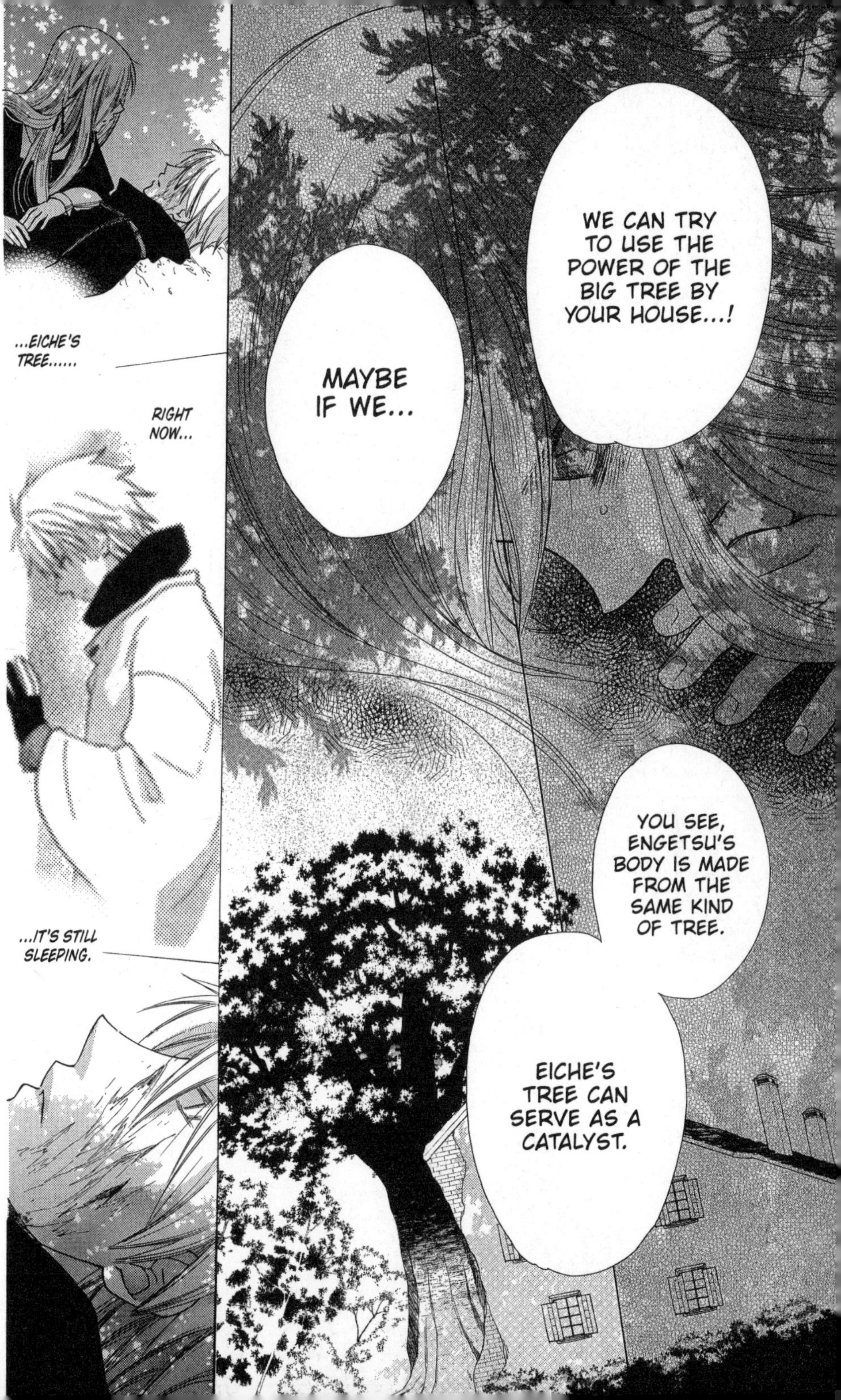
WE CAN TRY TO USE THE POWER OF THE BIG TREE BY YOUR HOUSE...!
MAYBE IF WE...
YOU SEE, ENGETSU'S BODY IS MADE FROM THE SAME KIND OF TREE.
EICHE'S TREE CAN SERVE AS A CATALYST.
...EICHE'S TREE......
RIGHT NOW...
...IT'S STILL SLEEPING.

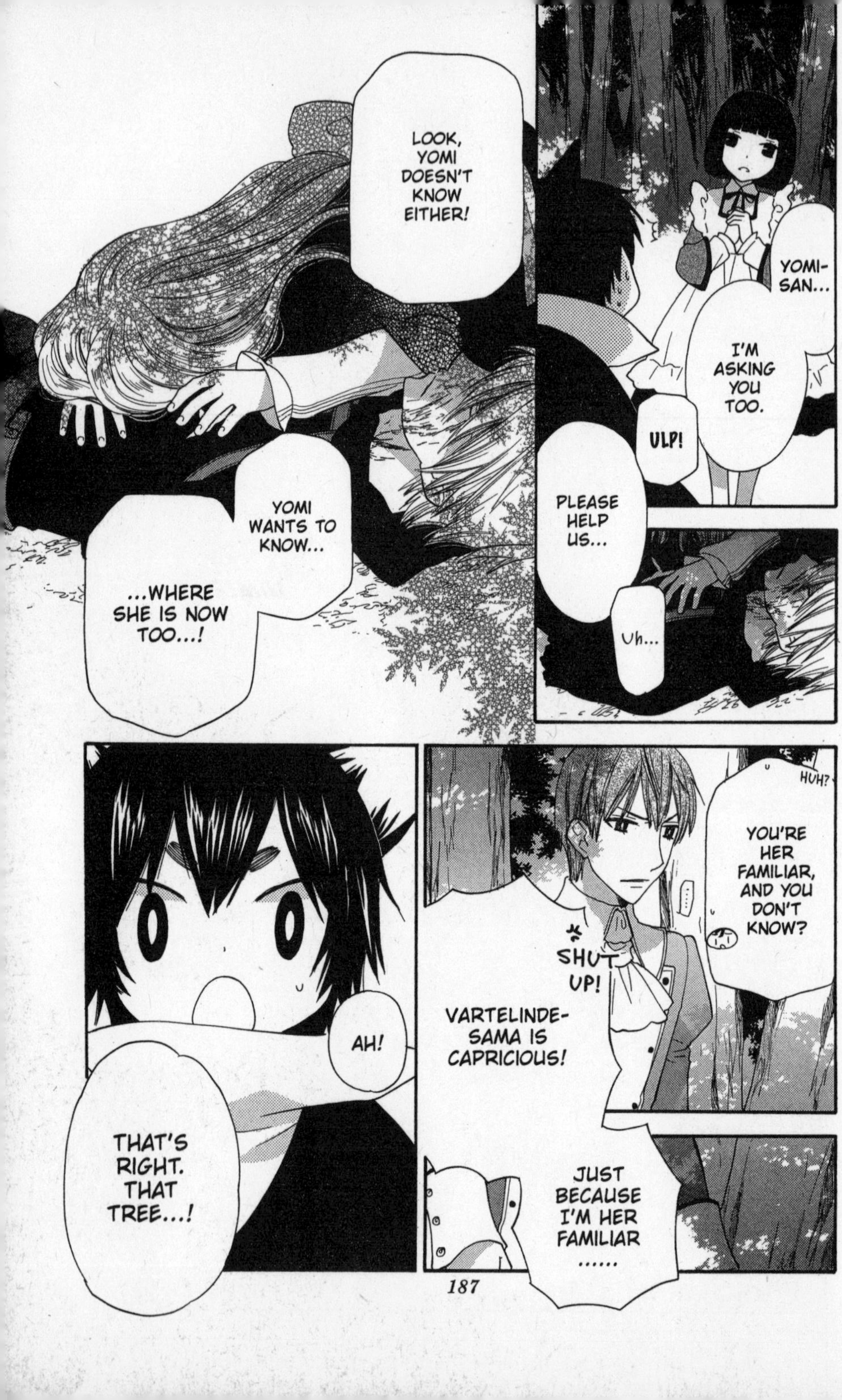
YOMI-SAN...
I'M ASKING YOU TOO.
ULP!
PLEASE HELP US...
Uh...
LOOK, YOMI DOESN'T KNOW EITHER!
YOMI WANTS TO KNOW...
...WHERE SHE IS NOW TOO...!
HUH?
YOU'RE HER FAMILIAR, AND YOU DON'T KNOW?
SHUT UP!
VARTELINDE-SAMA IS CAPRICIOUS!
JUST BECAUSE I'M HER FAMILIAR ......
AH!
THAT'S RIGHT. THAT TREE...!

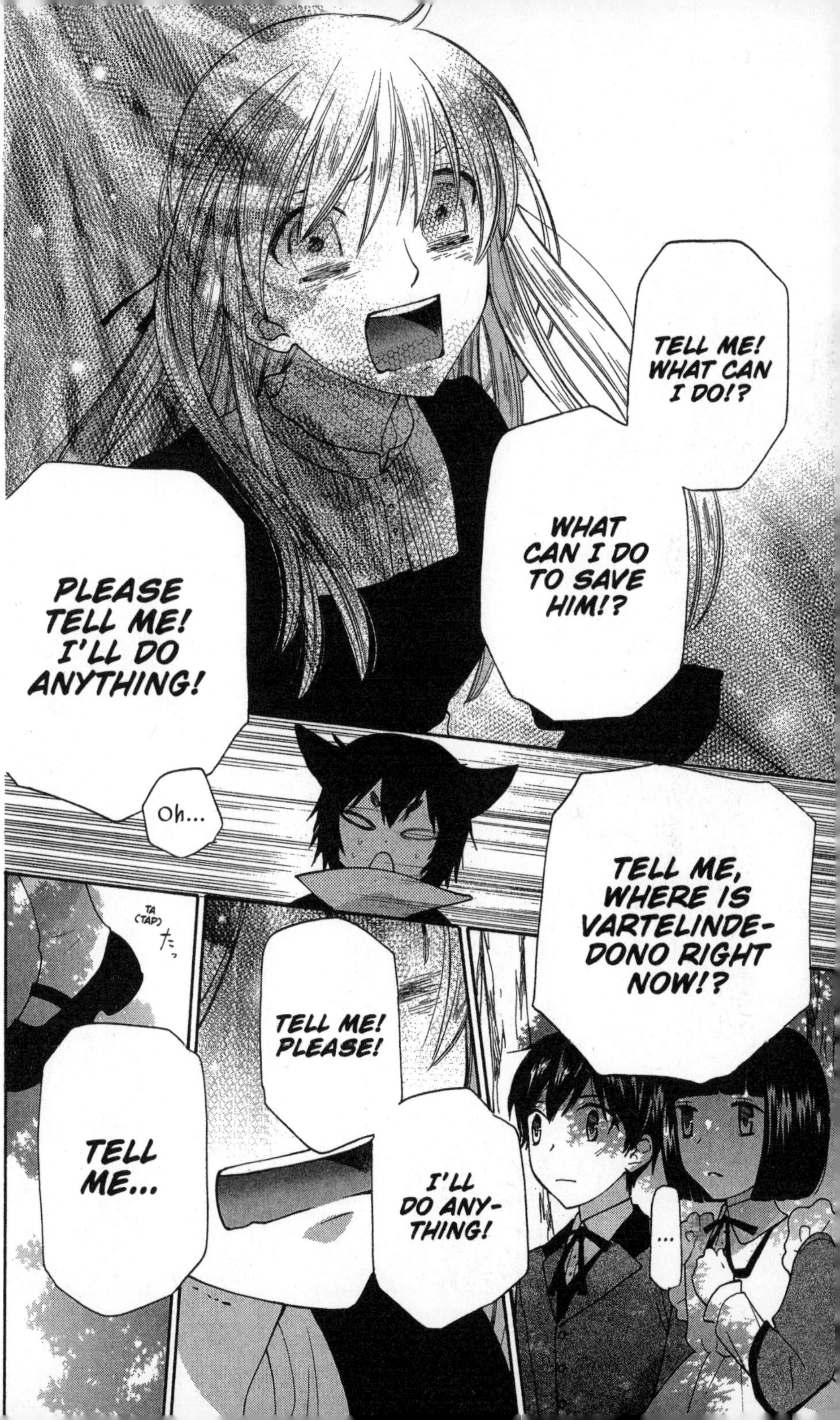
TELL ME! WHAT CAN I DO!?
WHAT CAN I DO TO SAVE HIM!?
PLEASE TELL ME! I'LL DO ANYTHING!
TELL ME, WHERE IS VARTELINDE-DONO RIGHT NOW!?
Oh...
TA (TAP)
TELL ME! PLEASE!
I'LL DO ANYTHING!
...
TELL ME...

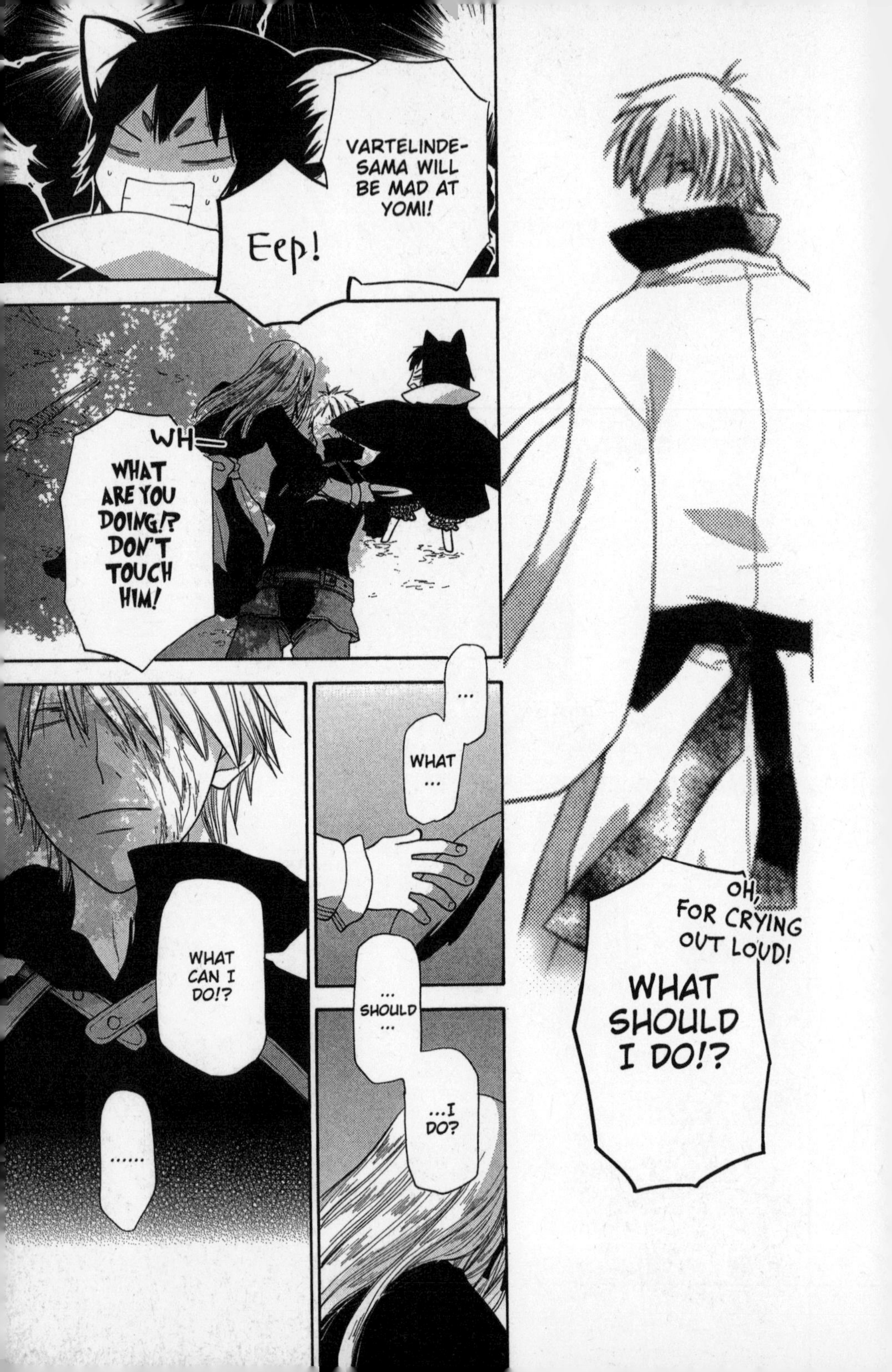
OH, FOR CRYING OUT LOUD!
WHAT SHOULD I DO!?
VARTELINDE-SAMA WILL BE MAD AT YOMI!
Eep!
WH—
WHAT ARE YOU DOING!? DON'T TOUCH HIM!
...
WHAT ...
... SHOULD ...
...I DO?
WHAT CAN I DO!?
......

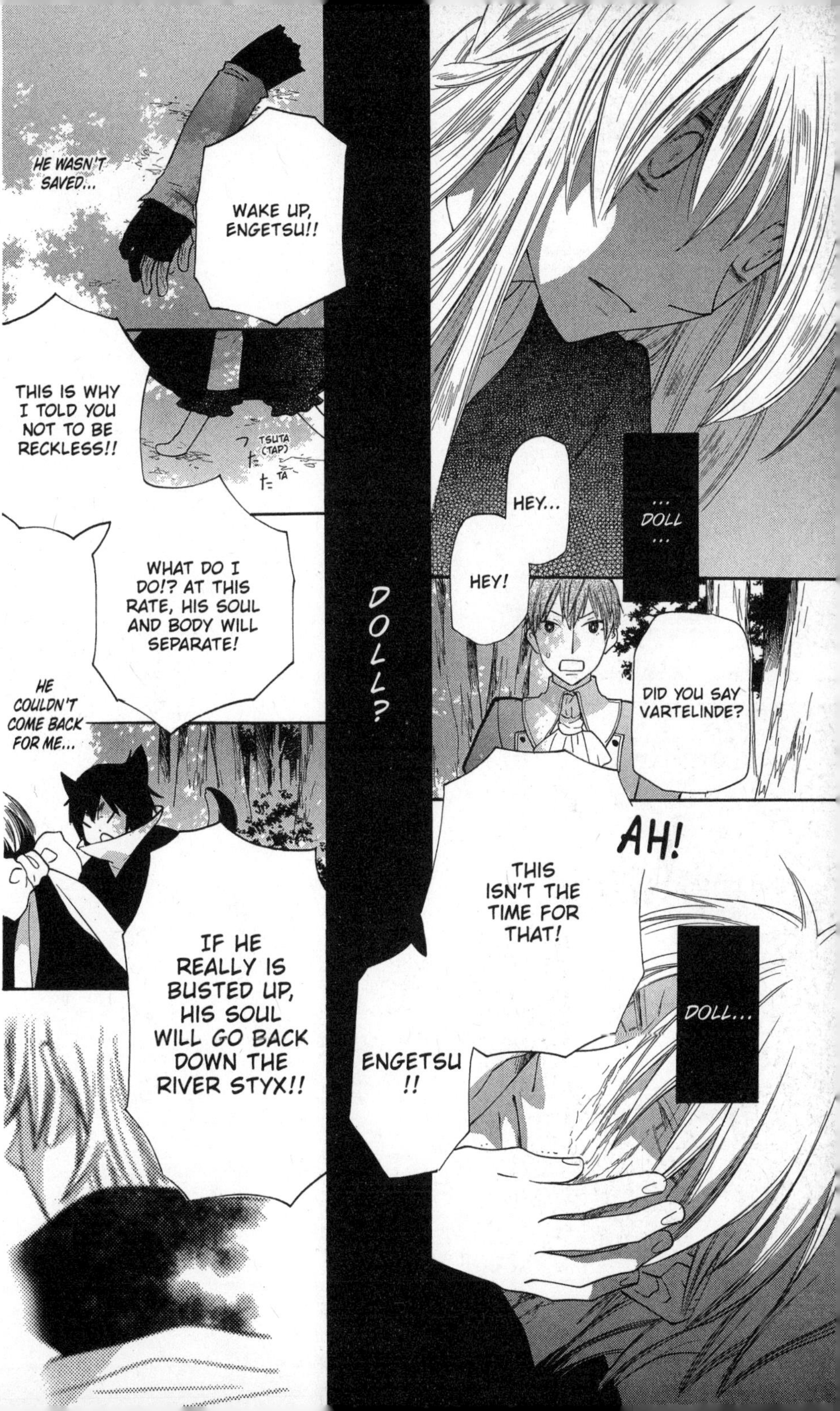
...DOLL...
HEY...
HEY!
DID YOU SAY VARTELINDE?
AH!
DOLL...
THIS ISN'T THE TIME FOR THAT!
ENGETSU!!
DOLL?
WAKE UP, ENGETSU!!
HE WASN'T SAVED...
THIS IS WHY I TOLD YOU NOT TO BE RECKLESS!!
TSUTA (TAP) TA
WHAT DO I DO!? AT THIS RATE, HIS SOUL AND BODY WILL SEPARATE!
HE COULDN'T COME BACK FOR ME...
IF HE REALLY IS BUSTED UP, HIS SOUL WILL GO BACK DOWN THE RIVER STYX!!

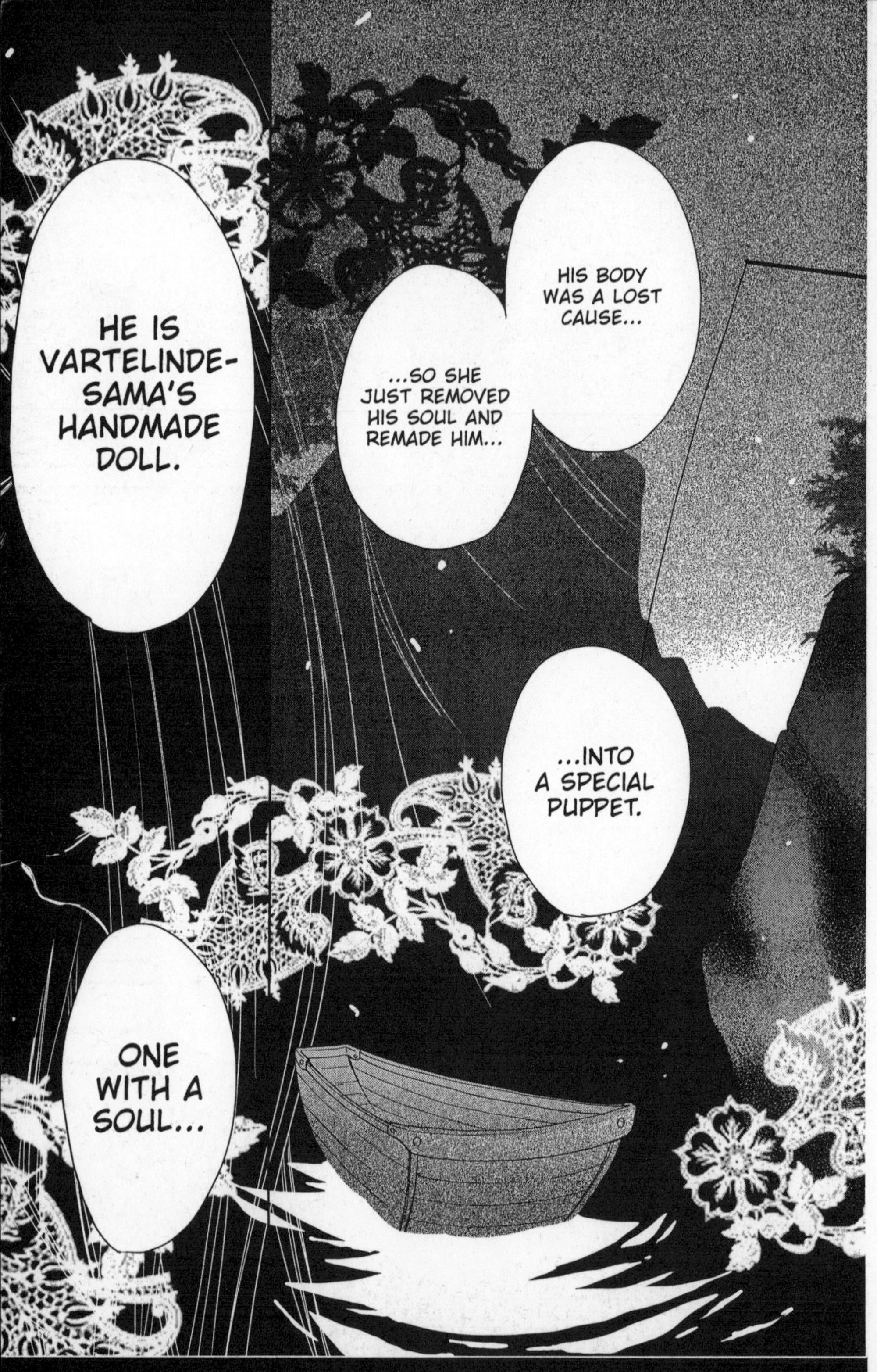
HIS BODY WAS A LOST CAUSE...
...SO SHE JUST REMOVED HIS SOUL AND REMADE HIM...
...INTO A SPECIAL PUPPET.
HE IS VARTELINDE-SAMA'S HANDMADE DOLL.
ONE WITH A SOUL...

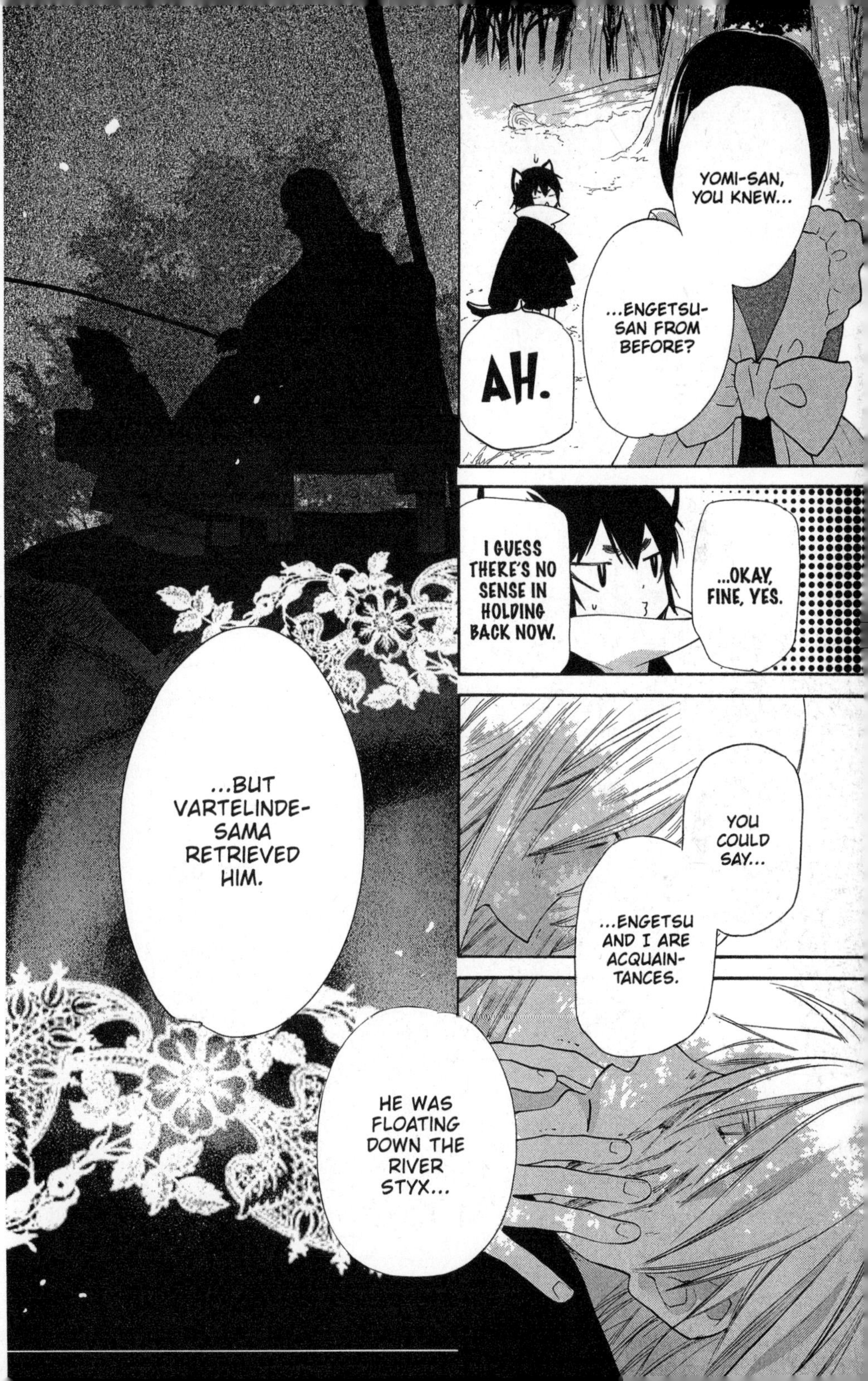
YOMI-SAN, YOU KNEW...
...ENGETSU-SAN FROM BEFORE?
AH.
...OKAY, FINE, YES.
I GUESS THERE'S NO SENSE IN HOLDING BACK NOW.
YOU COULD SAY...
...ENGETSU AND I ARE ACQUAINTANCES.
HE WAS FLOATING DOWN THE RIVER STYX...
...BUT VARTELINDE-SAMA RETRIEVED HIM.

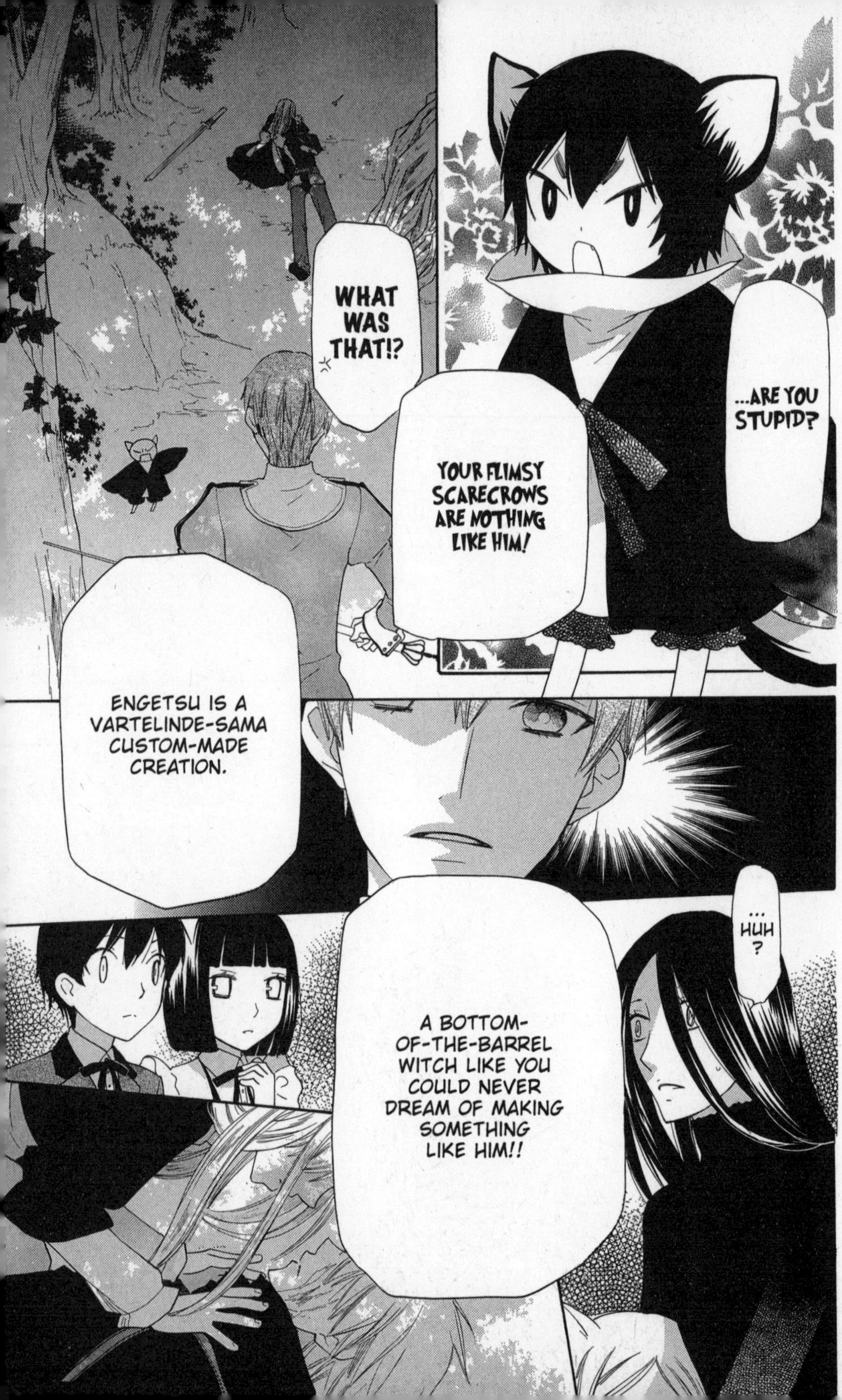
...ARE YOU STUPID?
WHAT WAS THAT!?
YOUR FLIMSY SCARECROWS ARE NOTHING LIKE HIM!
ENGETSU IS A VARTELINDE-SAMA CUSTOM-MADE CREATION.
... HUH?
A BOTTOM-OF-THE-BARREL WITCH LIKE YOU COULD NEVER DREAM OF MAKING SOMETHING LIKE HIM!!

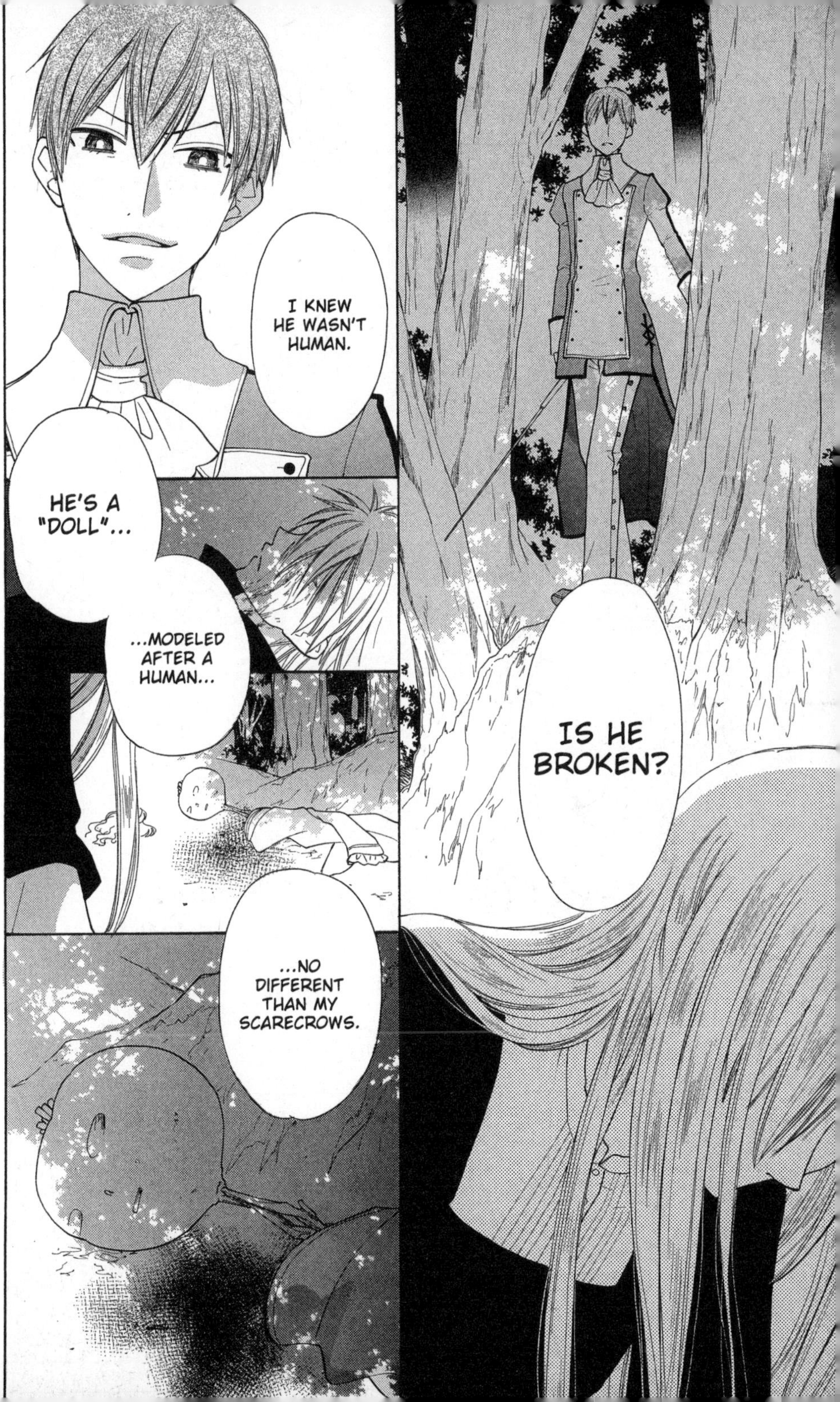
IS HE BROKEN?
I KNEW HE WASN'T HUMAN.
HE'S A "DOLL"...
...MODELED AFTER A HUMAN...
...NO DIFFERENT THAN MY SCARECROWS.

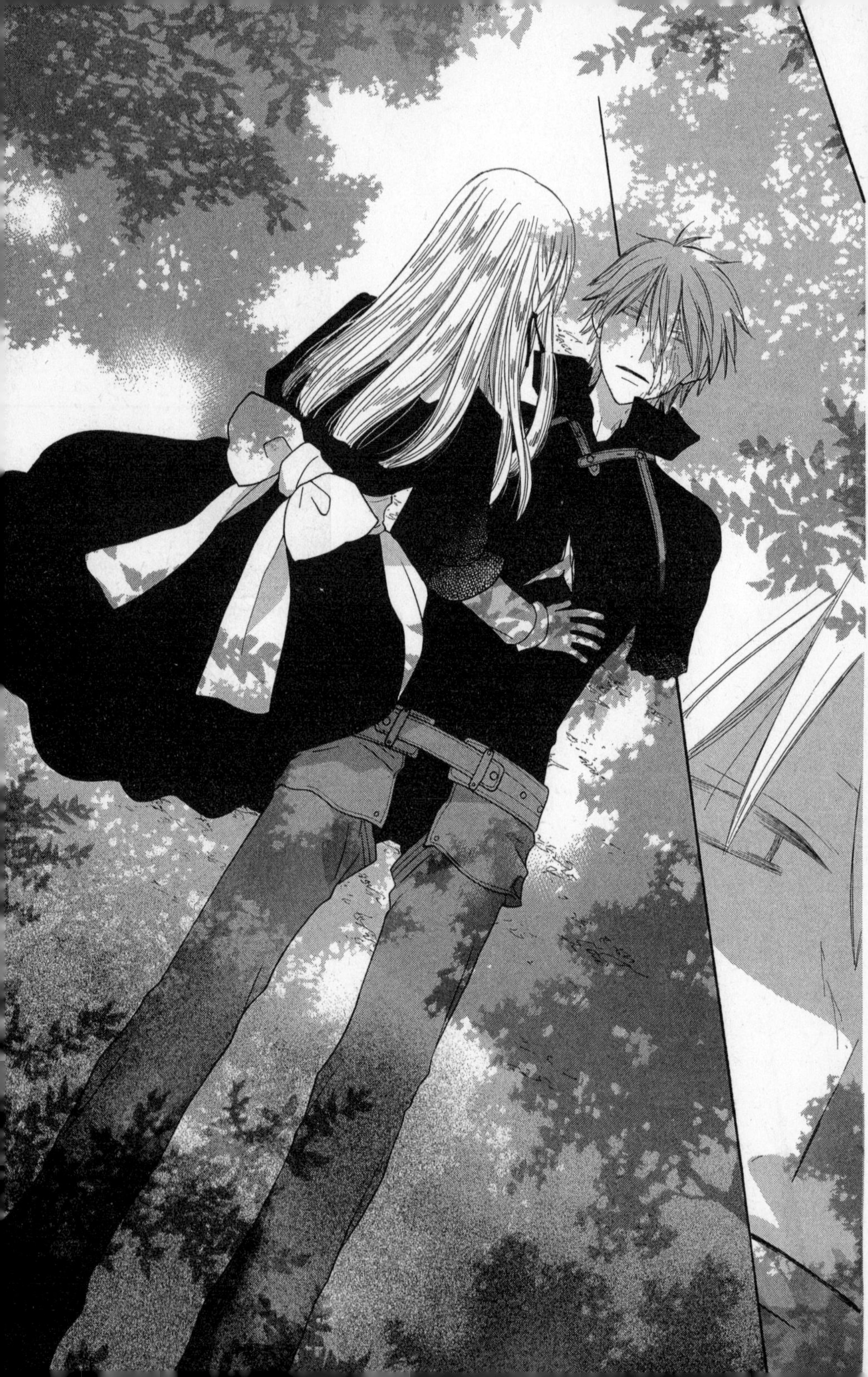

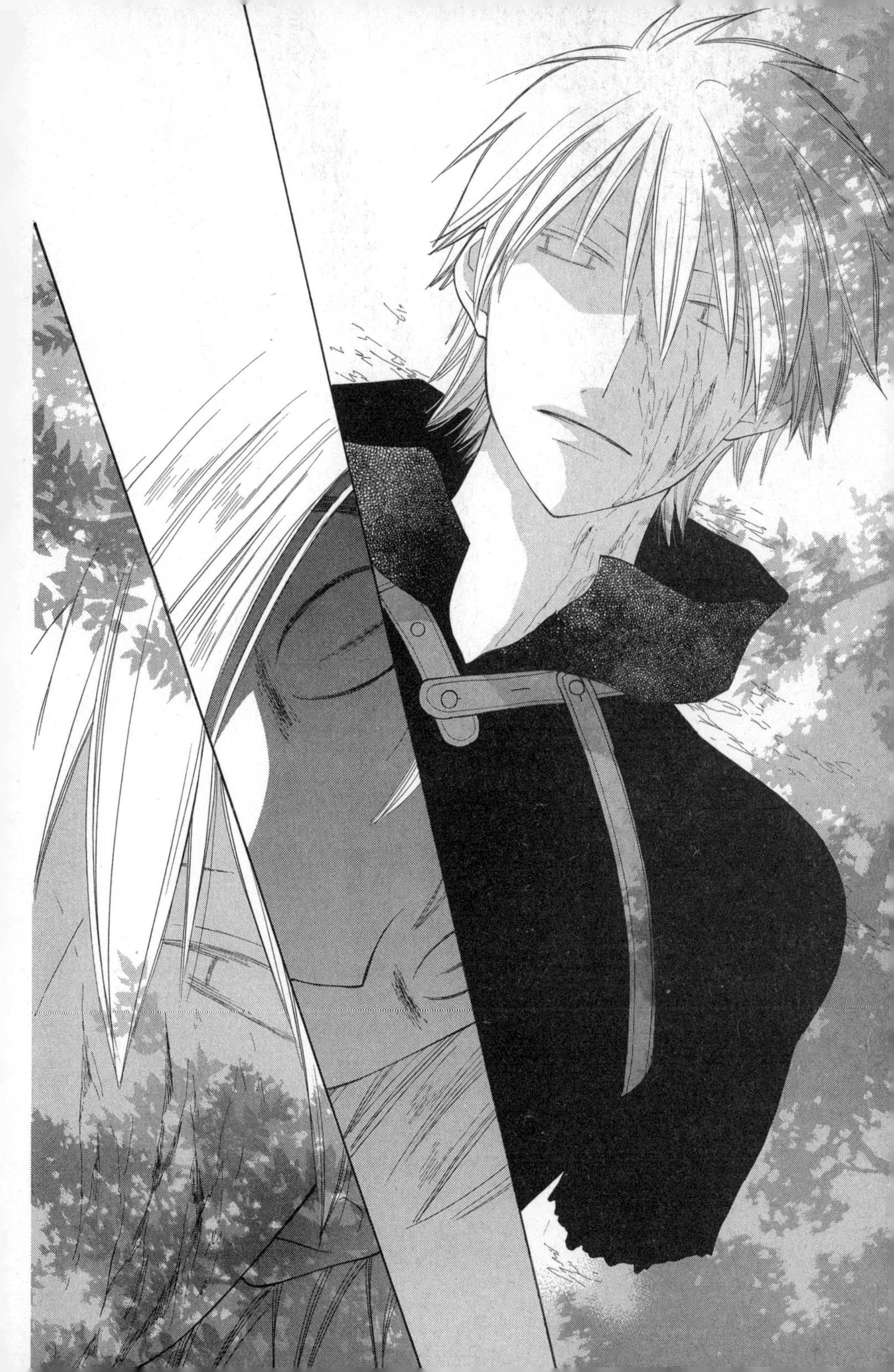

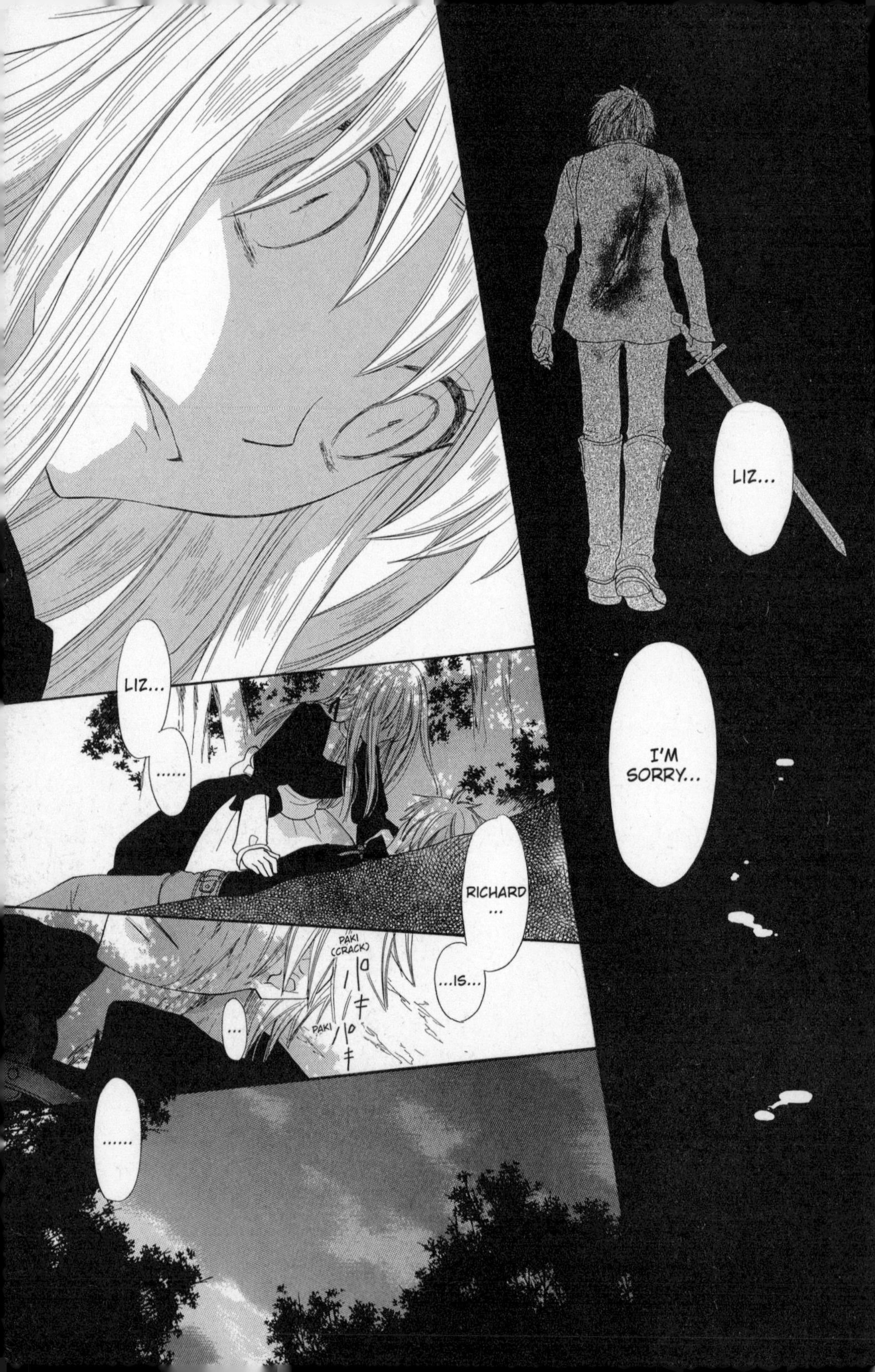
LIZ...
I'M SORRY...
LIZ...
......
RICHARD ...
...IS...
PAKI (CRACK)
PAKI
...
......

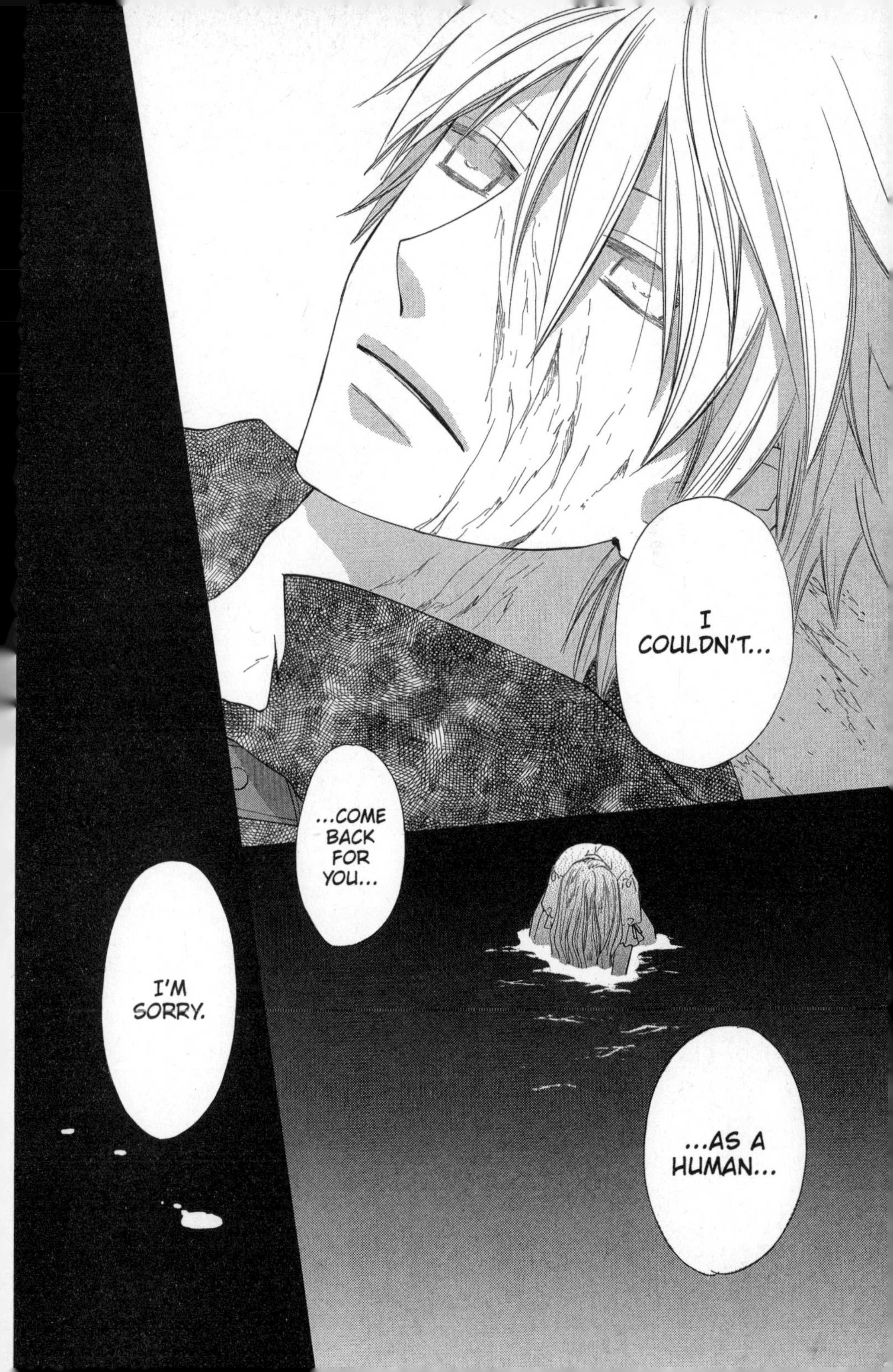
I COULDN'T...
...COME BACK FOR YOU...
...AS A HUMAN...
I'M SORRY.

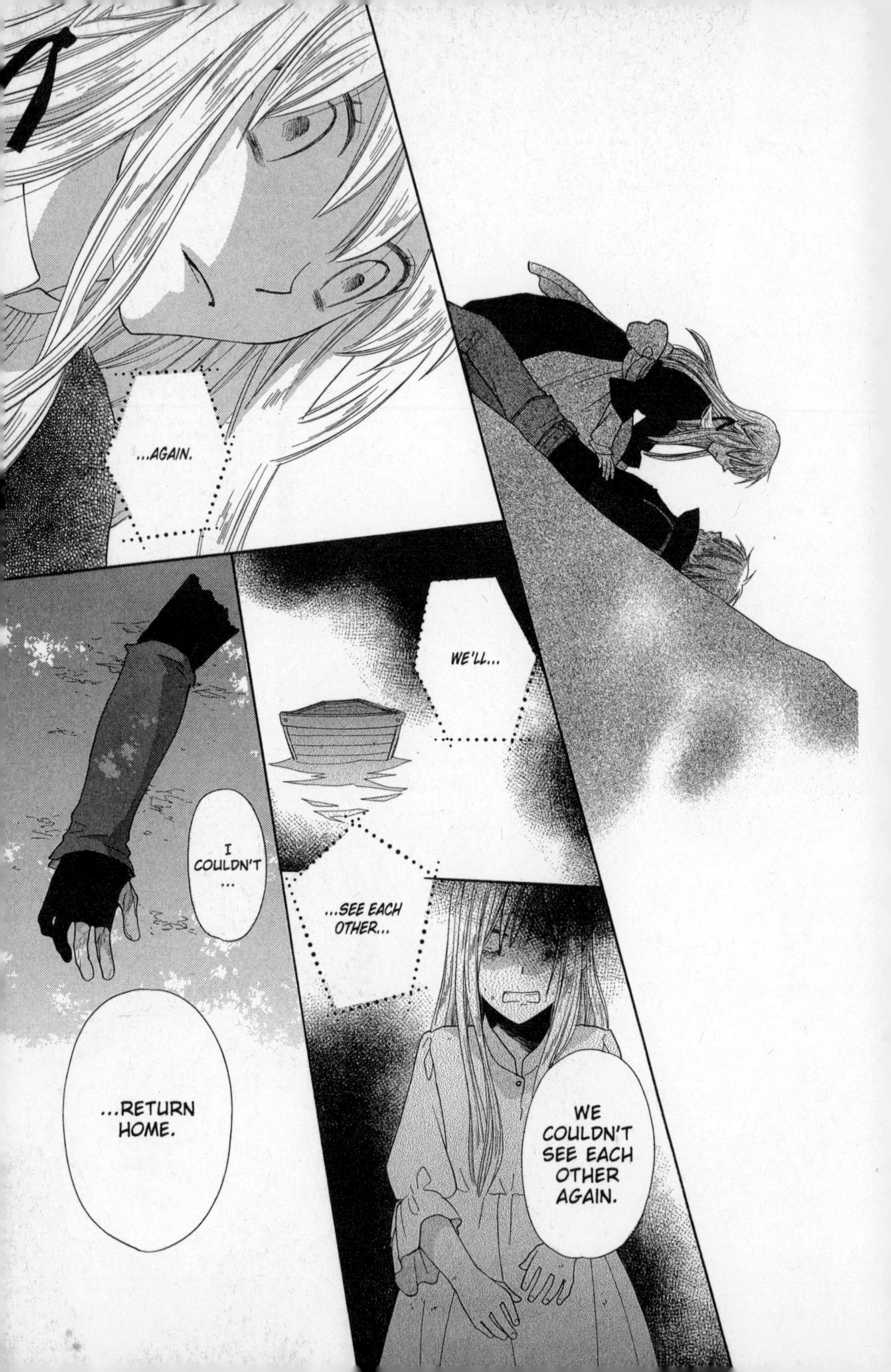
...AGAIN.
WE'LL...
...SEE EACH OTHER...
WE COULDN'T SEE EACH OTHER AGAIN.
I COULDN'T ...
...RETURN HOME.

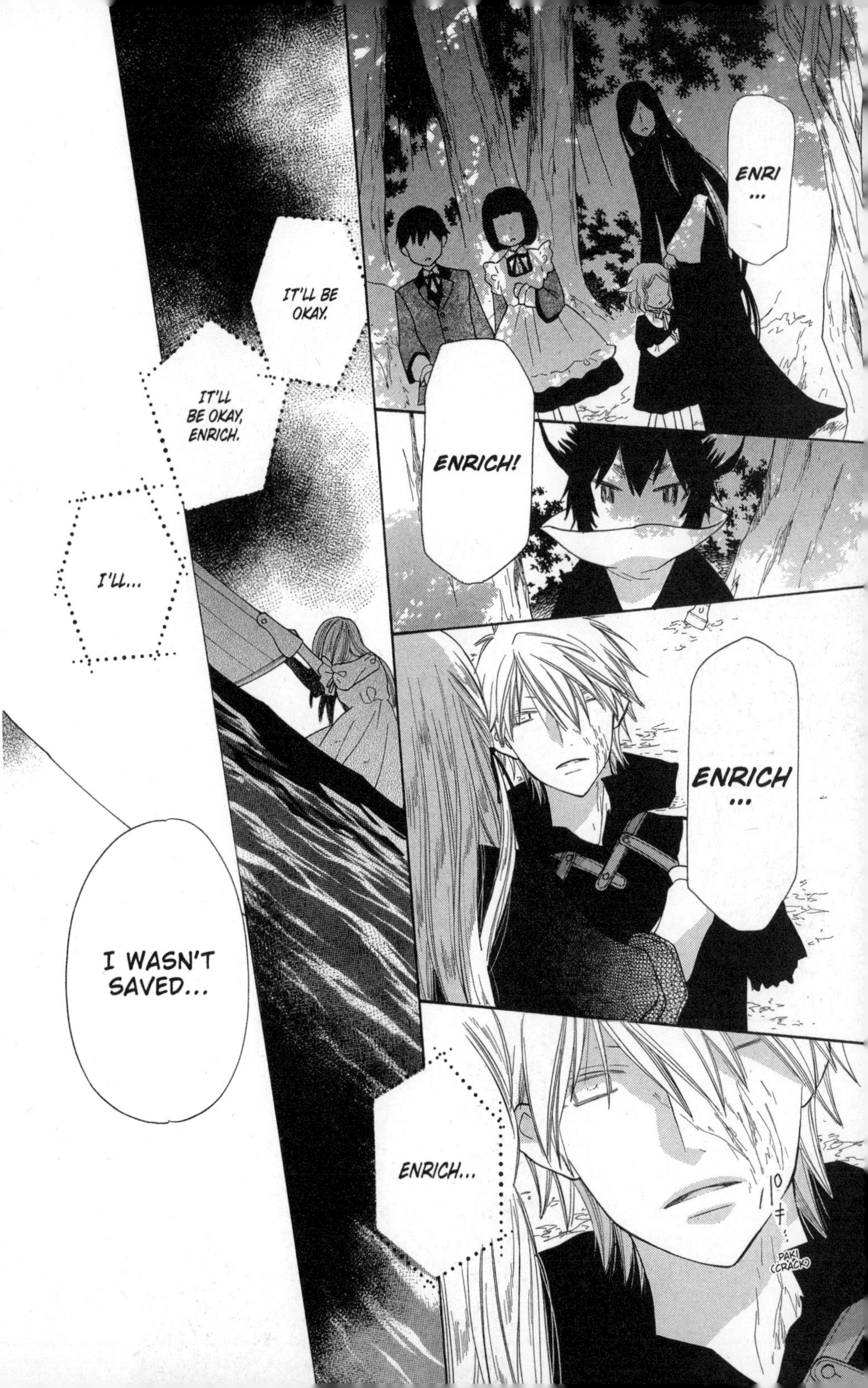
ENRI...
ENRICH!
ENRICH...
ENRICH...
PAKI (CRACK)
IT'LL BE OKAY.
IT'LL BE OKAY, ENRICH.
I'LL...
I WASN'T SAVED...

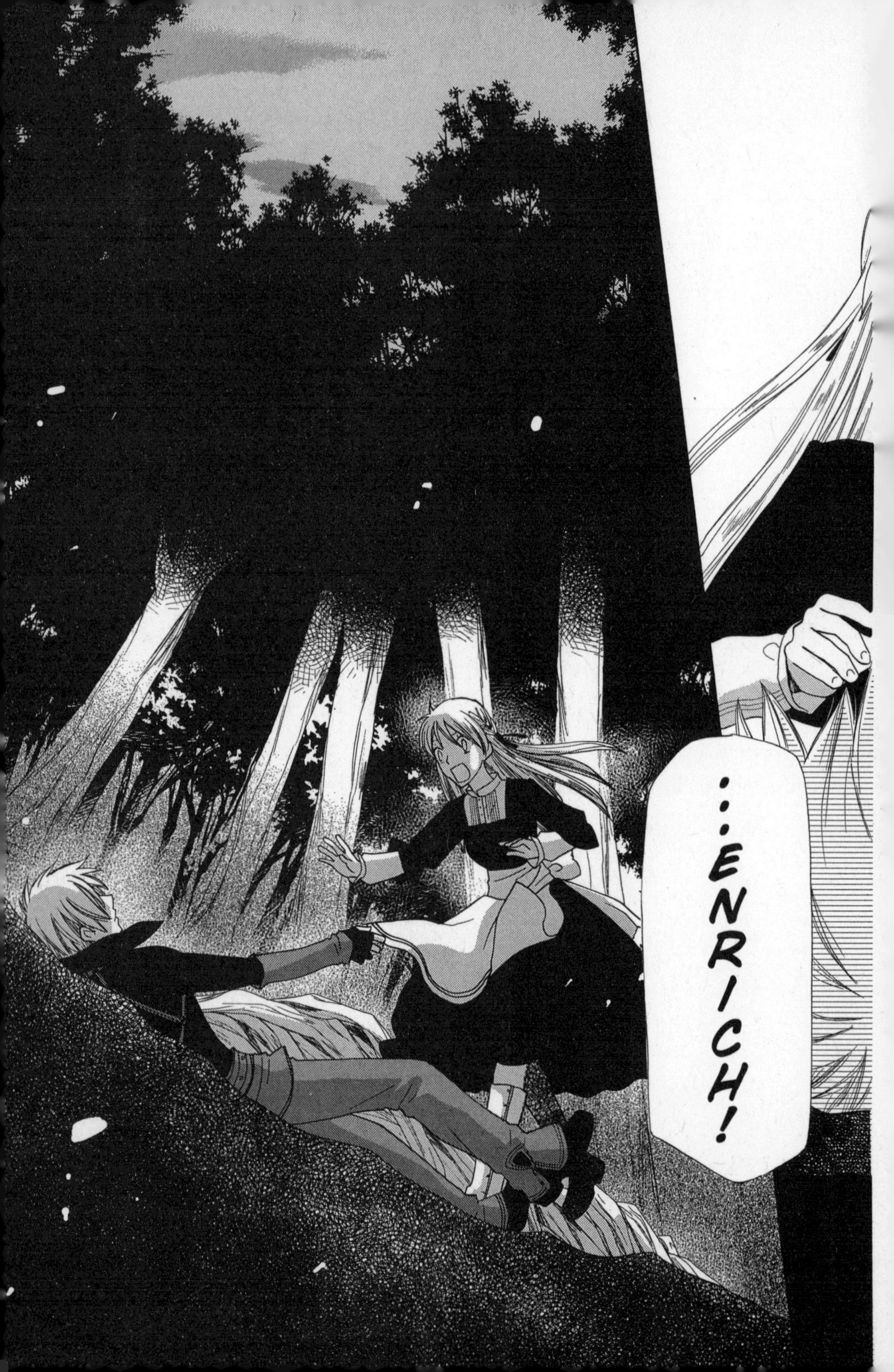
...ENRICH!

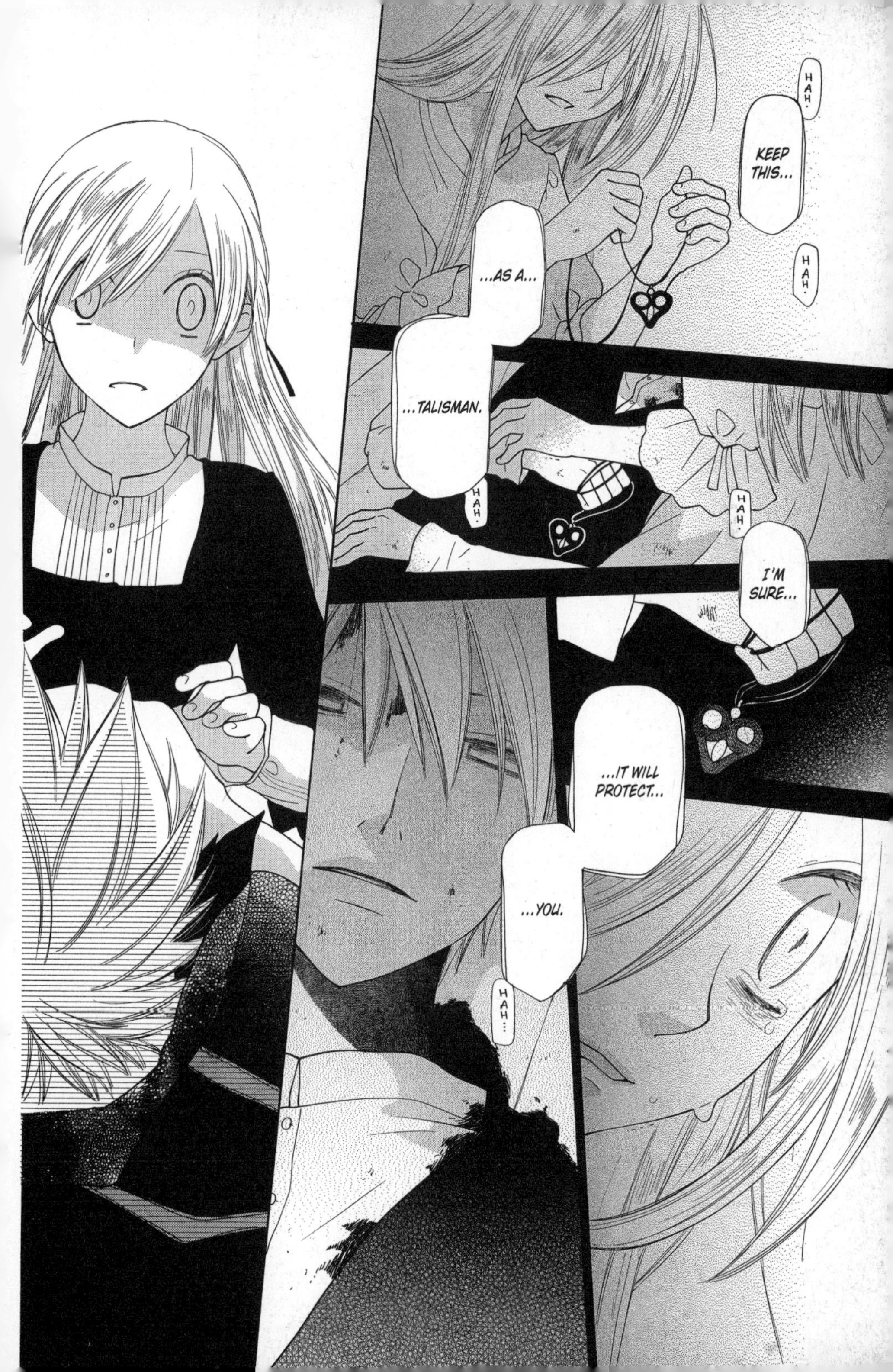
HAH.
KEEP THIS...
HAH.
...AS A...
...TALISMAN.
HAH.
HAH.
I'M SURE...
...IT WILL PROTECT...
...YOU.
HAH...

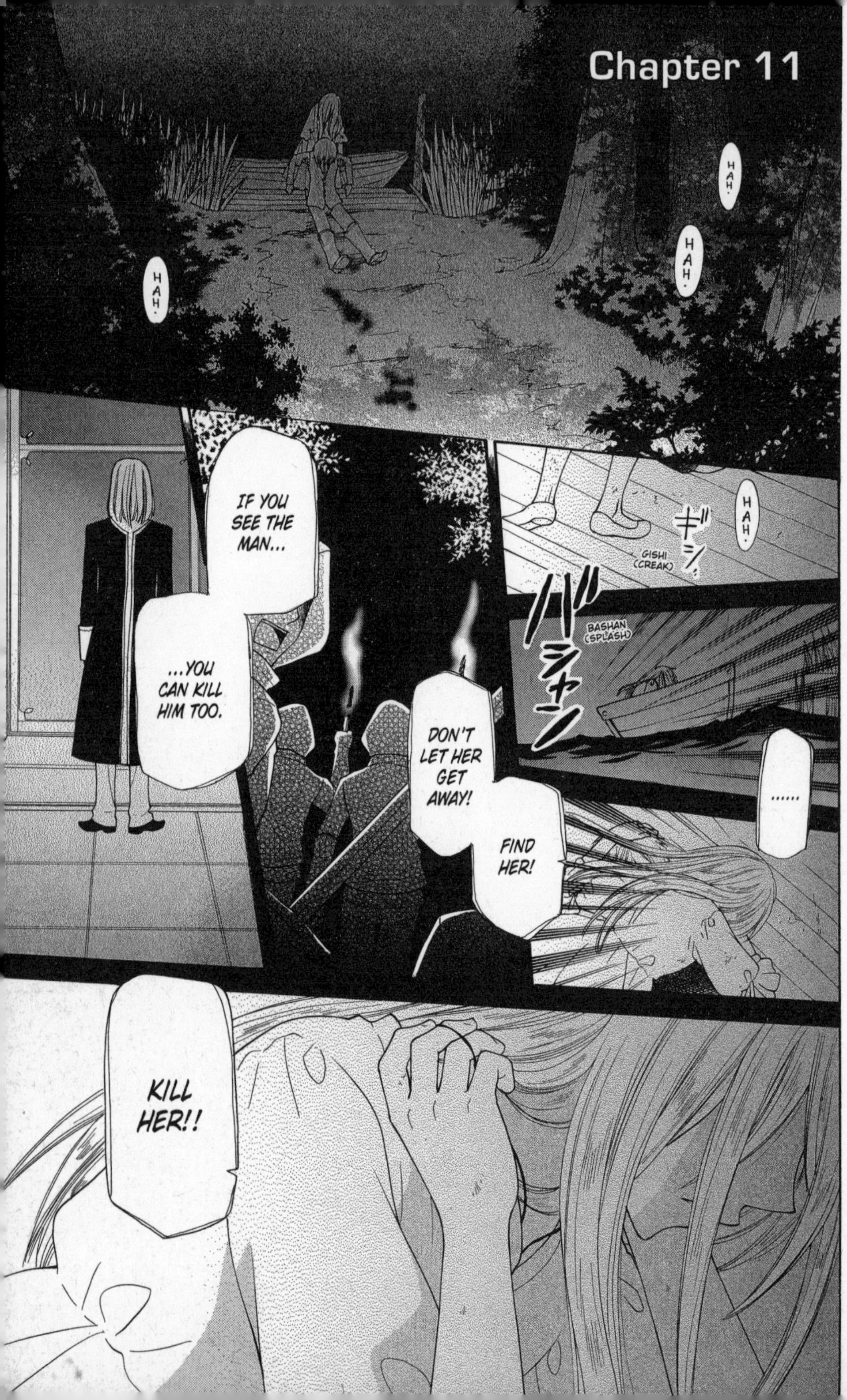
Chapter 11
HAH.
HAH.
HAH.
HAH.
GISHI (CREAK)
BASHAN (SPLASH)
......
DON'T LET HER GET AWAY!
FIND HER!
IF YOU SEE THE MAN...
...YOU CAN KILL HIM TOO.
KILL HER!!

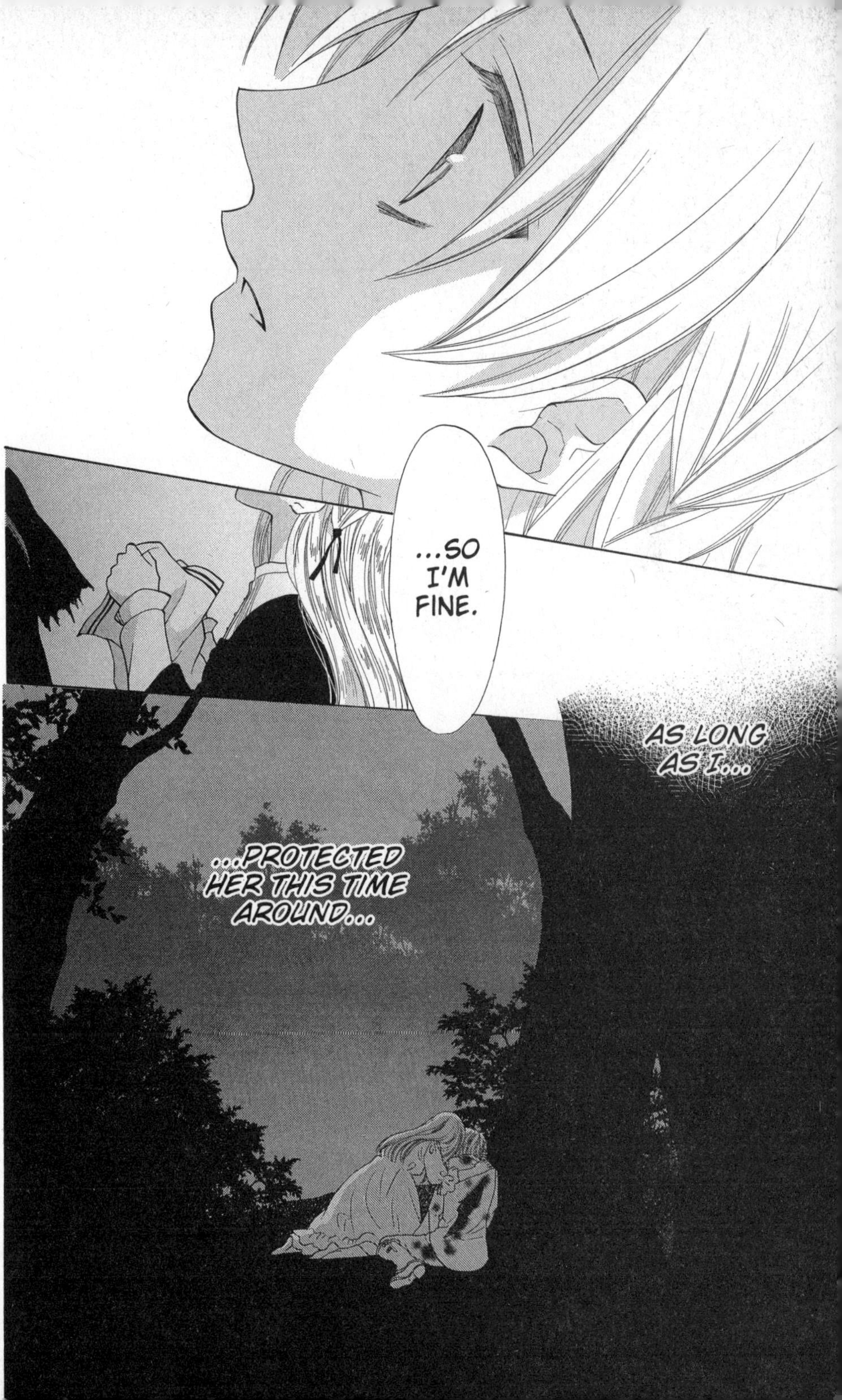
...SO I'M FINE.
AS LONG AS I...
...PROTECTED HER THIS TIME AROUND...

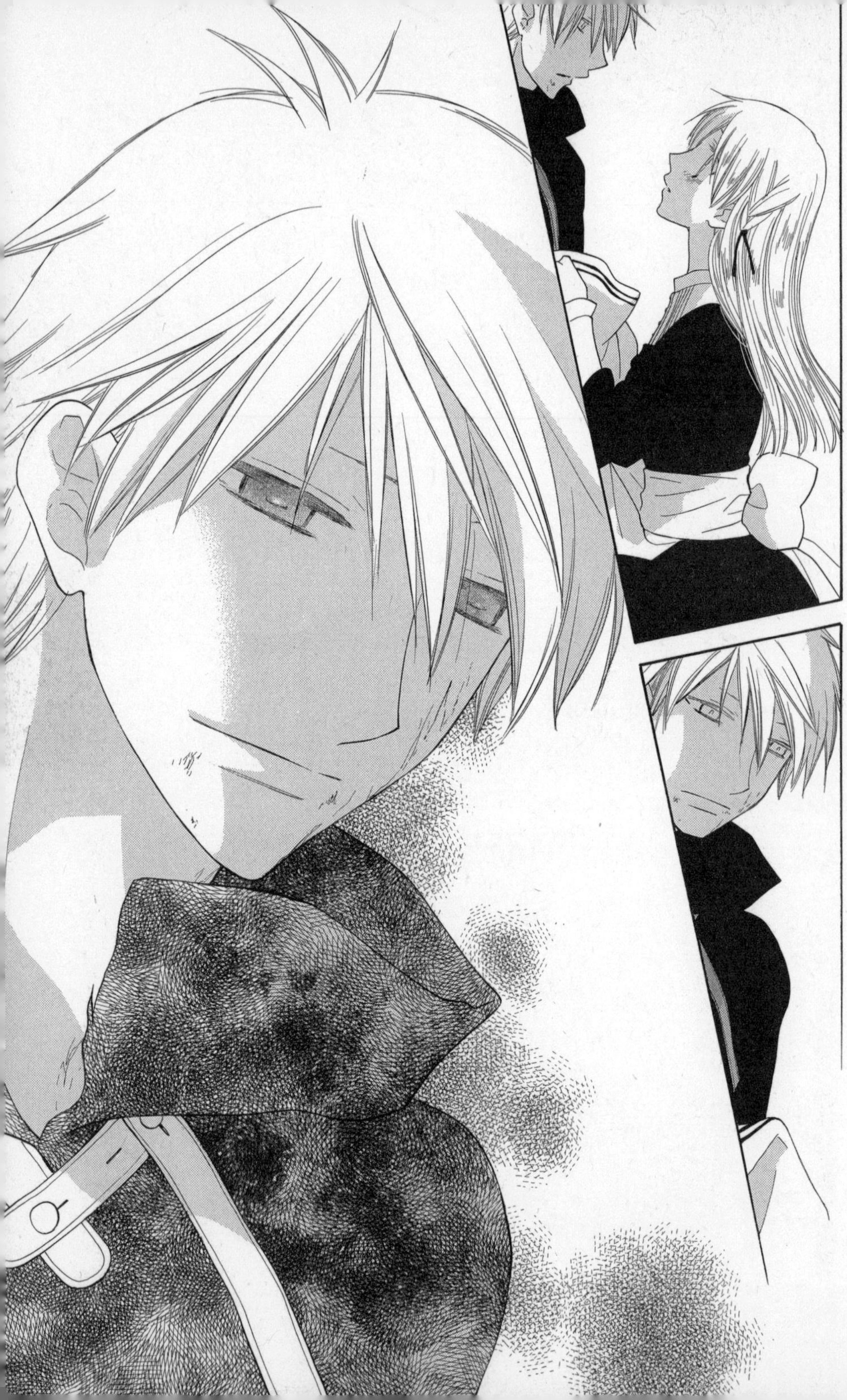

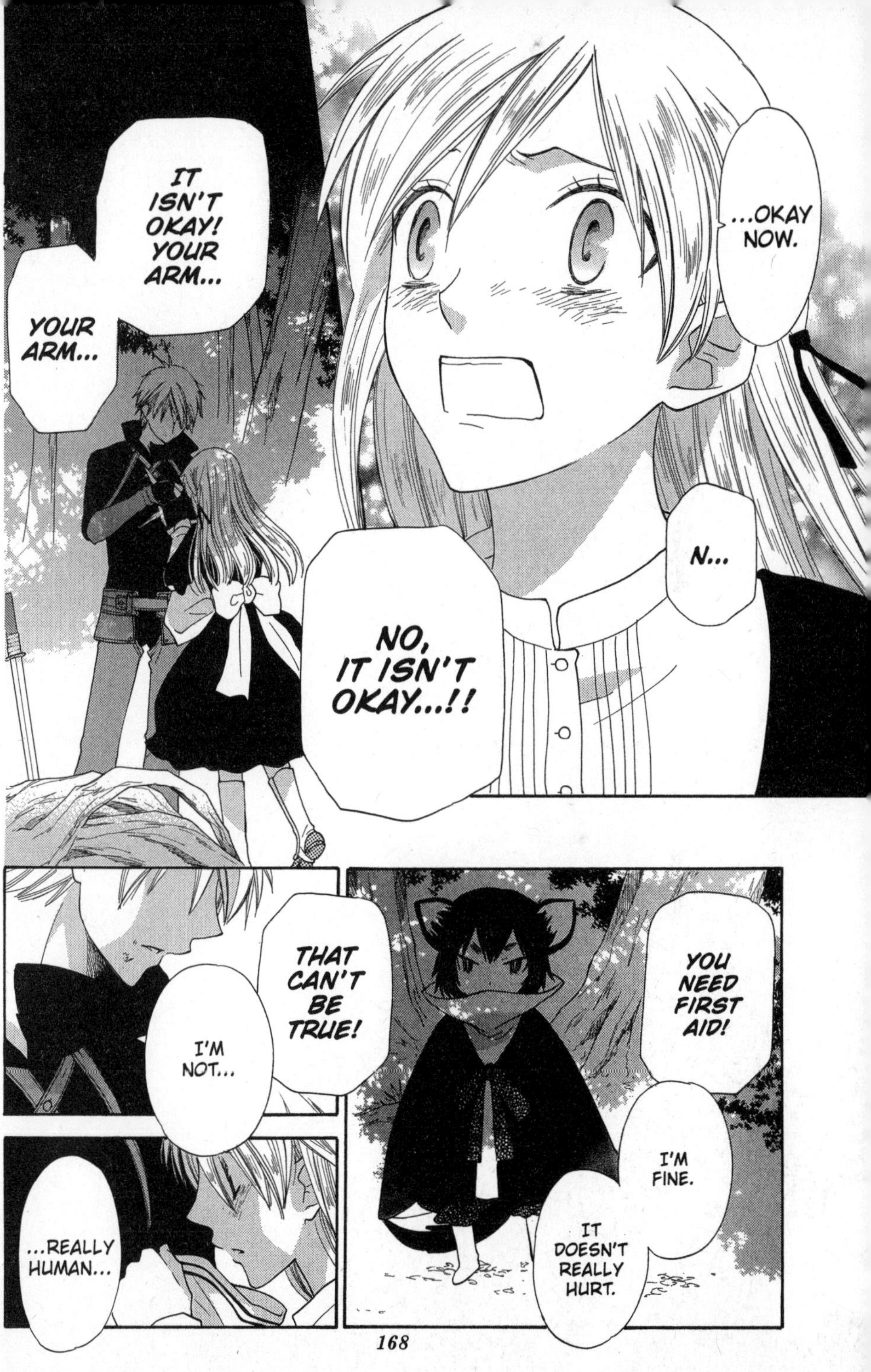
...OKAY NOW.
N...
NO, IT ISN'T OKAY...!!
IT ISN'T OKAY! YOUR ARM...
YOUR ARM...
YOU NEED FIRST AID!
I'M FINE.
IT DOESN'T REALLY HURT.
THAT CAN'T BE TRUE!
I'M NOT...
...REALLY HUMAN...

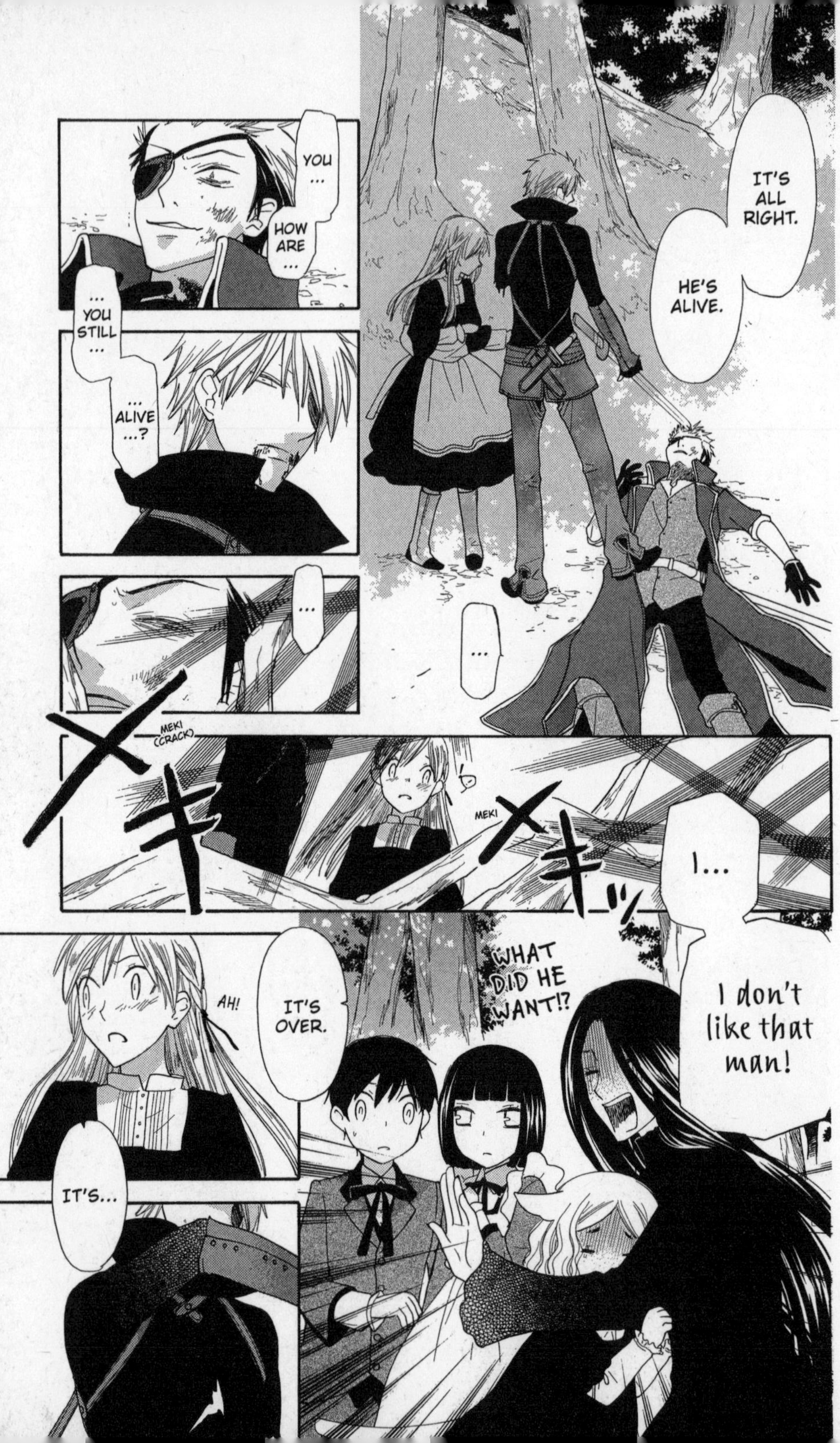
IT'S ALL RIGHT.
HE'S ALIVE.
...
YOU ... HOW ARE ...
... YOU STILL ...
... ALIVE ...?
...
MEKI
!
MEKI (CRACK)
I...
I don't like that man!
WHAT DID HE WANT!?
IT'S OVER.
AH!
IT'S...

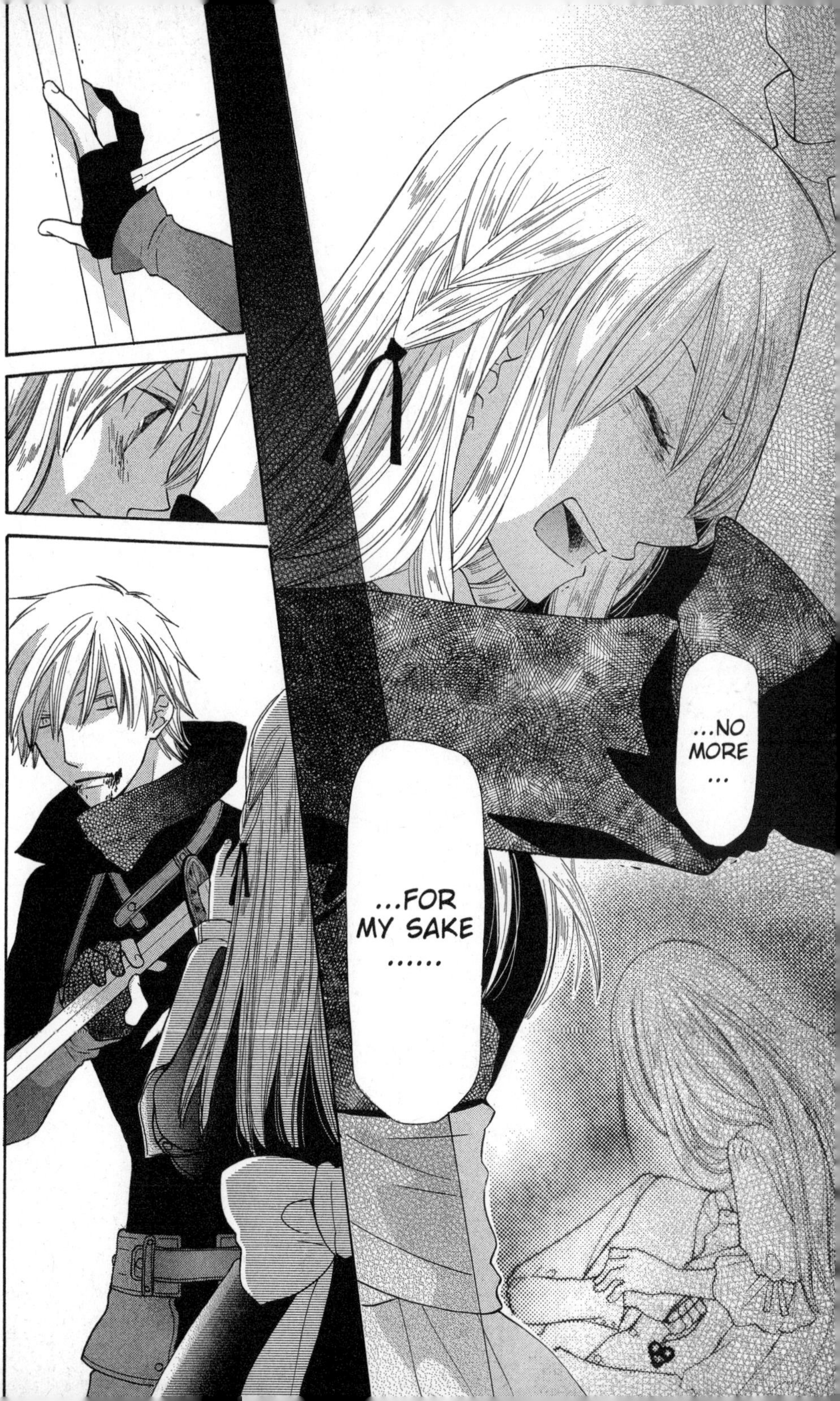
...NO MORE ...
...FOR MY SAKE ......

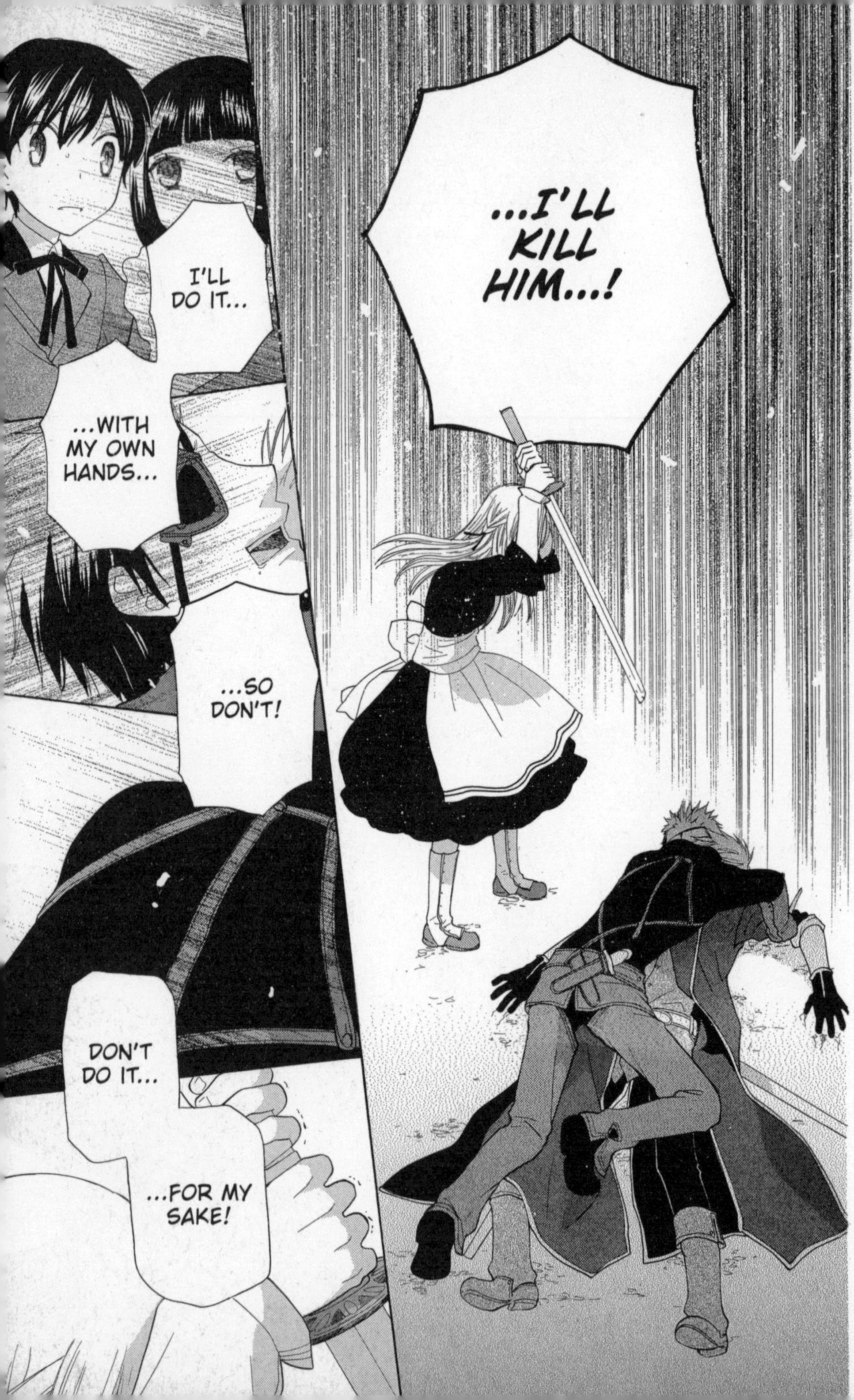
...I'LL KILL HIM...!
I'LL DO IT...
...WITH MY OWN HANDS...
...SO DON'T!
DON'T DO IT...
...FOR MY SAKE!

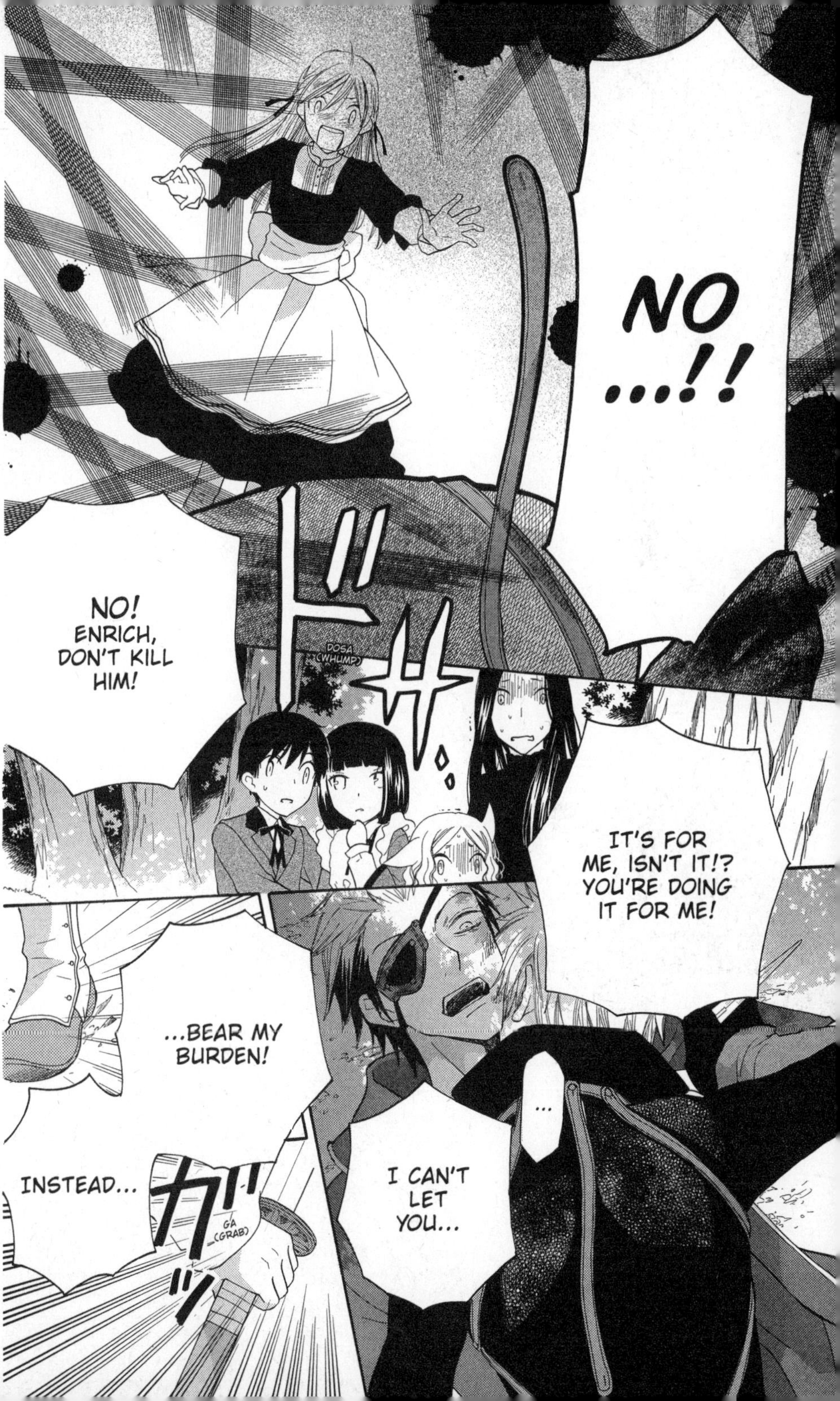
NO ...!!
NO! ENRICH, DON'T KILL HIM!
DOSA (WHUMP)
IT'S FOR ME, ISN'T IT!? YOU'RE DOING IT FOR ME!
...
I CAN'T LET YOU...
...BEAR MY BURDEN!
INSTEAD...
GA (GRAB)

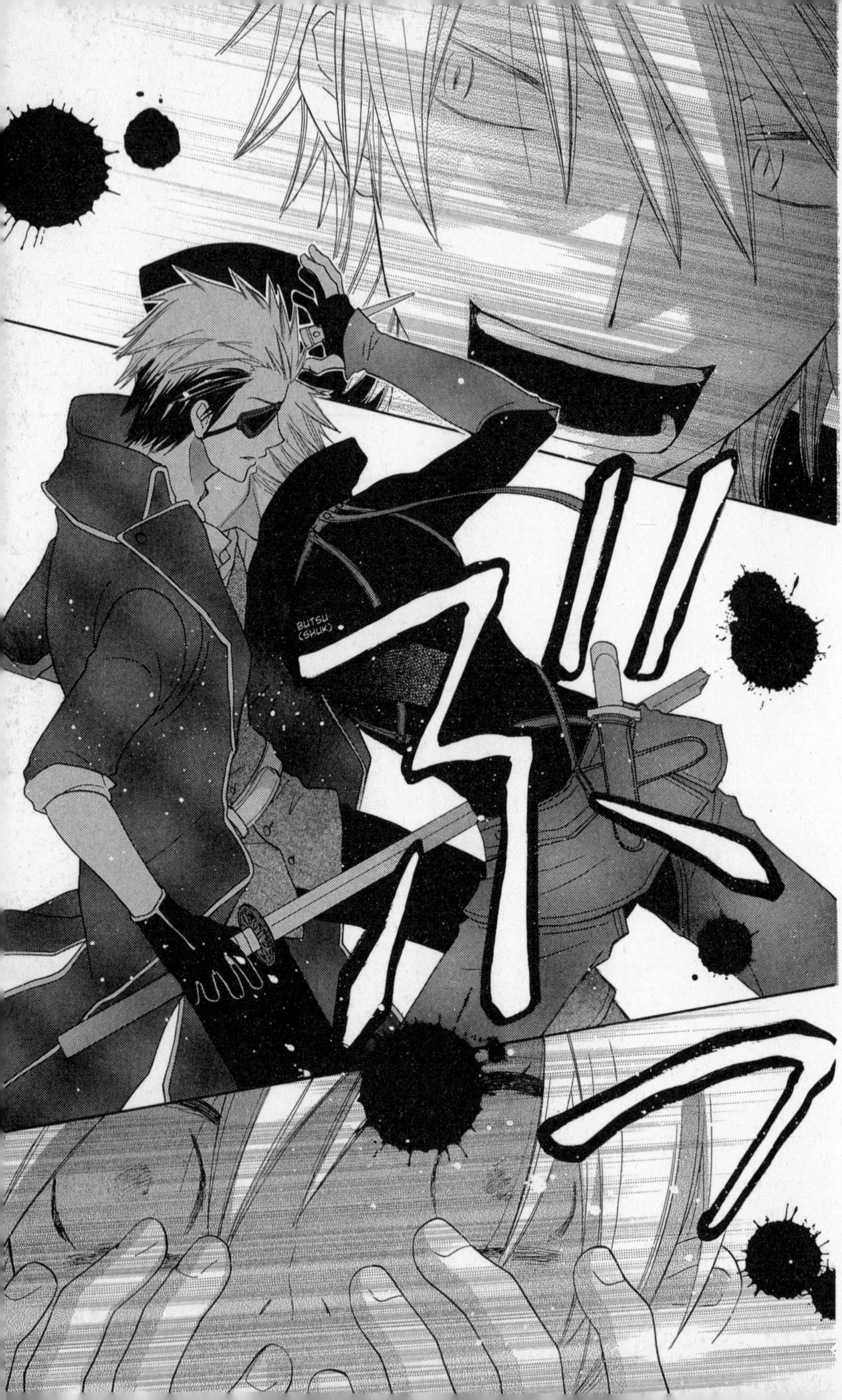
BUTSU
(SHUK)

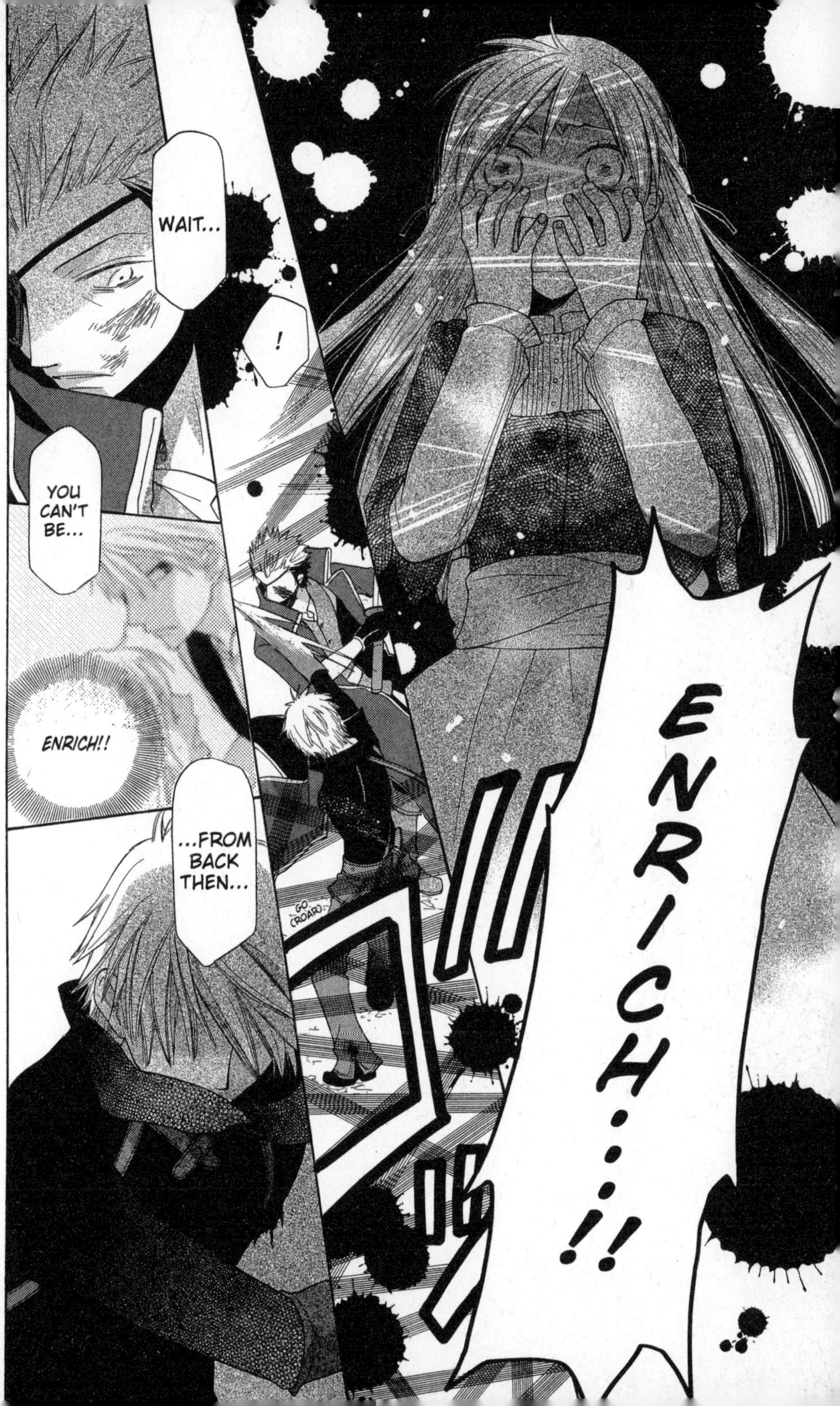
ENRICH...!!
!
GO (ROAR)
WAIT...
YOU CAN'T BE...
ENRICH!!
...FROM BACK THEN...

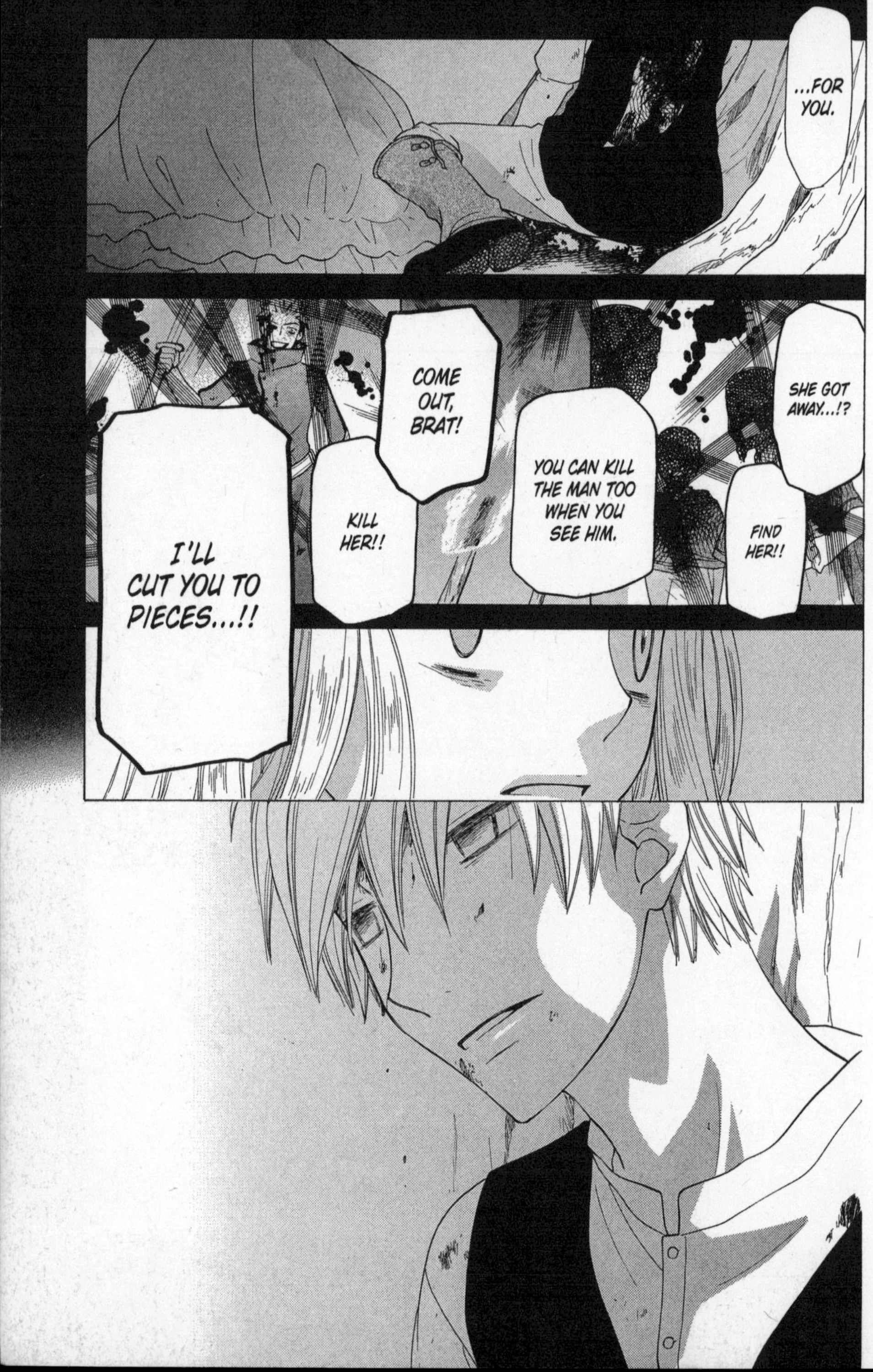
...FOR YOU.
SHE GOT AWAY...!?
FIND HER!!
YOU CAN KILL THE MAN TOO WHEN YOU SEE HIM.
COME OUT, BRAT!
KILL HER!!
I'LL CUT YOU TO PIECES...!!

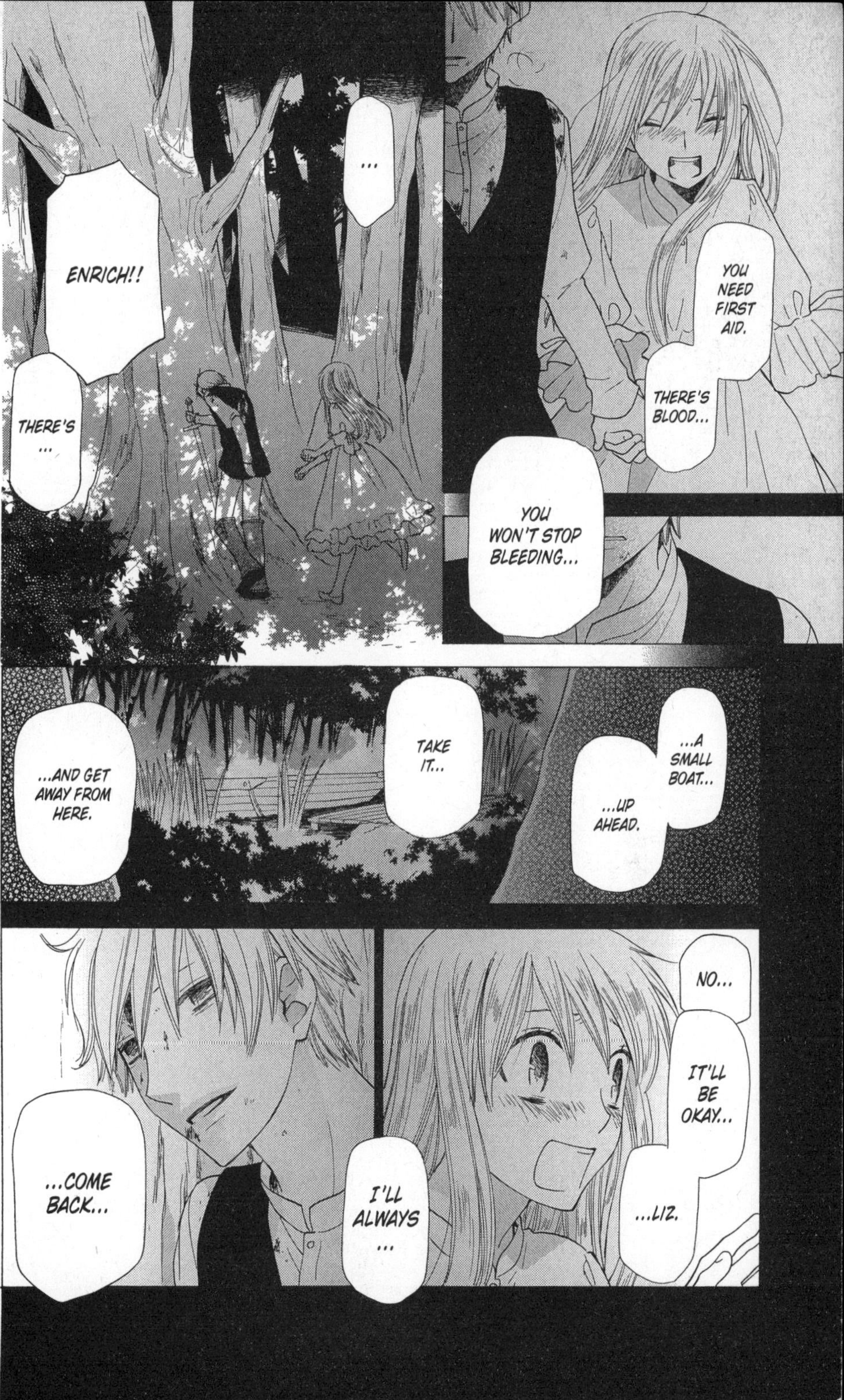
YOU NEED FIRST AID.
THERE'S BLOOD...
YOU WON'T STOP BLEEDING...
...
ENRICH!!
THERE'S ...
...A SMALL BOAT...
...UP AHEAD.
TAKE IT...
...AND GET AWAY FROM HERE.
NO...
IT'LL BE OKAY...
...LIZ.
I'LL ALWAYS ...
...COME BACK...

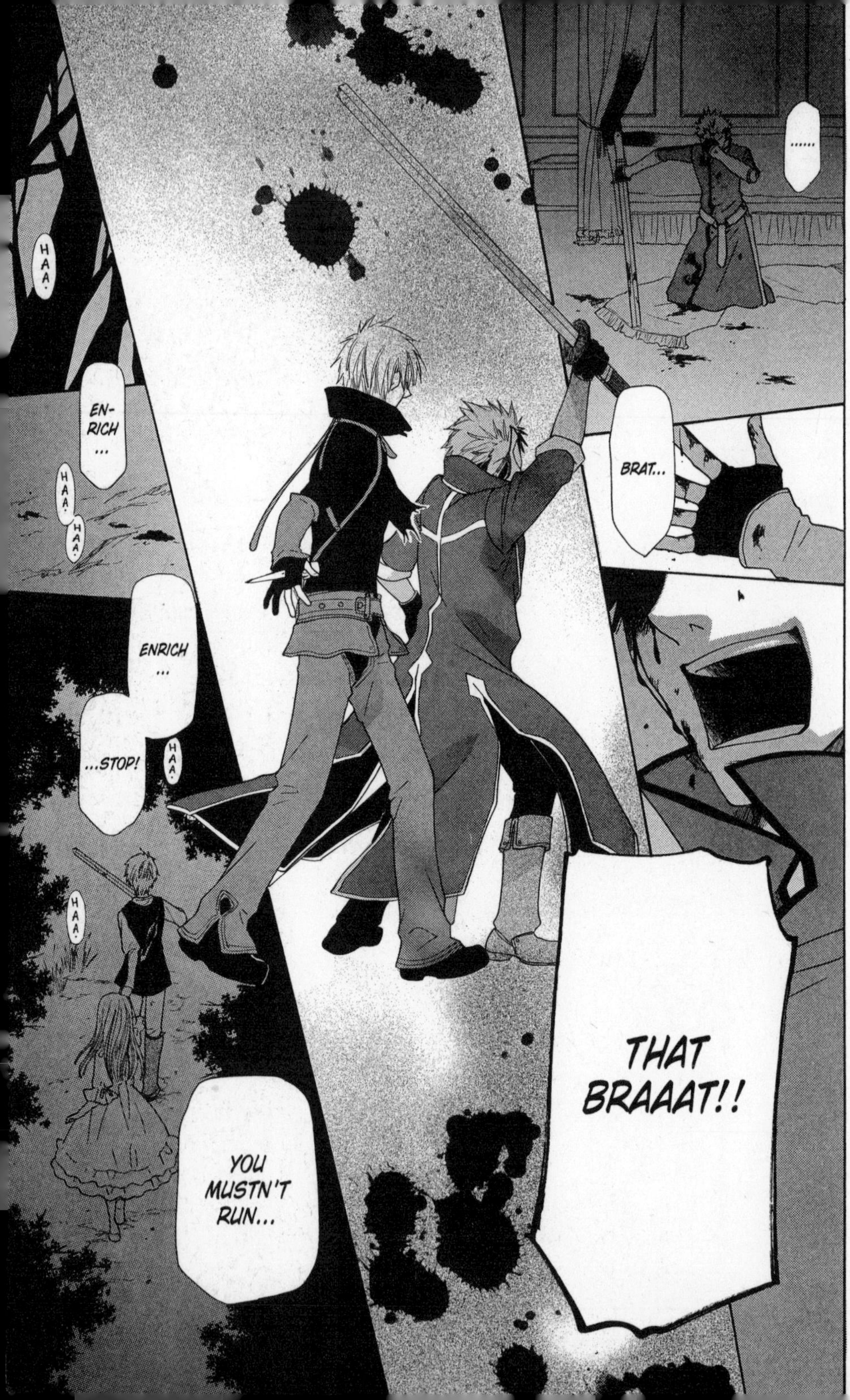
......
BRAT...
THAT BRAAAT!!
HAA.
EN-RICH...
HAA.
HAA.
ENRICH...
...STOP!
HAA.
HAA.
YOU MUSTN'T RUN...

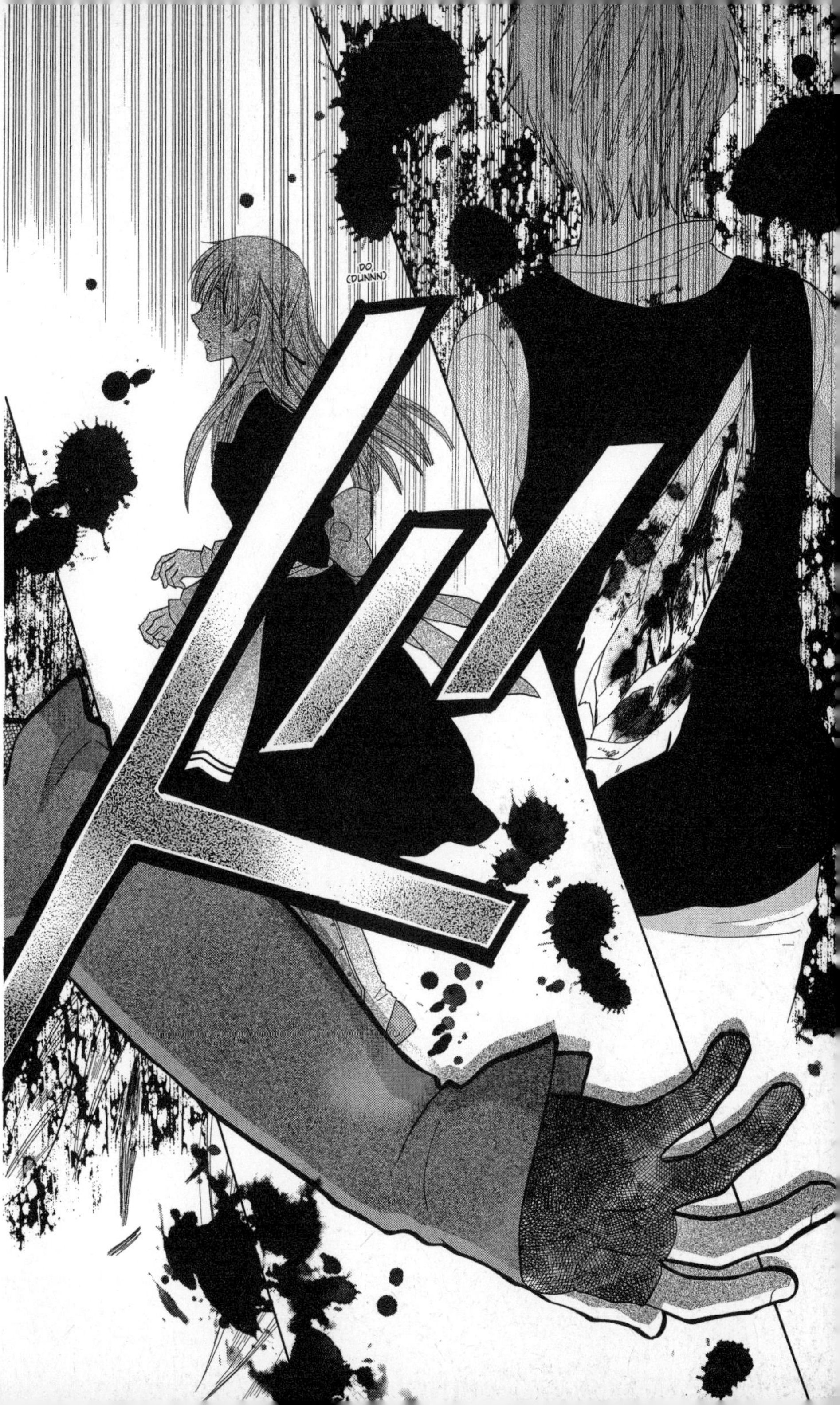
DO
(DUNNN)

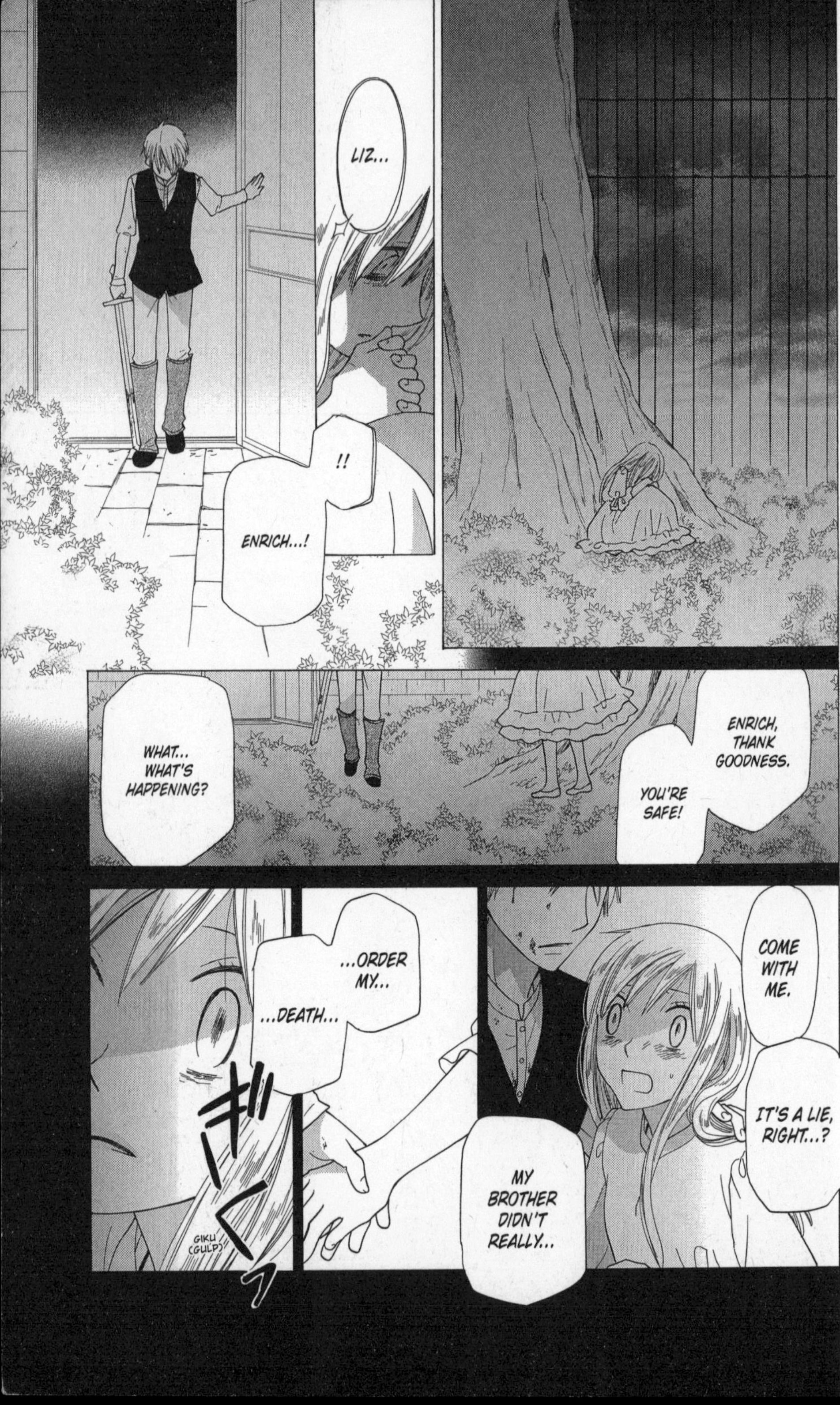
LIZ...
!!
ENRICH...!
ENRICH, THANK GOODNESS.
YOU'RE SAFE!
WHAT... WHAT'S HAPPENING?
COME WITH ME.
IT'S A LIE, RIGHT...?
MY BROTHER DIDN'T REALLY...
...ORDER MY...
...DEATH...
GIKU (GULP)

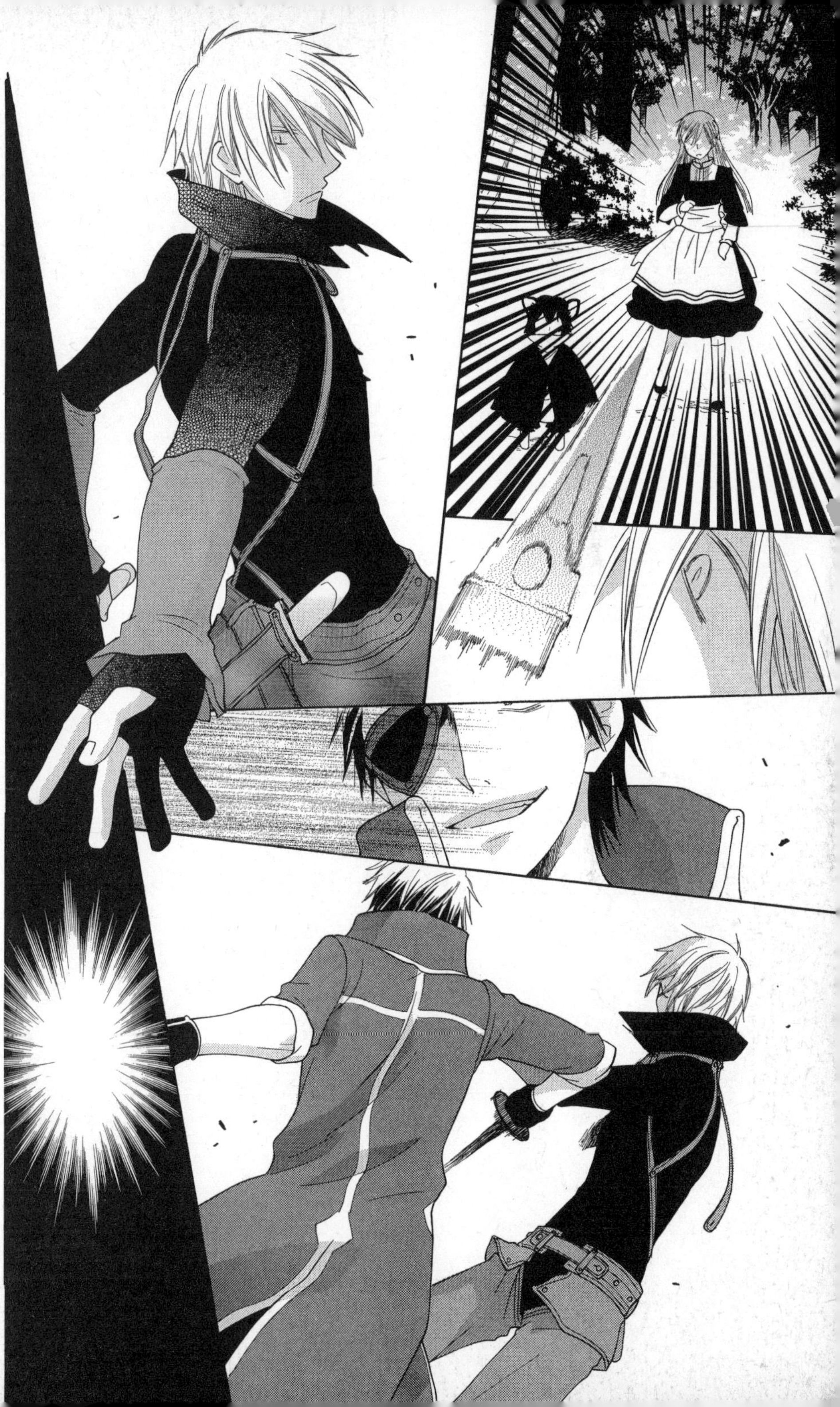

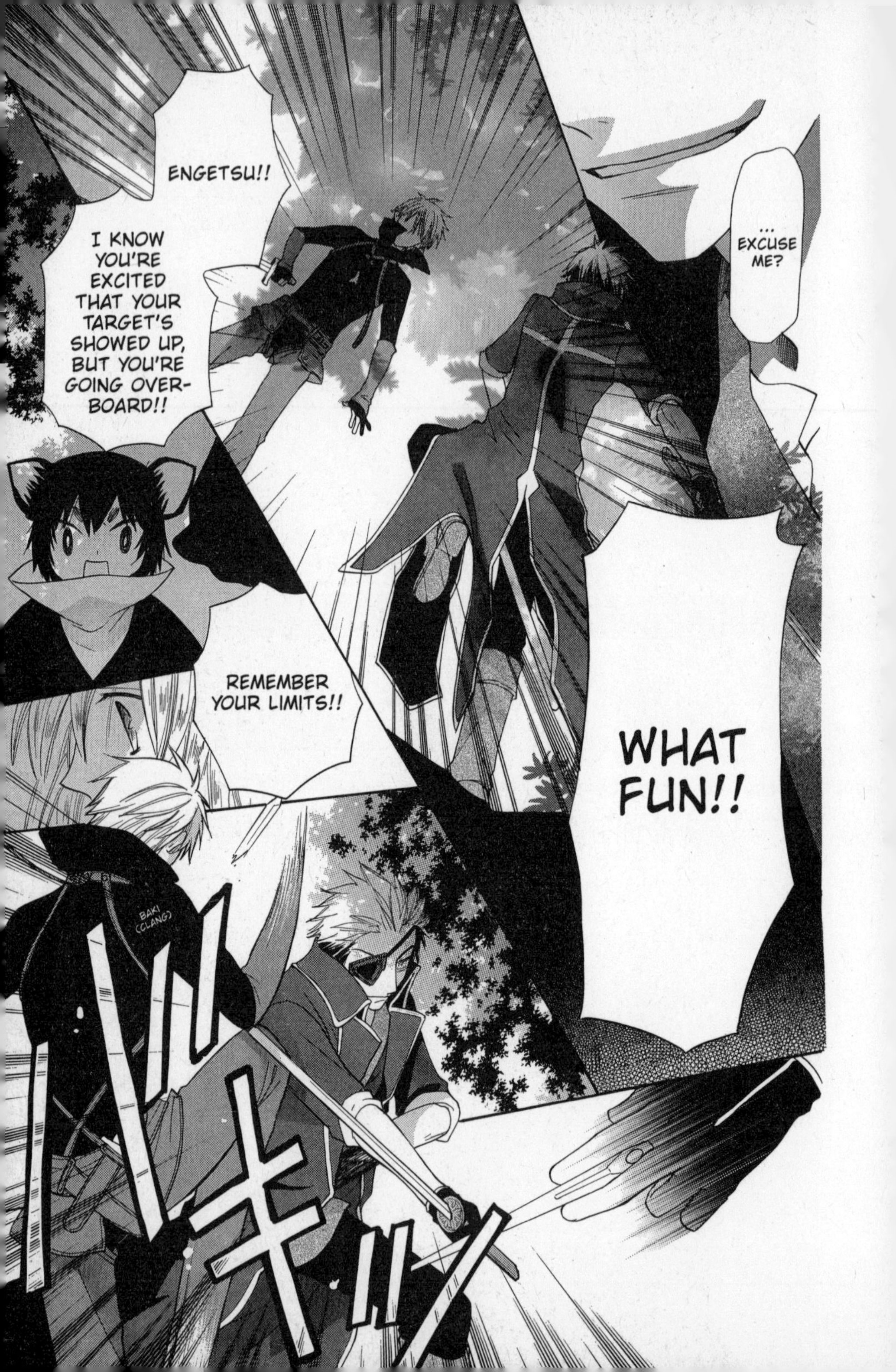

...EXCUSE ME?
WHAT FUN!!
ENGETSU!!
I KNOW YOU'RE EXCITED THAT YOUR TARGET'S SHOWED UP, BUT YOU'RE GOING OVER-BOARD!!
REMEMBER YOUR LIMITS!!
BAKI (CLANG)

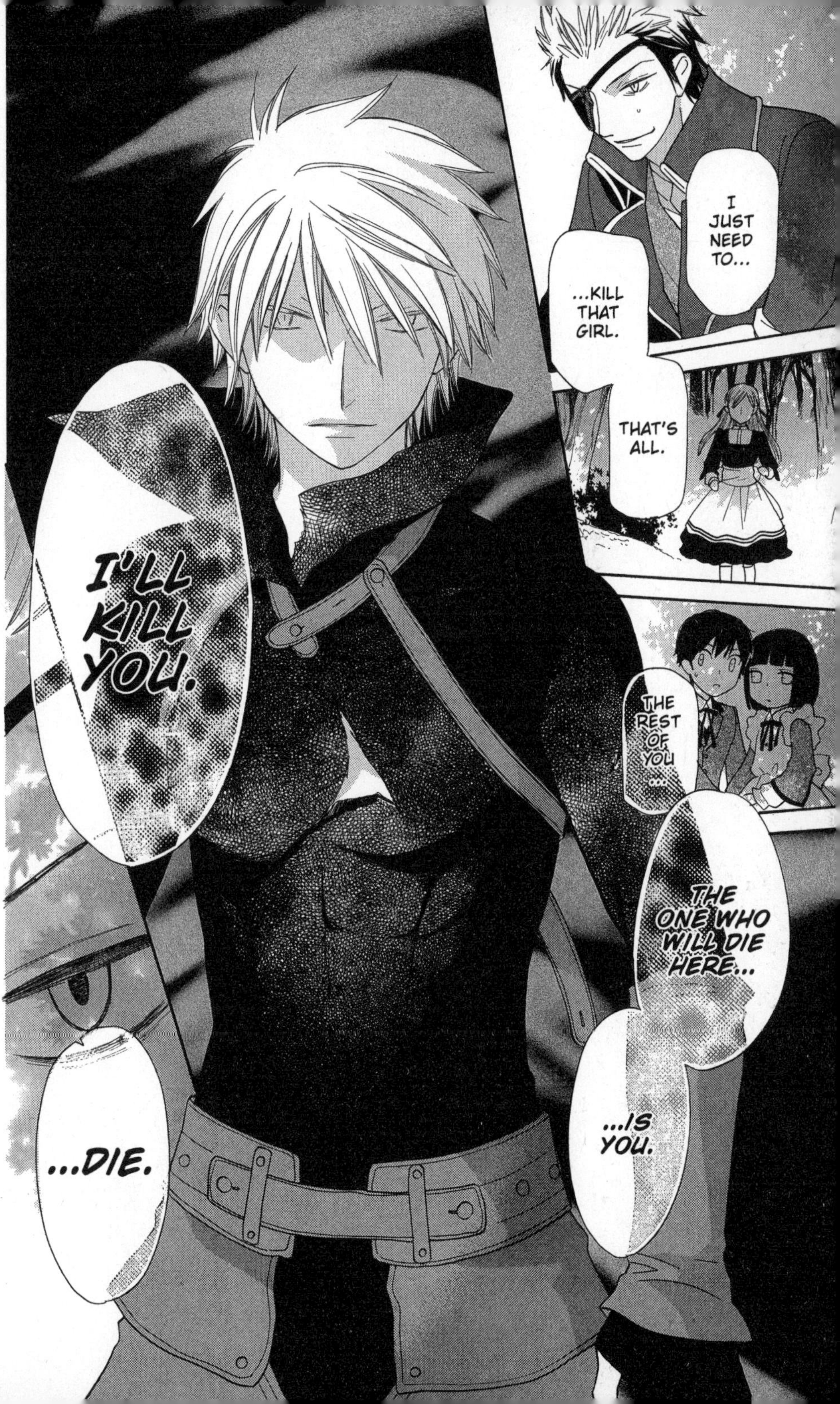
I JUST NEED TO...
...KILL THAT GIRL.
THAT'S ALL.
THE REST OF YOU...
I'LL KILL YOU.
THE ONE WHO WILL DIE HERE...
...IS YOU.
...DIE.

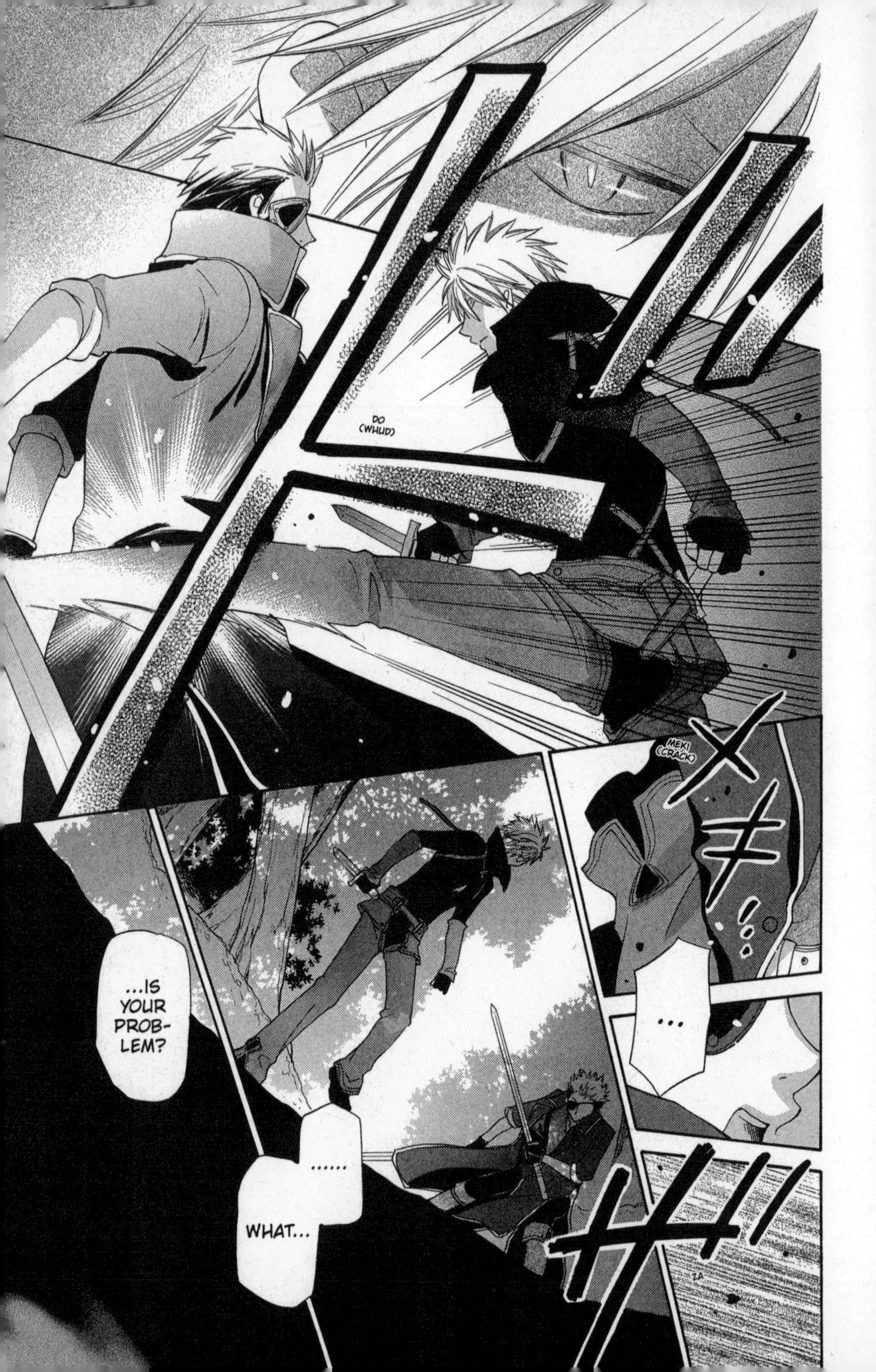
DO (WHUD)
MEKI (CRACK)
...
......
WHAT...
...IS YOUR PROB-LEM?
ZA

AND THEN ...
... ENRICH WAS...
IT ISN'T WISE TO GET BETWEEN ...
...A HUNTER AND HIS PREY!!
ZAN (SLASH)
!!

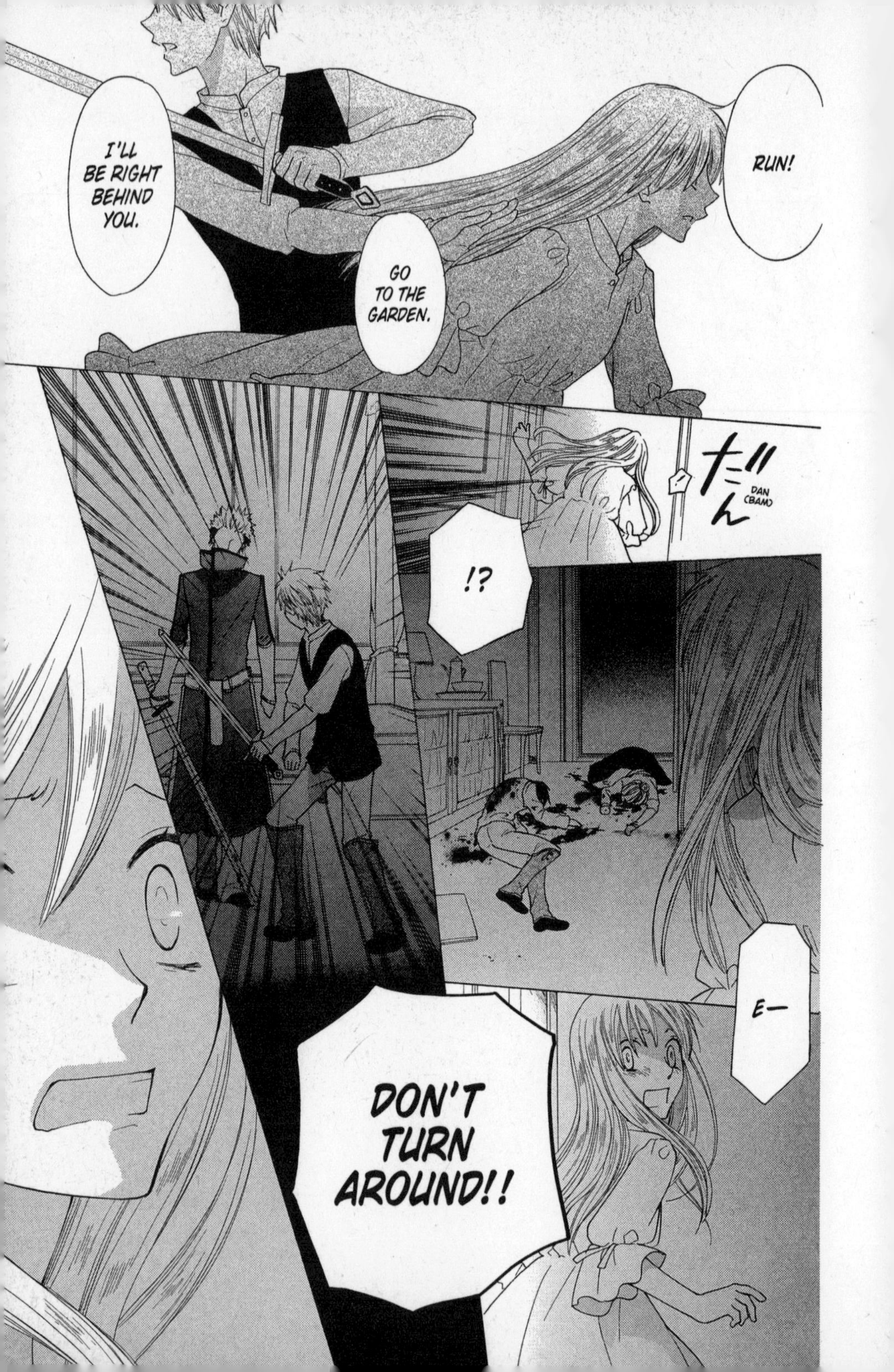
RUN!
GO TO THE GARDEN.
I'LL BE RIGHT BEHIND YOU.
だん
DAN (BAM)
!?
E—
DON'T TURN AROUND!!

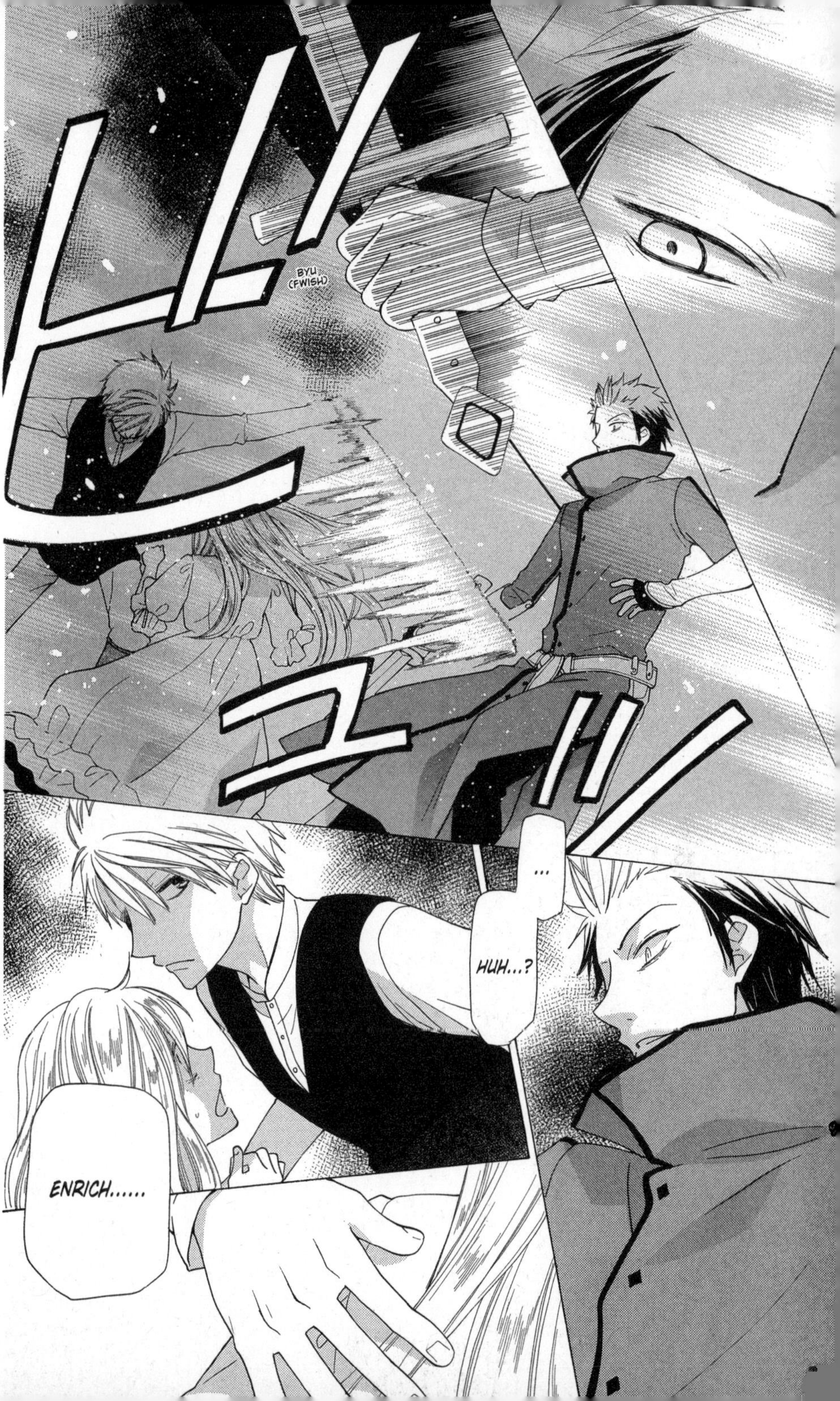
BYU (FWISH)
...
HUH...?
ENRICH......

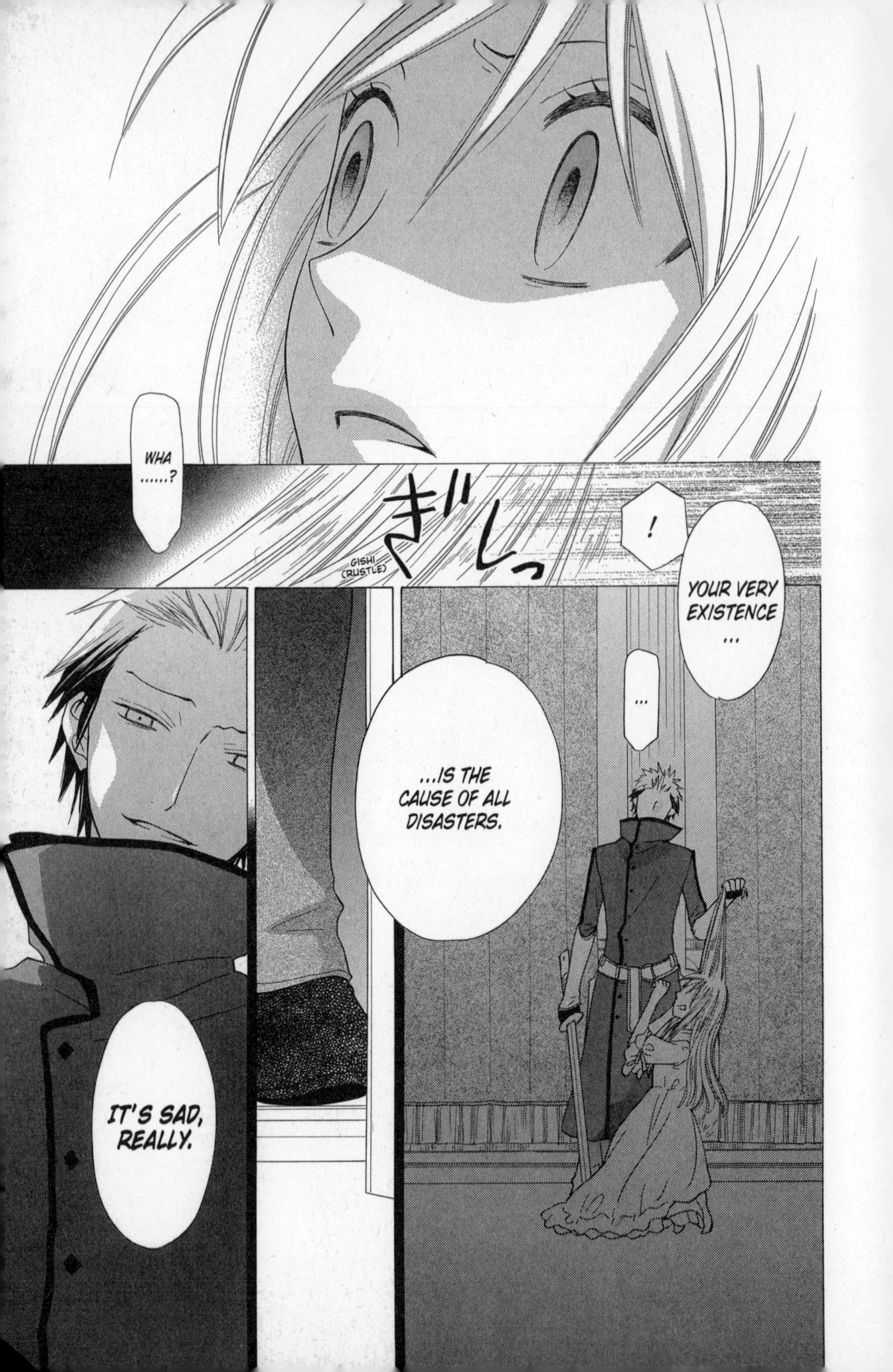
WHA ......?
!
ぎしっ
GISHI (RUSTLE)
YOUR VERY EXISTENCE ...
...
...IS THE CAUSE OF ALL DISASTERS.
IT'S SAD, REALLY.

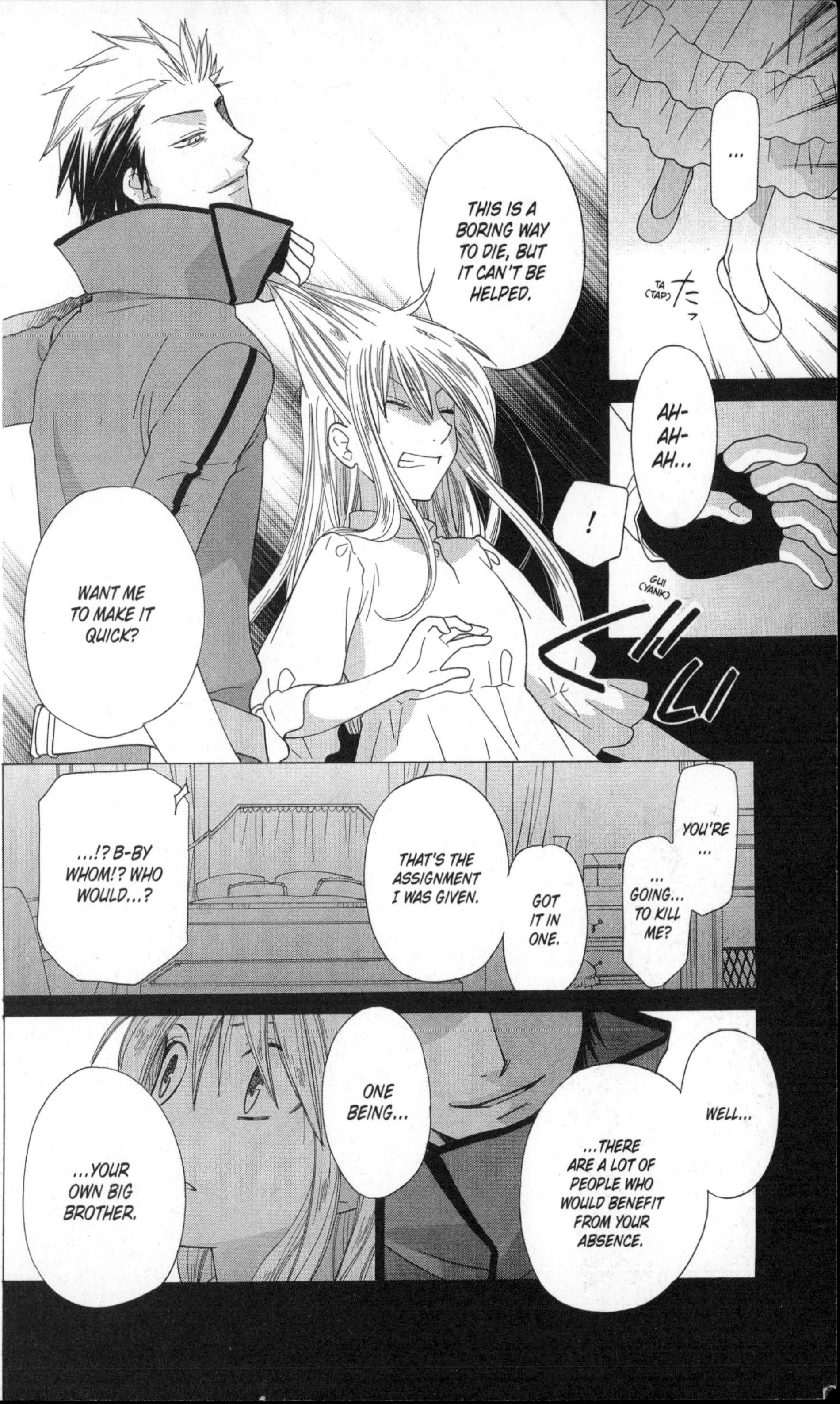
...
TA (TAP)
AH-AH-AH...
!
GUI (YANK)
THIS IS A BORING WAY TO DIE, BUT IT CAN'T BE HELPED.
WANT ME TO MAKE IT QUICK?
YOU'RE... ...GOING... TO KILL ME?
GOT IT IN ONE.
THAT'S THE ASSIGNMENT I WAS GIVEN.
...!? B-BY WHOM!? WHO WOULD...?
WELL...
...THERE ARE A LOT OF PEOPLE WHO WOULD BENEFIT FROM YOUR ABSENCE.
ONE BEING...
...YOUR OWN BIG BROTHER.

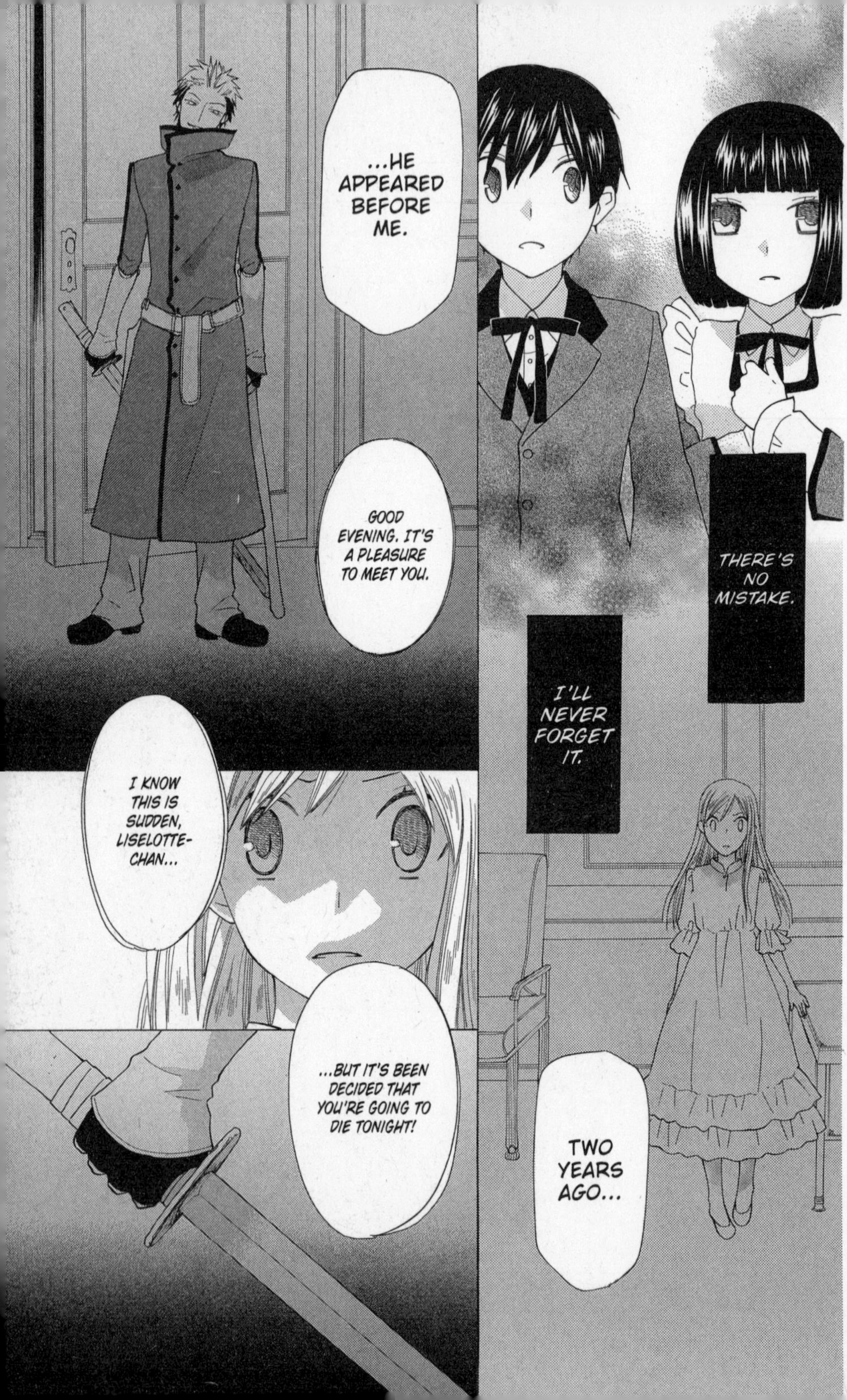
THERE'S NO MISTAKE.
I'LL NEVER FORGET IT.
TWO YEARS AGO...
...HE APPEARED BEFORE ME.
GOOD EVENING. IT'S A PLEASURE TO MEET YOU.
I KNOW THIS IS SUDDEN, LISELOTTE-CHAN...
...BUT IT'S BEEN DECIDED THAT YOU'RE GOING TO DIE TONIGHT!

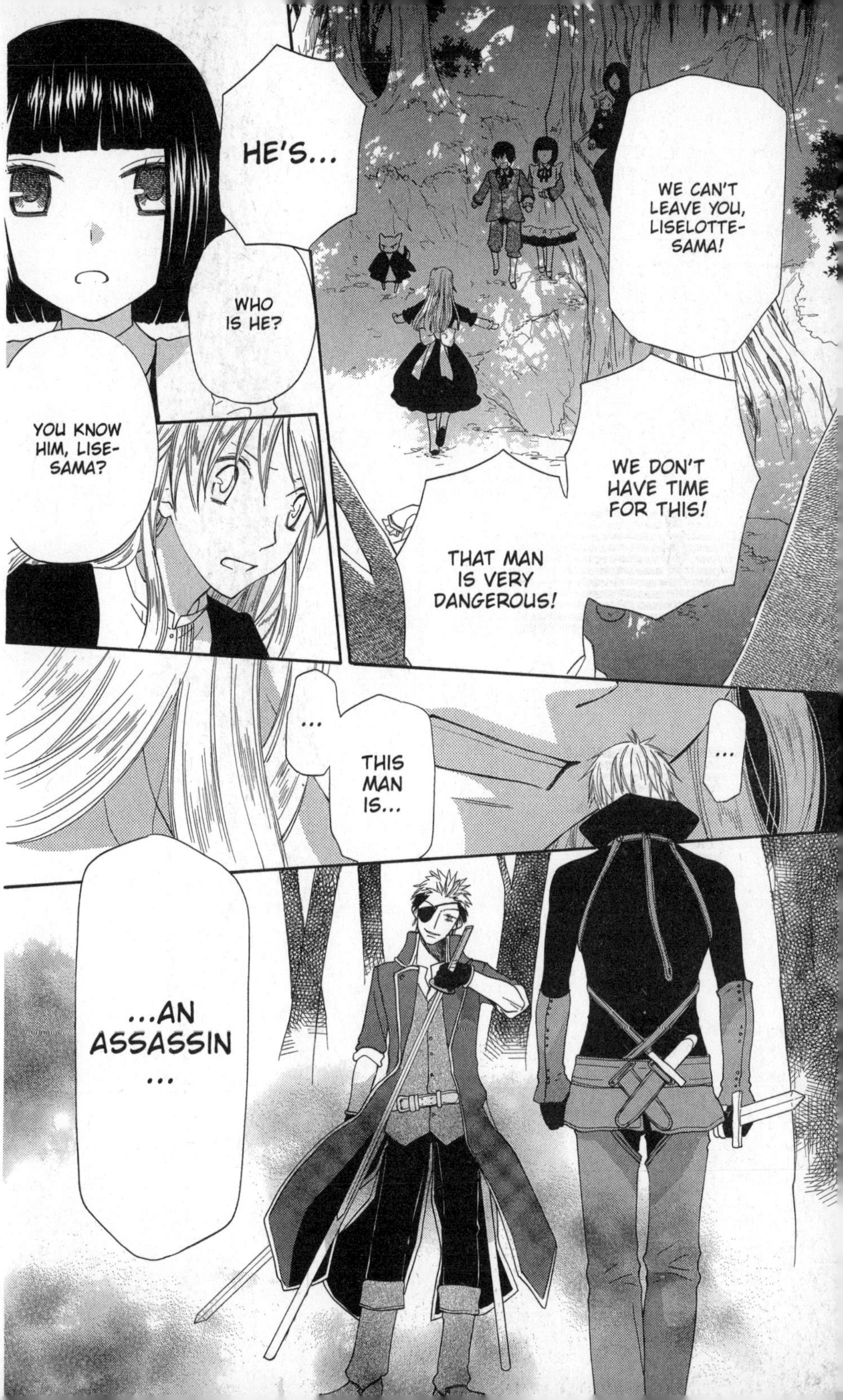
WE CAN'T LEAVE YOU, LISELOTTE-SAMA!
WE DON'T HAVE TIME FOR THIS!
THAT MAN IS VERY DANGEROUS!
HE'S...
WHO IS HE?
YOU KNOW HIM, LISE-SAMA?
...
...
THIS MAN IS...
...AN ASSASSIN ...

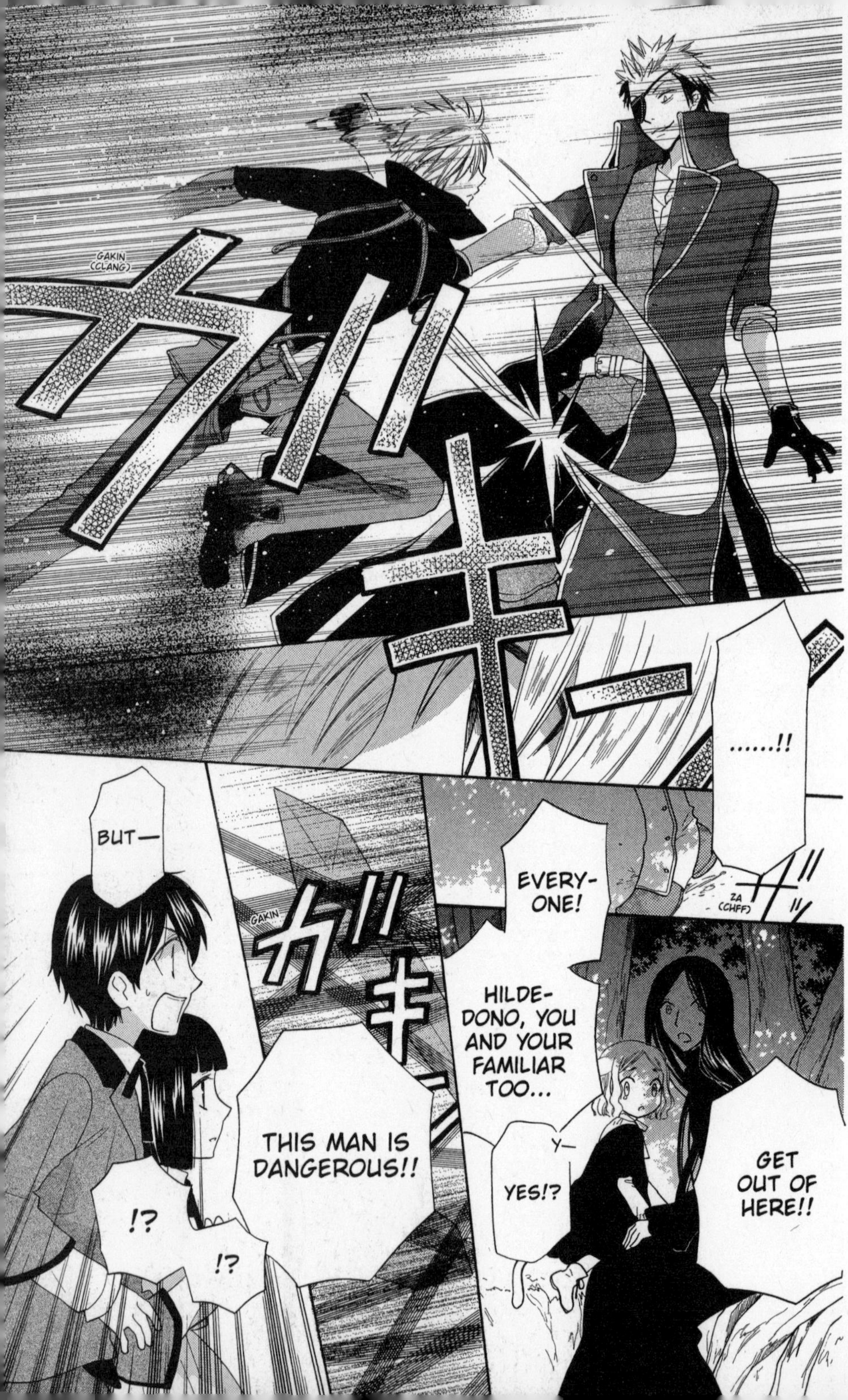
GAKIN (CLANG)
......!!
ZA (CHFF)
EVERY-ONE!
HILDE-DONO, YOU AND YOUR FAMILIAR TOO...
GET OUT OF HERE!!
Y—
YES!?
GAKIN
BUT—
THIS MAN IS DANGEROUS!!
!?
!?

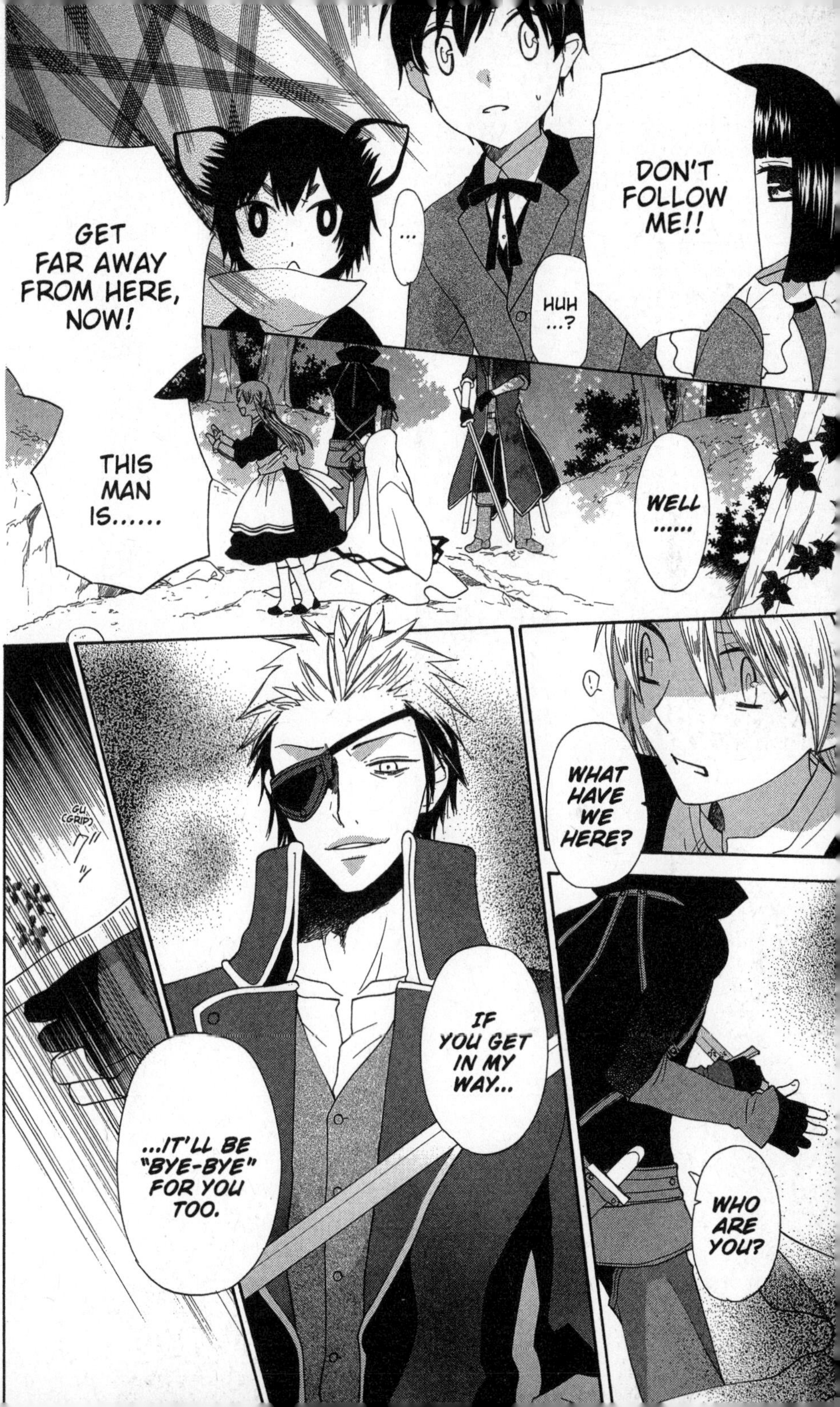
DON'T FOLLOW ME!!
HUH ...?
...
GET FAR AWAY FROM HERE, NOW!
WELL ......
THIS MAN IS......
!
WHAT HAVE WE HERE?
WHO ARE YOU?
IF YOU GET IN MY WAY...
...IT'LL BE "BYE-BYE" FOR YOU TOO.
GU (GRIP)

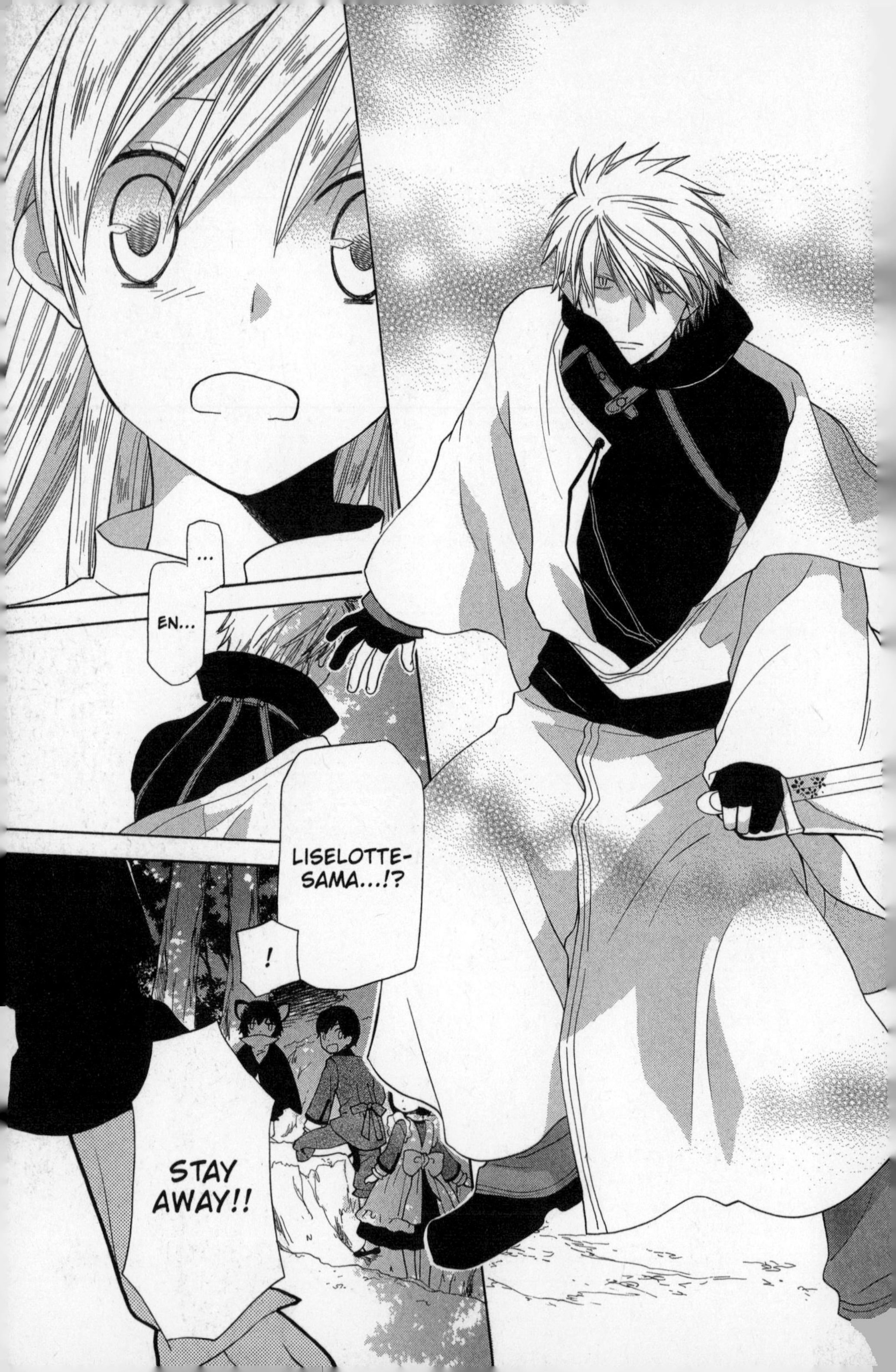
...
EN...
LISELOTTE-SAMA...!?
!
STAY AWAY!!

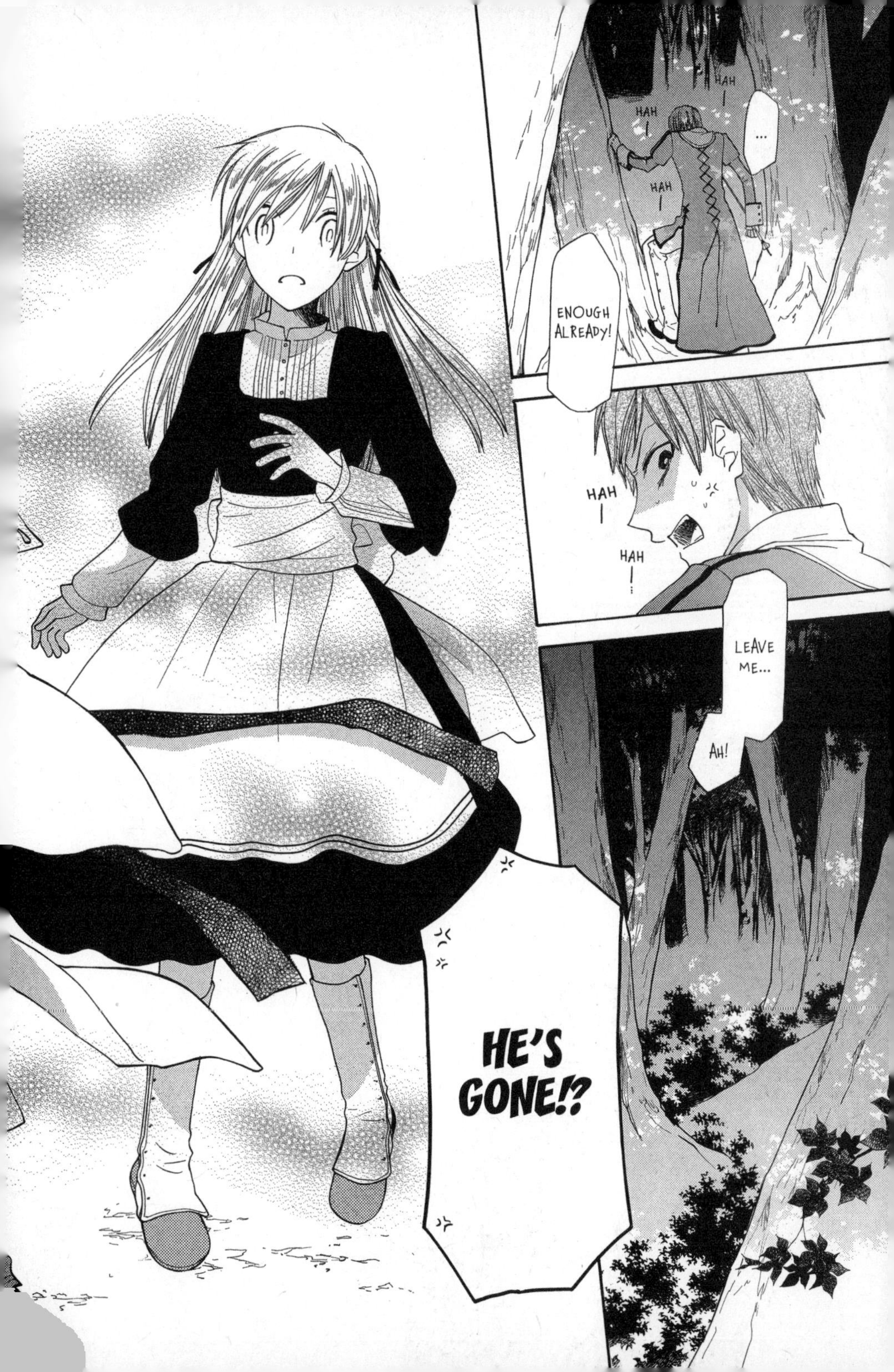
HAH
...
HAH
HAH
ENOUGH ALREADY!
HAH
HAH
LEAVE ME...
AH!
HE'S GONE!?

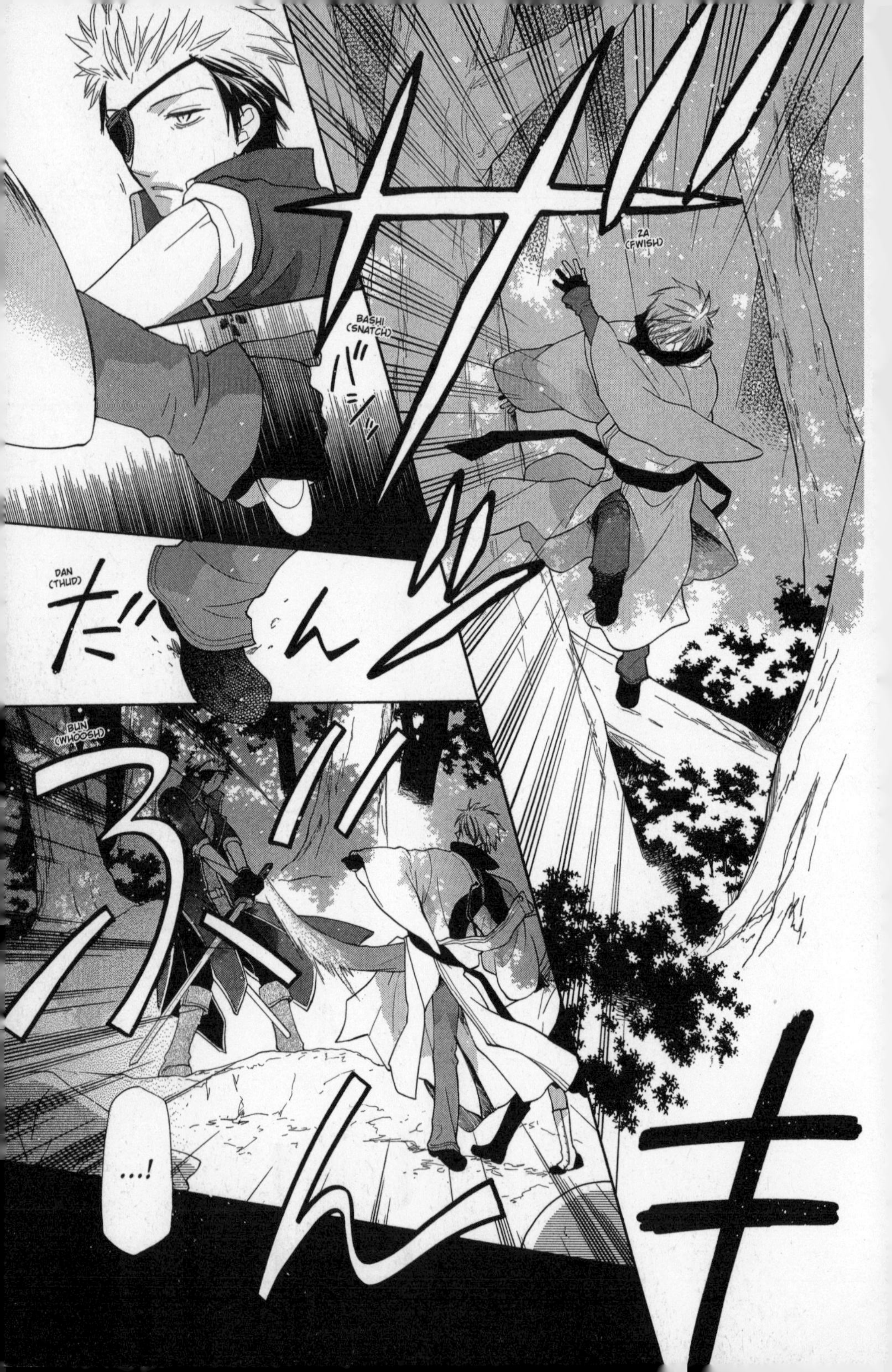
ZA
(FWISH)
BASHI
(SNATCH)
DAN
(THUD)
BUN
(WHOOSH)
...!

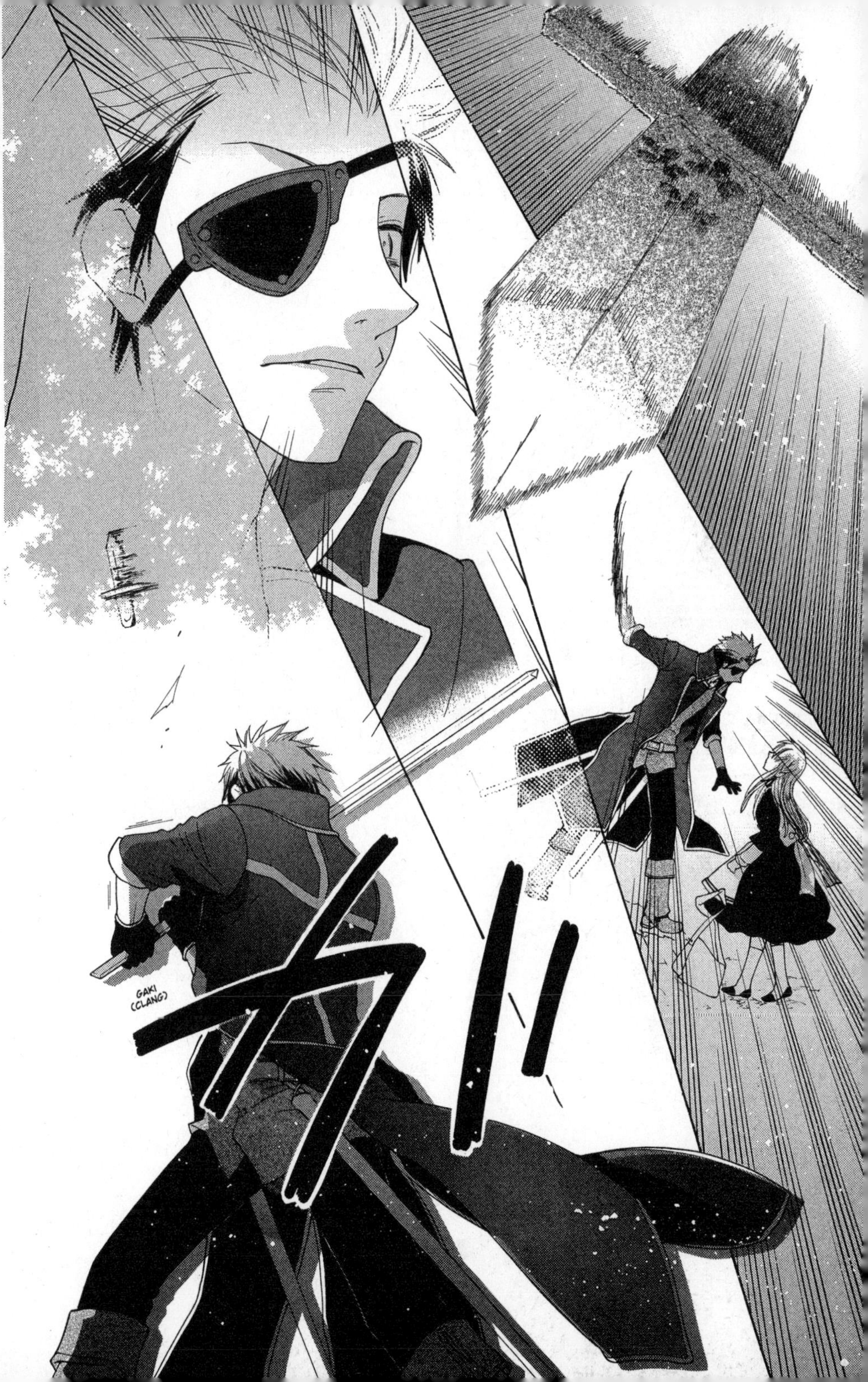
GAKI
(CLANG)

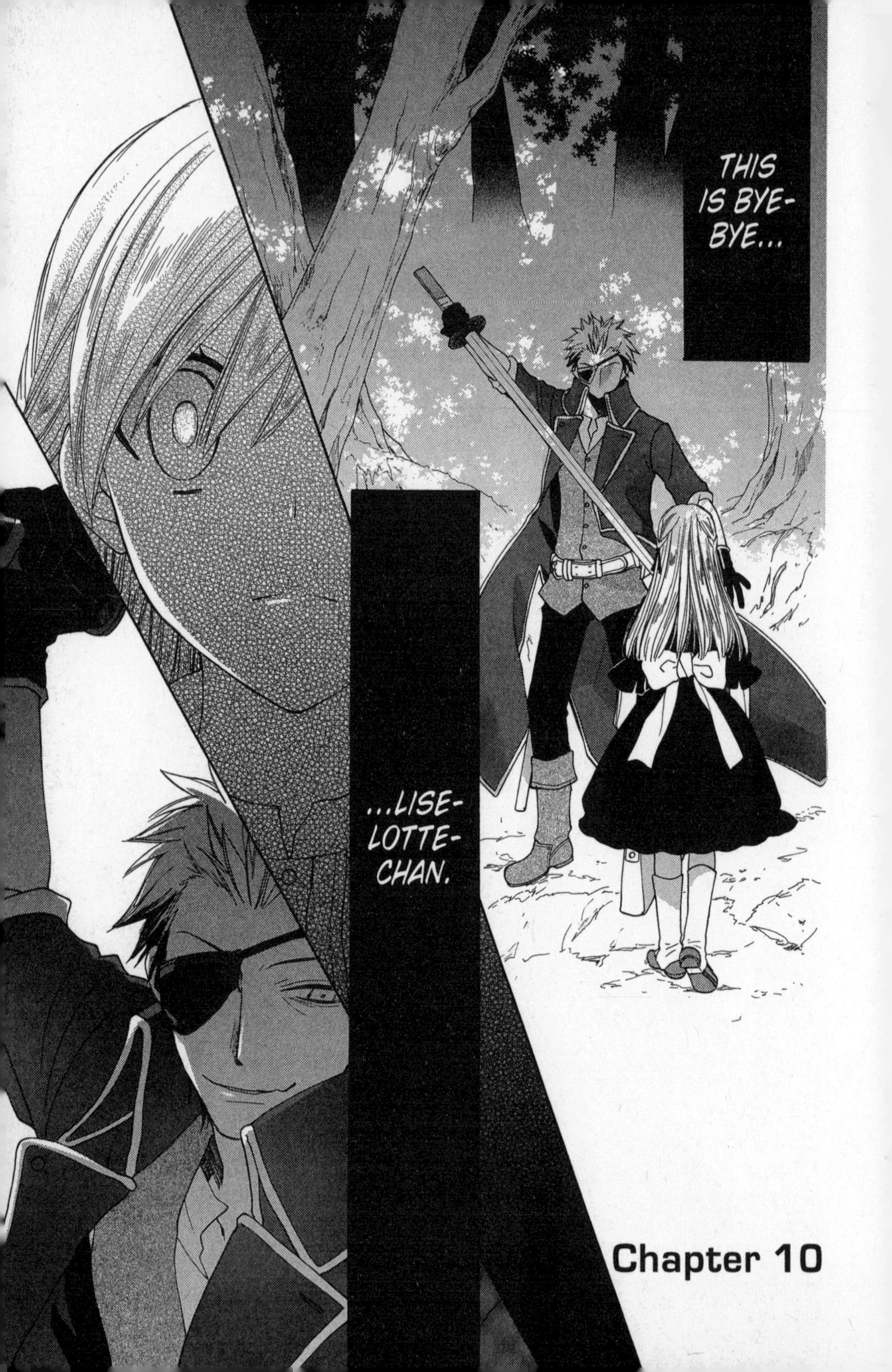
THIS IS BYE-BYE...
...LISE-LOTTE-CHAN.
Chapter 10

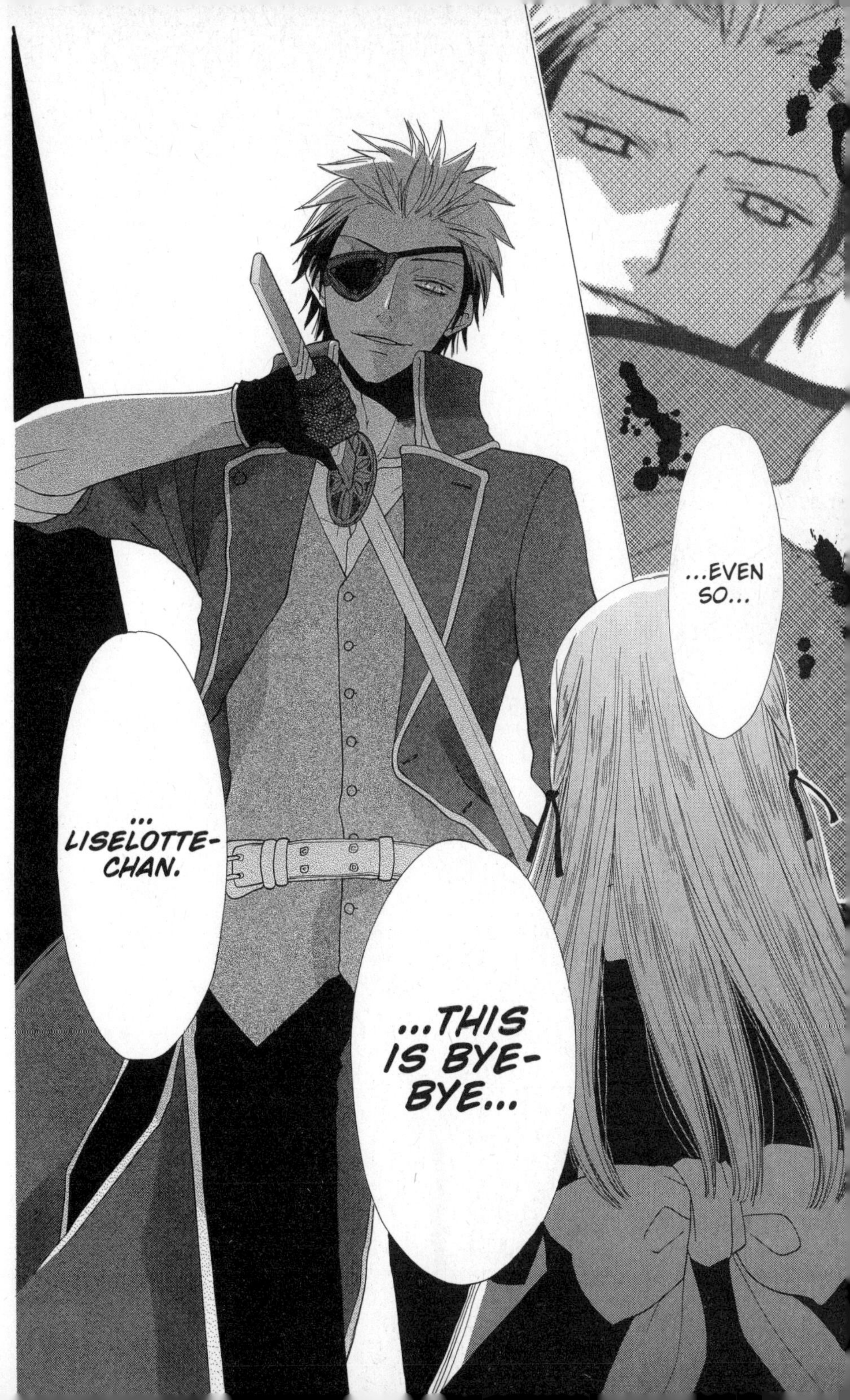
...EVEN SO...
...LISELÖTTE-CHAN.
...THIS IS BYE-BYE...

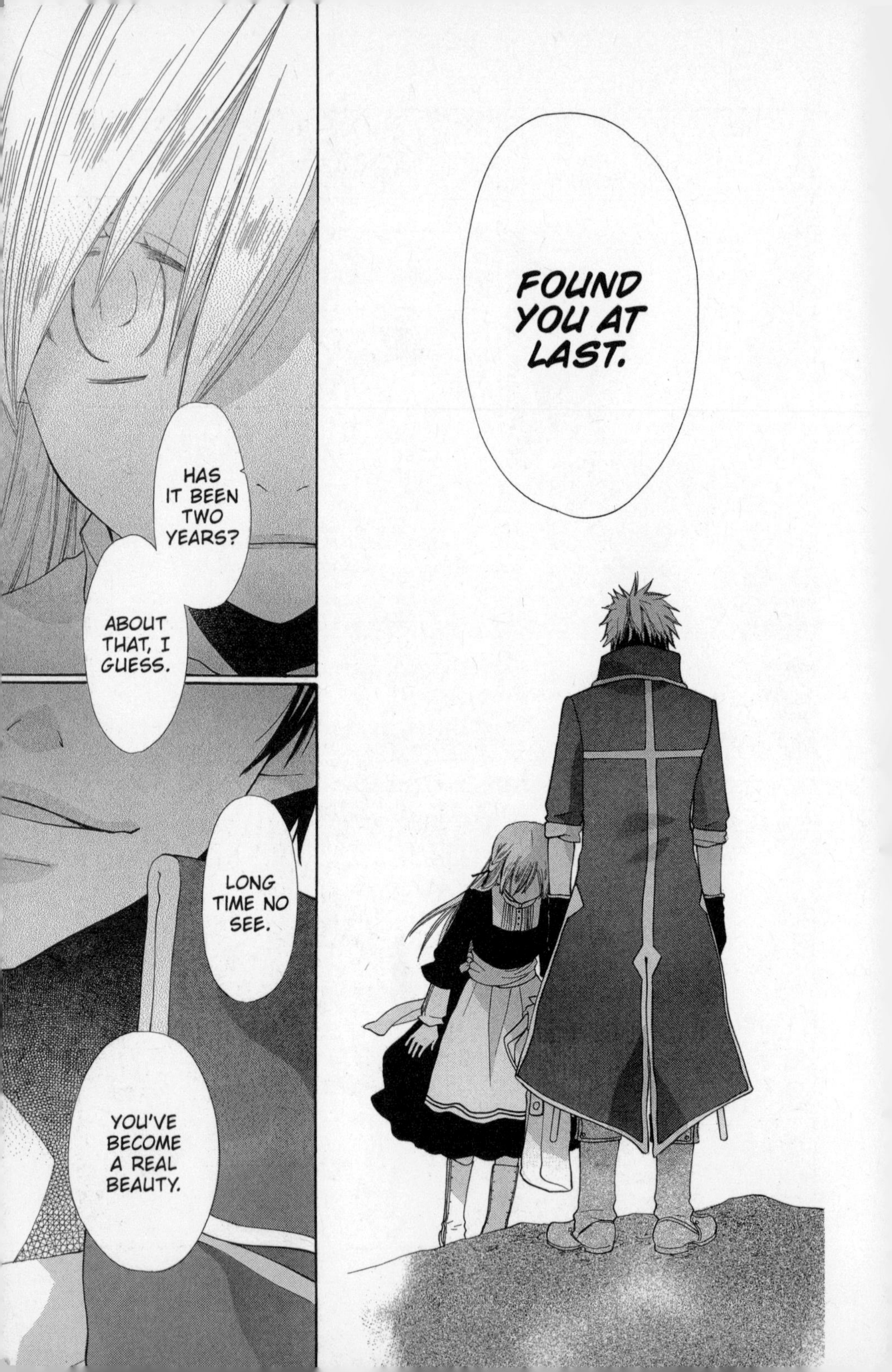
FOUND YOU AT LAST.
HAS IT BEEN TWO YEARS?
ABOUT THAT, I GUESS.
LONG TIME NO SEE.
YOU'VE BECOME A REAL BEAUTY.

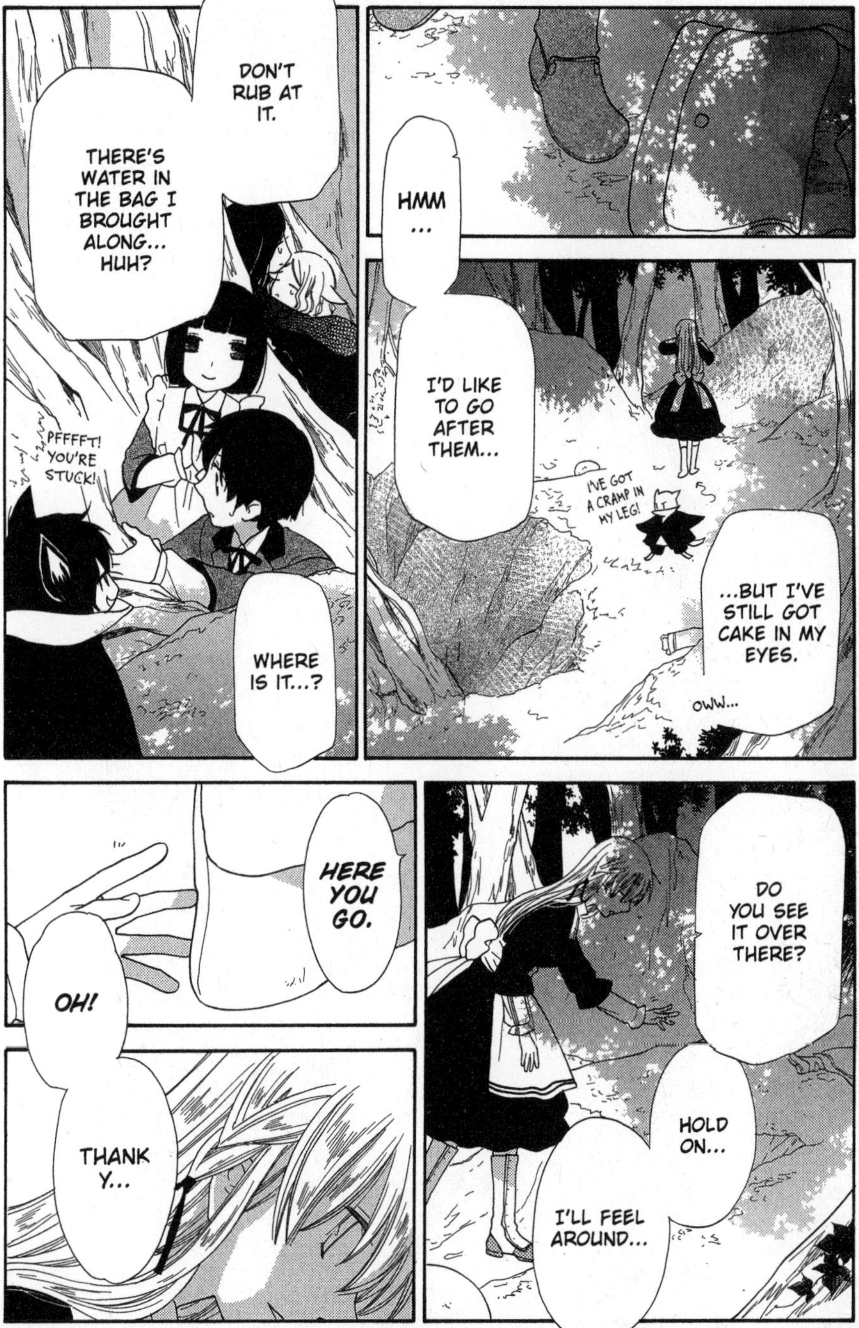
HMM...
I'D LIKE TO GO AFTER THEM...
...BUT I'VE STILL GOT CAKE IN MY EYES.
OWW...
I'VE GOT A CRAMP IN MY LEG!
DON'T RUB AT IT.
THERE'S WATER IN THE BAG I BROUGHT ALONG... HUH?
PFFFFT! YOU'RE STUCK!
WHERE IS IT...?
DO YOU SEE IT OVER THERE?
HOLD ON...
I'LL FEEL AROUND...
HERE YOU GO.
OH!
THANK Y...

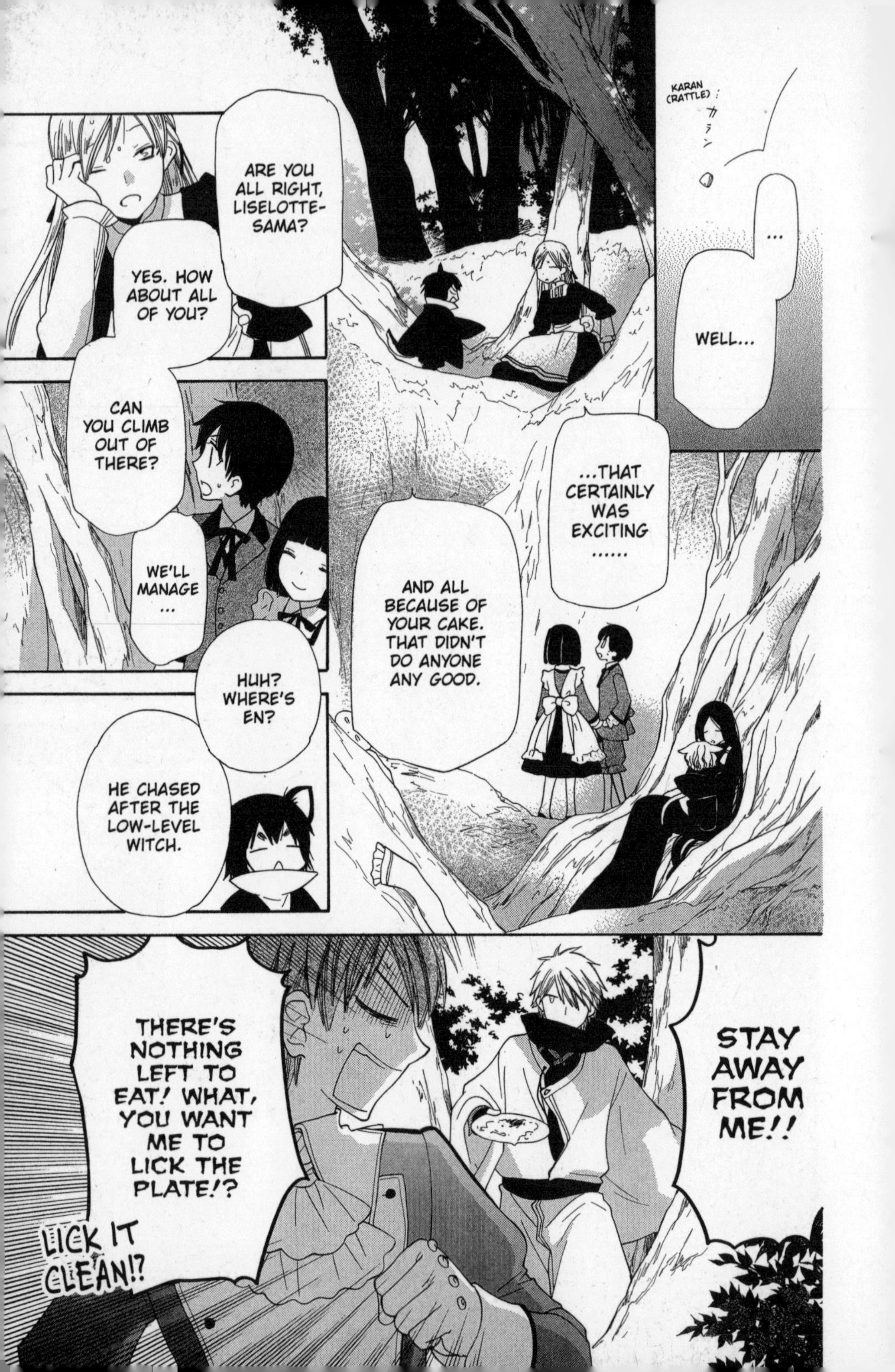
KARAN (RATTLE)
カラン
...
WELL...
...THAT CERTAINLY WAS EXCITING ......
AND ALL BECAUSE OF YOUR CAKE. THAT DIDN'T DO ANYONE ANY GOOD.
ARE YOU ALL RIGHT, LISELOTTE-SAMA?
YES. HOW ABOUT ALL OF YOU?
CAN YOU CLIMB OUT OF THERE?
WE'LL MANAGE ...
HUH? WHERE'S EN?
HE CHASED AFTER THE LOW-LEVEL WITCH.
STAY AWAY FROM ME!!
THERE'S NOTHING LEFT TO EAT! WHAT, YOU WANT ME TO LICK THE PLATE!?
LICK IT CLEAN!?

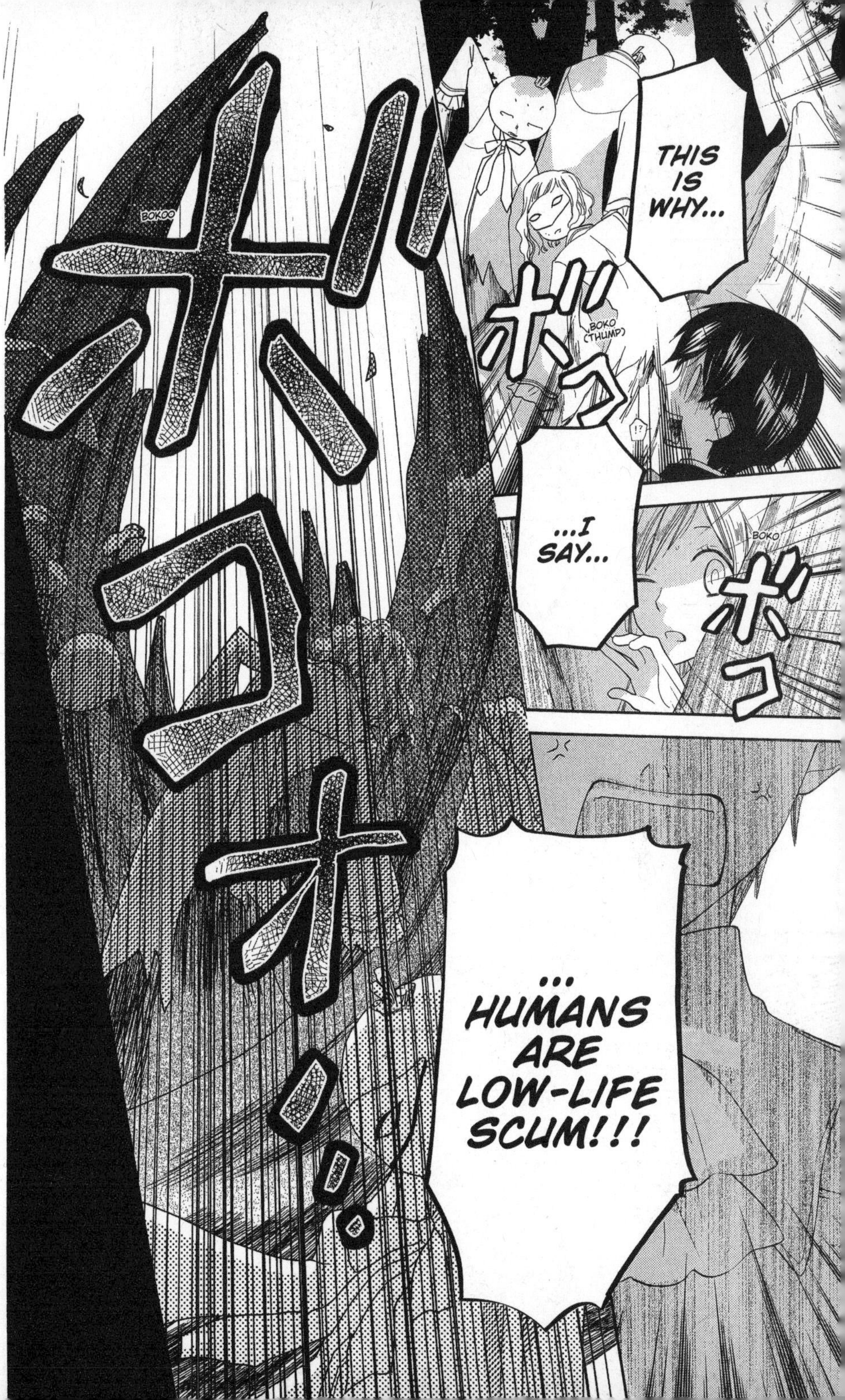
THIS IS WHY...
BOKO (THUMP)
!?
...I SAY...
BOKO
...HUMANS ARE LOW-LIFE SCUM!!!
BOKOO

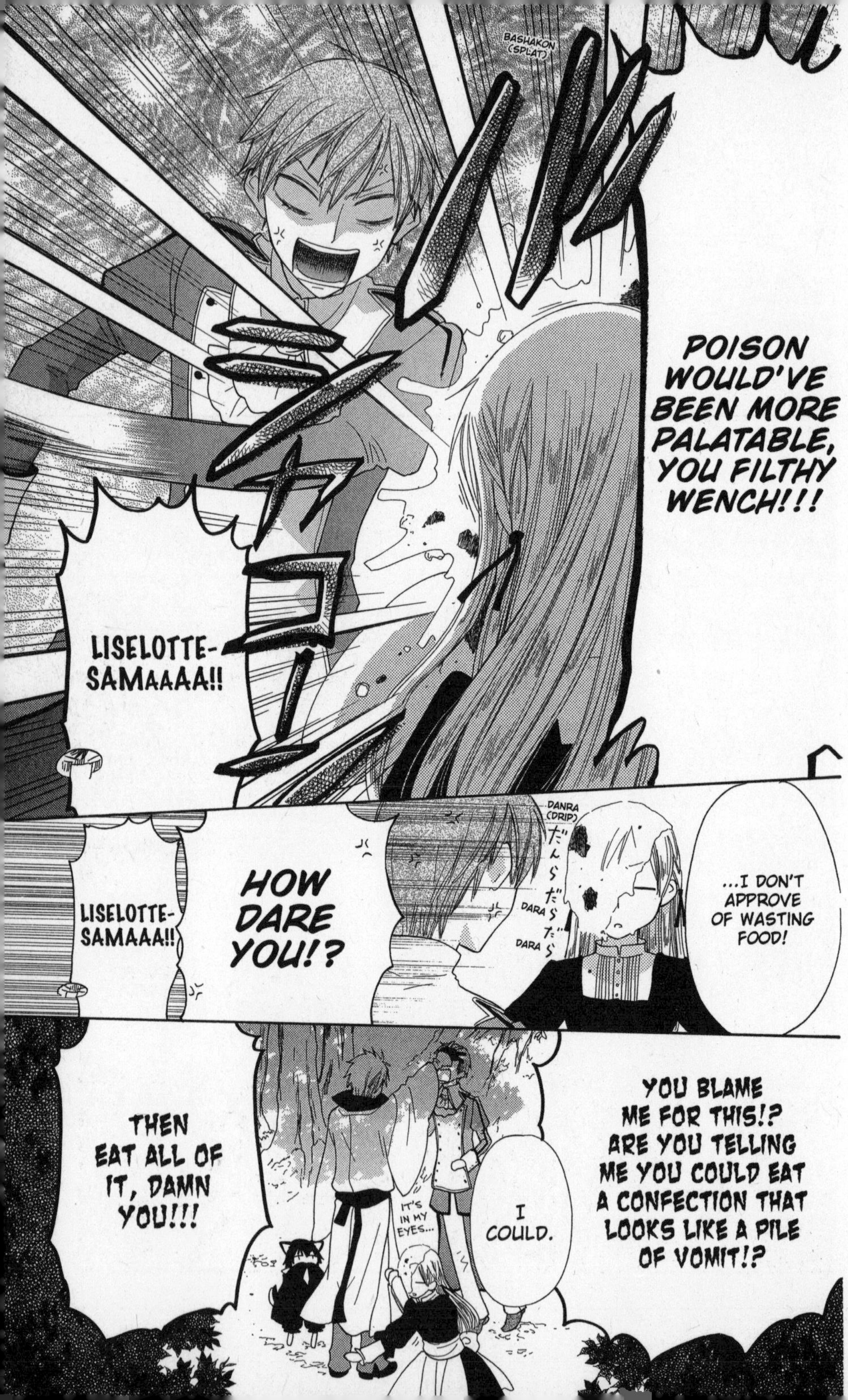
BASHAKON (SPLAT)
POISON WOULD'VE BEEN MORE PALATABLE, YOU FILTHY WENCH!!!
LISELOTTE-SAMAaaaa!!
...I DON'T APPROVE OF WASTING FOOD!
DANRA (DRIP)
だんらだらだら
DARA DARA
HOW DARE YOU!?
LISELOTTE-SAMAAA!!
YOU BLAME ME FOR THIS!? ARE YOU TELLING ME YOU COULD EAT A CONFECTION THAT LOOKS LIKE A PILE OF VOMIT!?
I COULD.
IT'S IN MY EYES...
THEN EAT ALL OF IT, DAMN YOU!!!

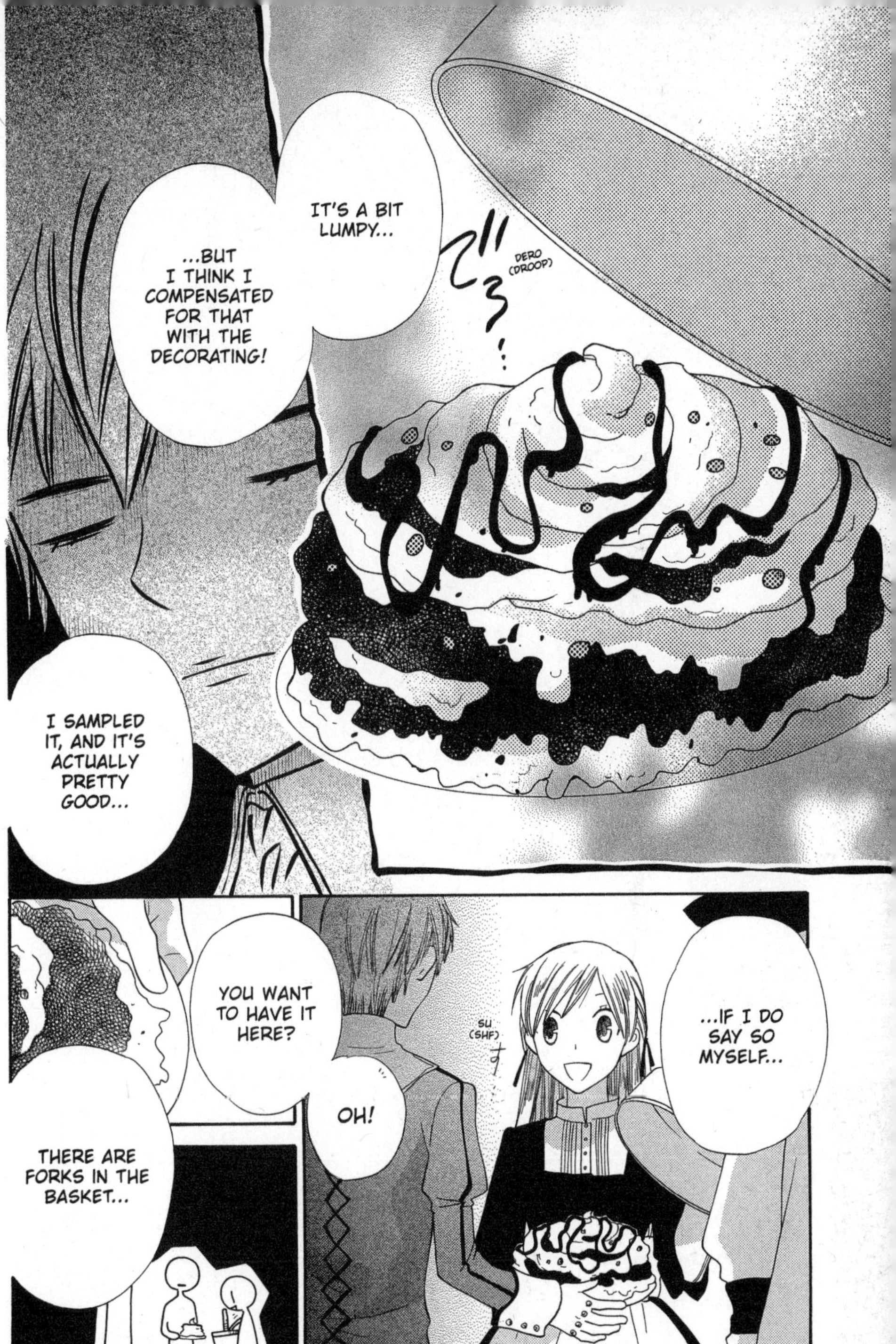
DERO (DROOP)
IT'S A BIT LUMPY...
...BUT I THINK I COMPENSATED FOR THAT WITH THE DECORATING!
I SAMPLED IT, AND IT'S ACTUALLY PRETTY GOOD...
...IF I DO SAY SO MYSELF...
SU (SHF)
OH!
YOU WANT TO HAVE IT HERE?
THERE ARE FORKS IN THE BASKET...

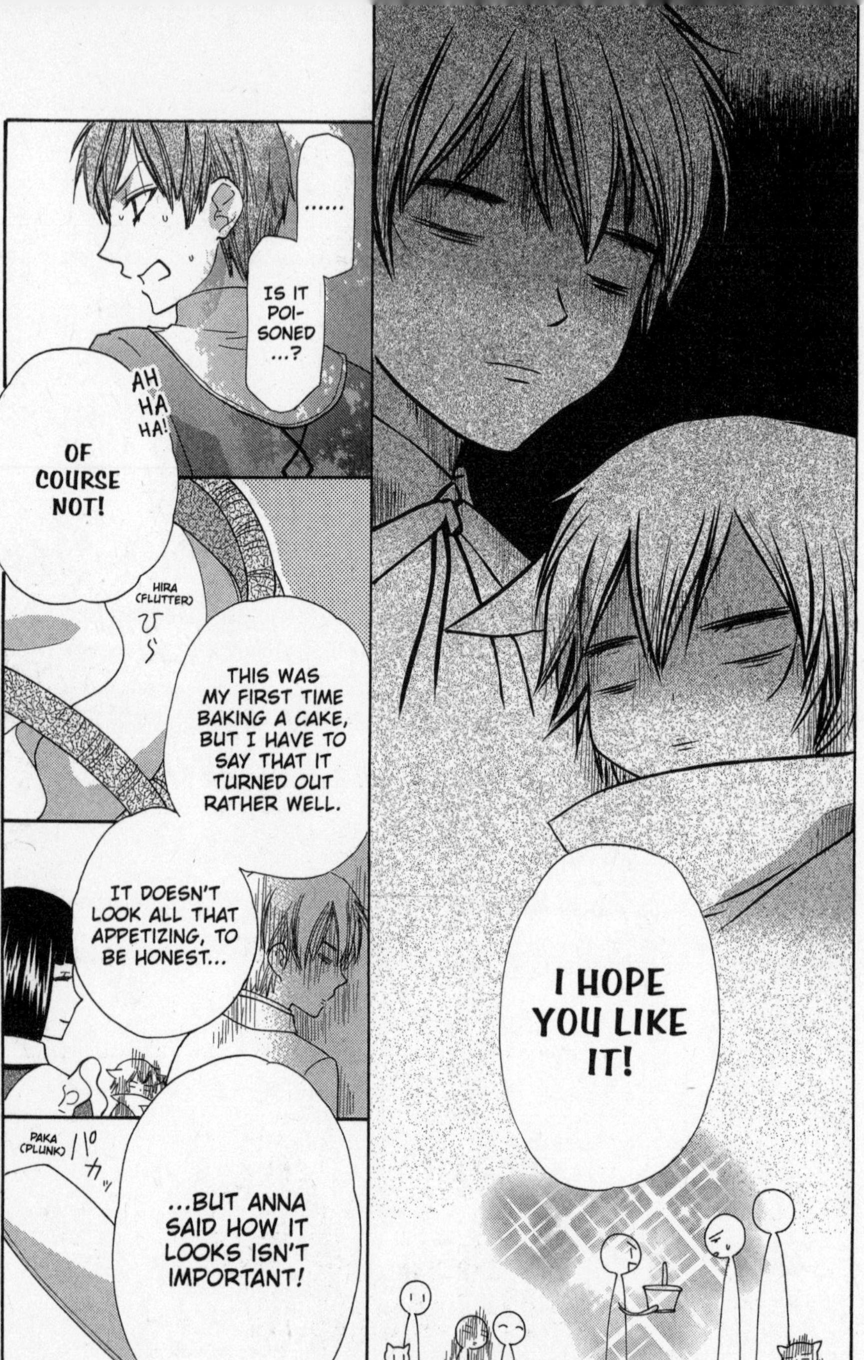
I HOPE YOU LIKE IT!
......
IS IT POI-SONED ...?
AH HA HA!
OF COURSE NOT!
HIRA (FLUTTER)
ひら
THIS WAS MY FIRST TIME BAKING A CAKE, BUT I HAVE TO SAY THAT IT TURNED OUT RATHER WELL.
IT DOESN'T LOOK ALL THAT APPETIZING, TO BE HONEST...
PAKA (PLUNK)
パカッ
...BUT ANNA SAID HOW IT LOOKS ISN'T IMPORTANT!

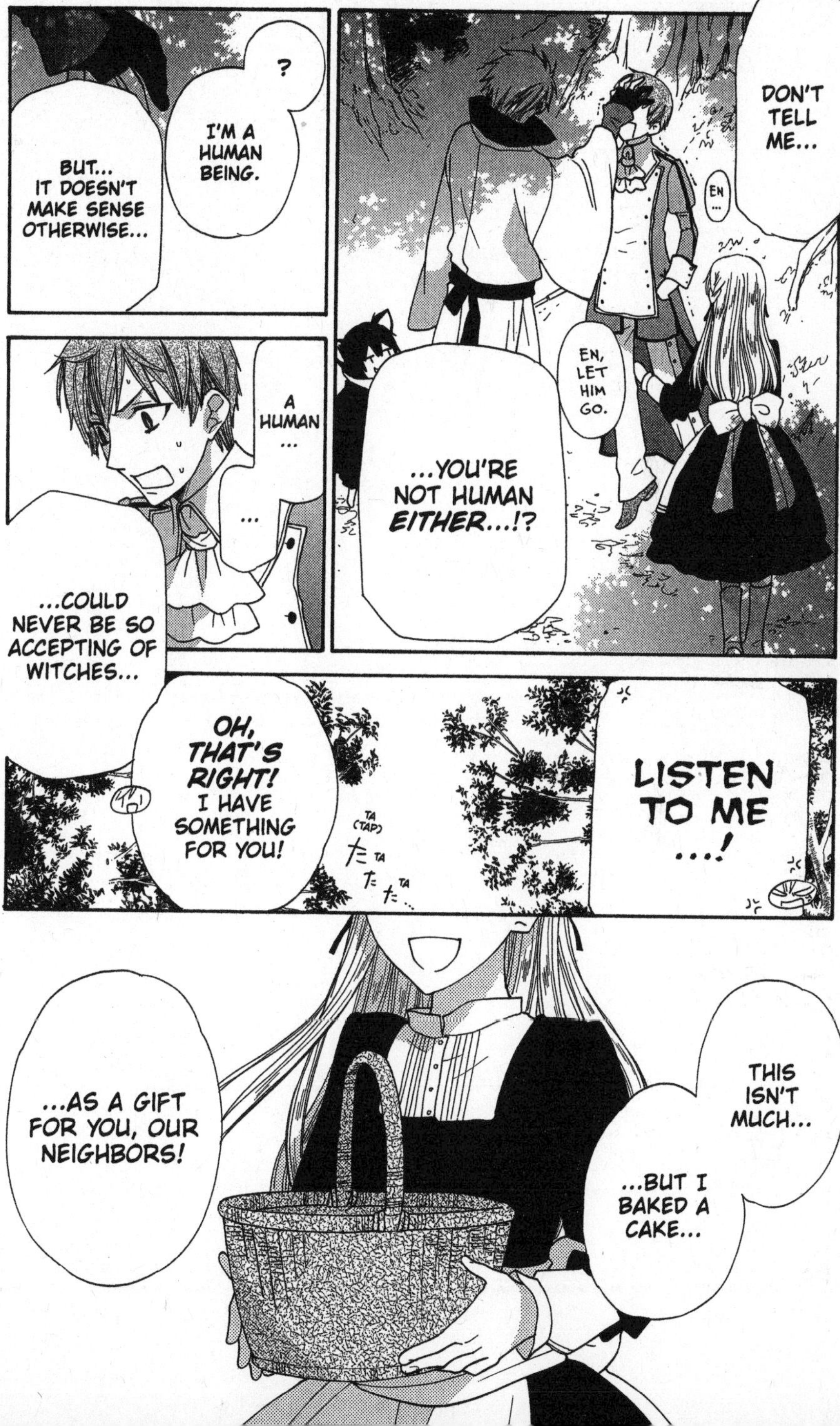
DON'T TELL ME...
EN...
EN, LET HIM GO.
...YOU'RE NOT HUMAN *EITHER*...!?
?
I'M A HUMAN BEING.
BUT... IT DOESN'T MAKE SENSE OTHERWISE...
A HUMAN...
...
...COULD NEVER BE SO ACCEPTING OF WITCHES...
LISTEN TO ME...!
TA (TAP) TA TA TA
OH, THAT'S RIGHT! I HAVE SOMETHING FOR YOU!
THIS ISN'T MUCH...
...BUT I BAKED A CAKE...
...AS A GIFT FOR YOU, OUR NEIGHBORS!

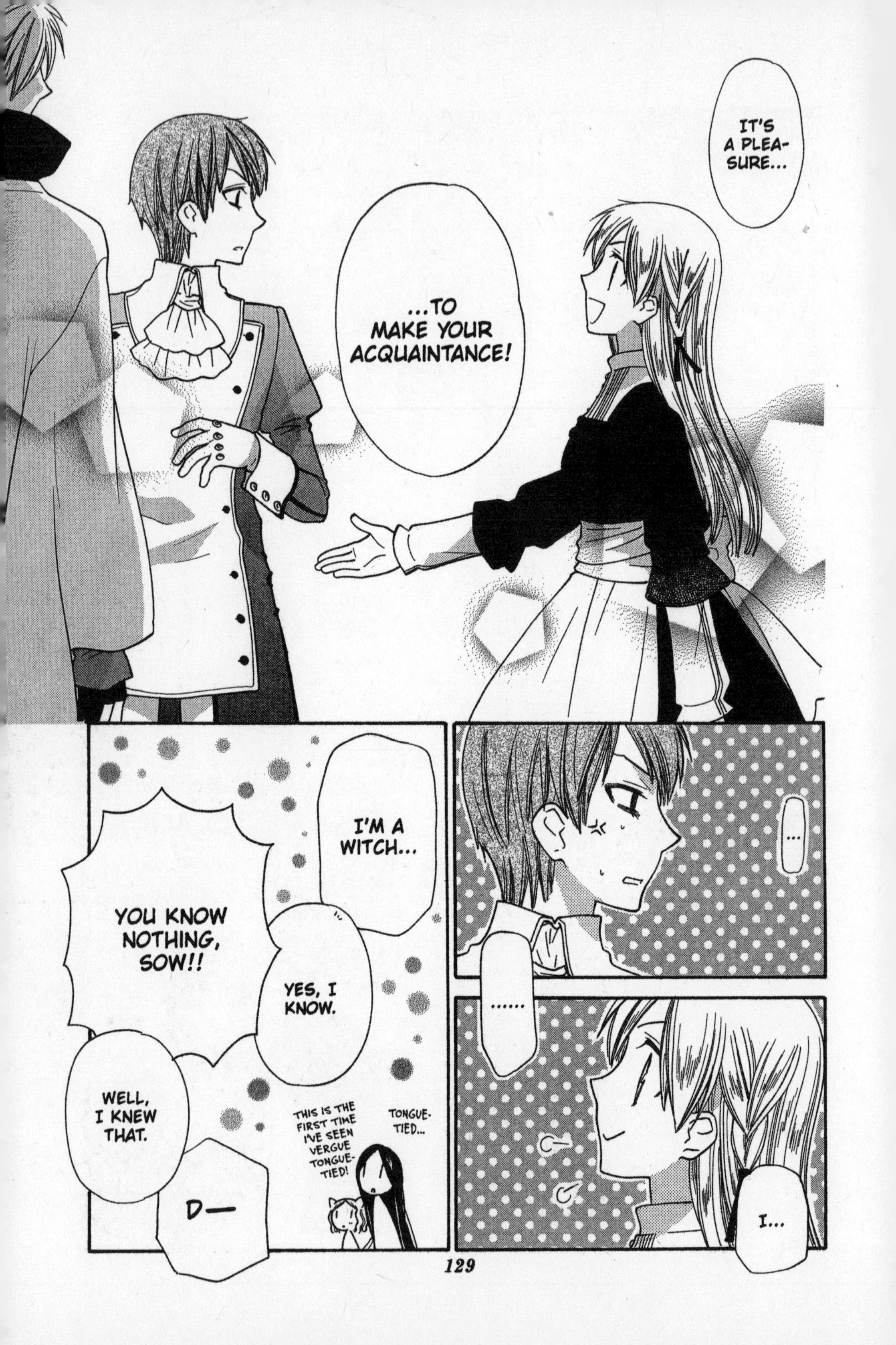
IT'S A PLEASURE...
...TO MAKE YOUR ACQUAINTANCE!
...
......
I...
I'M A WITCH...
YES, I KNOW.
YOU KNOW NOTHING, SOW!!
WELL, I KNEW THAT.
D—
TONGUE-TIED...
THIS IS THE FIRST TIME I'VE SEEN VERGUE TONGUE-TIED!

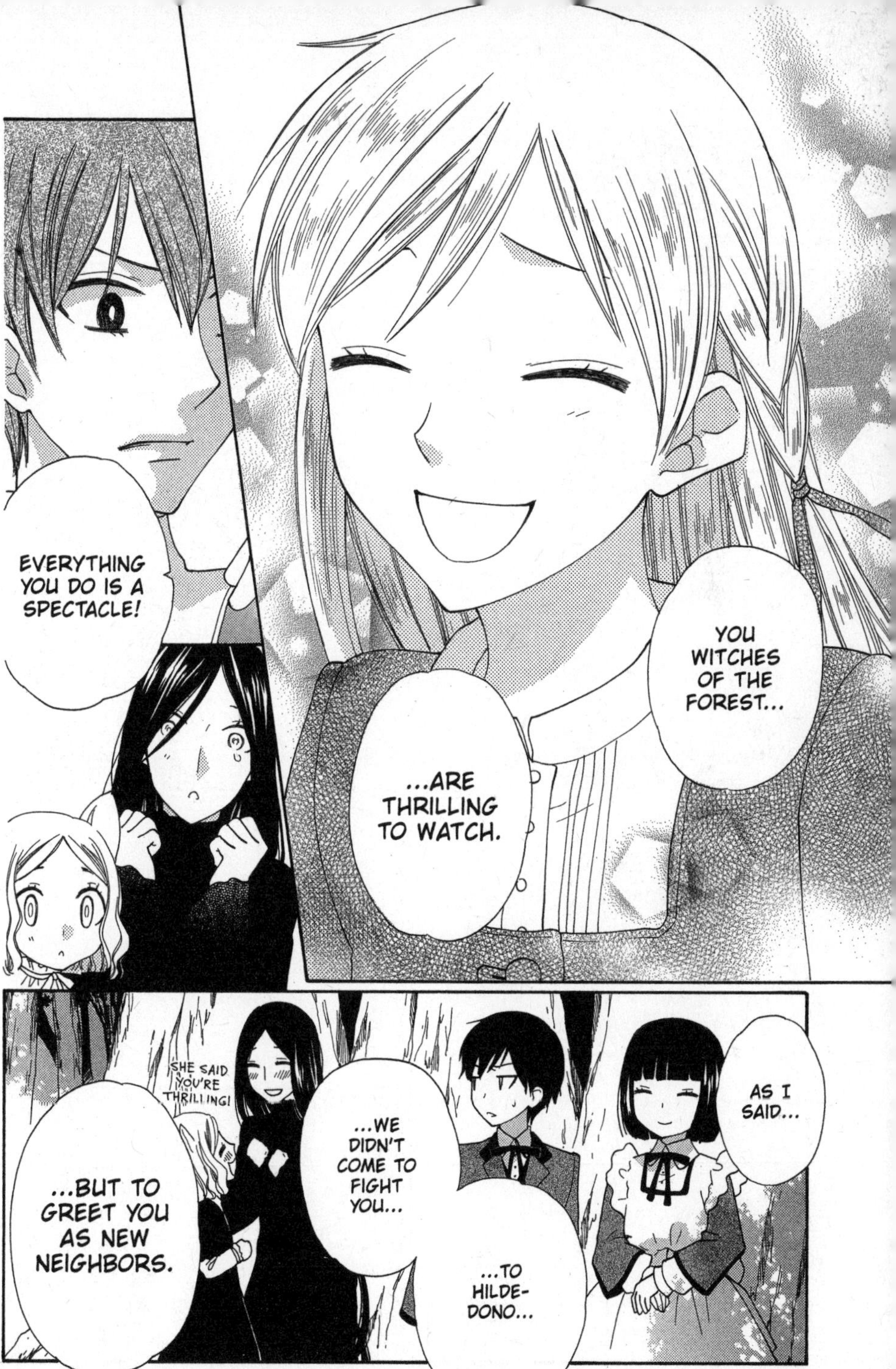
YOU WITCHES OF THE FOREST...
...ARE THRILLING TO WATCH.
EVERYTHING YOU DO IS A SPECTACLE!
AS I SAID...
...WE DIDN'T COME TO FIGHT YOU...
...TO HILDE-DONO...
...BUT TO GREET YOU AS NEW NEIGHBORS.
SHE SAID YOU'RE THRILLING!

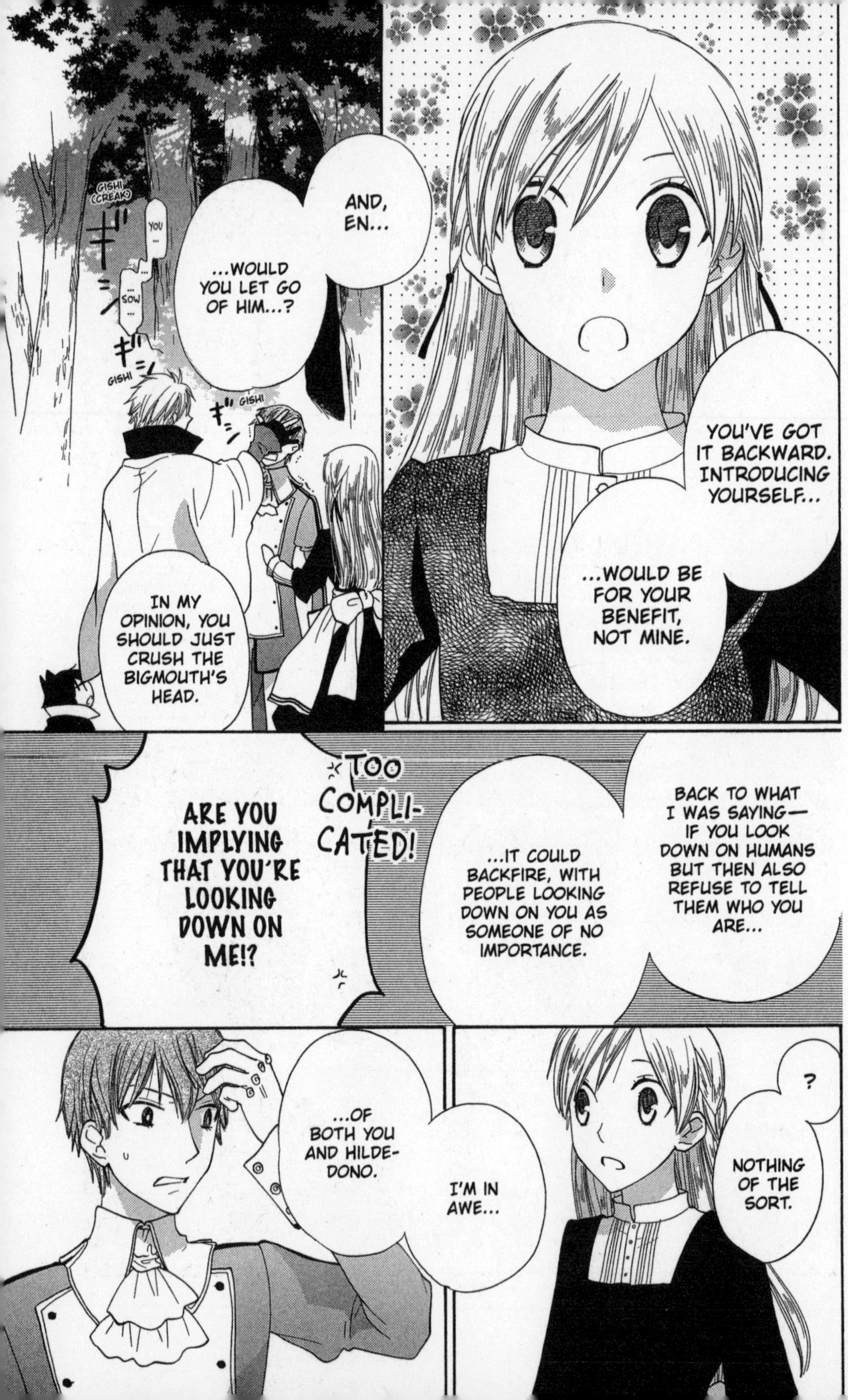
YOU'VE GOT IT BACKWARD. INTRODUCING YOURSELF...
...WOULD BE FOR YOUR BENEFIT, NOT MINE.
AND, EN...
...WOULD YOU LET GO OF HIM...?
GISHI (CREAK)
YOU...
...
...SOW...
GISHI
GISHI
IN MY OPINION, YOU SHOULD JUST CRUSH THE BIGMOUTH'S HEAD.
BACK TO WHAT I WAS SAYING—IF YOU LOOK DOWN ON HUMANS BUT THEN ALSO REFUSE TO TELL THEM WHO YOU ARE...
...IT COULD BACKFIRE, WITH PEOPLE LOOKING DOWN ON YOU AS SOMEONE OF NO IMPORTANCE.
TOO COMPLI-CATED!
ARE YOU IMPLYING THAT YOU'RE LOOKING DOWN ON ME!?
?
NOTHING OF THE SORT.
I'M IN AWE...
...OF BOTH YOU AND HILDE-DONO.

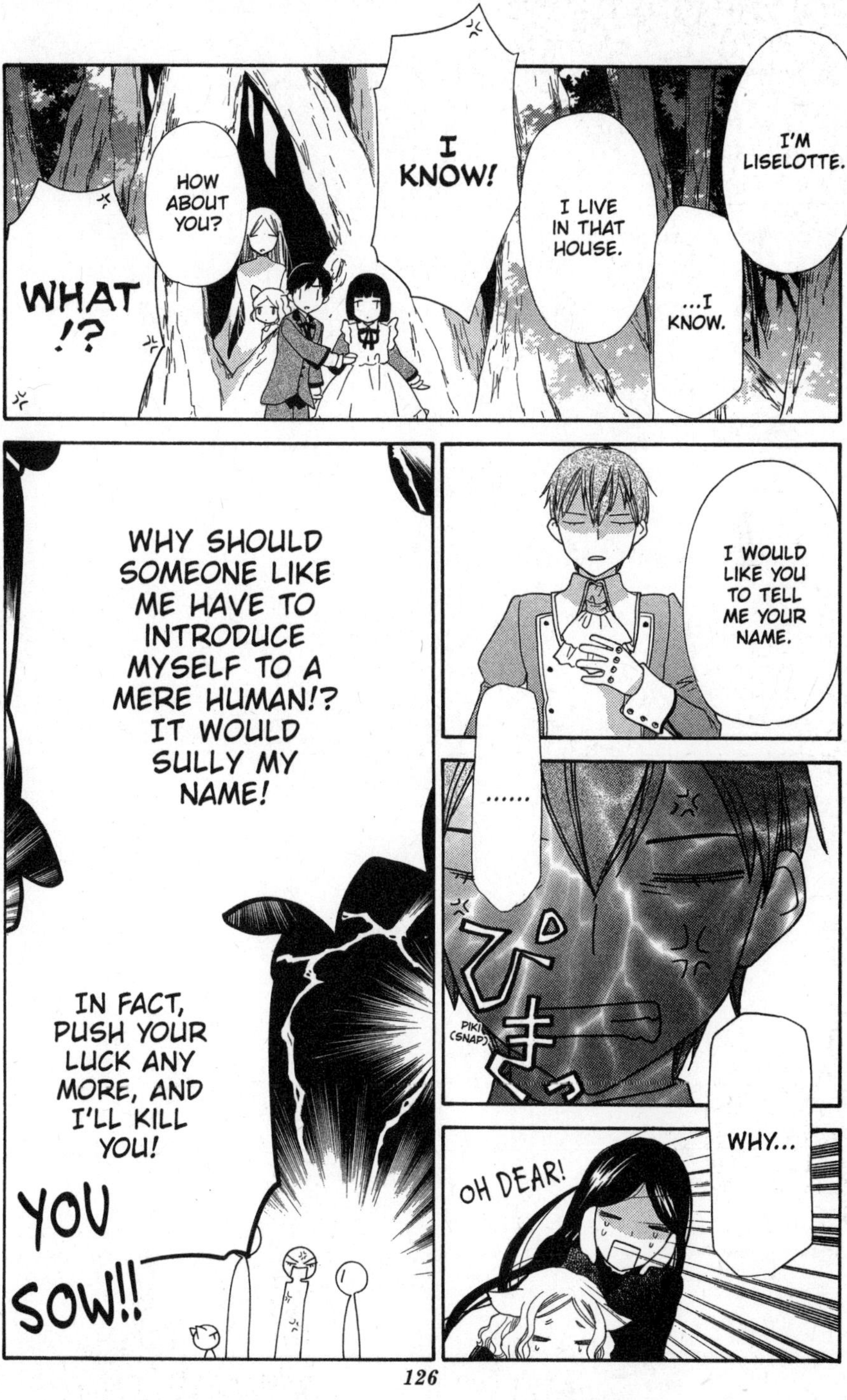
I'M LISELOTTE.
...I KNOW.
I LIVE IN THAT HOUSE.
I KNOW!
HOW ABOUT YOU?
WHAT!?
I WOULD LIKE YOU TO TELL ME YOUR NAME.
......
PIKI (SNAP)
WHY...
OH DEAR!
WHY SHOULD SOMEONE LIKE ME HAVE TO INTRODUCE MYSELF TO A MERE HUMAN!? IT WOULD SULLY MY NAME!
IN FACT, PUSH YOUR LUCK ANY MORE, AND I'LL KILL YOU!
YOU SOW!!

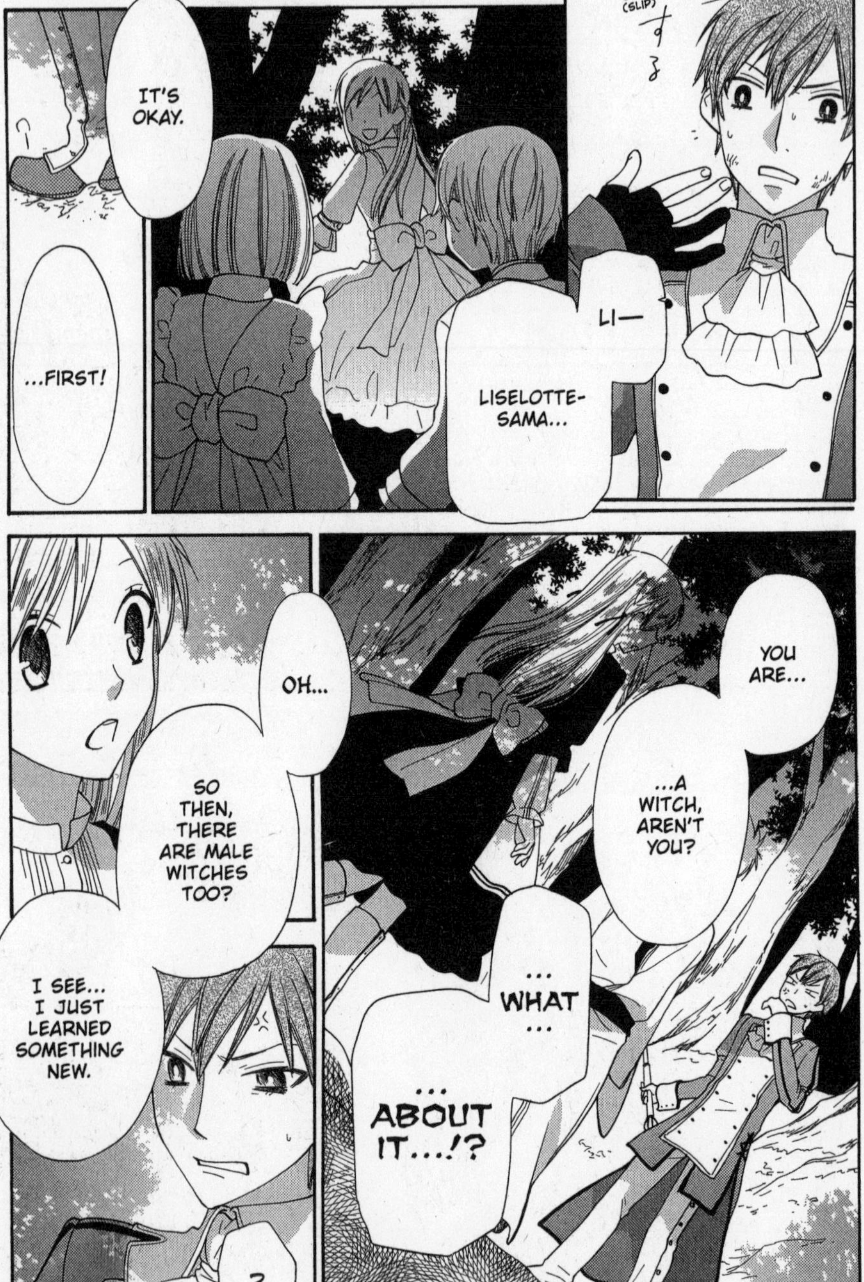
SURU (SLIP)
LI—
LISELOTTE-SAMA...
IT'S OKAY.
...FIRST!
YOU ARE...
...A WITCH, AREN'T YOU?
...WHAT...
...ABOUT IT...!?
OH...
SO THEN, THERE ARE MALE WITCHES TOO?
I SEE... I JUST LEARNED SOMETHING NEW.
?

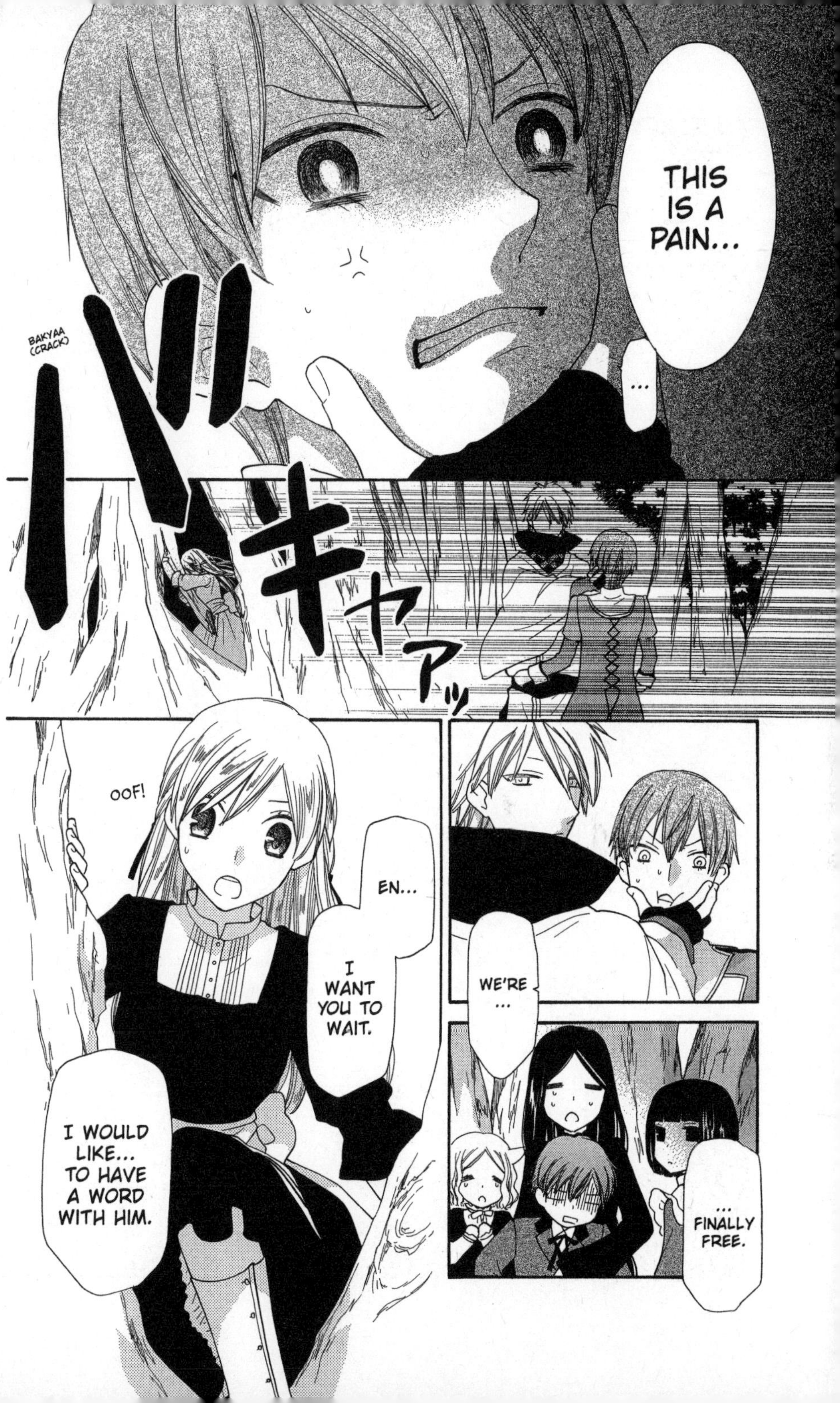
THIS IS A PAIN...
...
BAKYAA (CRACK)
バキャアッ
WE'RE ...
... FINALLY FREE.
OOF!
EN...
I WANT YOU TO WAIT.
I WOULD LIKE... TO HAVE A WORD WITH HIM.

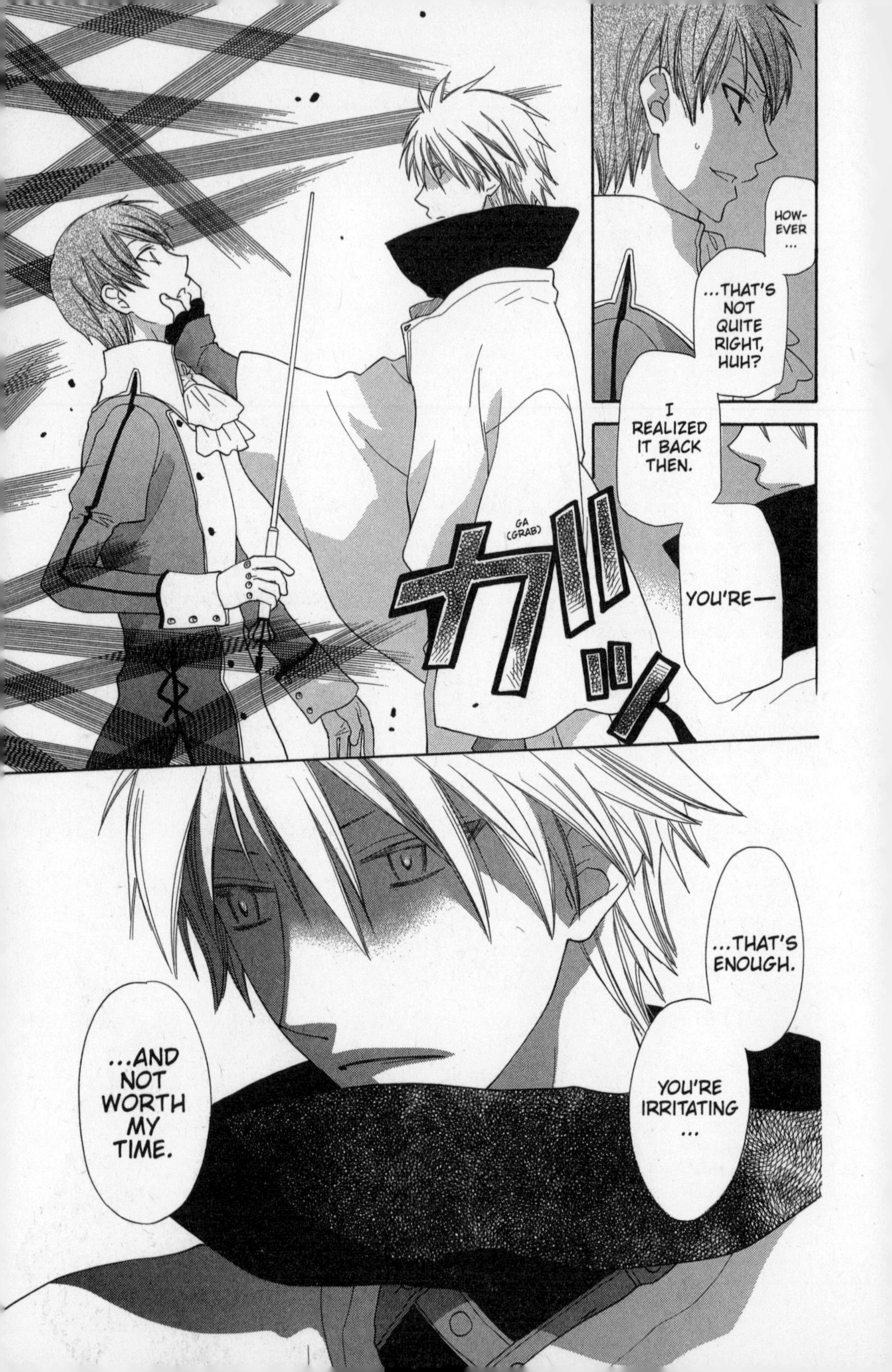
HOW-EVER...
...THAT'S NOT QUITE RIGHT, HUH?
I REALIZED IT BACK THEN.
YOU'RE—
ガッ
GA (GRAB)
...THAT'S ENOUGH.
YOU'RE IRRITATING...
...AND NOT WORTH MY TIME.

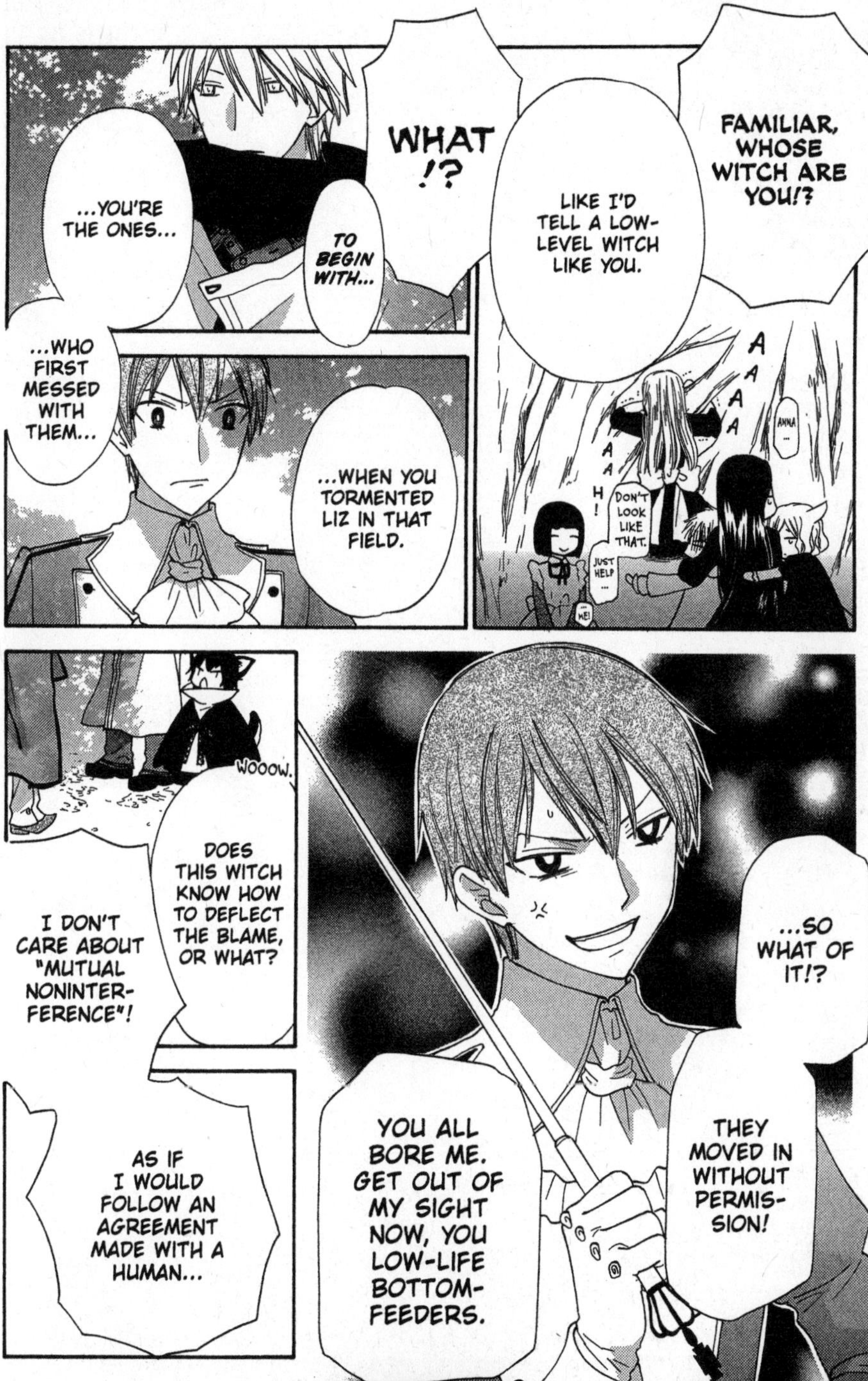
FAMILIAR, WHOSE WITCH ARE YOU!?
WHAT!?
LIKE I'D TELL A LOW-LEVEL WITCH LIKE YOU.
AAAAAAAH!
ANNA...
DON'T LOOK LIKE THAT.
JUST HELP...
...ME!
TO BEGIN WITH...
...YOU'RE THE ONES...
...WHO FIRST MESSED WITH THEM...
...WHEN YOU TORMENTED LIZ IN THAT FIELD.
...SO WHAT OF IT!?
THEY MOVED IN WITHOUT PERMISSION!
YOU ALL BORE ME. GET OUT OF MY SIGHT NOW, YOU LOW-LIFE BOTTOM-FEEDERS.
WOOOW.
DOES THIS WITCH KNOW HOW TO DEFLECT THE BLAME, OR WHAT?
I DON'T CARE ABOUT "MUTUAL NONINTERFERENCE"!
AS IF I WOULD FOLLOW AN AGREEMENT MADE WITH A HUMAN...

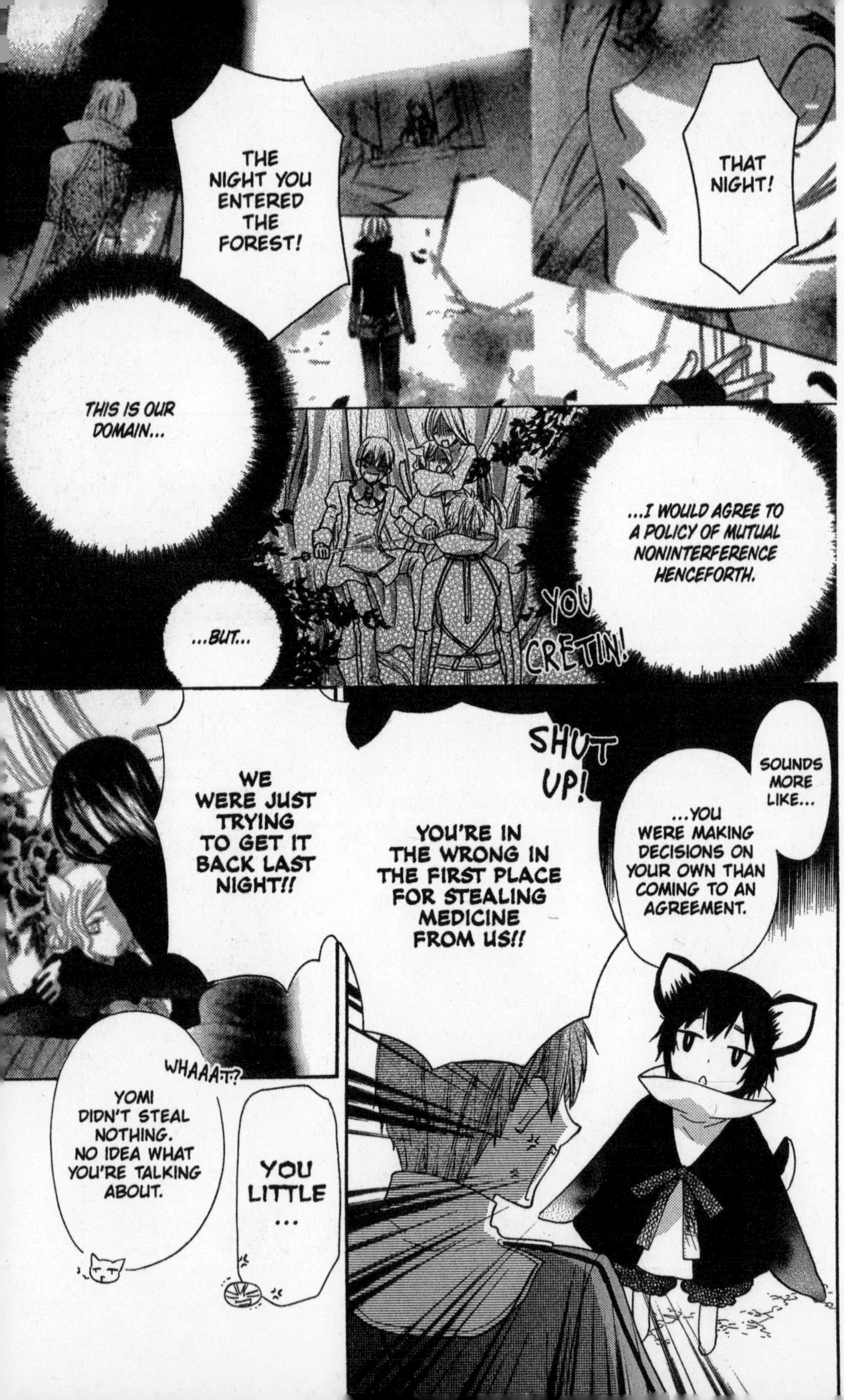
THAT NIGHT!
THE NIGHT YOU ENTERED THE FOREST!
THIS IS OUR DOMAIN...
...BUT...
...I WOULD AGREE TO A POLICY OF MUTUAL NONINTERFERENCE HENCEFORTH.
YOU CRETIN!
SOUNDS MORE LIKE...
...YOU WERE MAKING DECISIONS ON YOUR OWN THAN COMING TO AN AGREEMENT.
SHUT UP!
YOU'RE IN THE WRONG IN THE FIRST PLACE FOR STEALING MEDICINE FROM US!!
WE WERE JUST TRYING TO GET IT BACK LAST NIGHT!!
YOU LITTLE...
WHAAAT!?
YOMI DIDN'T STEAL NOTHING. NO IDEA WHAT YOU'RE TALKING ABOUT.

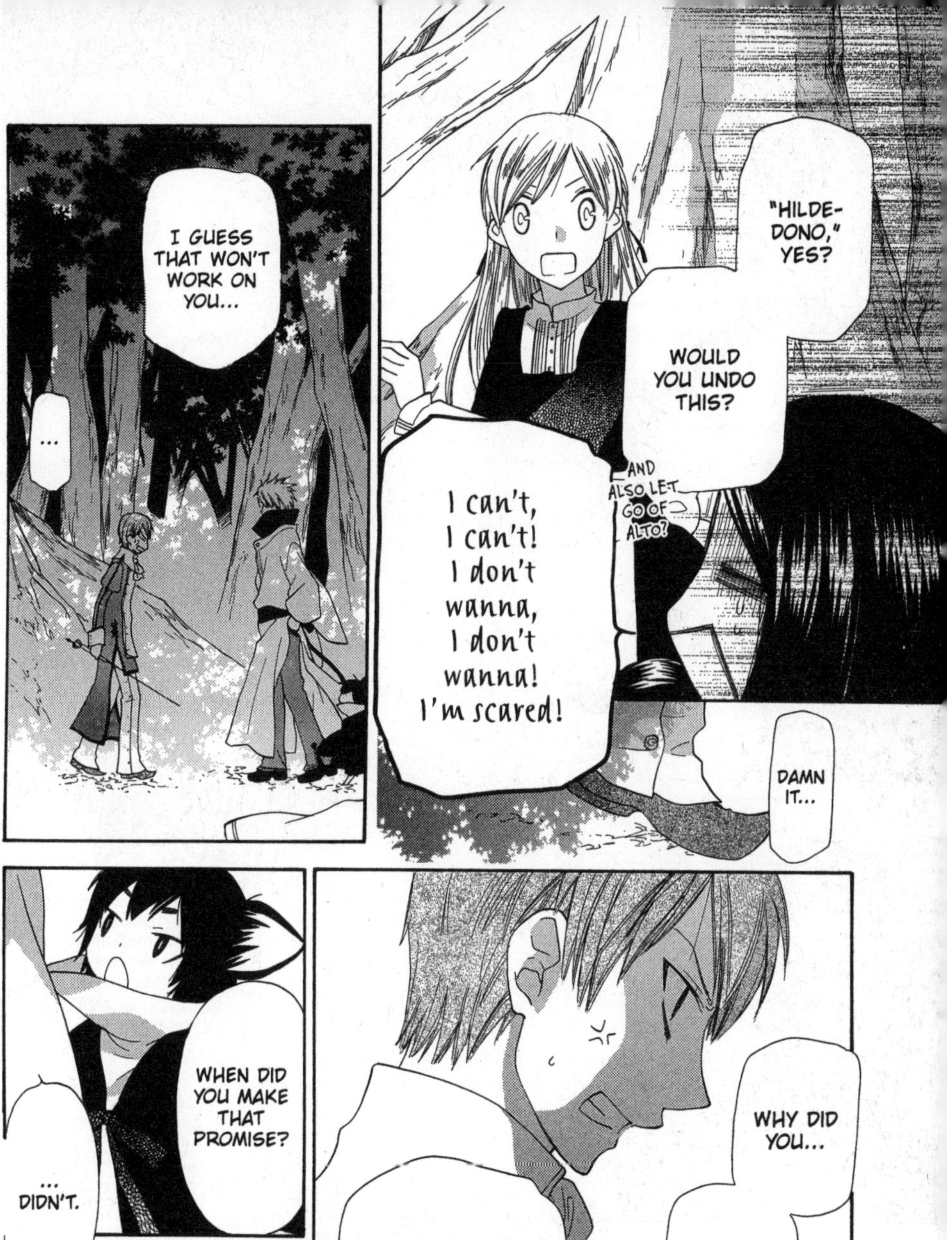
"HILDE-DONO," YES?
WOULD YOU UNDO THIS?
AND ALSO LET GO OF ALTO?
I can't, I can't! I don't wanna, I don't wanna! I'm scared!
DAMN IT...
I GUESS THAT WON'T WORK ON YOU...
...
WHY DID YOU...
...COME BACK TO THE FOREST?
WASN'T IT DECIDED THAT BOTH SIDES WOULD STEER CLEAR OF EACH OTHER?
WHEN DID YOU MAKE THAT PROMISE?
... DIDN'T.
YES, YOU DID!!

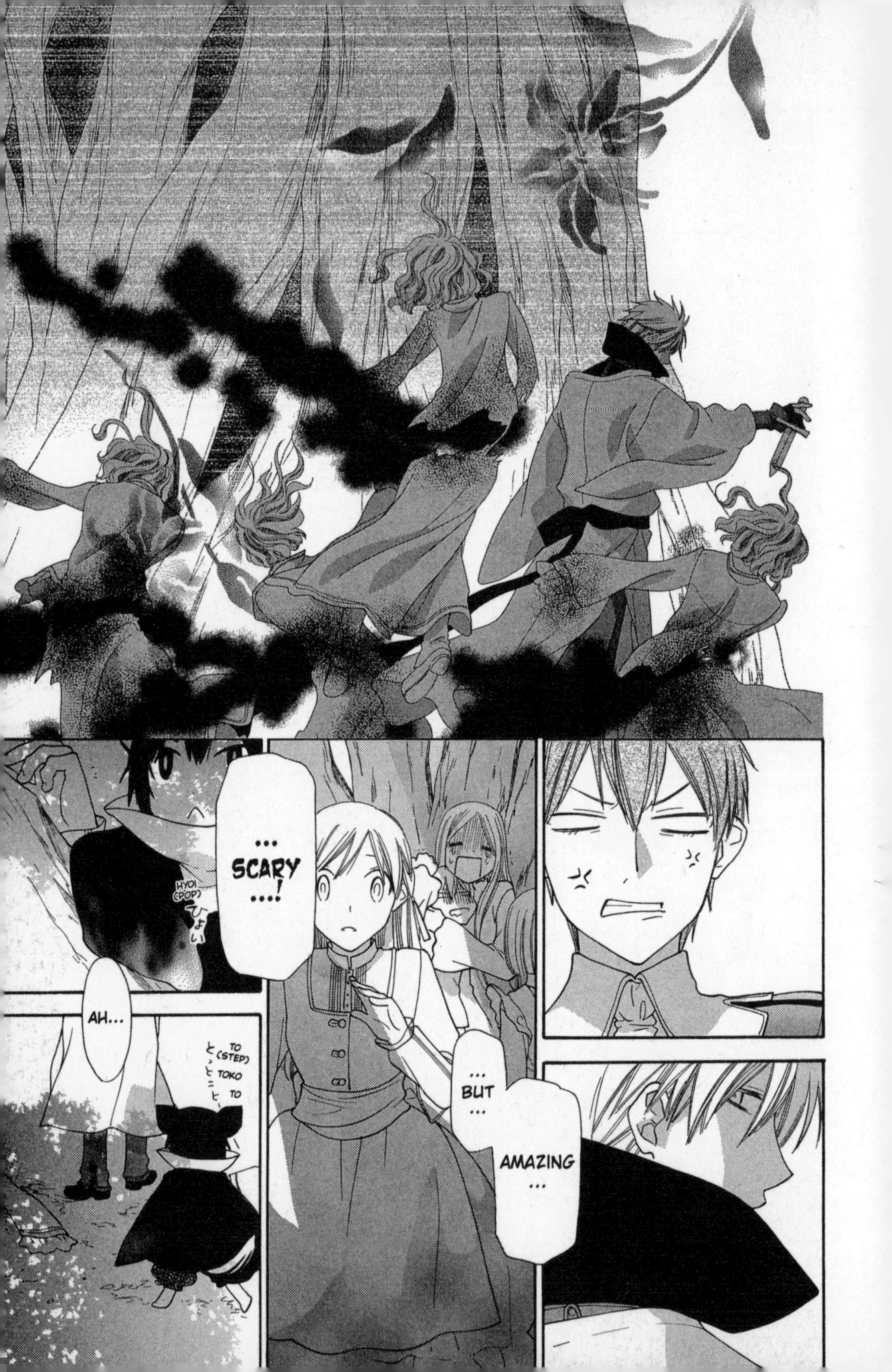

...SCARY....!
...BUT... AMAZING...
HYOI (POP)
ひょい
AH...
TO (STEP) TOKO TO

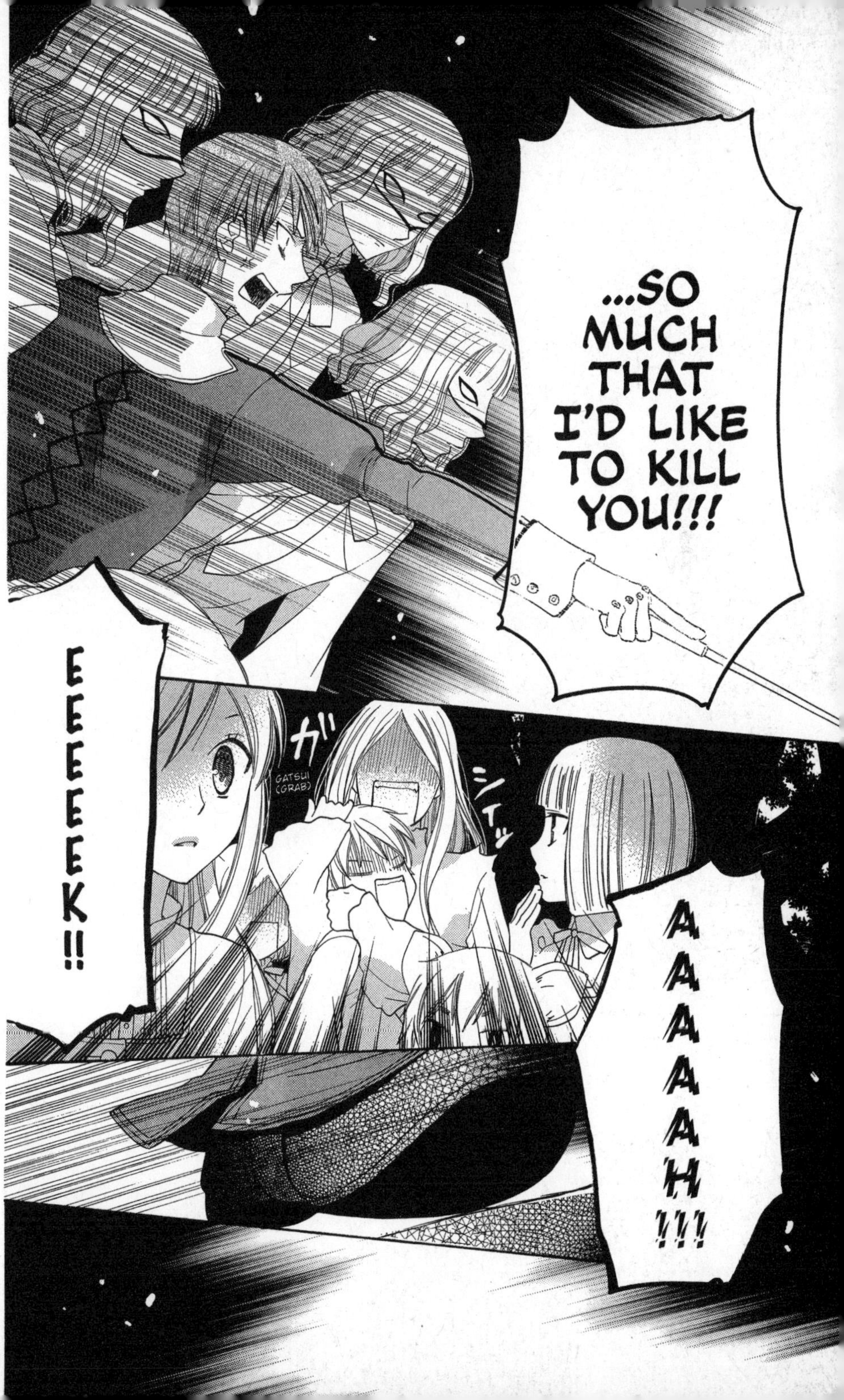
...SO MUCH THAT I'D LIKE TO KILL YOU!!!
AAAAAH!!!
ガッ
GATSU! (GRAB)
EEEEEEK!!

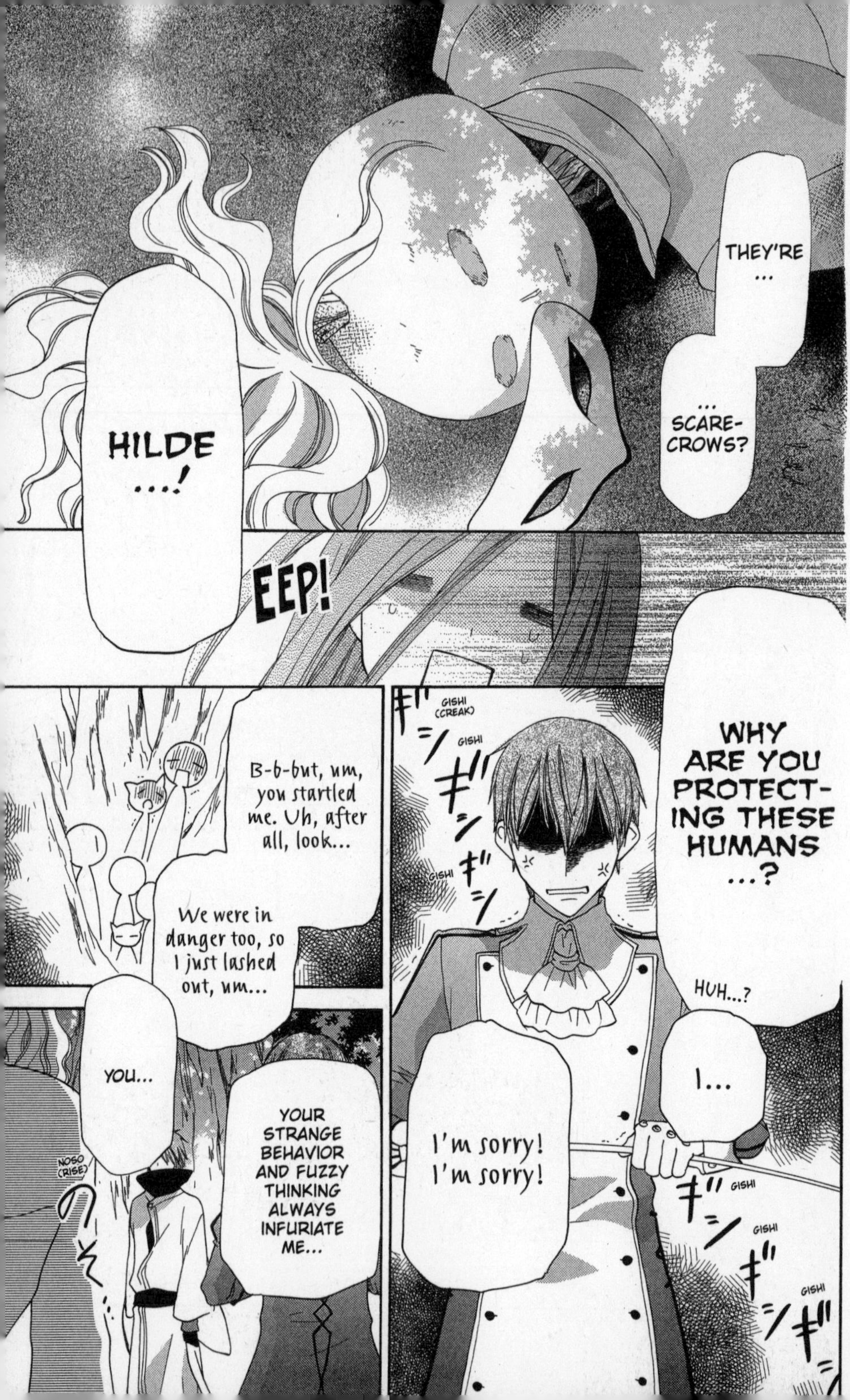
THEY'RE ...
... SCARECROWS?
HILDE ...!
EEP!
WHY ARE YOU PROTECTING THESE HUMANS ...?
GISHI (CREAK)
GISHI
GISHI
HUH...?
I...
I'm sorry! I'm sorry!
GISHI
GISHI
GISHI
B-b-but, um, you startled me. Uh, after all, look...
We were in danger too, so I just lashed out, um...
YOU...
YOUR STRANGE BEHAVIOR AND FUZZY THINKING ALWAYS INFURIATE ME...
NOSO (RISE)

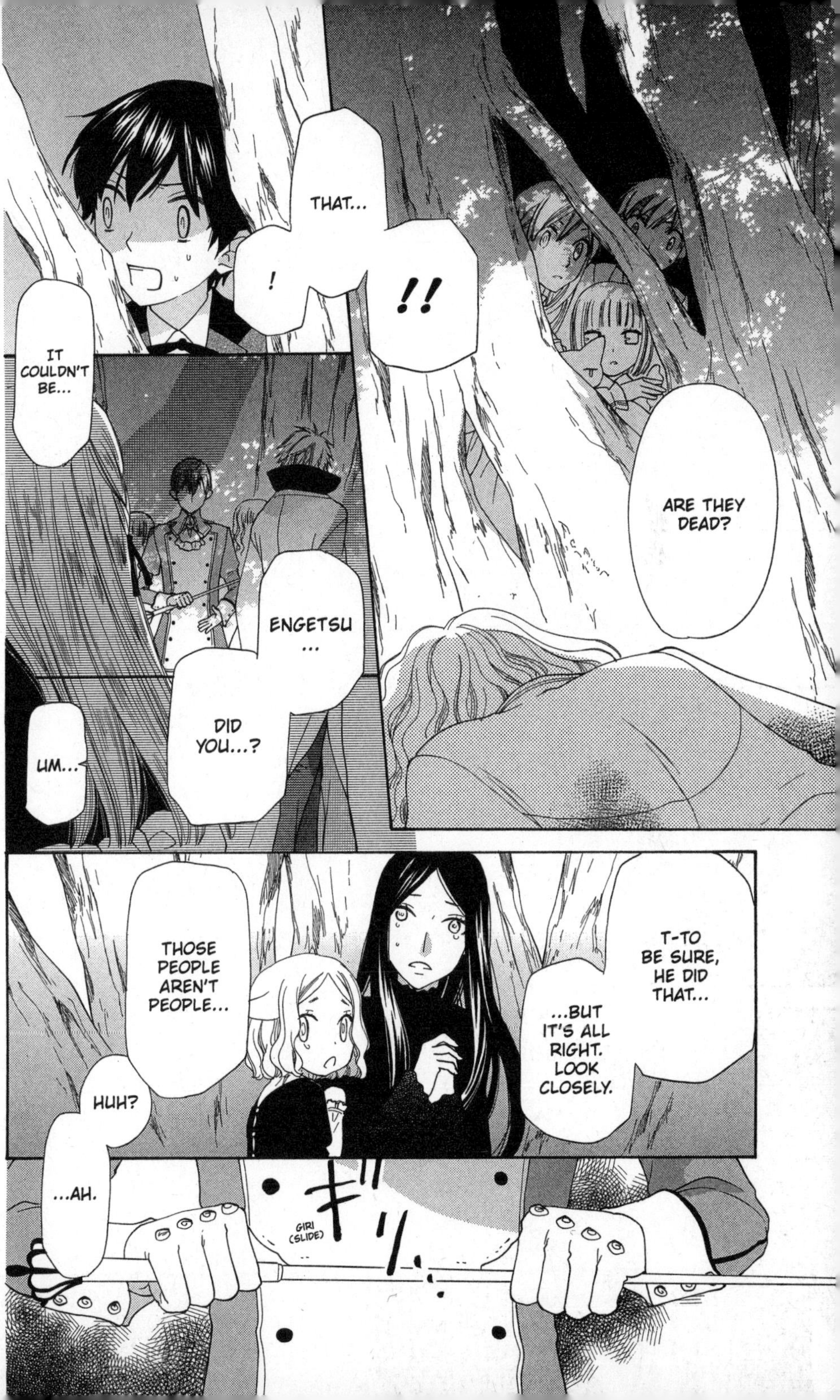
ARE THEY DEAD?
THAT...
!
!!
IT COULDN'T BE...
ENGETSU...
DID YOU...?
UM...
T-TO BE SURE, HE DID THAT...
...BUT IT'S ALL RIGHT. LOOK CLOSELY.
THOSE PEOPLE AREN'T PEOPLE...
HUH?
GIRI (SLIDE)
...AH.

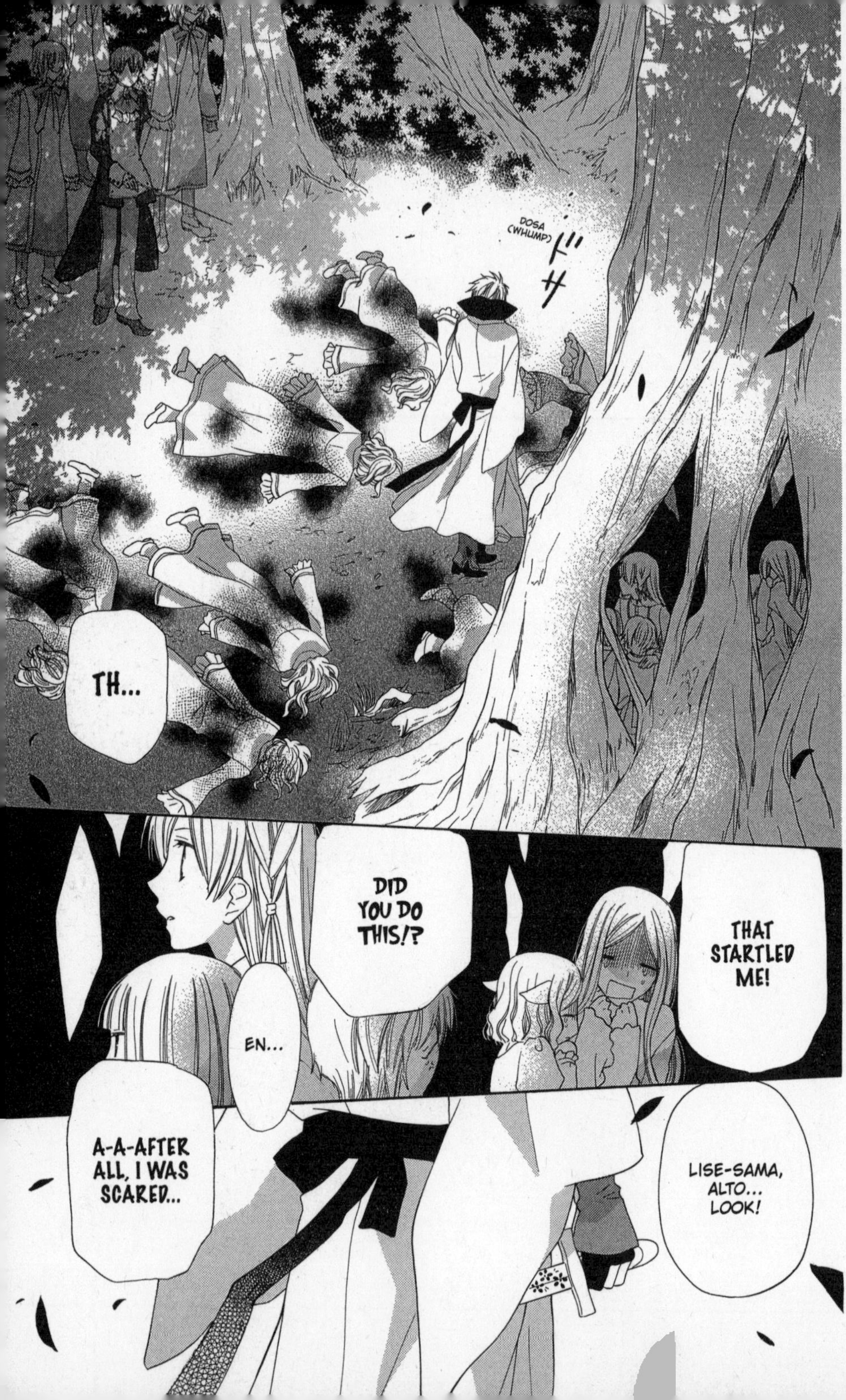
DOSA (WHUMP)
ドサ
TH...
THAT STARTLED ME!
DID YOU DO THIS!?
EN...
LISE-SAMA, ALTO... LOOK!
A-A-AFTER ALL, I WAS SCARED...

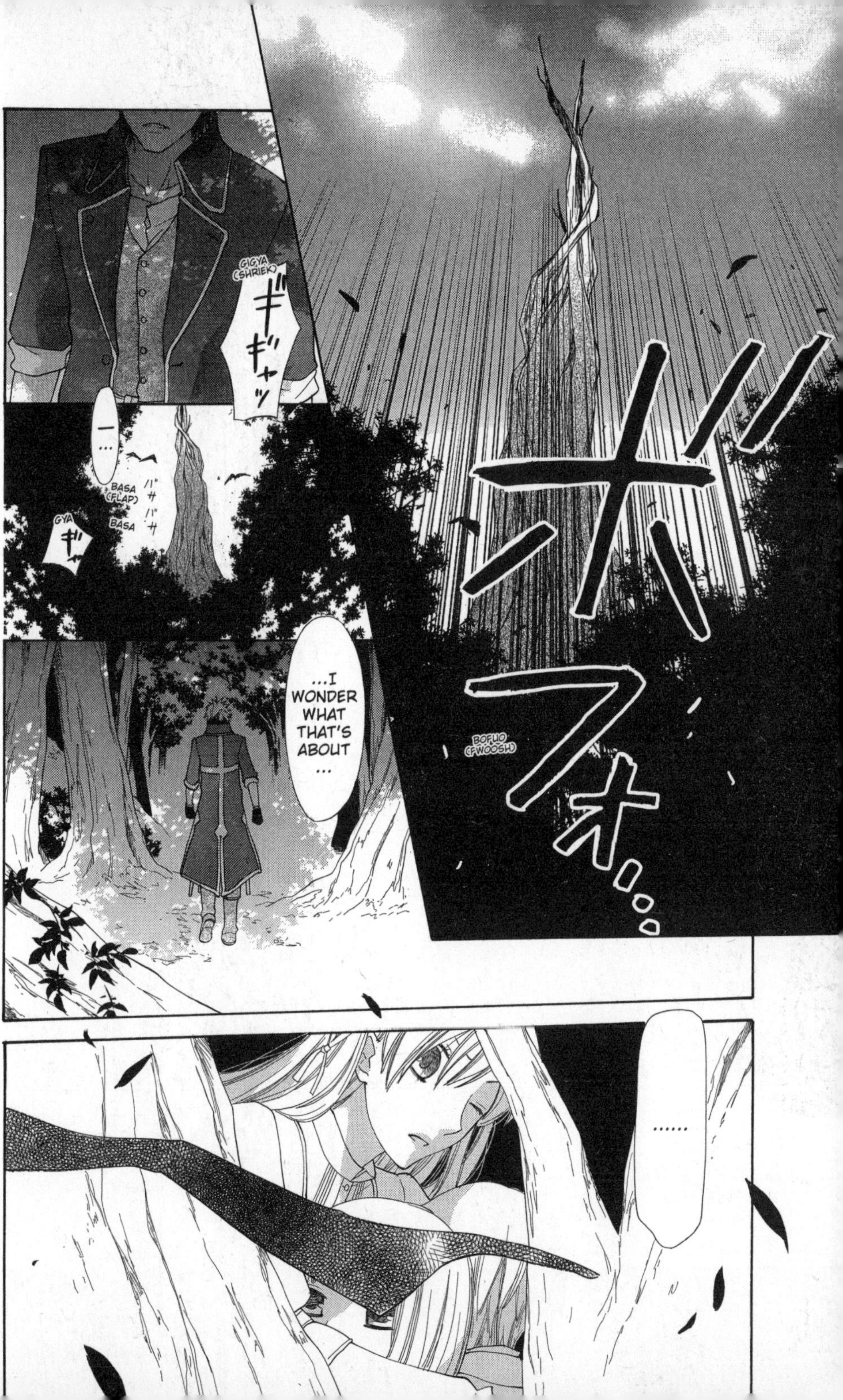
BOFUO (FWOOSH)
ボフォ…
GIGYA (SHRIEK)
ギギャッ
—…
BASA (FLAP)
バサバサ
BASA
GYA
ギャ
…I WONDER WHAT THAT'S ABOUT …
……

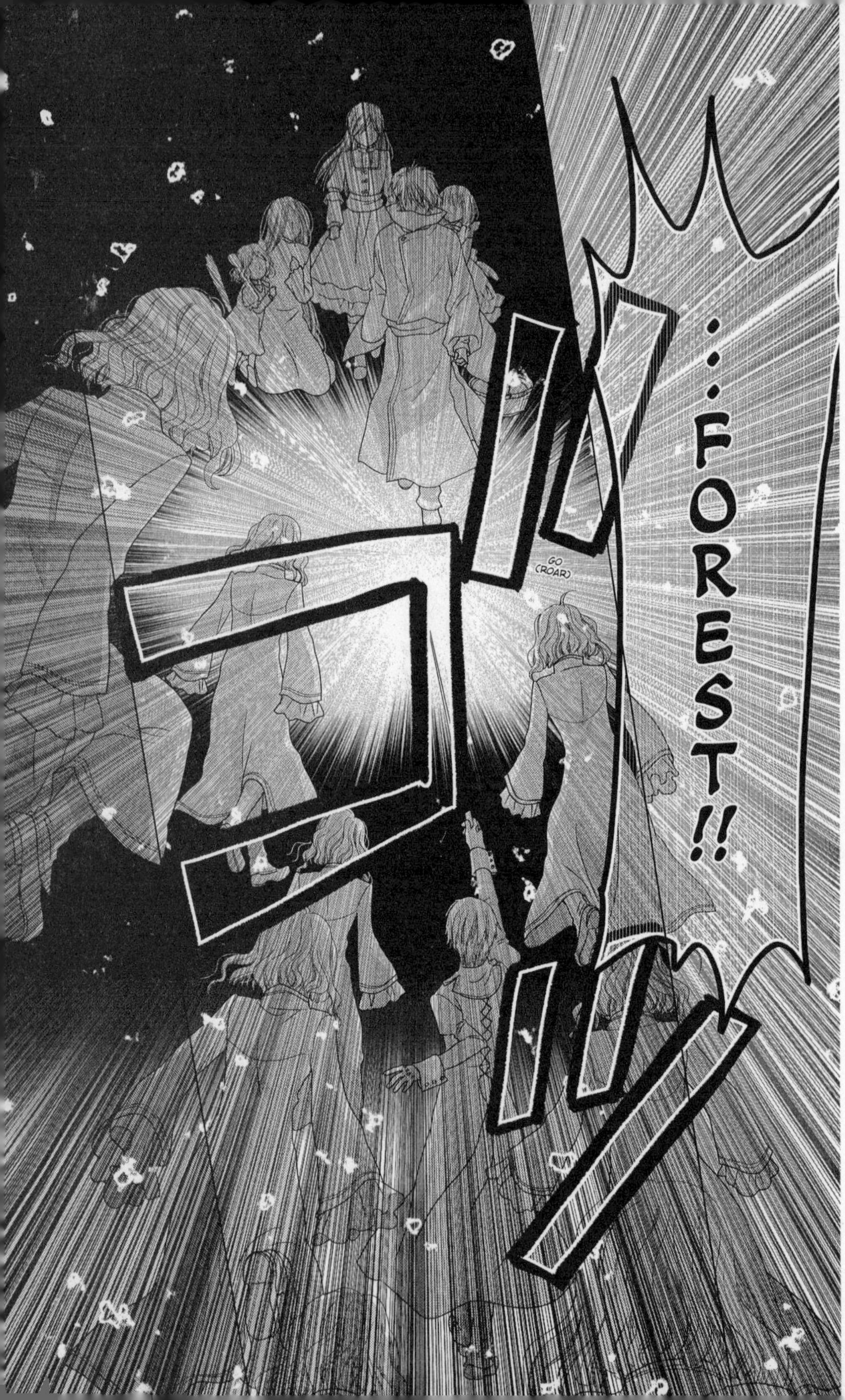
...FOREST!!
GO (ROAR)

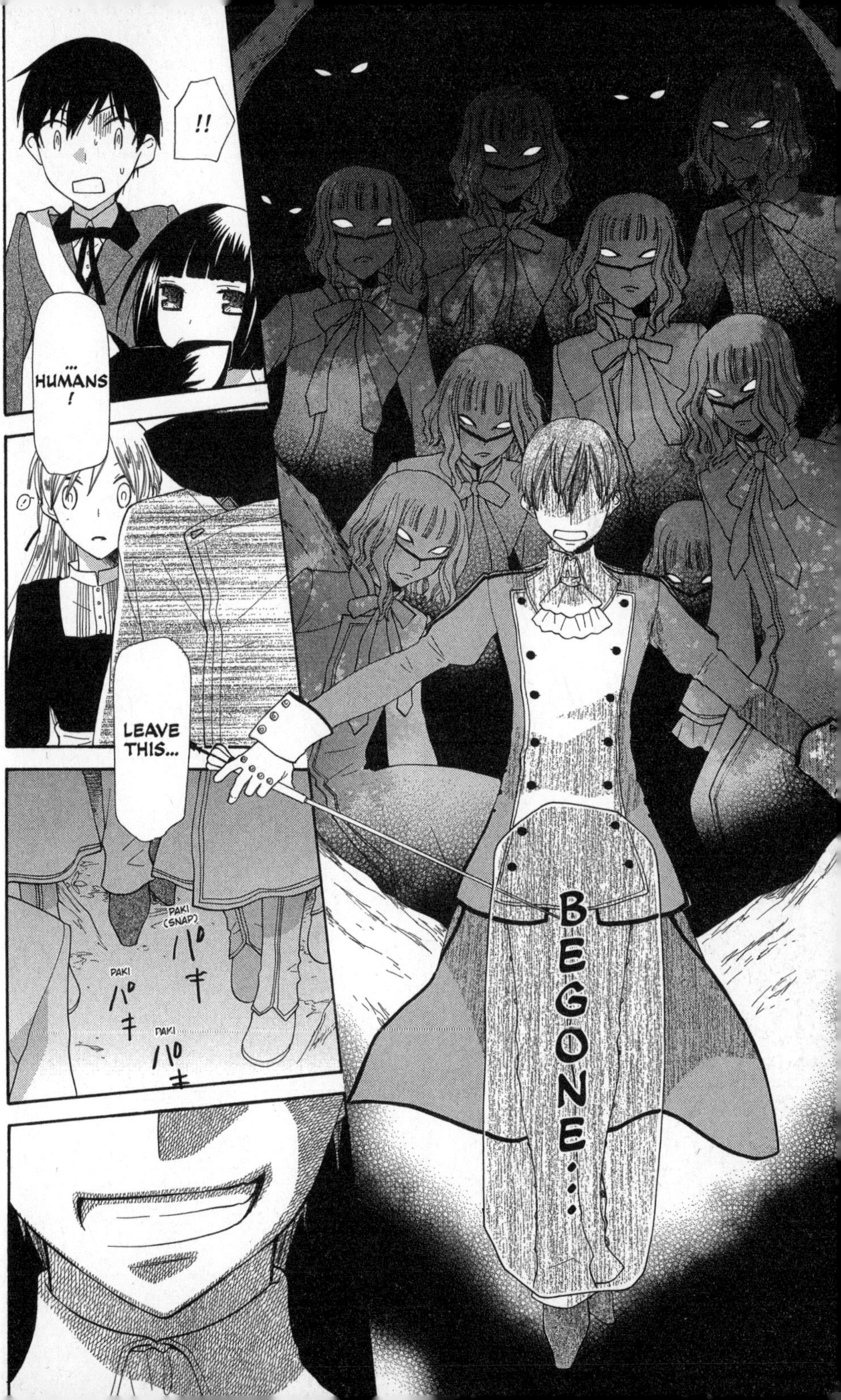
!!
...HUMANS!
LEAVE THIS...
BEGONE...
PAKI (SNAP)
パキ
PAKI
パキ
PAKI
パキ

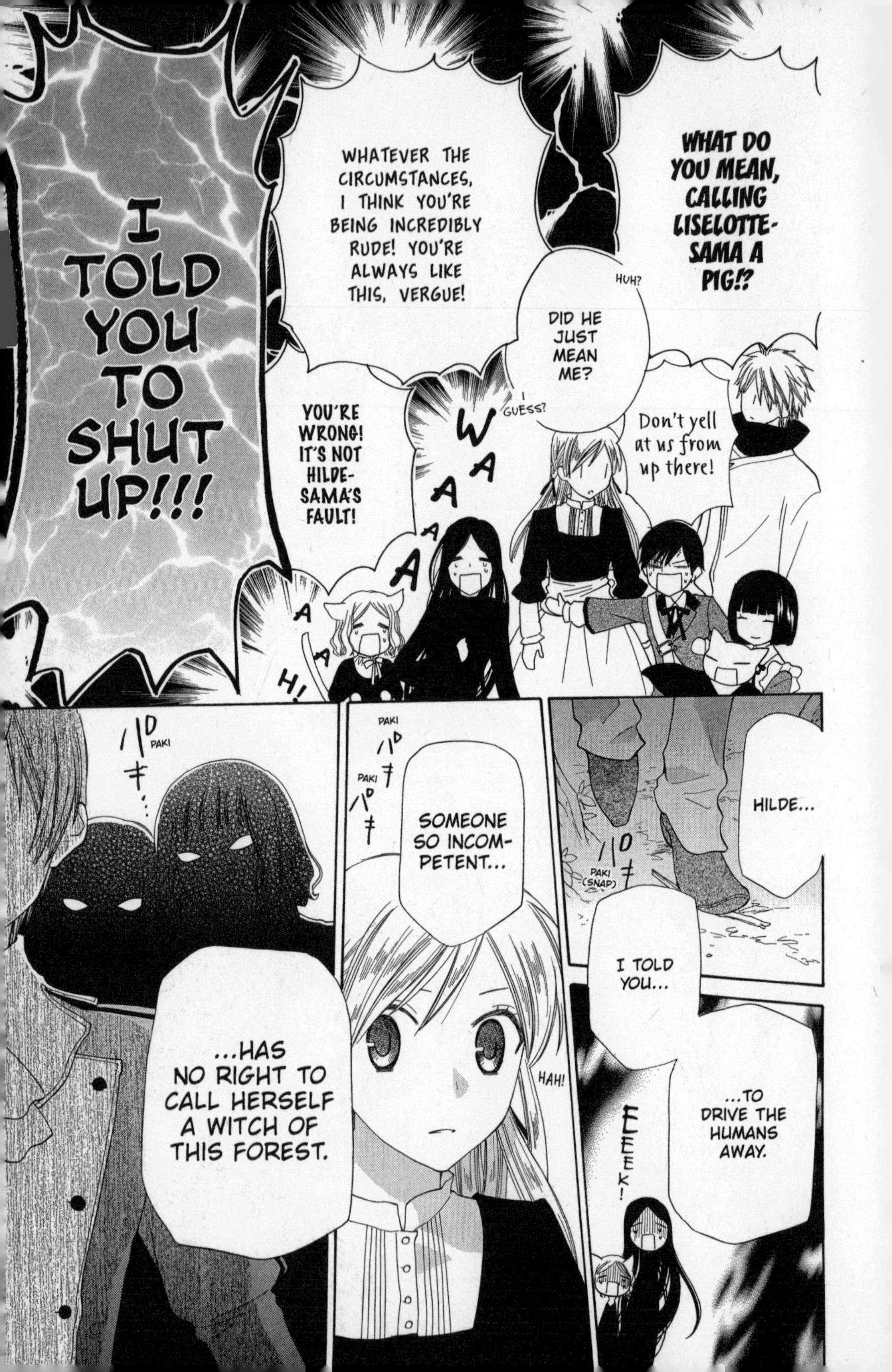
WHAT DO YOU MEAN, CALLING LISELOTTE-SAMA A PIG!?
HUH?
DID HE JUST MEAN ME?
I GUESS?
Don't yell at us from up there!
WHATEVER THE CIRCUMSTANCES, I THINK YOU'RE BEING INCREDIBLY RUDE! YOU'RE ALWAYS LIKE THIS, VERGUE!
YOU'RE WRONG! IT'S NOT HILDE-SAMA'S FAULT!
WAAAAAAAH!
I TOLD YOU TO SHUT UP!!!
HILDE...
パキ PAKI (SNAP)
I TOLD YOU...
...TO DRIVE THE HUMANS AWAY.
EEEEK!
パキ PAKI
パキ PAKI
SOMEONE SO INCOMPETENT...
HAH!
パキ PAKI
...HAS NO RIGHT TO CALL HERSELF A WITCH OF THIS FOREST.

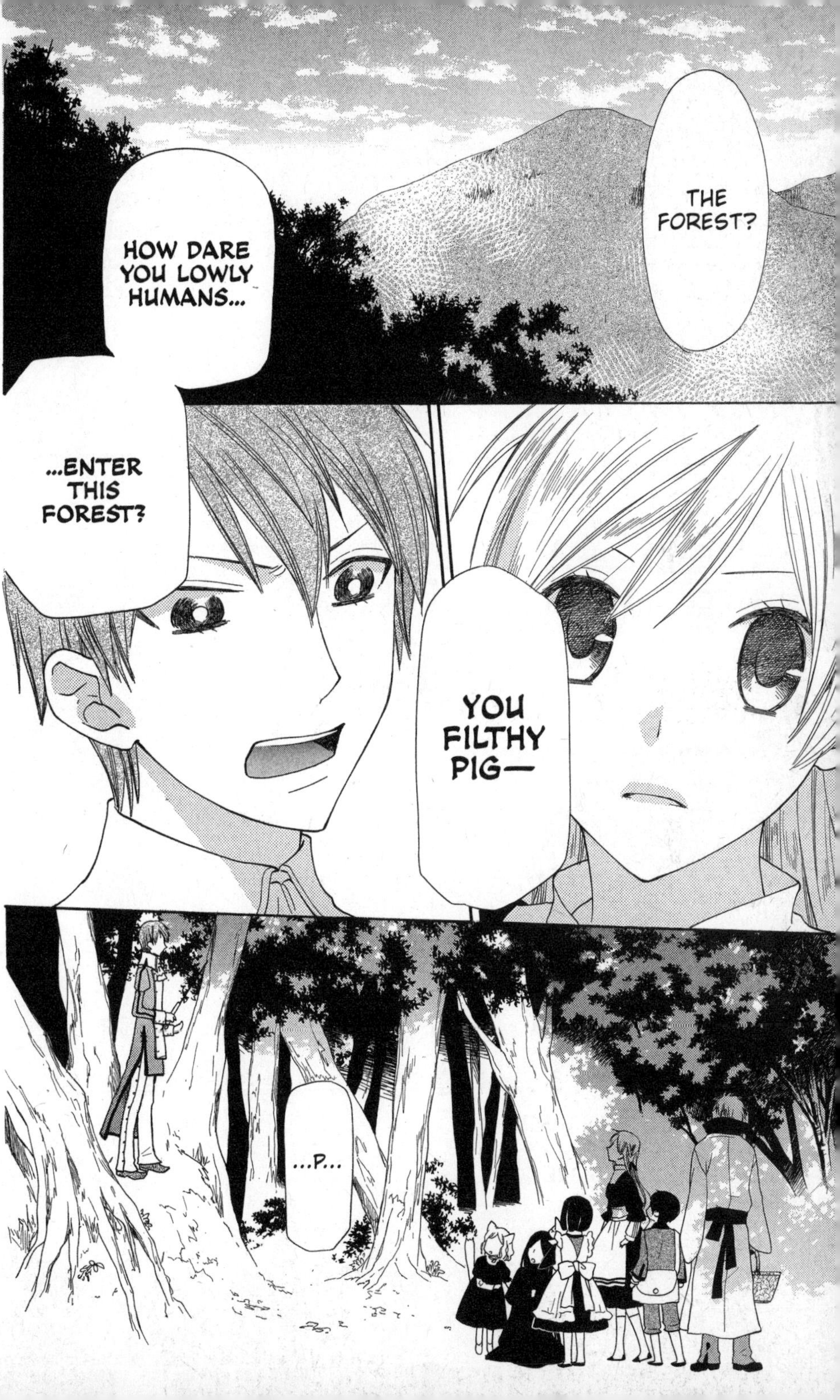
THE FOREST?
HOW DARE YOU LOWLY HUMANS...
...ENTER THIS FOREST?
YOU FILTHY PIG—
...P...

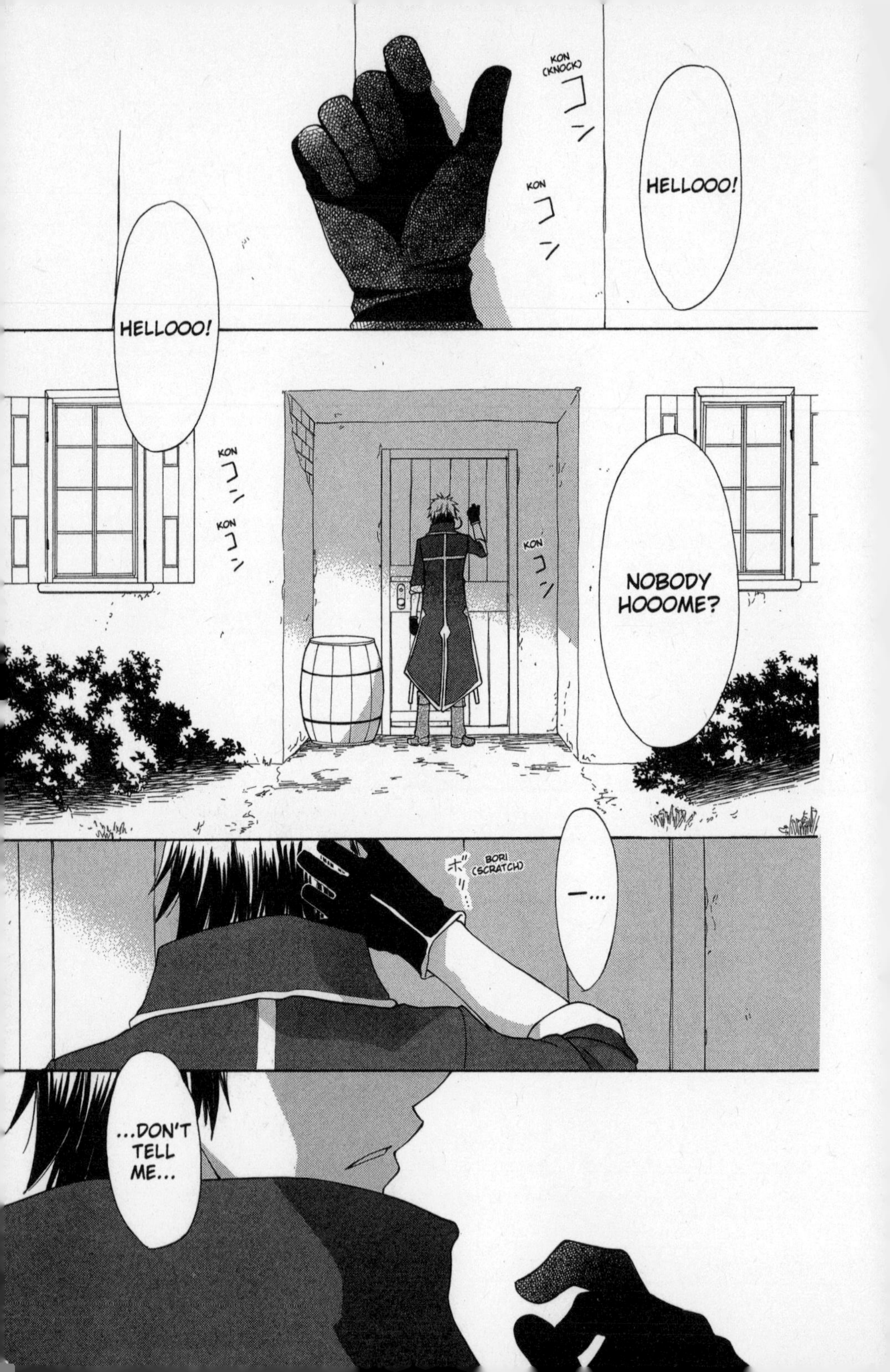
HELLOOO!
KON (KNOCK)
コン
KON
コン
HELLOOO!
NOBODY HOOOME?
KON
コン
KON
コン
KON
コン
—...
BORI (SCRATCH)
ボリ
...DON'T TELL ME...

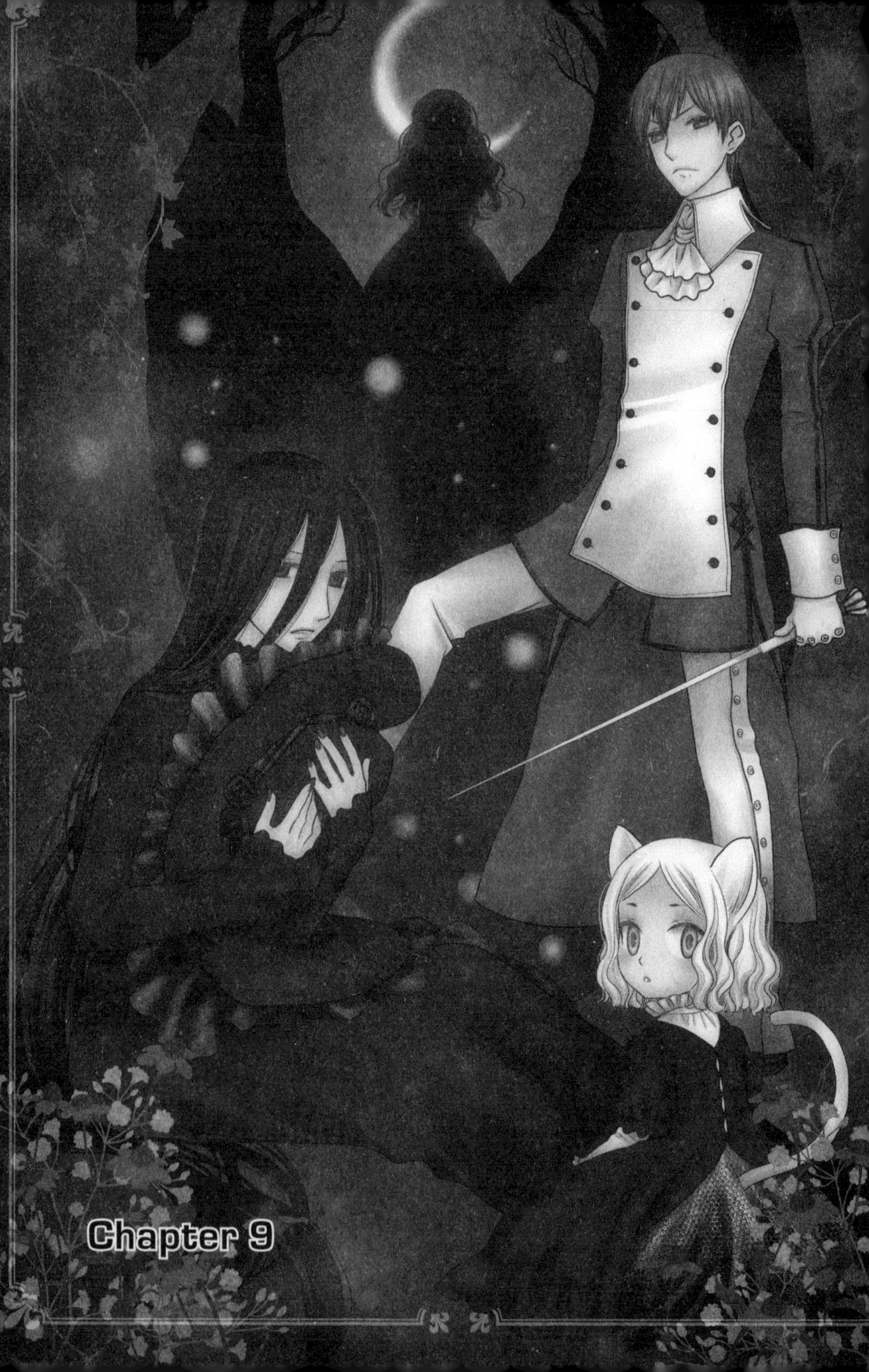
Chapter 9

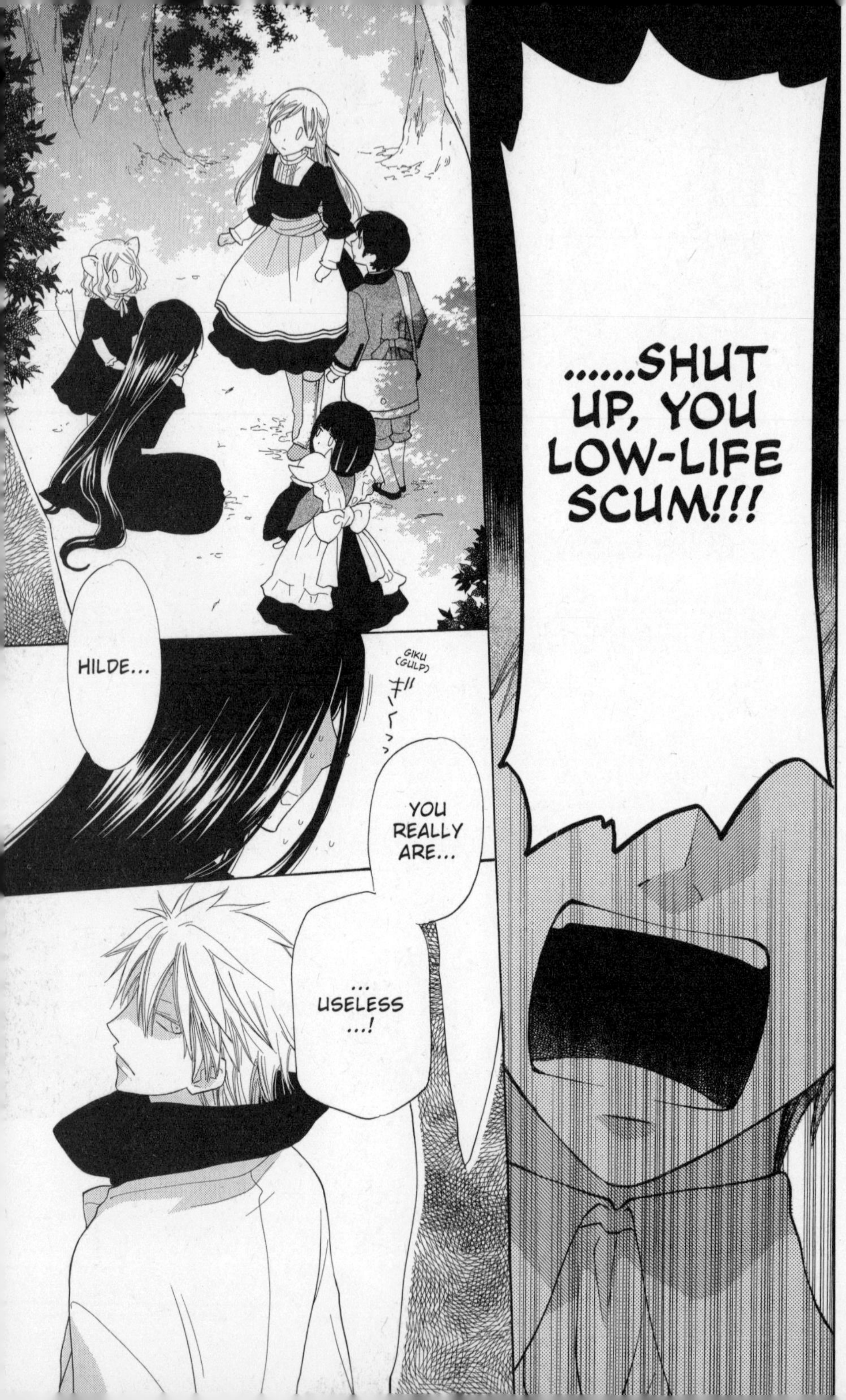

......SHUT UP, YOU LOW-LIFE SCUM!!!
HILDE...
GIKU (GULP)
YOU REALLY ARE...
... USELESS ...!

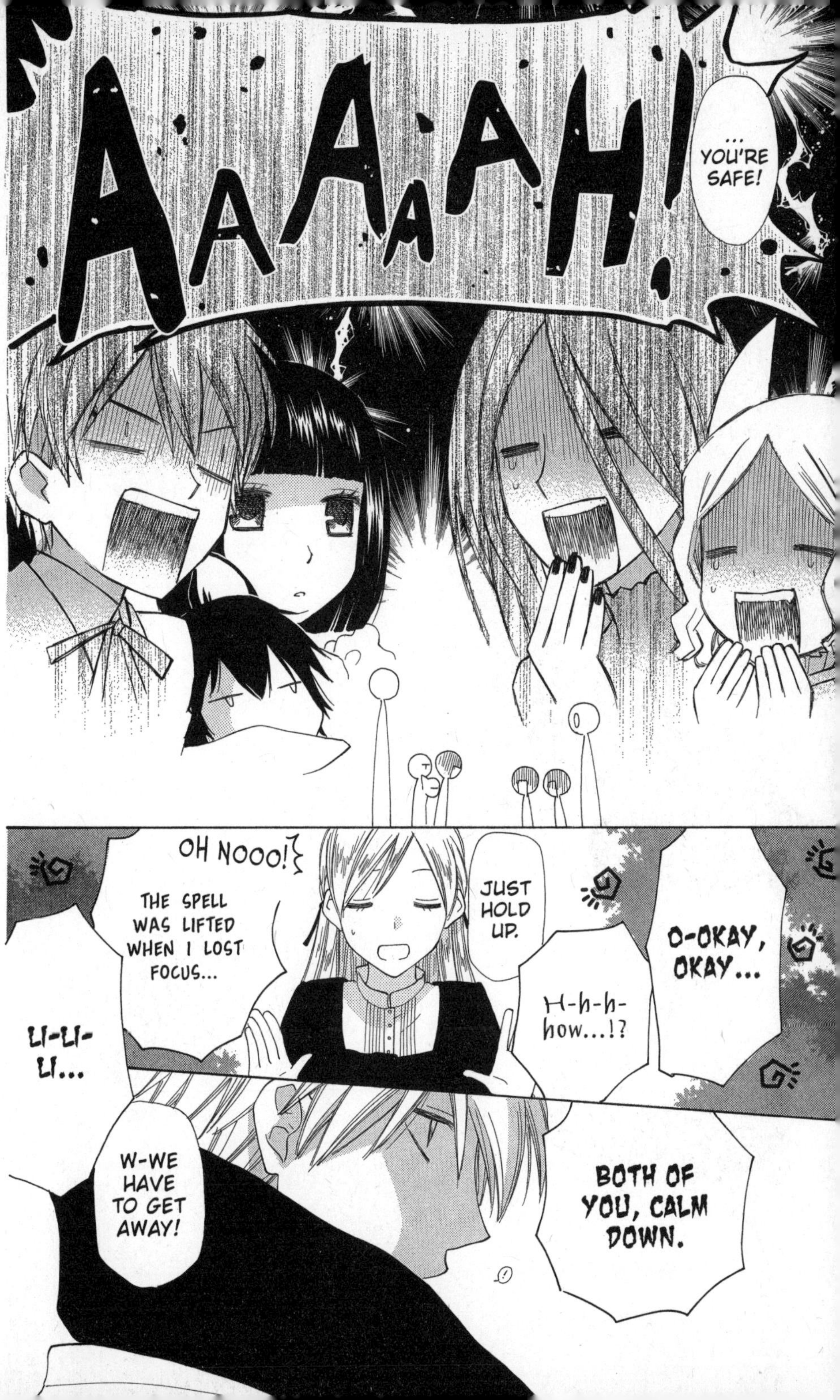
... YOU'RE SAFE!
AAAAAH!
O-OKAY, OKAY...
H-h-h-how...!?
JUST HOLD UP.
OH NOOO!
THE SPELL WAS LIFTED WHEN I LOST FOCUS...
LI-LI-LI...
BOTH OF YOU, CALM DOWN.
W-WE HAVE TO GET AWAY!

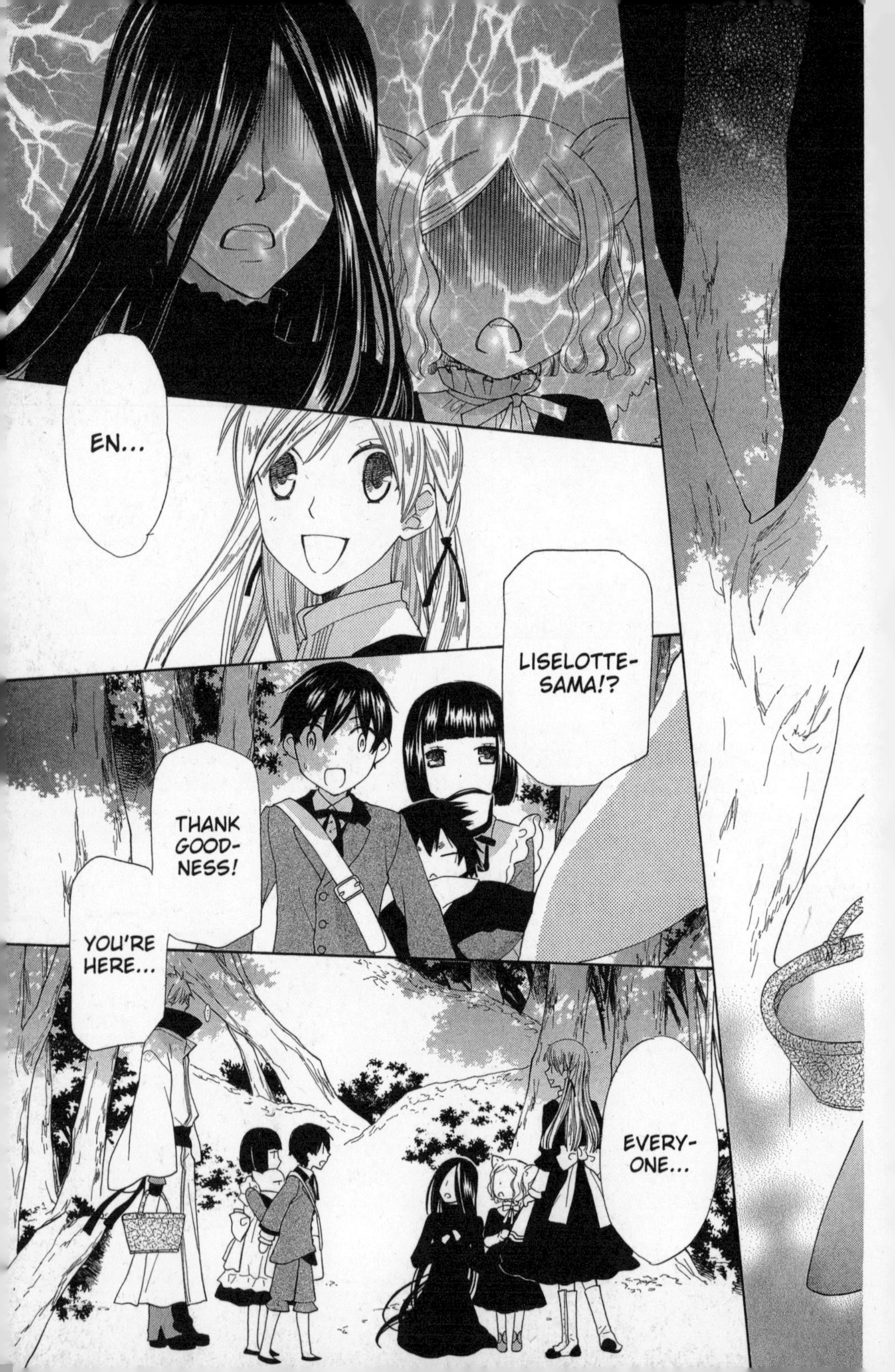
EN...
LISELOTTE-SAMA!?
THANK GOODNESS!
YOU'RE HERE...
EVERYONE...

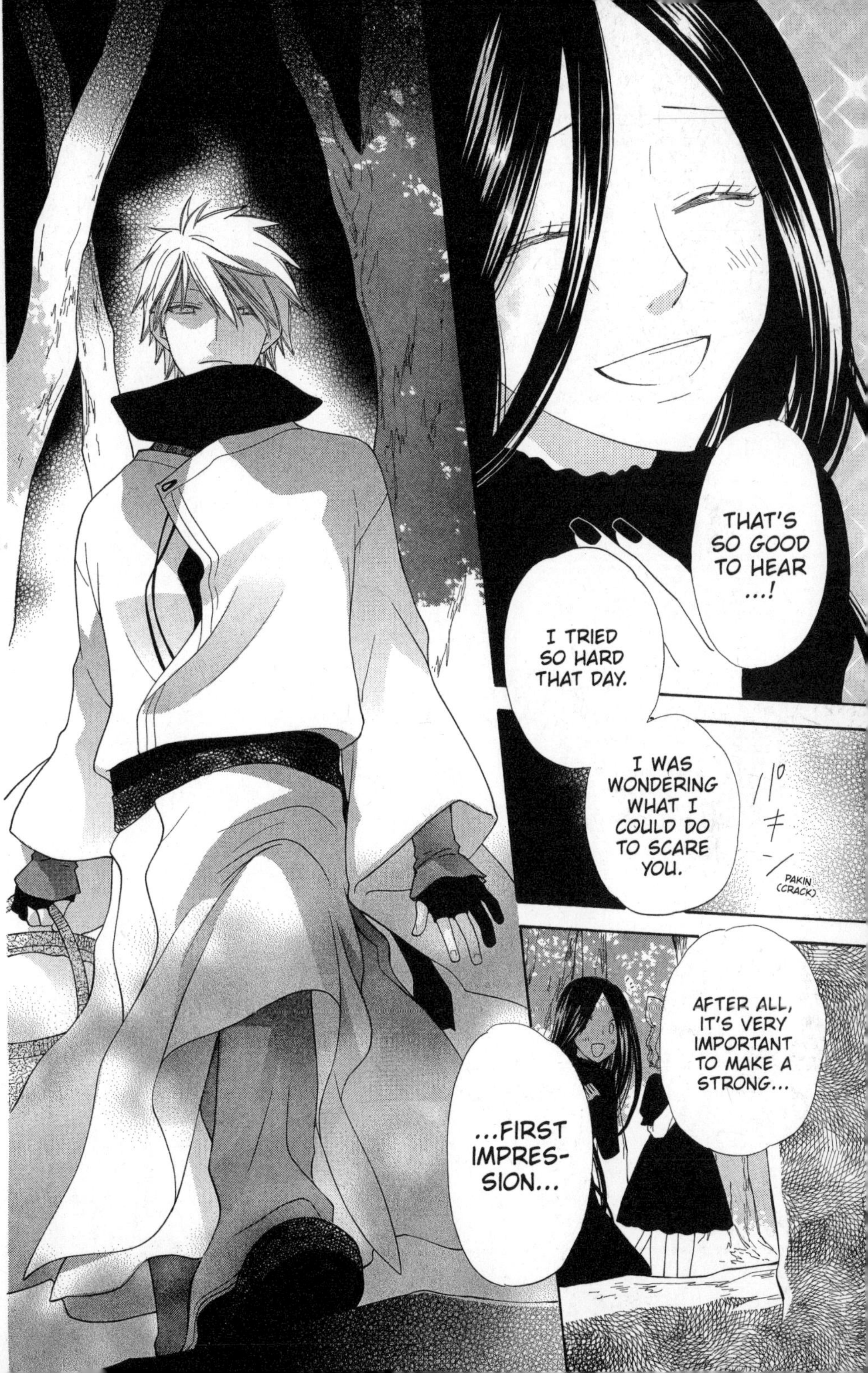
THAT'S SO GOOD TO HEAR ...!
I TRIED SO HARD THAT DAY.
I WAS WONDERING WHAT I COULD DO TO SCARE YOU.
パキン
PAKIN (CRACK)
AFTER ALL, IT'S VERY IMPORTANT TO MAKE A STRONG...
...FIRST IMPRES-SION...

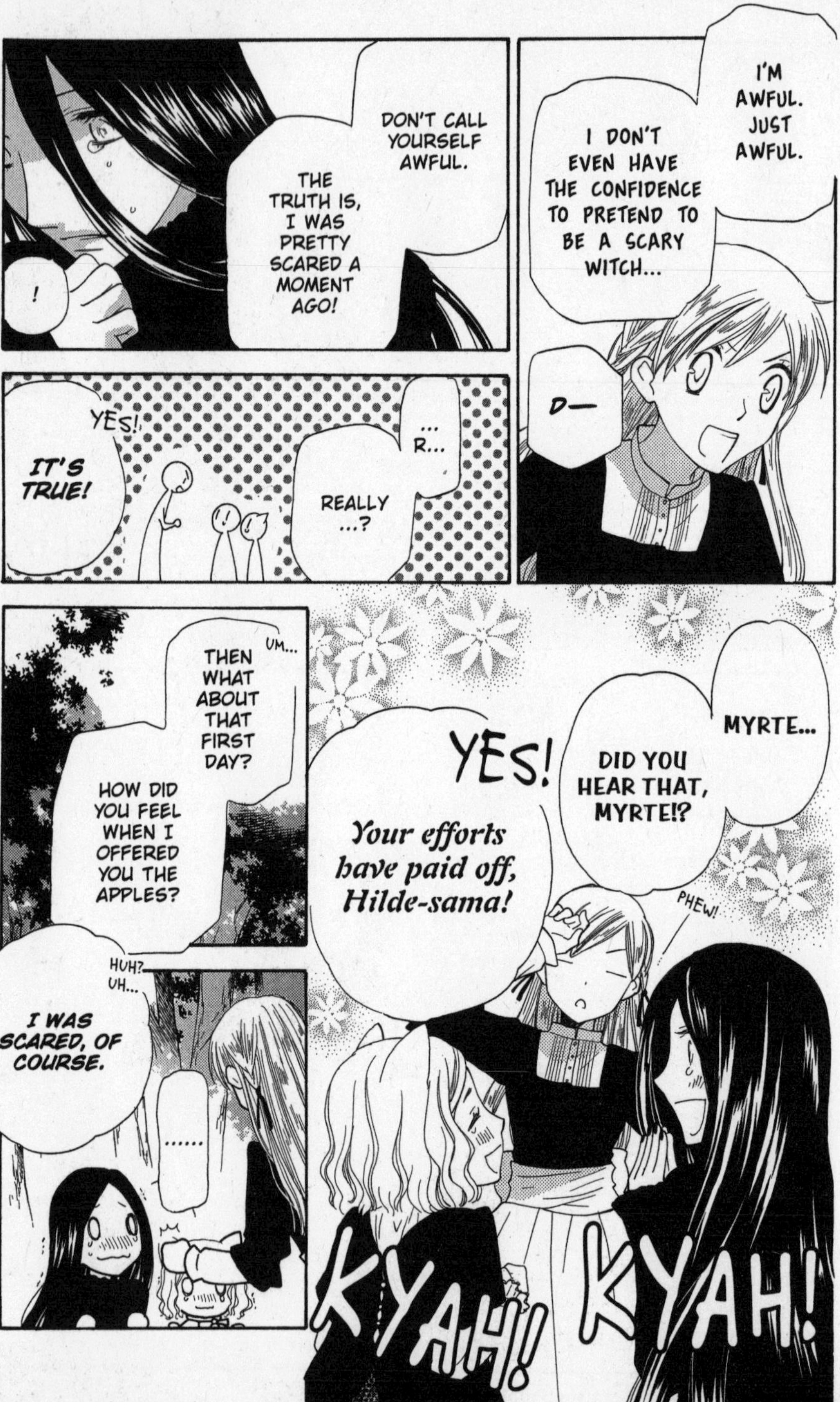
I'M AWFUL. JUST AWFUL.
I DON'T EVEN HAVE THE CONFIDENCE TO PRETEND TO BE A SCARY WITCH...
DON'T CALL YOURSELF AWFUL.
THE TRUTH IS, I WAS PRETTY SCARED A MOMENT AGO!
!
D—
... R...
REALLY ...?
YES!
IT'S TRUE!
MYRTE...
DID YOU HEAR THAT, MYRTE!?
YES!
Your efforts have paid off, Hilde-sama!
PHEW!
KYAH!
KYAH!
UM...
THEN WHAT ABOUT THAT FIRST DAY?
HOW DID YOU FEEL WHEN I OFFERED YOU THE APPLES?
HUH? UH...
I WAS SCARED, OF COURSE.
....

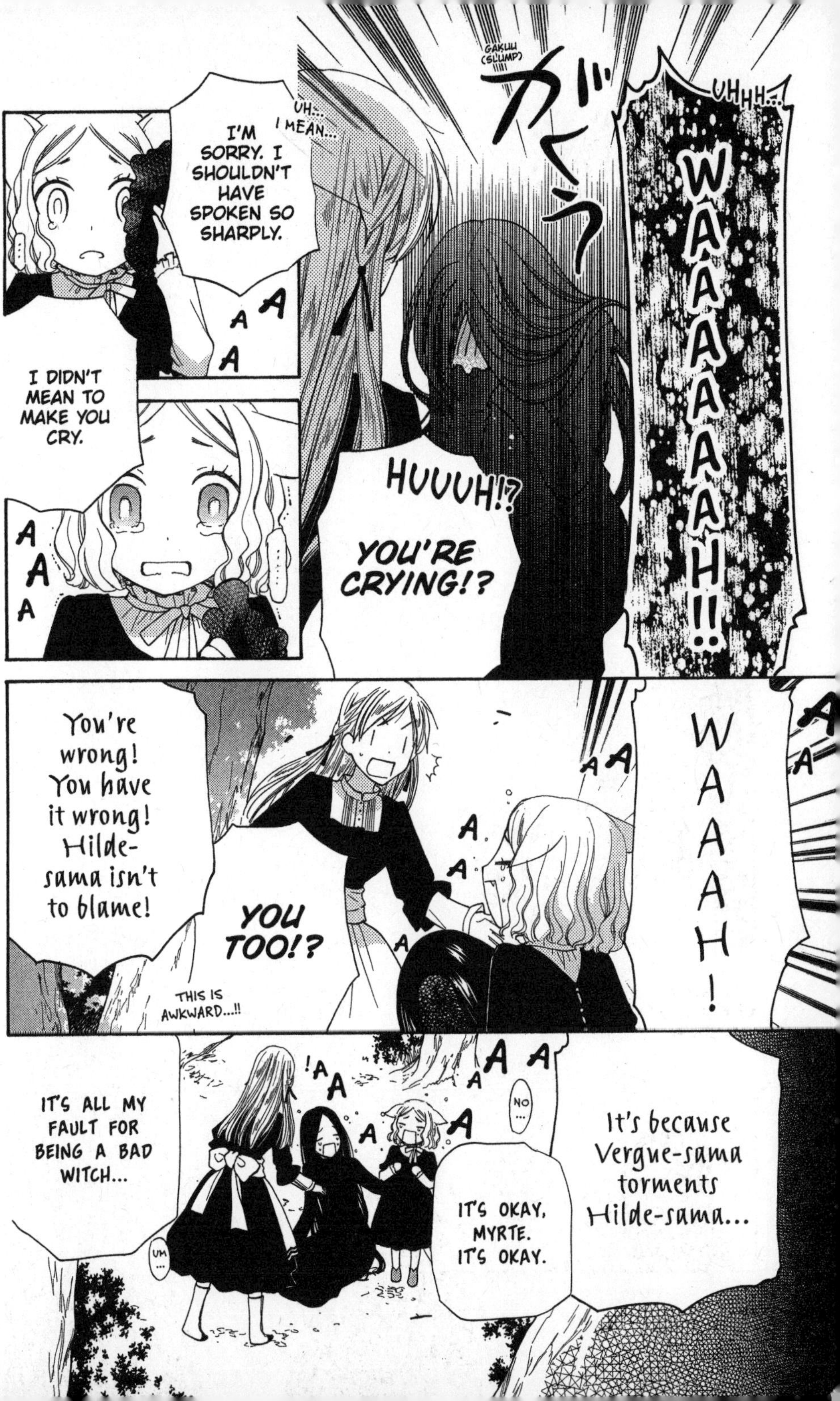
GAKUU (SLUMP)
UHHH...
WAAAAAAAAH!!
HUUUH!?
YOU'RE CRYING!?
UH... I MEAN...
I'M SORRY. I SHOULDN'T HAVE SPOKEN SO SHARPLY.
I DIDN'T MEAN TO MAKE YOU CRY.
WAAAAH!
YOU TOO!?
You're wrong! You have it wrong! Hilde-sama isn't to blame!
THIS IS AWKWARD...!!
It's because Vergue-sama torments Hilde-sama...
NO...
IT'S OKAY, MYRTE. IT'S OKAY.
IT'S ALL MY FAULT FOR BEING A BAD WITCH...
UH...

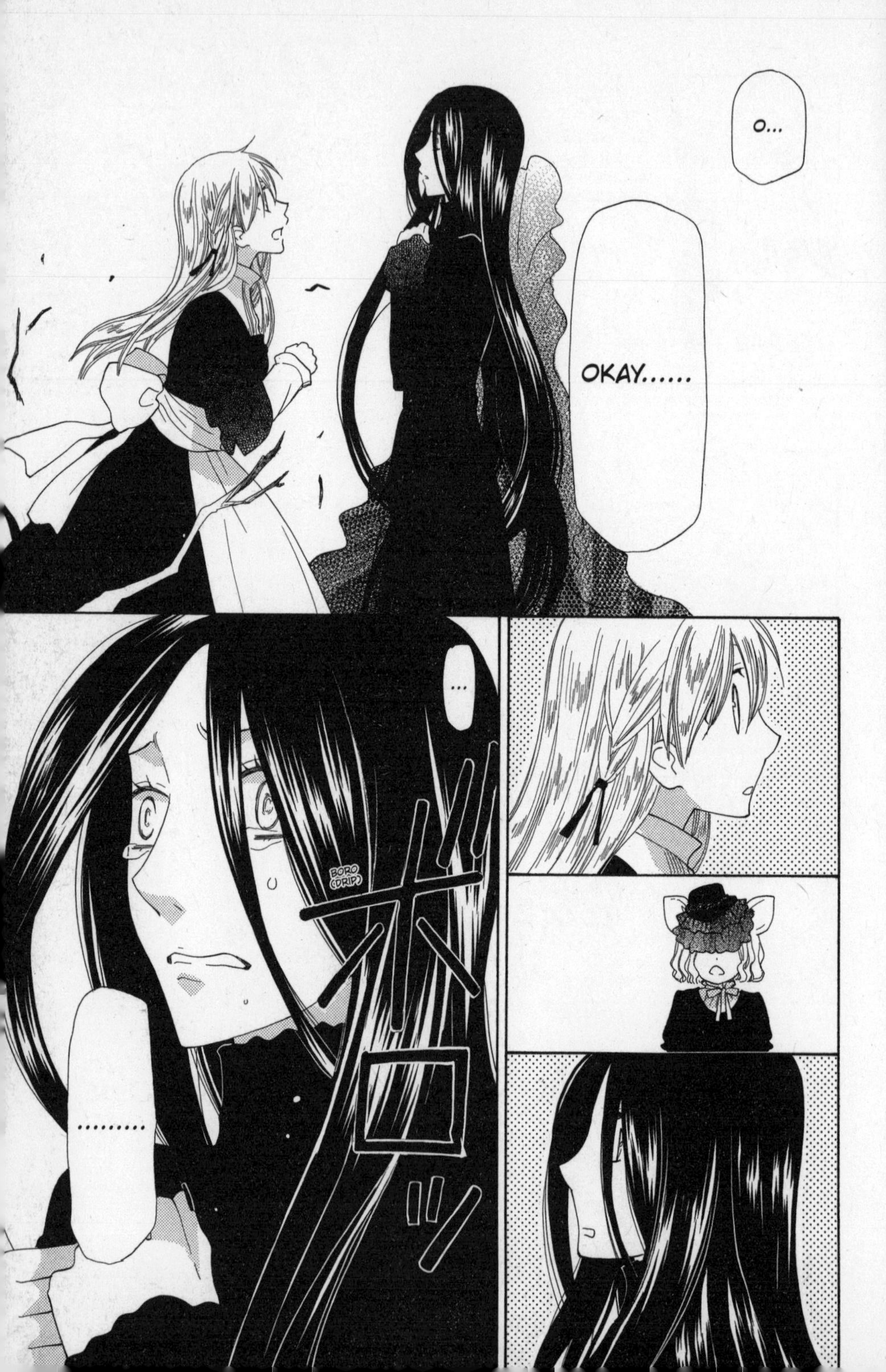
O...
OKAY......
...
BORO (DRIP)
....

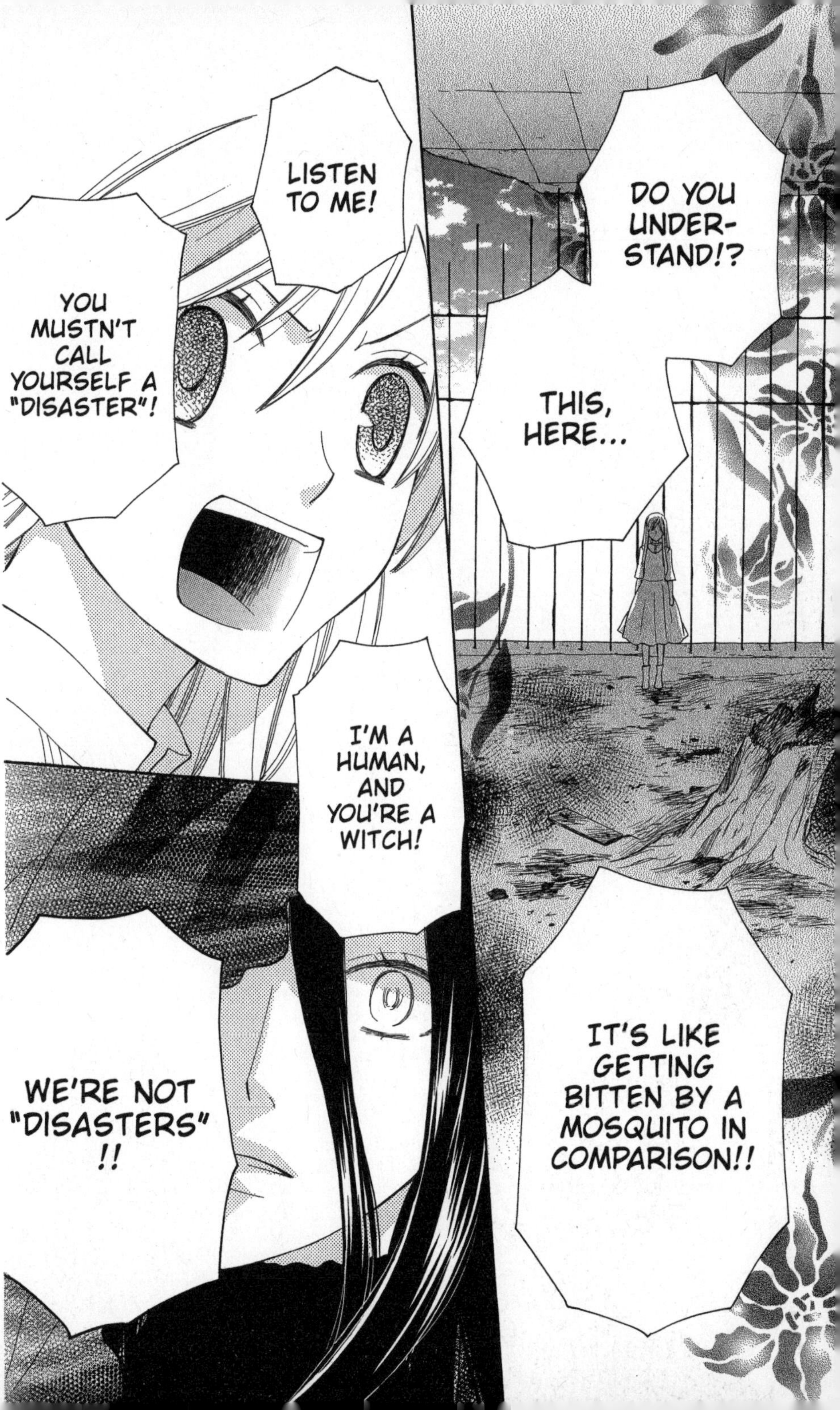
DO YOU UNDER-STAND!?
THIS, HERE...
IT'S LIKE GETTING BITTEN BY A MOSQUITO IN COMPARISON!!
LISTEN TO ME!
YOU MUSTN'T CALL YOURSELF A "DISASTER"!
I'M A HUMAN, AND YOU'RE A WITCH!
WE'RE NOT "DISASTERS" !!

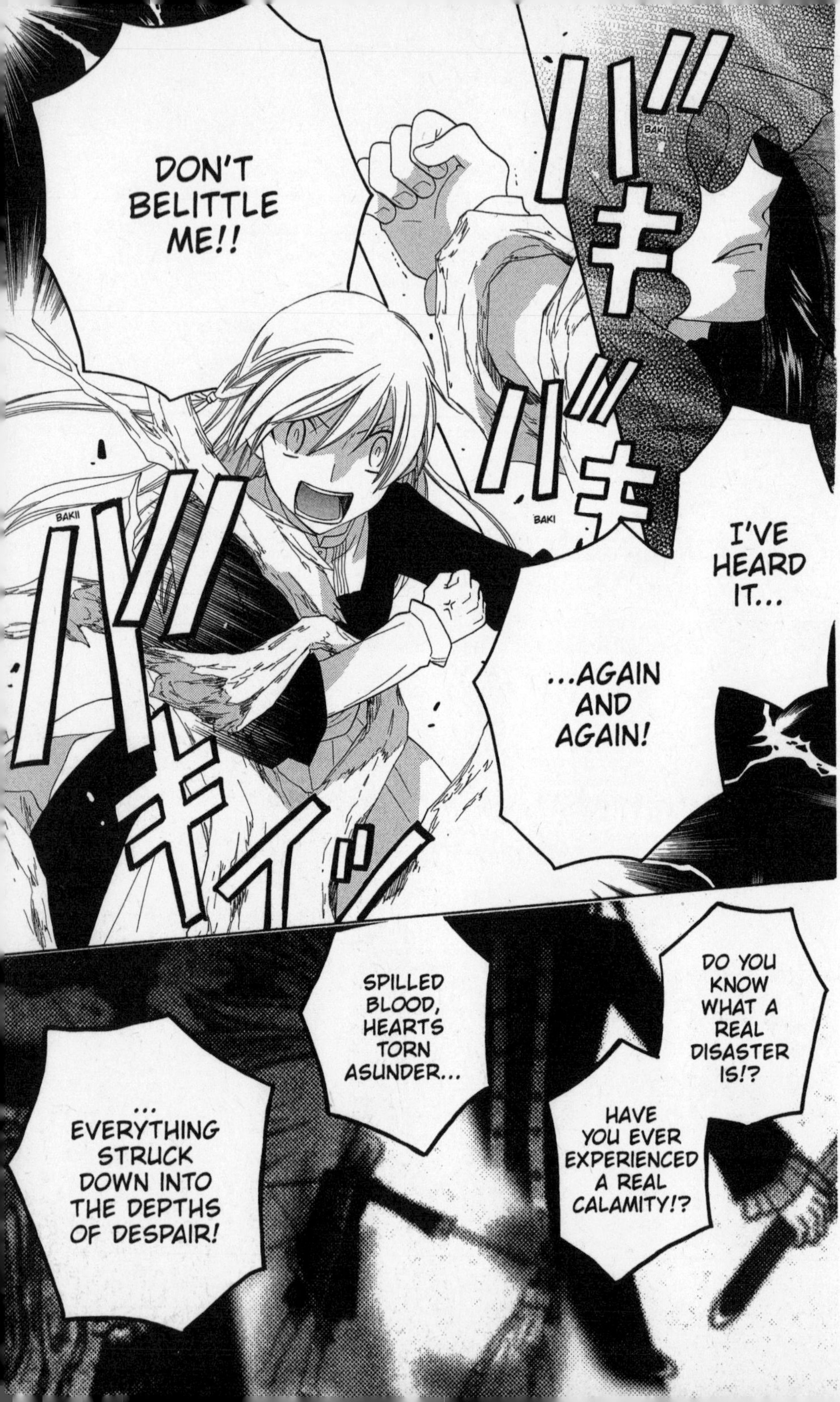
バキ
BAKI
DON'T BELITTLE ME!!
バキ
BAKI
バギィッ
BAKII
I'VE HEARD IT...
...AGAIN AND AGAIN!
DO YOU KNOW WHAT A REAL DISASTER IS!?
HAVE YOU EVER EXPERIENCED A REAL CALAMITY!?
SPILLED BLOOD, HEARTS TORN ASUNDER...
... EVERYTHING STRUCK DOWN INTO THE DEPTHS OF DESPAIR!

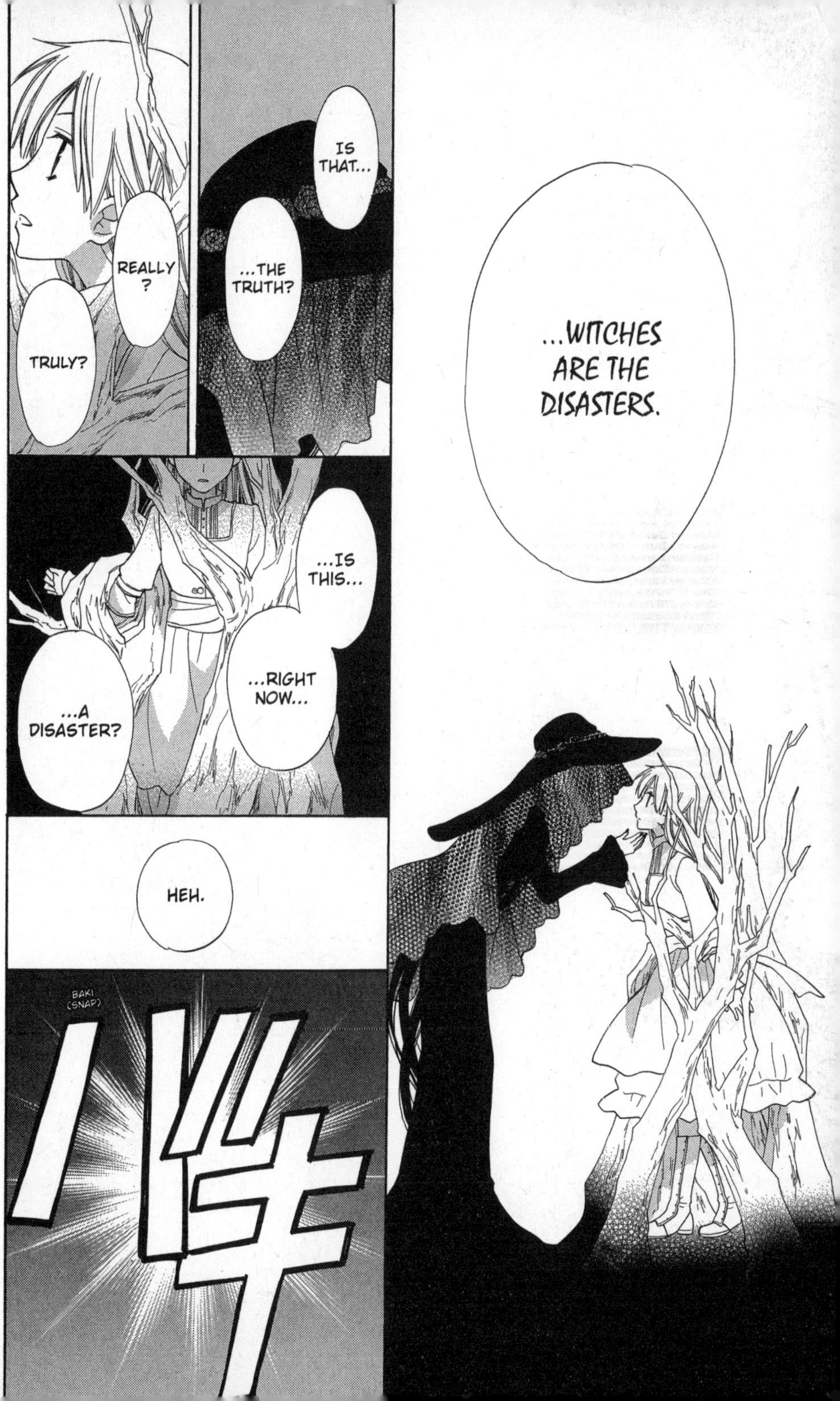
...WITCHES ARE THE DISASTERS.
IS THAT...
...THE TRUTH?
REALLY?
TRULY?
...IS THIS...
...RIGHT NOW...
...A DISASTER?
HEH.
BAKI (SNAP)

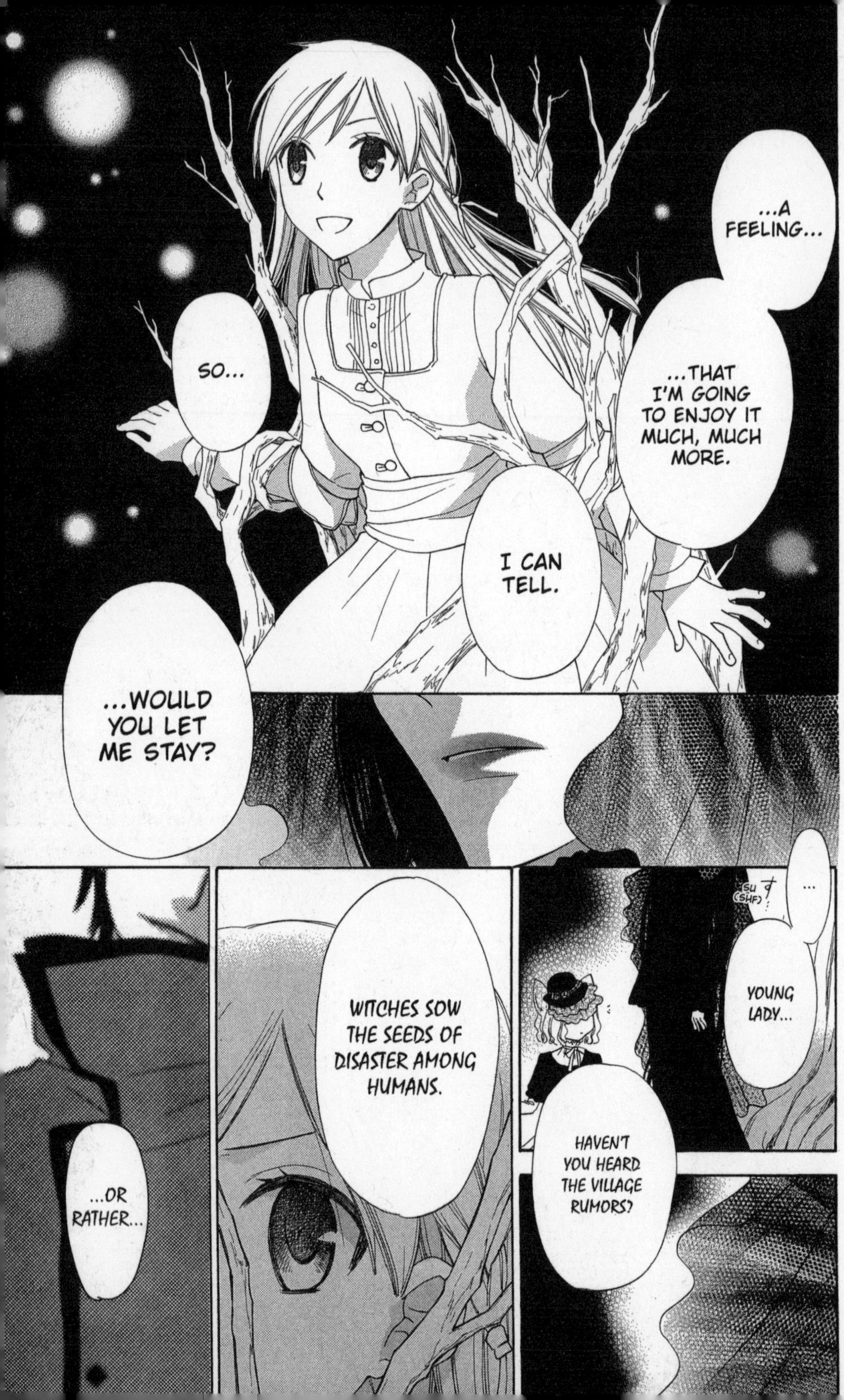
...A FEELING...
...THAT I'M GOING TO ENJOY IT MUCH, MUCH MORE.
I CAN TELL.
SO...
...WOULD YOU LET ME STAY?
...
す (SU SHF)
YOUNG LADY...
HAVEN'T YOU HEARD THE VILLAGE RUMORS?
WITCHES SOW THE SEEDS OF DISASTER AMONG HUMANS.
...OR RATHER...

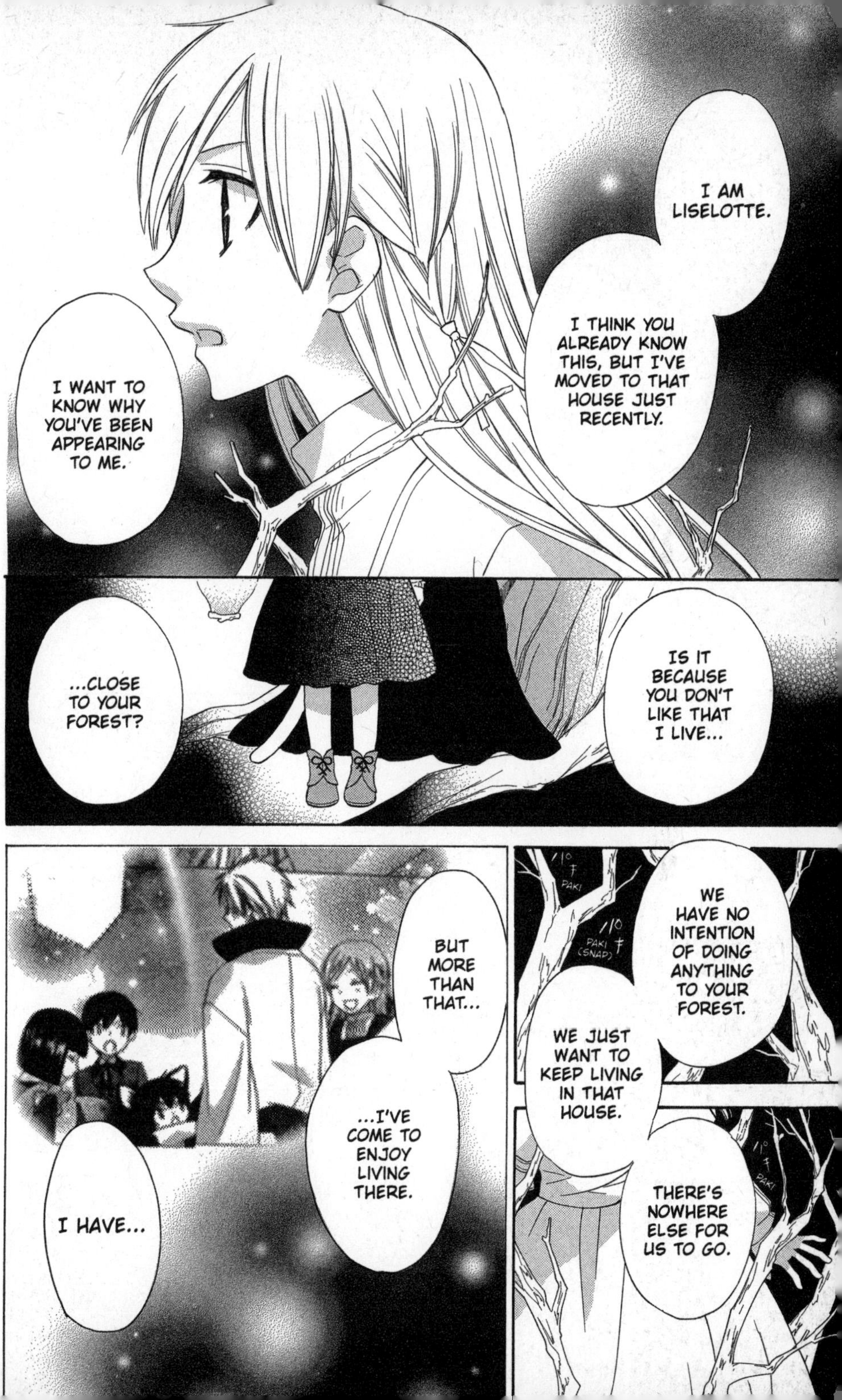
I AM LISELOTTE.
I THINK YOU ALREADY KNOW THIS, BUT I'VE MOVED TO THAT HOUSE JUST RECENTLY.
I WANT TO KNOW WHY YOU'VE BEEN APPEARING TO ME.
IS IT BECAUSE YOU DON'T LIKE THAT I LIVE...
...CLOSE TO YOUR FOREST?
PAKI
PAKI (SNAP)
WE HAVE NO INTENTION OF DOING ANYTHING TO YOUR FOREST.
WE JUST WANT TO KEEP LIVING IN THAT HOUSE.
PAKI
THERE'S NOWHERE ELSE FOR US TO GO.
BUT MORE THAN THAT...
...I'VE COME TO ENJOY LIVING THERE.
I HAVE...

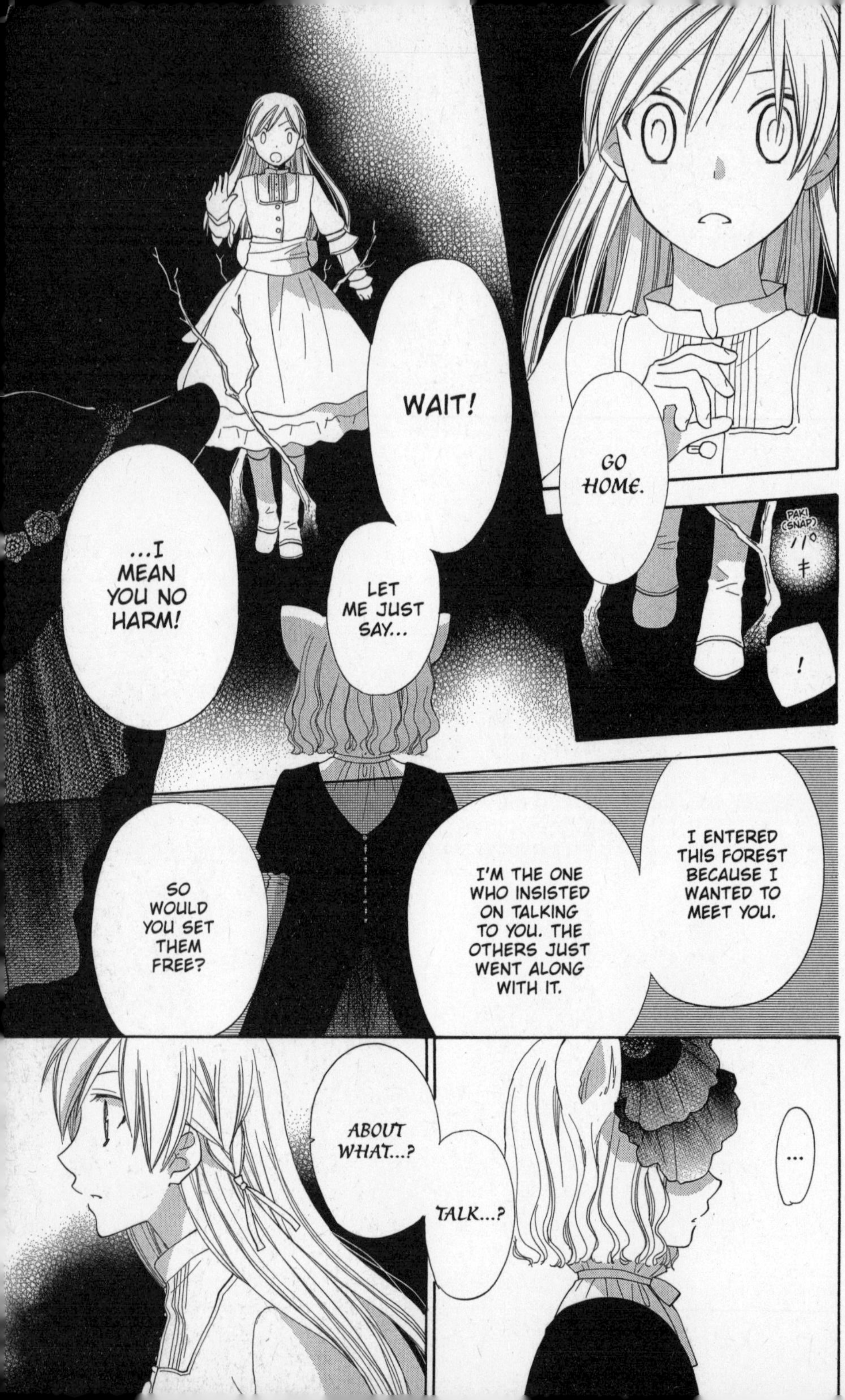
GO HOME.
PAKI (SNAP)
!
WAIT!
...I MEAN YOU NO HARM!
LET ME JUST SAY...
I ENTERED THIS FOREST BECAUSE I WANTED TO MEET YOU.
I'M THE ONE WHO INSISTED ON TALKING TO YOU. THE OTHERS JUST WENT ALONG WITH IT.
SO WOULD YOU SET THEM FREE?
...
TALK...?
ABOUT WHAT...?

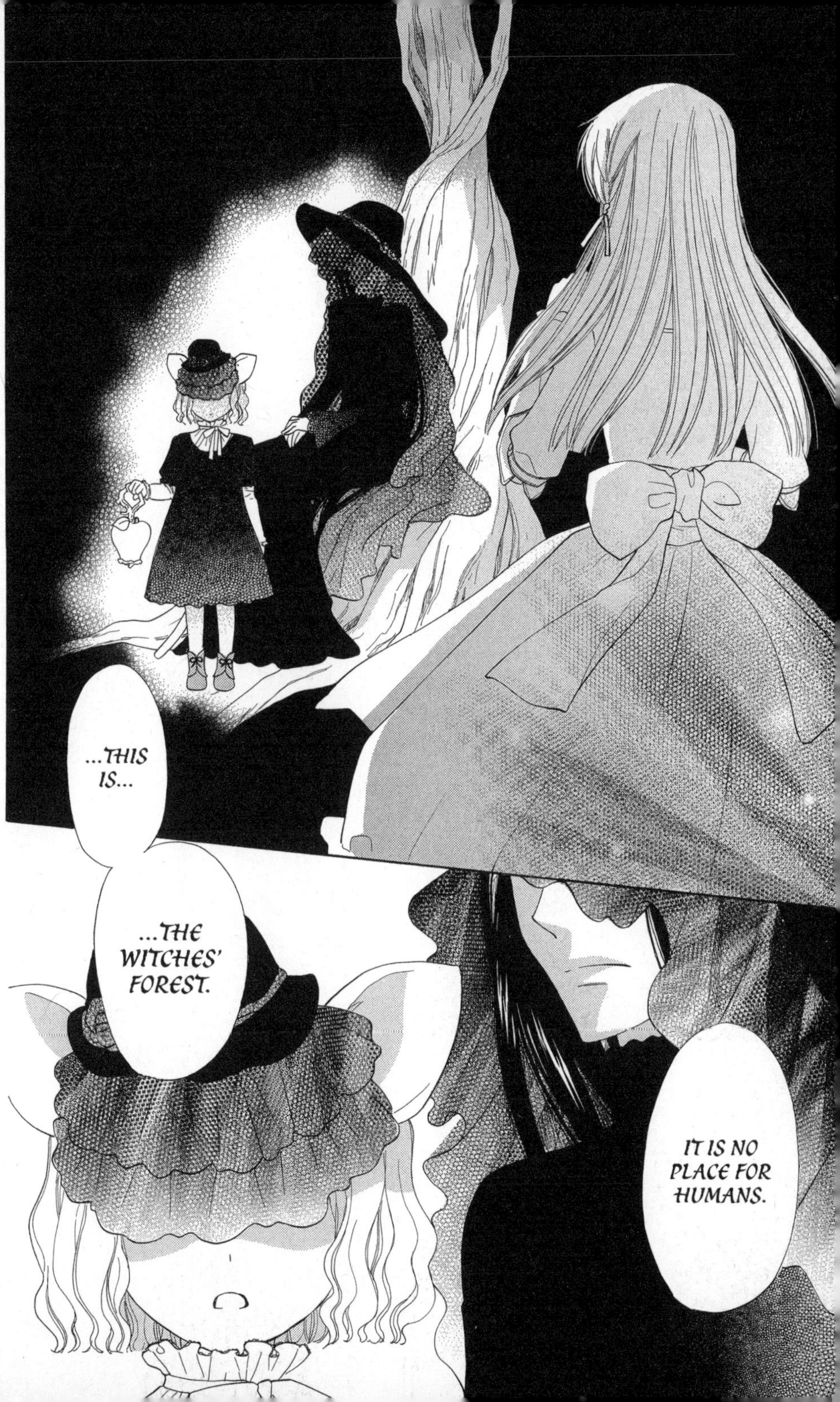

...THIS IS...
...THE WITCHES' FOREST.
IT IS NO PLACE FOR HUMANS.

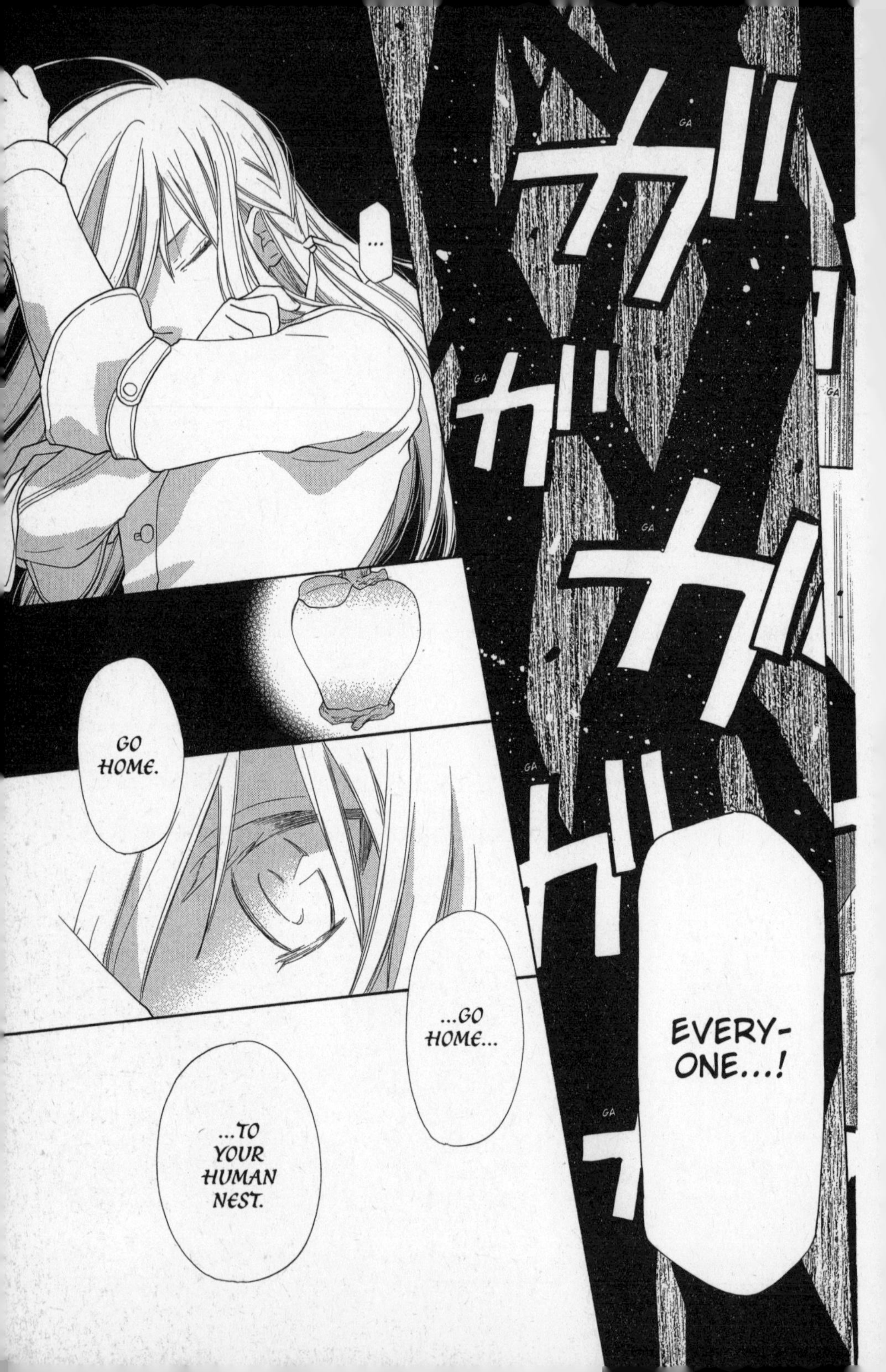
GA
GA
GA
GA
GA
EVERY-ONE...!
...
GO HOME.
...GO HOME...
...TO YOUR HUMAN NEST.

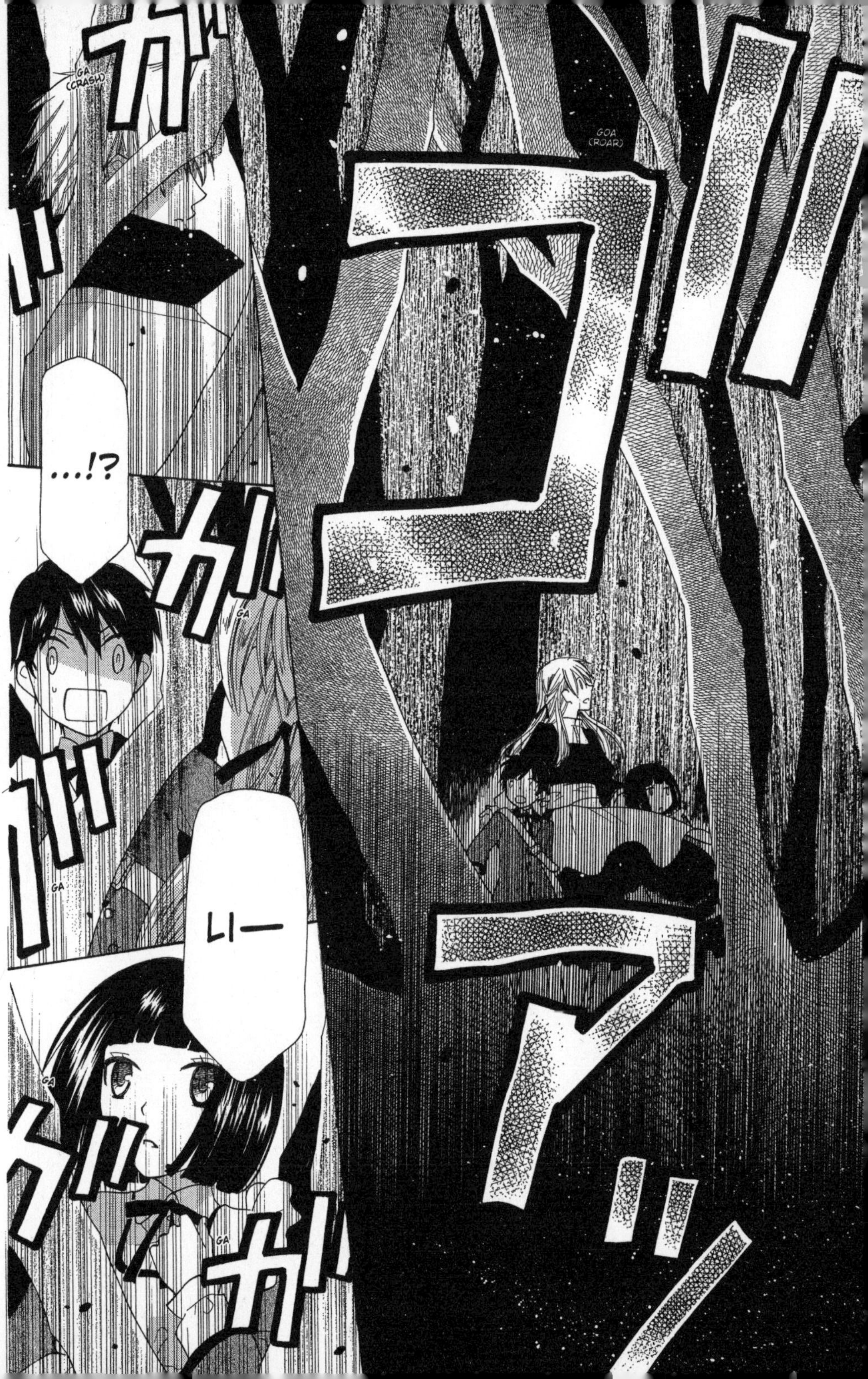
GOA (ROAR)
GA (CRASH)
...!?
GA
GA
LI—
GA
GA

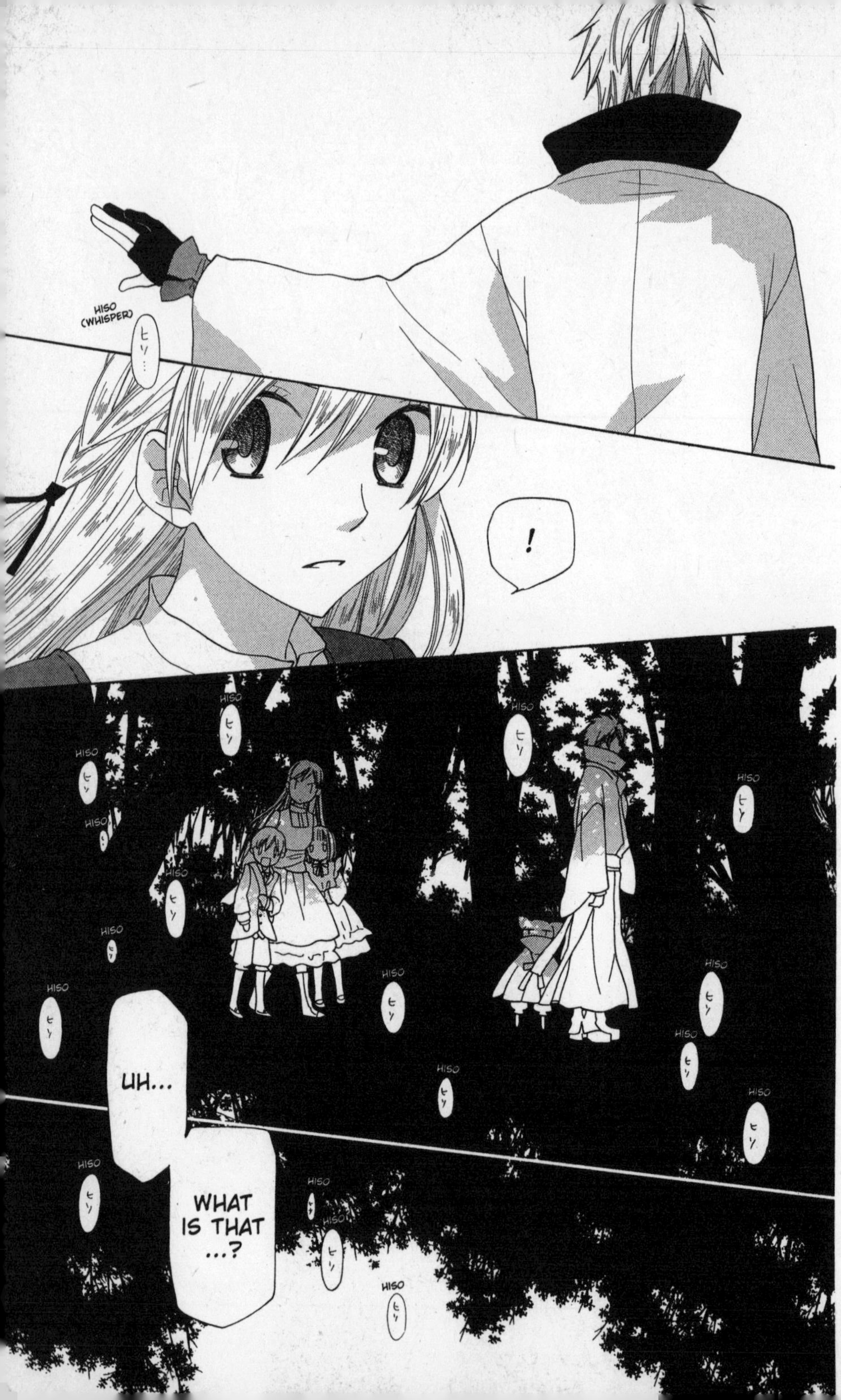

HISO (WHISPER)
ヒソ…
!
HISO
ヒソ
HISO
ヒソ
HISO
ヒソ
HISO
ヒソ
HISO
ヒソ
UH...
WHAT IS THAT ...?
HISO
ヒソ

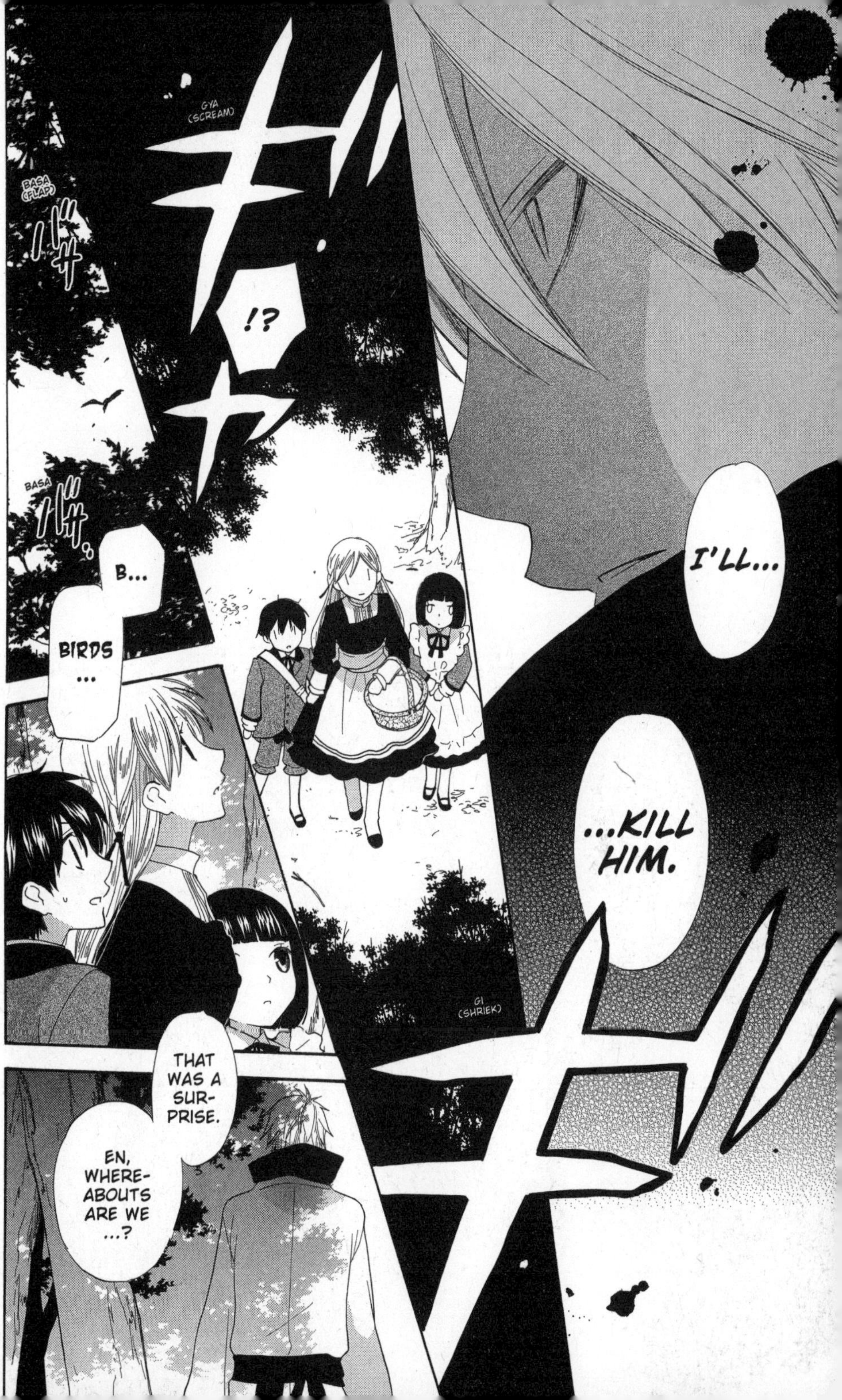
I'LL...
...KILL HIM.
GYA (SCREAM)
BASA (FLAP)
!?
BASA
B...
BIRDS...
GI (SHRIEK)
THAT WAS A SUR-PRISE.
EN, WHERE-ABOUTS ARE WE ...?

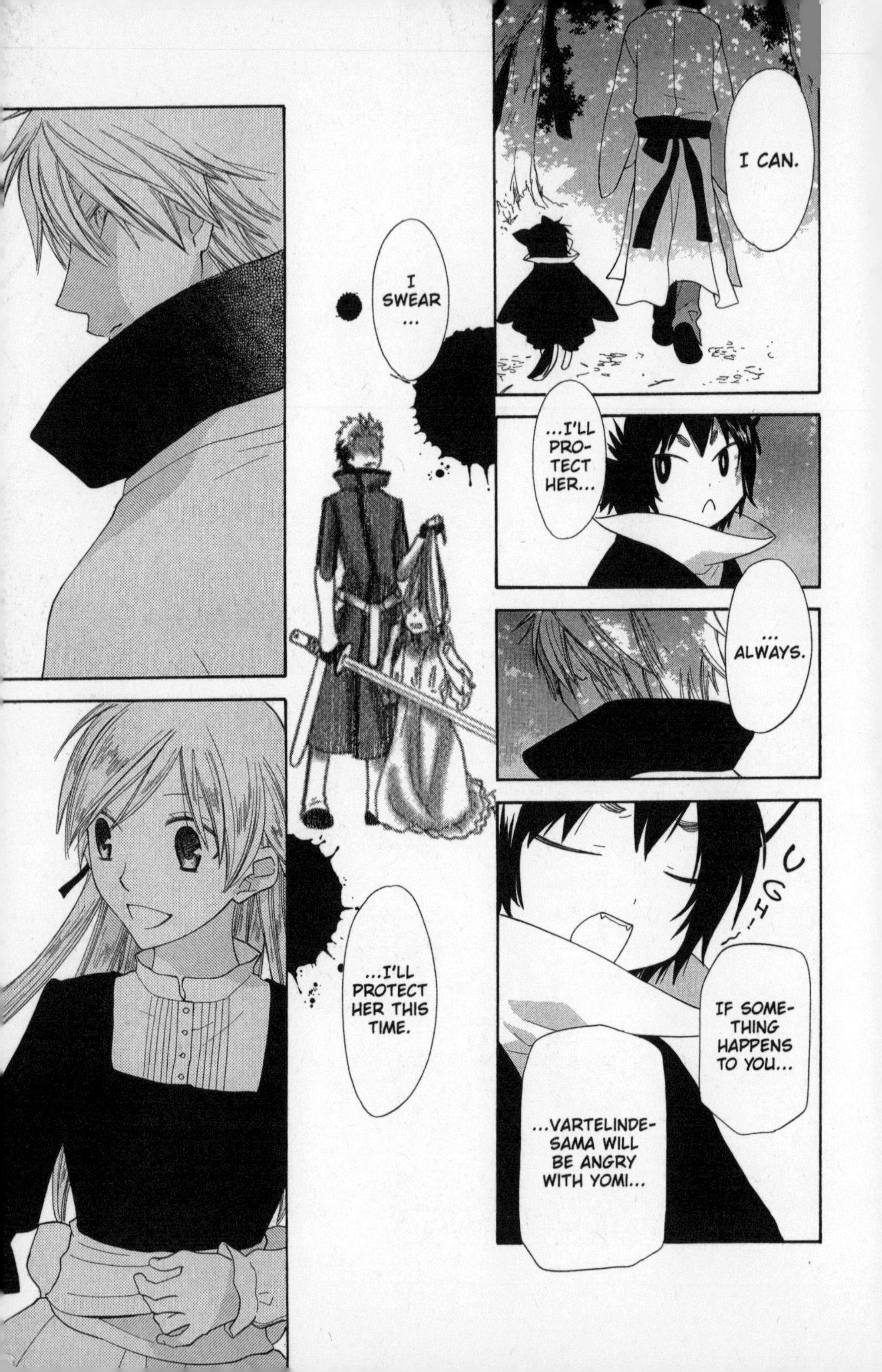
I CAN.
...I'LL PROTECT HER...
...ALWAYS.
UGH...!
IF SOMETHING HAPPENS TO YOU...
...VARTELINDE-SAMA WILL BE ANGRY WITH YOMI...
I SWEAR...
...I'LL PROTECT HER THIS TIME.

YOUR "REAL TARGET," I MEAN.
... EVEN SO...
...IF SHE WISHES IT...
...I'LL MAKE IT SO.
... THIS IS WHY I CAN'T STAND THE ROMANTIC BRAIN...
LISTEN TO ME, ENGETSU.
YOMI WAS PUT IN CHARGE OF YOU.
YOU'RE NOT "100%" YET. WHAT IF SOMETHING HAPPENS BECAUSE OF THIS FOOLISH-NESS?
CAN YOU PROTECT THAT WOMAN FROM YOUR TARGET!?

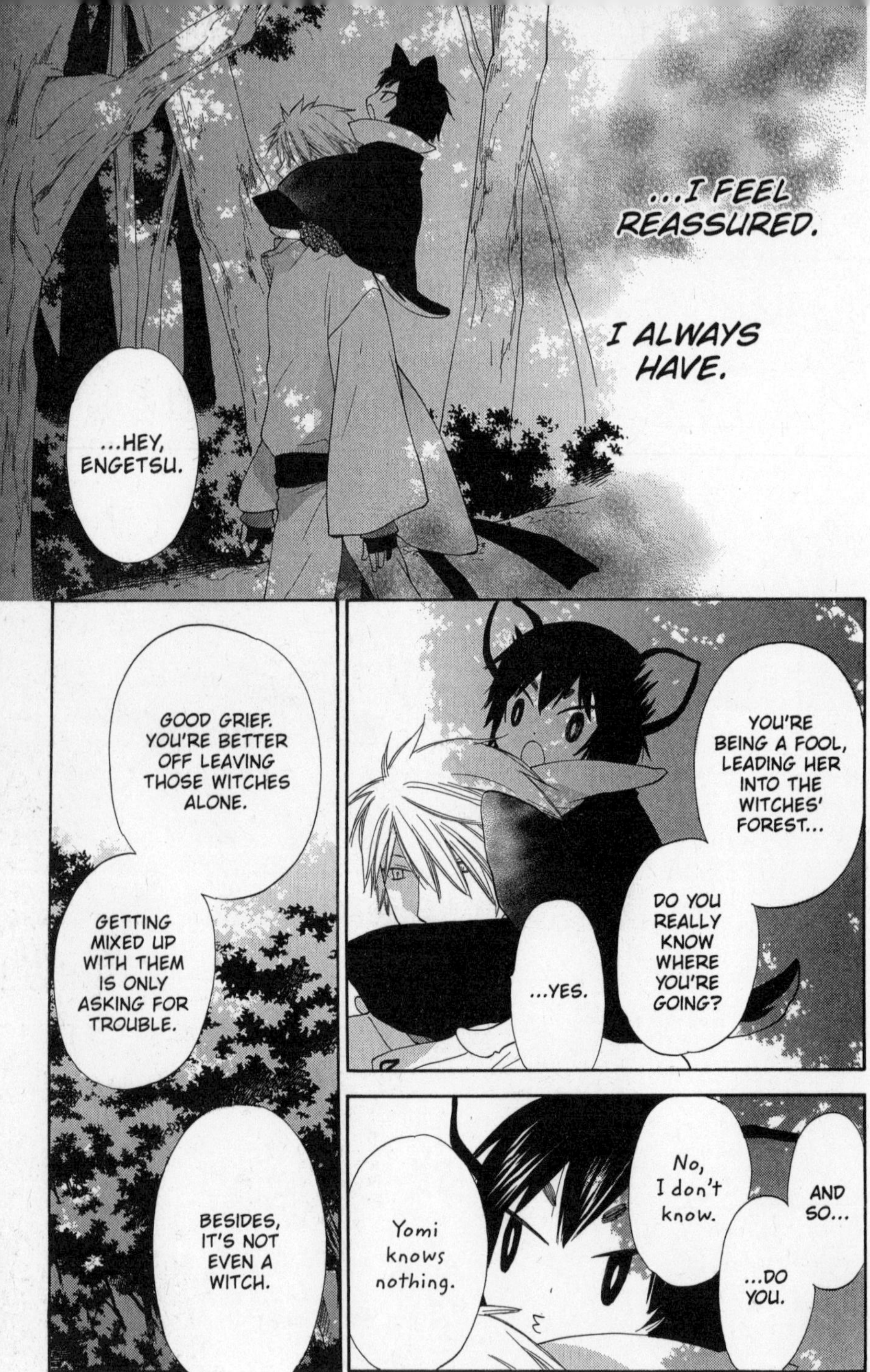
...I FEEL REASSURED.
I ALWAYS HAVE.
...HEY, ENGETSU.
YOU'RE BEING A FOOL, LEADING HER INTO THE WITCHES' FOREST...
DO YOU REALLY KNOW WHERE YOU'RE GOING?
...YES.
No, I don't know.
AND SO...
...DO YOU.
Yomi knows nothing.
GOOD GRIEF. YOU'RE BETTER OFF LEAVING THOSE WITCHES ALONE.
GETTING MIXED UP WITH THEM IS ONLY ASKING FOR TROUBLE.
BESIDES, IT'S NOT EVEN A WITCH.

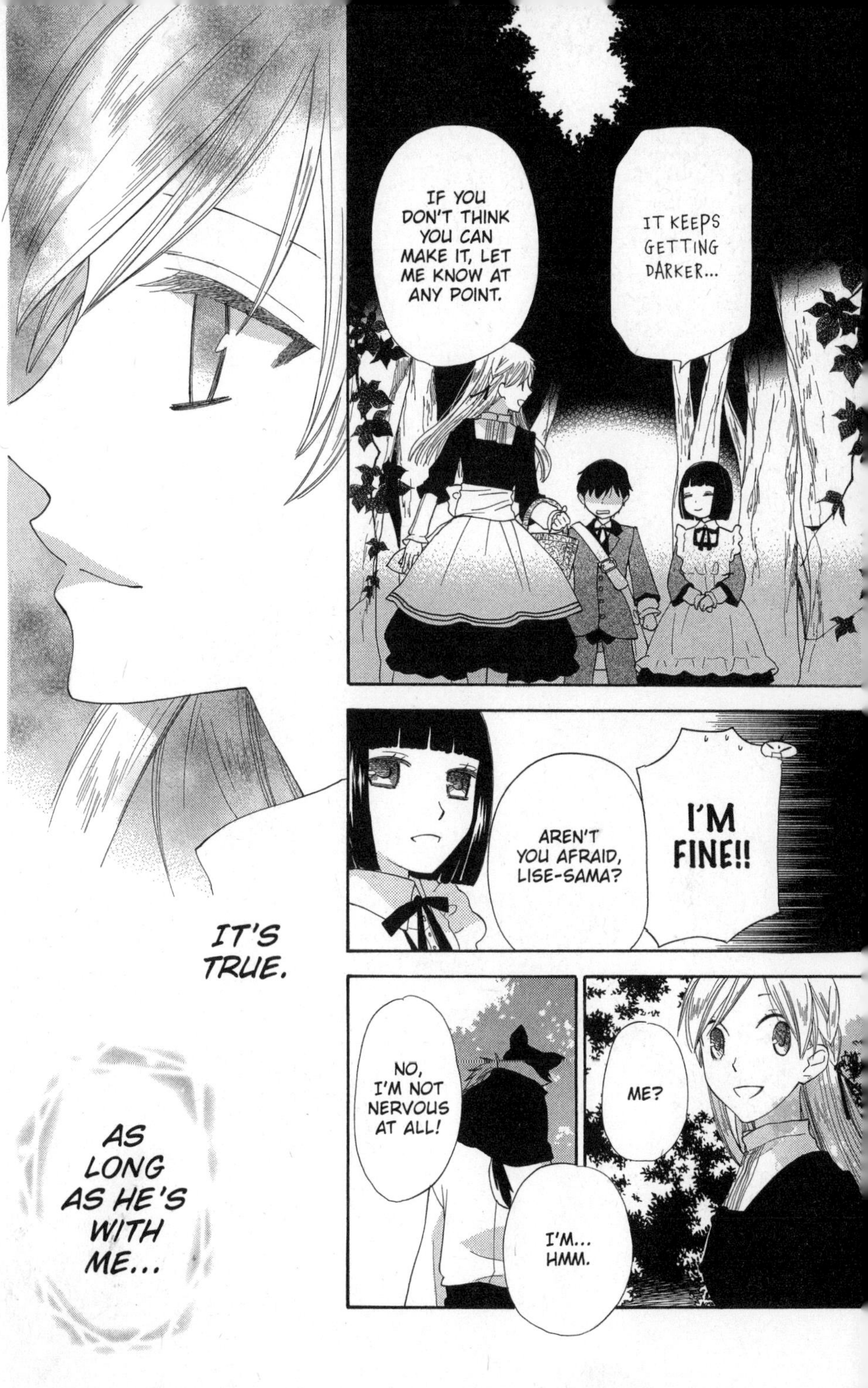
IT KEEPS GETTING DARKER...
IF YOU DON'T THINK YOU CAN MAKE IT, LET ME KNOW AT ANY POINT.
I'M FINE!!
AREN'T YOU AFRAID, LISE-SAMA?
ME?
I'M... HMM.
NO, I'M NOT NERVOUS AT ALL!
IT'S TRUE.
AS LONG AS HE'S WITH ME...

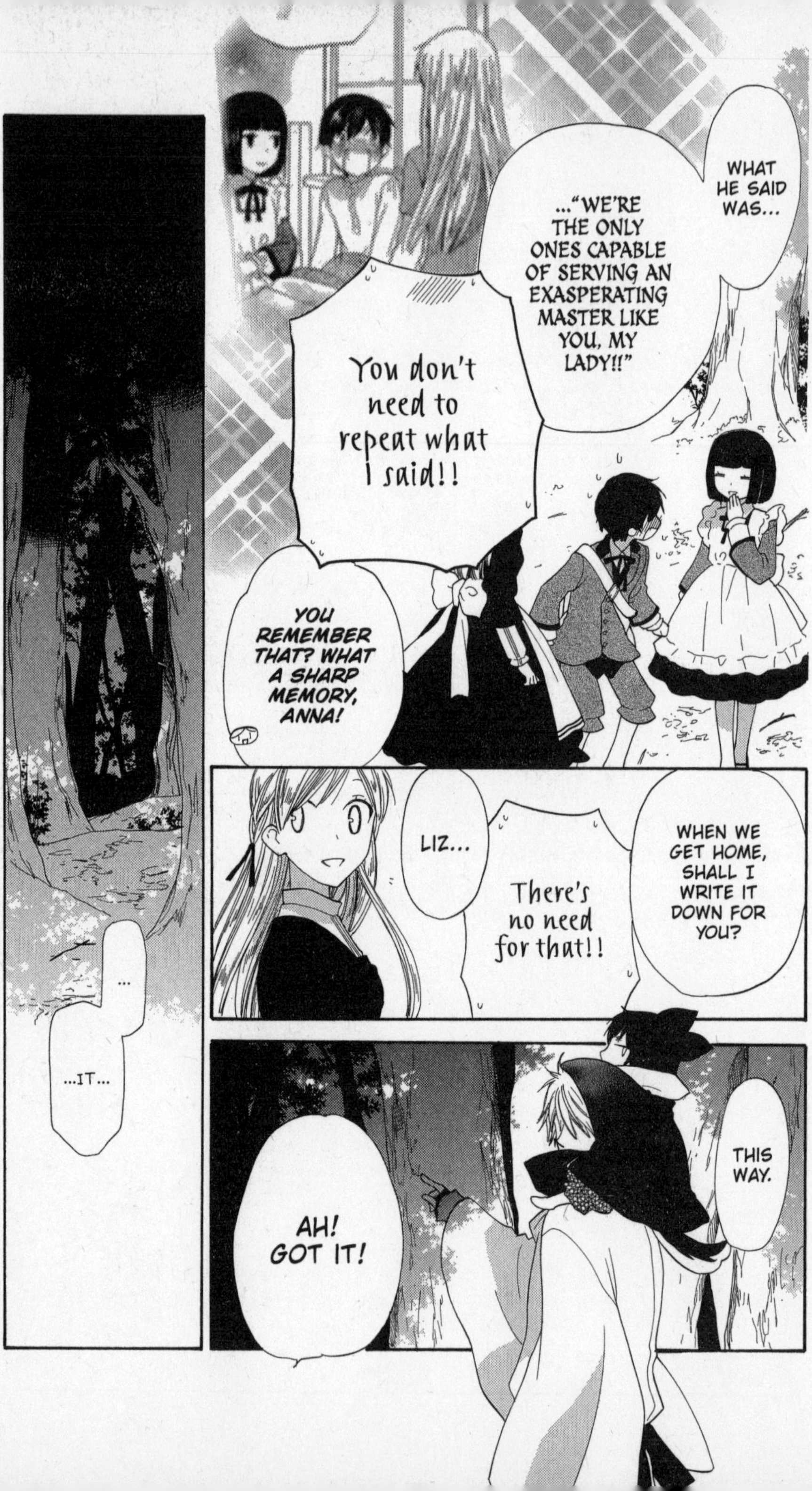
WHAT HE SAID WAS...
..."WE'RE THE ONLY ONES CAPABLE OF SERVING AN EXASPERATING MASTER LIKE YOU, MY LADY!!"
You don't need to repeat what I said!!
YOU REMEMBER THAT? WHAT A SHARP MEMORY, ANNA!
WHEN WE GET HOME, SHALL I WRITE IT DOWN FOR YOU?
There's no need for that!!
LIZ...
THIS WAY.
AH! GOT IT!
...
...IT...

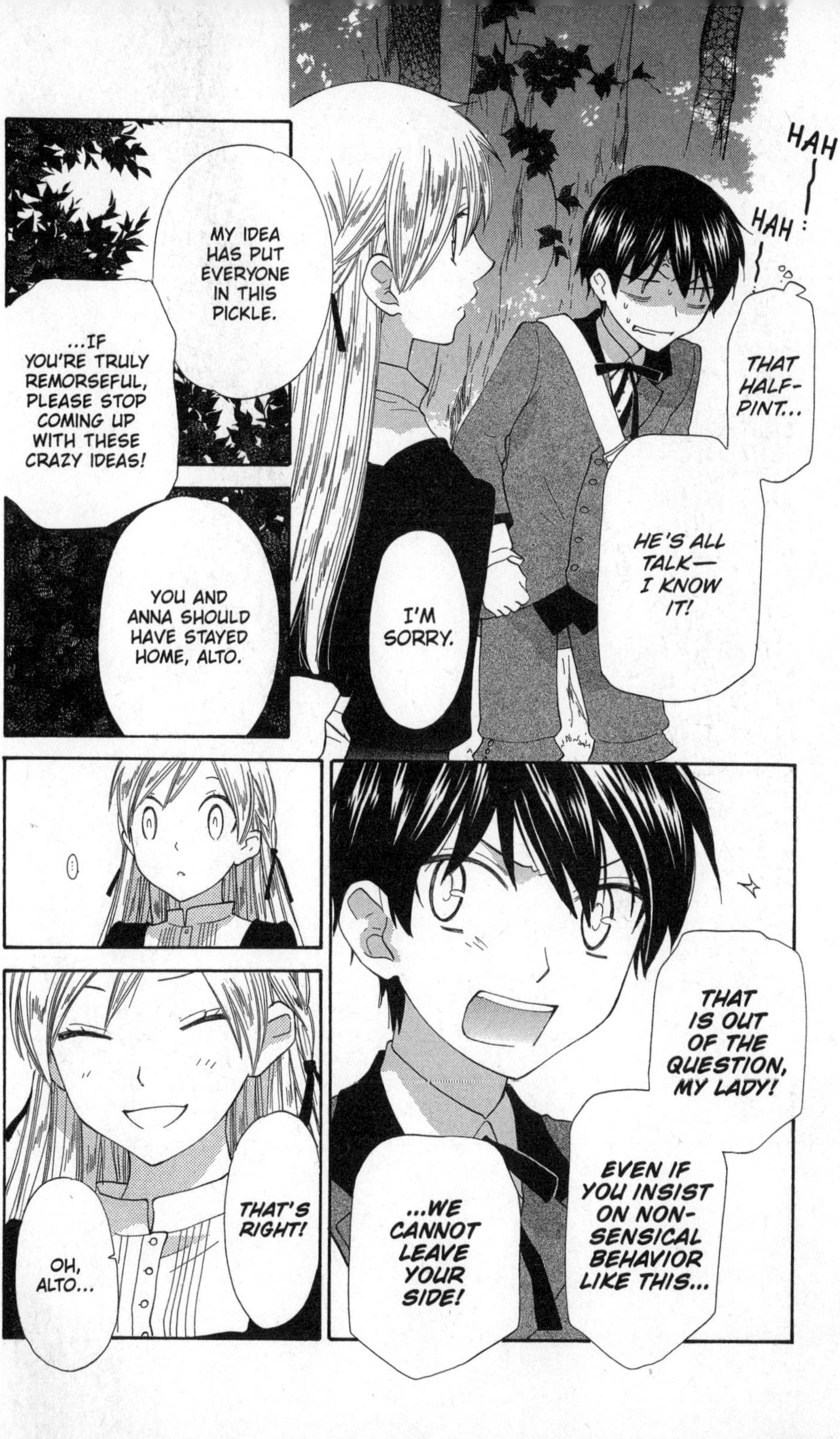
HAH
HAH
THAT HALF-PINT...
HE'S ALL TALK— I KNOW IT!
I'M SORRY.
MY IDEA HAS PUT EVERYONE IN THIS PICKLE.
...IF YOU'RE TRULY REMORSEFUL, PLEASE STOP COMING UP WITH THESE CRAZY IDEAS!
YOU AND ANNA SHOULD HAVE STAYED HOME, ALTO.
THAT IS OUT OF THE QUESTION, MY LADY!
EVEN IF YOU INSIST ON NON-SENSICAL BEHAVIOR LIKE THIS...
...WE CANNOT LEAVE YOUR SIDE!
THAT'S RIGHT!
OH, ALTO...

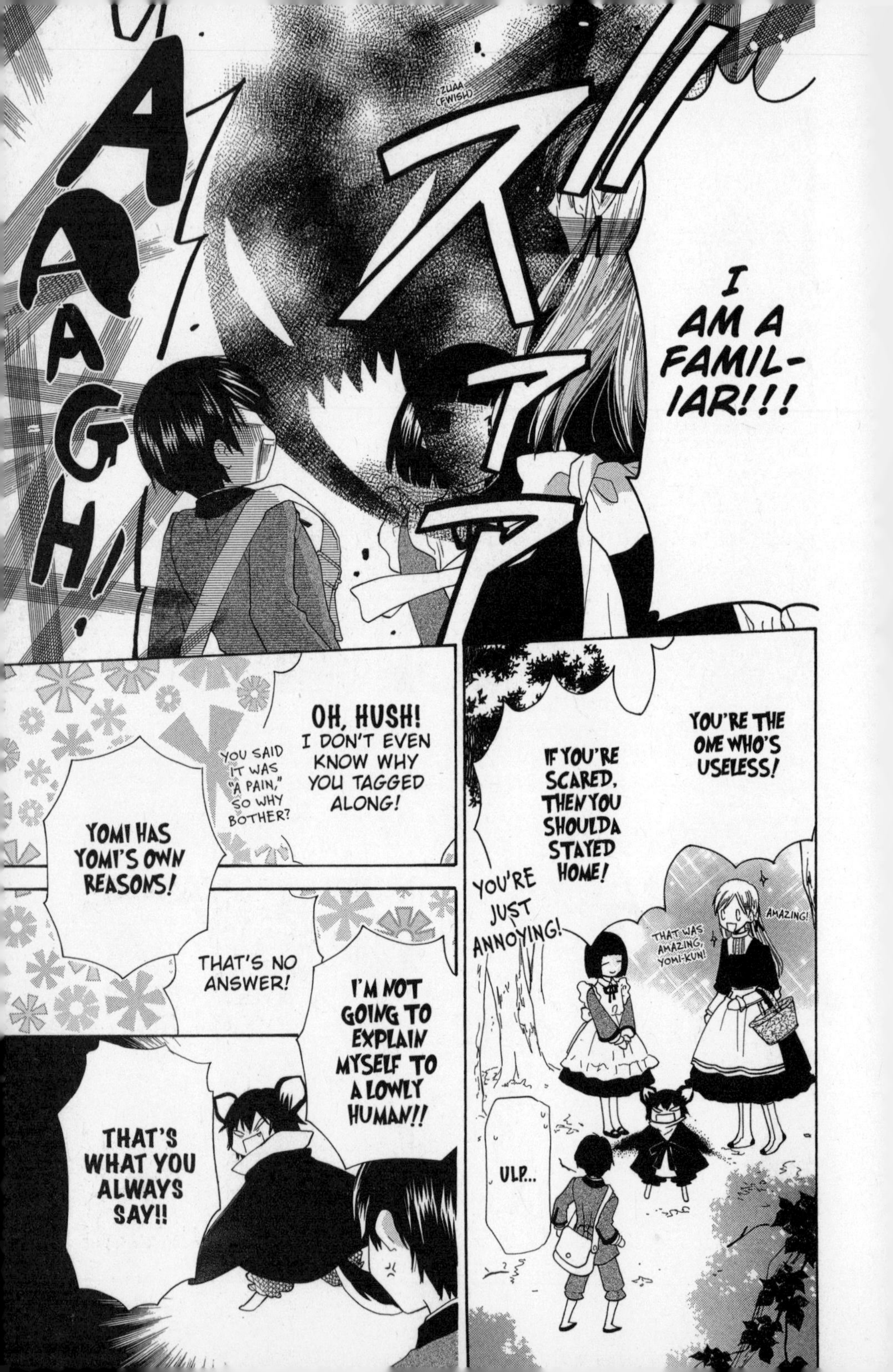

I AM A FAMILIAR!!!
ZUAA (FWISH)
AAAGH!
YOU'RE THE ONE WHO'S USELESS!
IF YOU'RE SCARED, THEN YOU SHOULDA STAYED HOME!
YOU'RE JUST ANNOYING!
AMAZING!
THAT WAS AMAZING, YOMI-KUN!
ULP...
OH, HUSH! I DON'T EVEN KNOW WHY YOU TAGGED ALONG!
YOU SAID IT WAS "A PAIN," SO WHY BOTHER?
YOMI HAS YOMI'S OWN REASONS!
THAT'S NO ANSWER!
I'M NOT GOING TO EXPLAIN MYSELF TO A LOWLY HUMAN!!
THAT'S WHAT YOU ALWAYS SAY!!

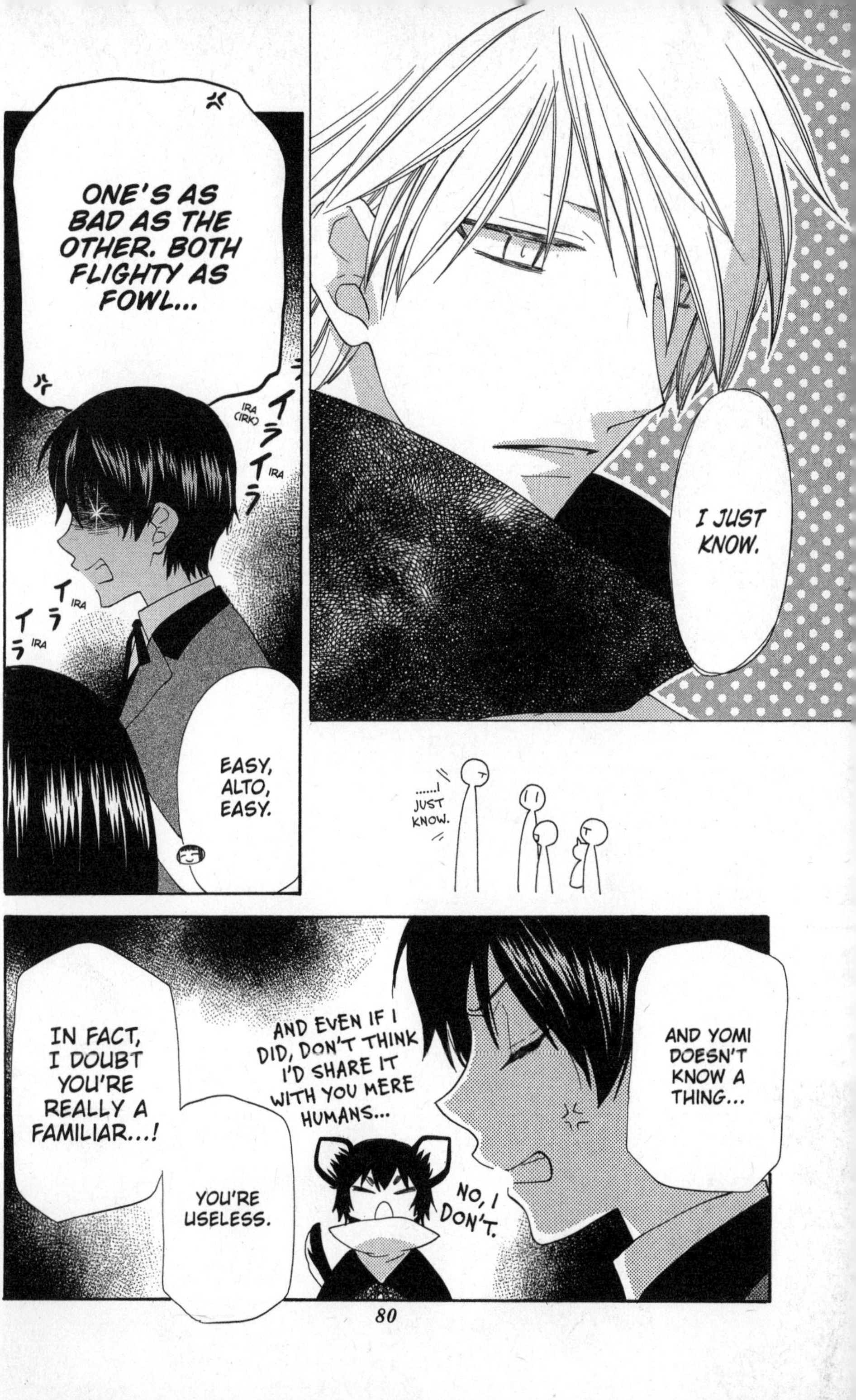
I JUST KNOW.
......I JUST KNOW.
ONE'S AS BAD AS THE OTHER. BOTH FLIGHTY AS FOWL...
イライラ
IRA (IRK)
IRA
イライラ
IRA
IRA
EASY, ALTO, EASY.
AND YOMI DOESN'T KNOW A THING...
NO, I DON'T.
AND EVEN IF I DID, DON'T THINK I'D SHARE IT WITH YOU MERE HUMANS...
IN FACT, I DOUBT YOU'RE REALLY A FAMILIAR...!
YOU'RE USELESS.

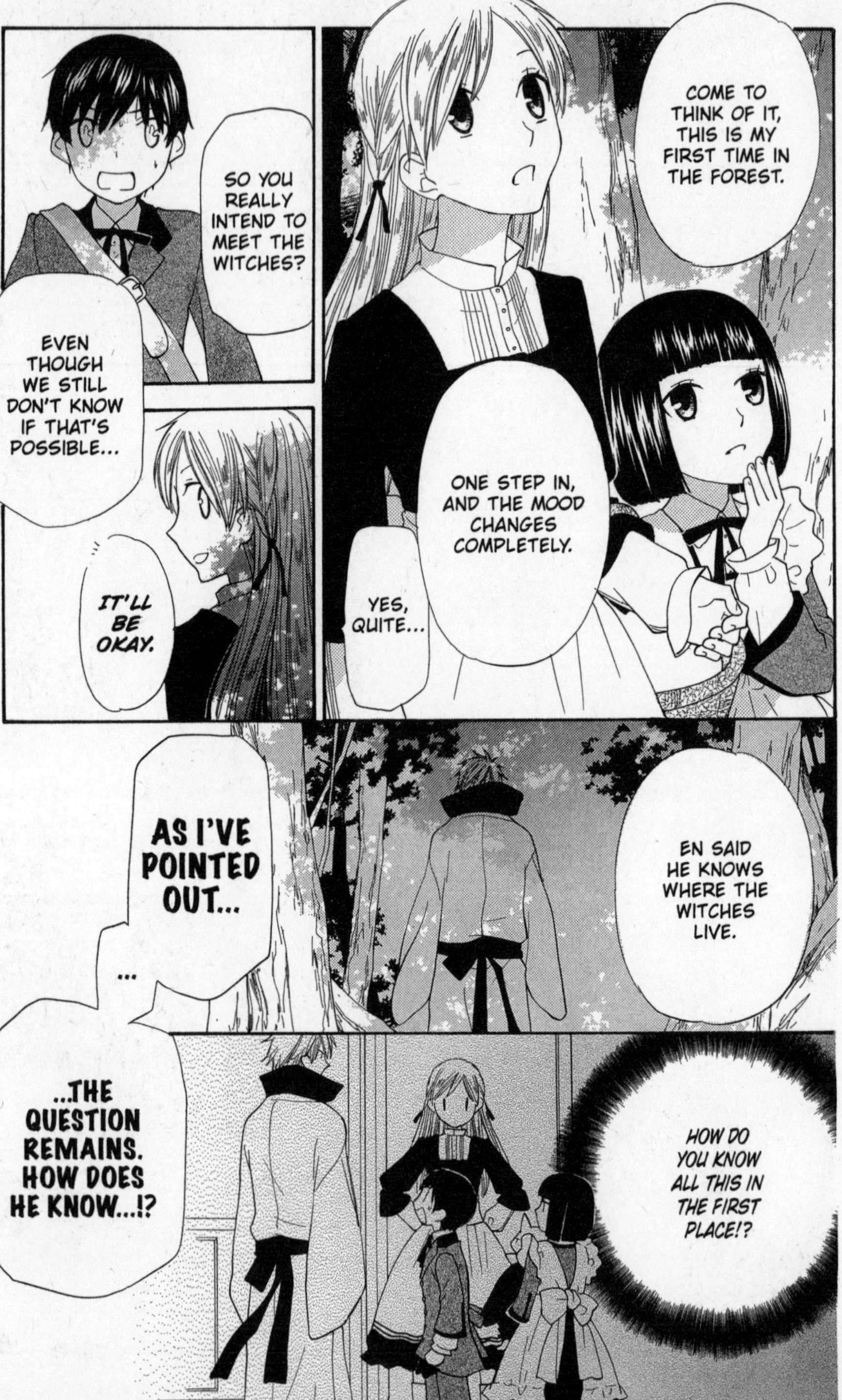
COME TO THINK OF IT, THIS IS MY FIRST TIME IN THE FOREST.
ONE STEP IN, AND THE MOOD CHANGES COMPLETELY.
YES, QUITE...
SO YOU REALLY INTEND TO MEET THE WITCHES?
EVEN THOUGH WE STILL DON'T KNOW IF THAT'S POSSIBLE...
IT'LL BE OKAY.
EN SAID HE KNOWS WHERE THE WITCHES LIVE.
AS I'VE POINTED OUT...
...
HOW DO YOU KNOW ALL THIS IN THE FIRST PLACE!?
...THE QUESTION REMAINS. HOW DOES HE KNOW...!?

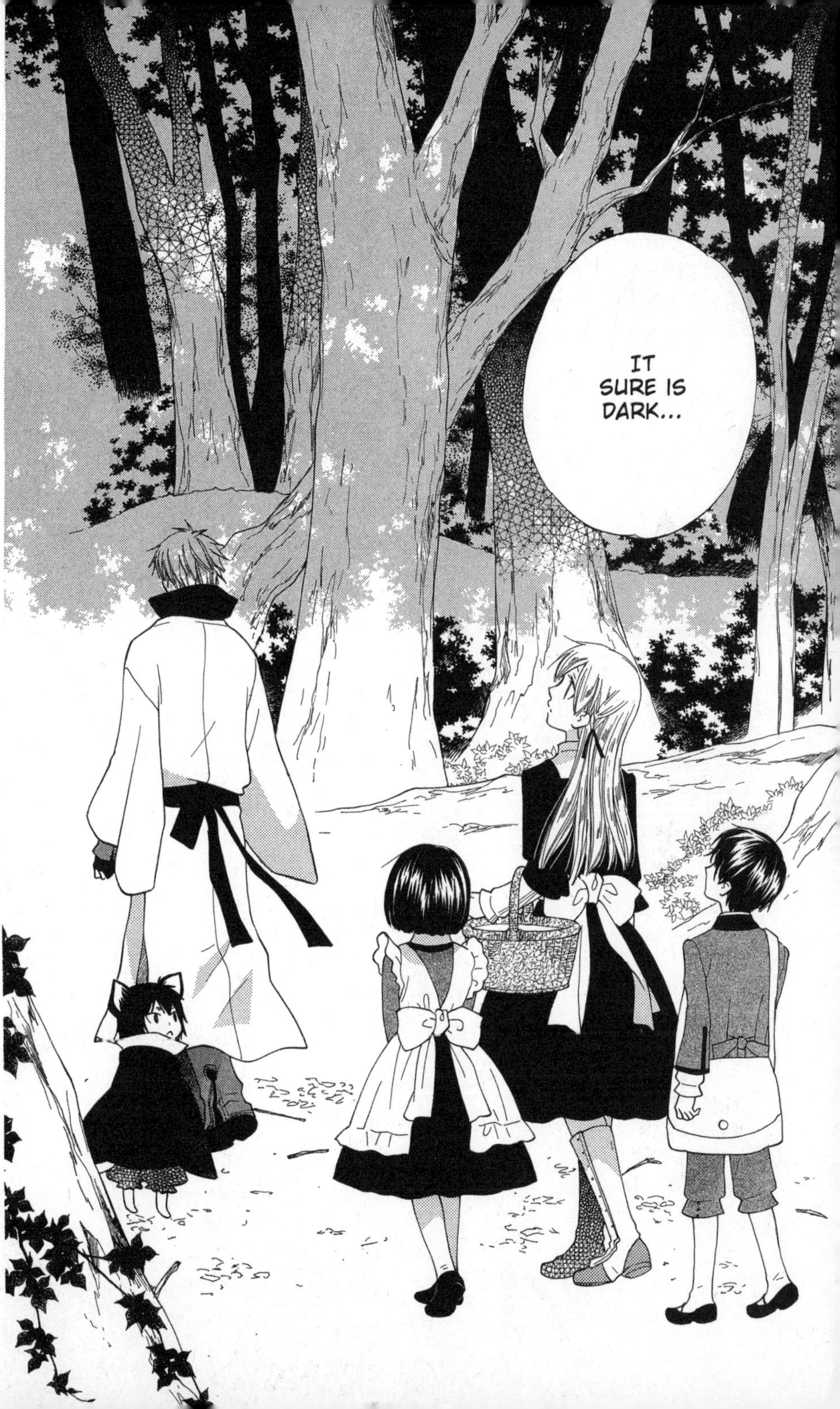
IT SURE IS DARK...

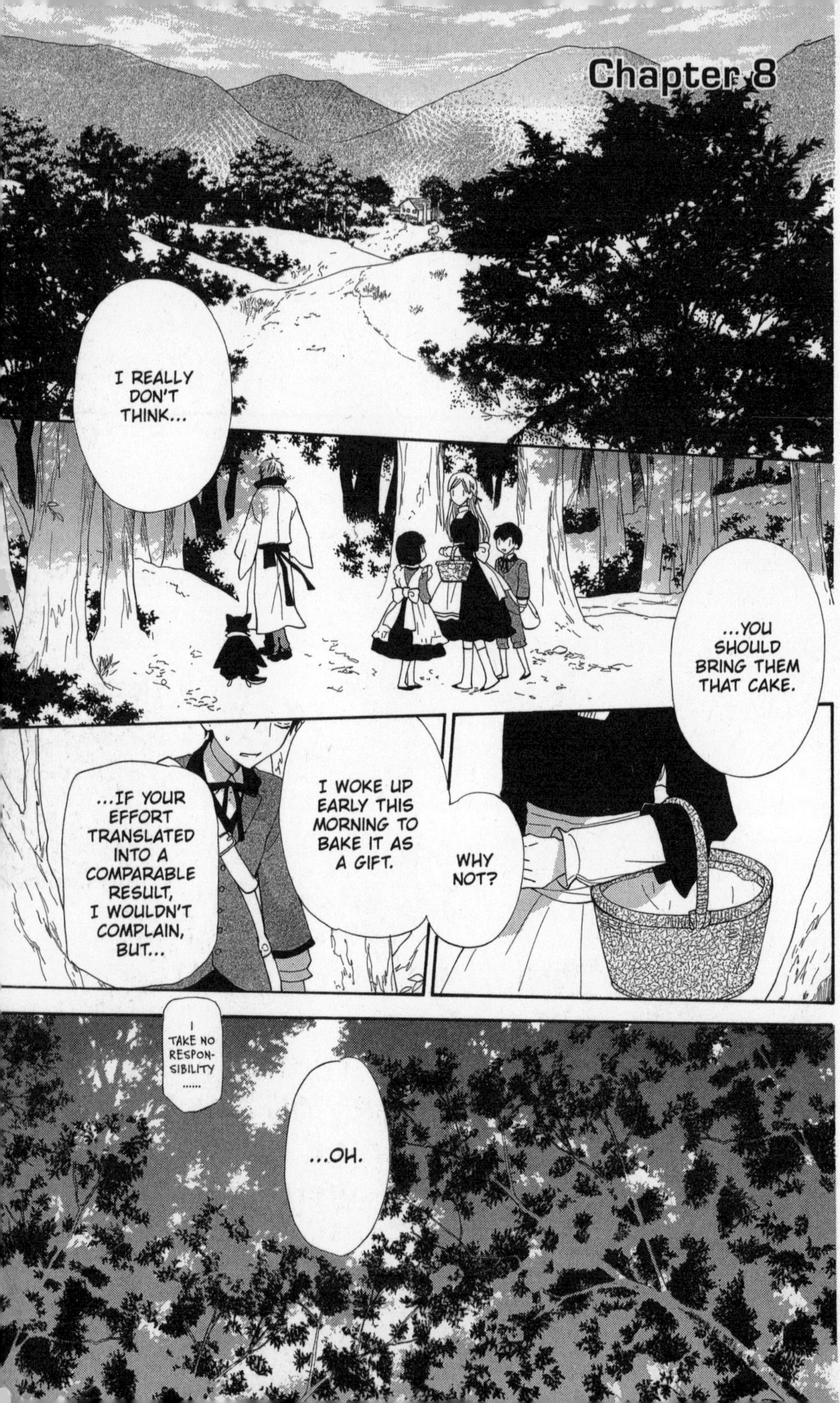
Chapter 8
I REALLY DON'T THINK...
...YOU SHOULD BRING THEM THAT CAKE.
WHY NOT?
I WOKE UP EARLY THIS MORNING TO BAKE IT AS A GIFT.
...IF YOUR EFFORT TRANSLATED INTO A COMPARABLE RESULT, I WOULDN'T COMPLAIN, BUT...
...OH.
I TAKE NO RESPON-SIBILITY ......

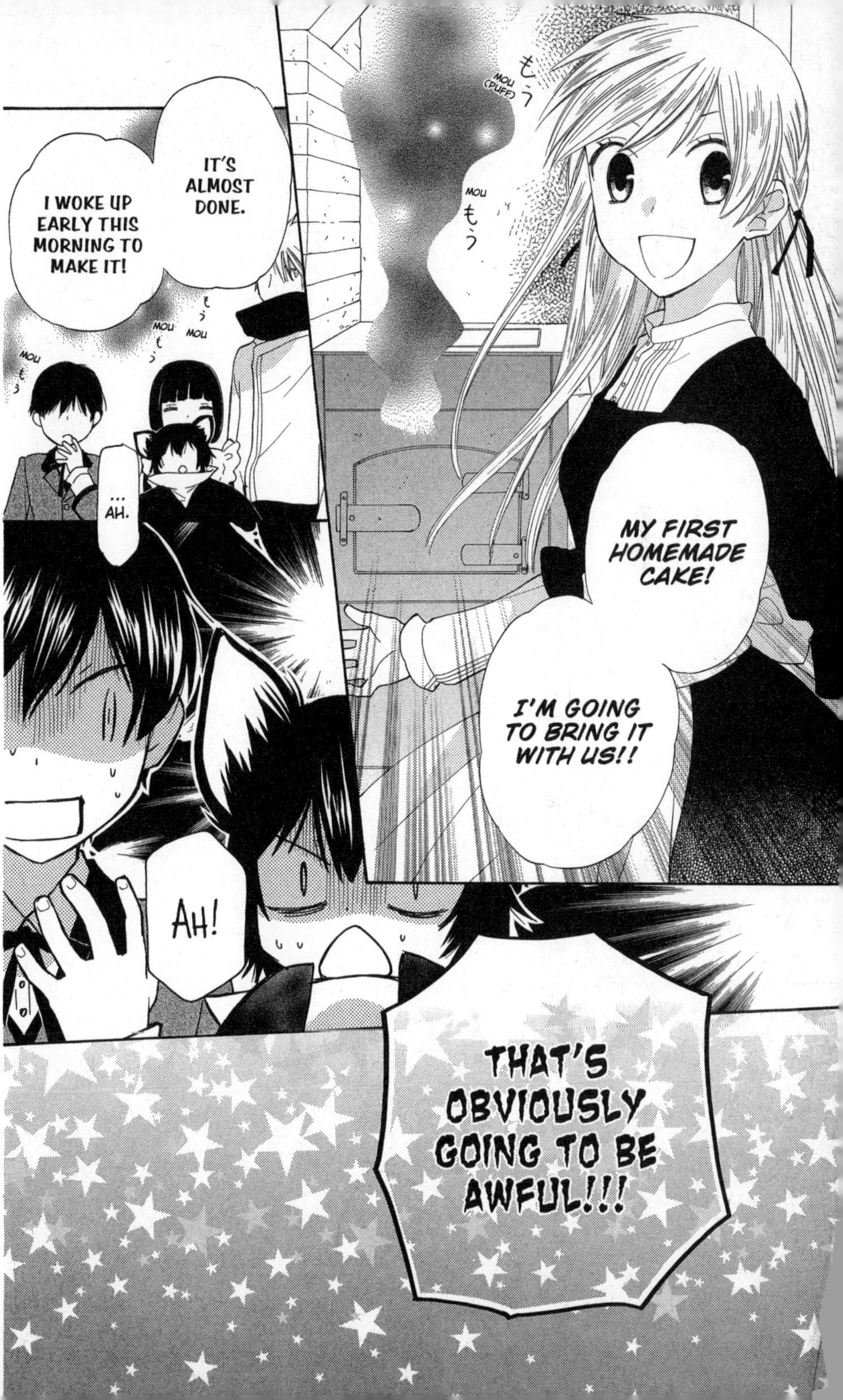
もう
MOU (PUFF)
MOU
もう
MY FIRST HOMEMADE CAKE!
I'M GOING TO BRING IT WITH US!!
IT'S ALMOST DONE.
I WOKE UP EARLY THIS MORNING TO MAKE IT!
もう
MOU
MOU
もう
MOU
もう
...AH.
AH!
THAT'S OBVIOUSLY GOING TO BE AWFUL!!!

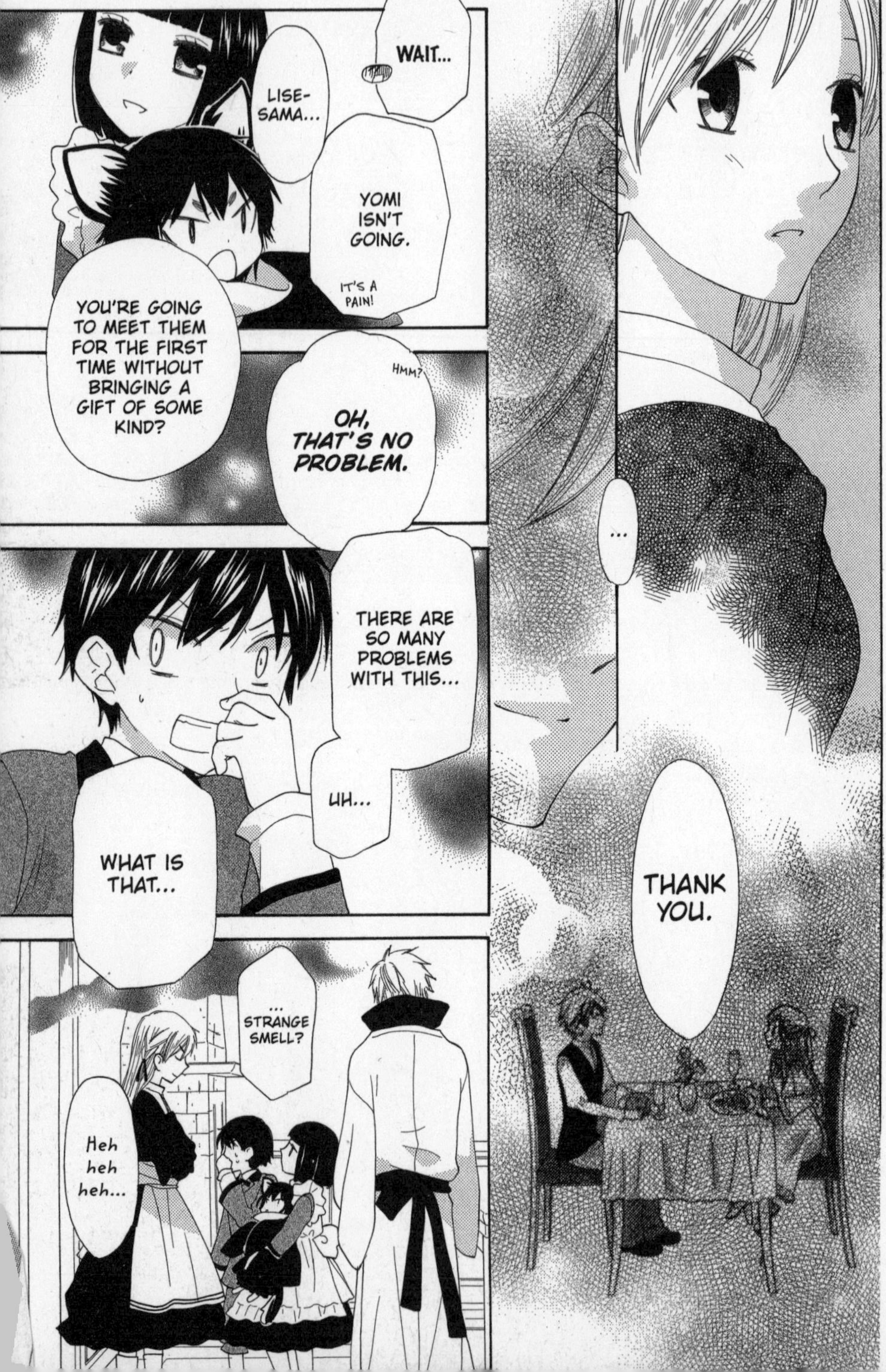
...
THANK YOU.
WAIT...
LISE-SAMA...
YOMI ISN'T GOING.
IT'S A PAIN!
YOU'RE GOING TO MEET THEM FOR THE FIRST TIME WITHOUT BRINGING A GIFT OF SOME KIND?
HMM?
OH, THAT'S NO PROBLEM.
THERE ARE SO MANY PROBLEMS WITH THIS...
UH...
WHAT IS THAT...
...STRANGE SMELL?
Heh heh heh...

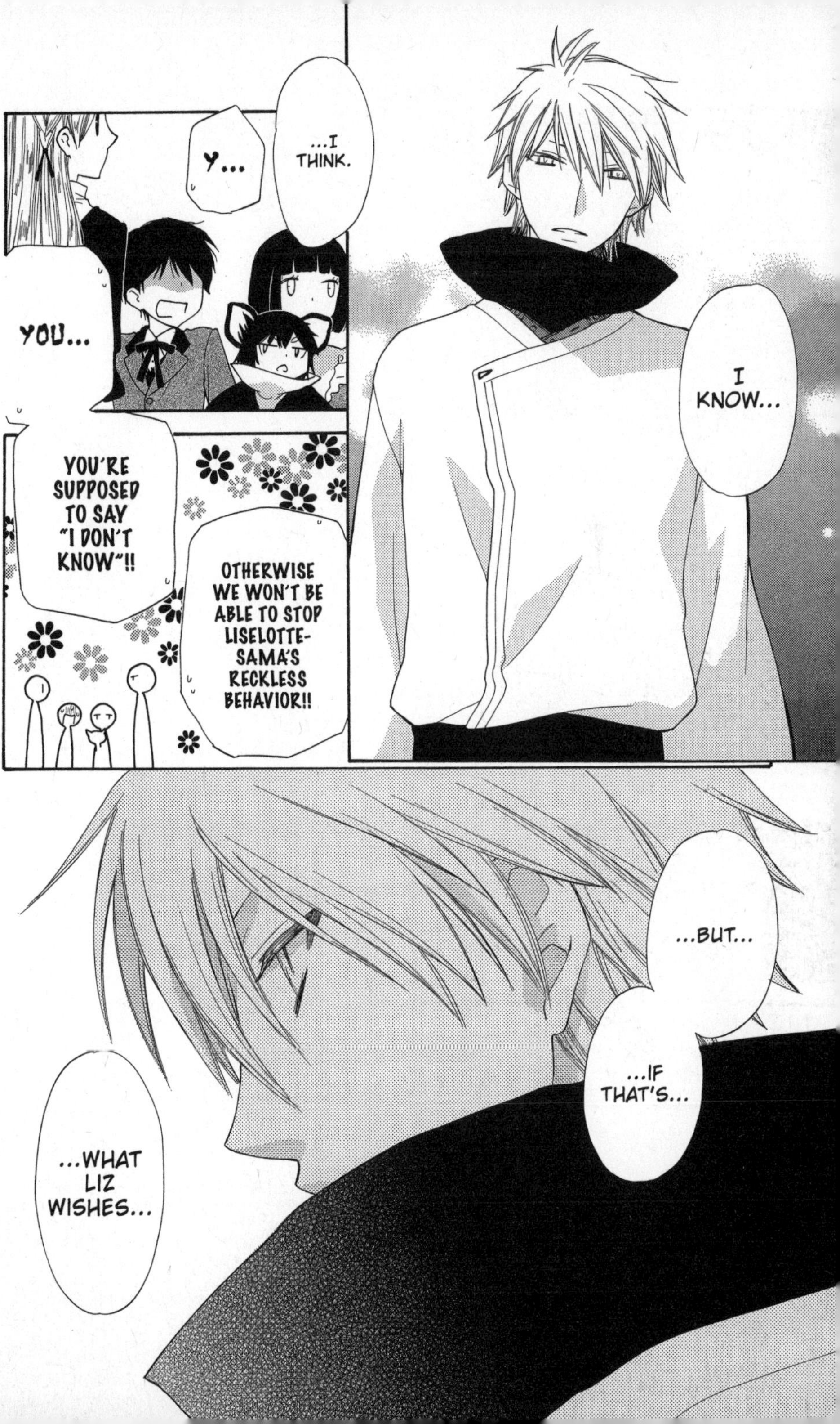
I KNOW...
...I THINK.
Y...
YOU...
YOU'RE SUPPOSED TO SAY "I DON'T KNOW"!!
OTHERWISE WE WON'T BE ABLE TO STOP LISELOTTE-SAMA'S RECKLESS BEHAVIOR!!
...BUT...
...IF THAT'S...
...WHAT LIZ WISHES...

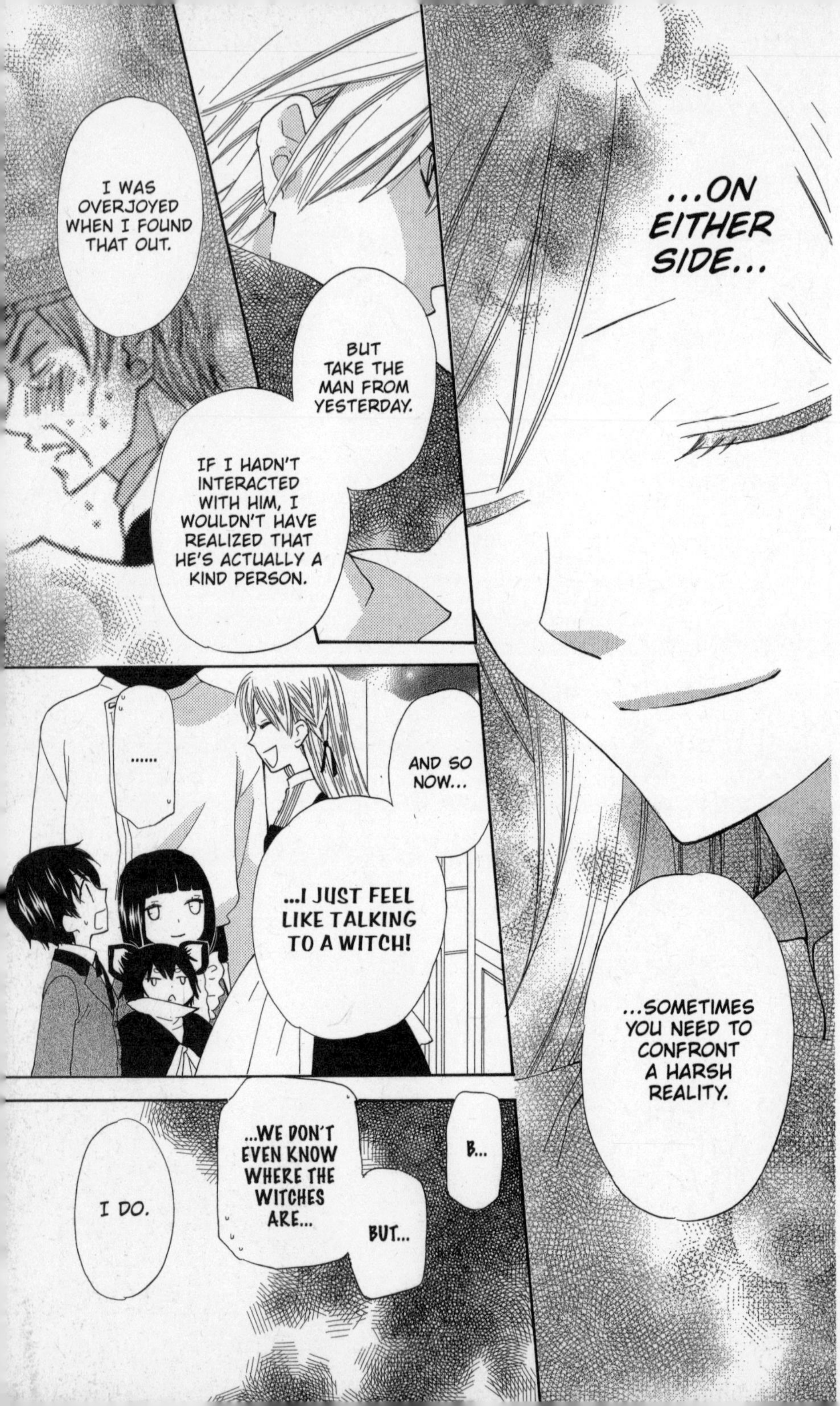
...ON EITHER SIDE...
...SOMETIMES YOU NEED TO CONFRONT A HARSH REALITY.
BUT TAKE THE MAN FROM YESTERDAY.
IF I HADN'T INTERACTED WITH HIM, I WOULDN'T HAVE REALIZED THAT HE'S ACTUALLY A KIND PERSON.
I WAS OVERJOYED WHEN I FOUND THAT OUT.
AND SO NOW...
...I JUST FEEL LIKE TALKING TO A WITCH!
......
B...
BUT...
...WE DON'T EVEN KNOW WHERE THE WITCHES ARE...
I DO.

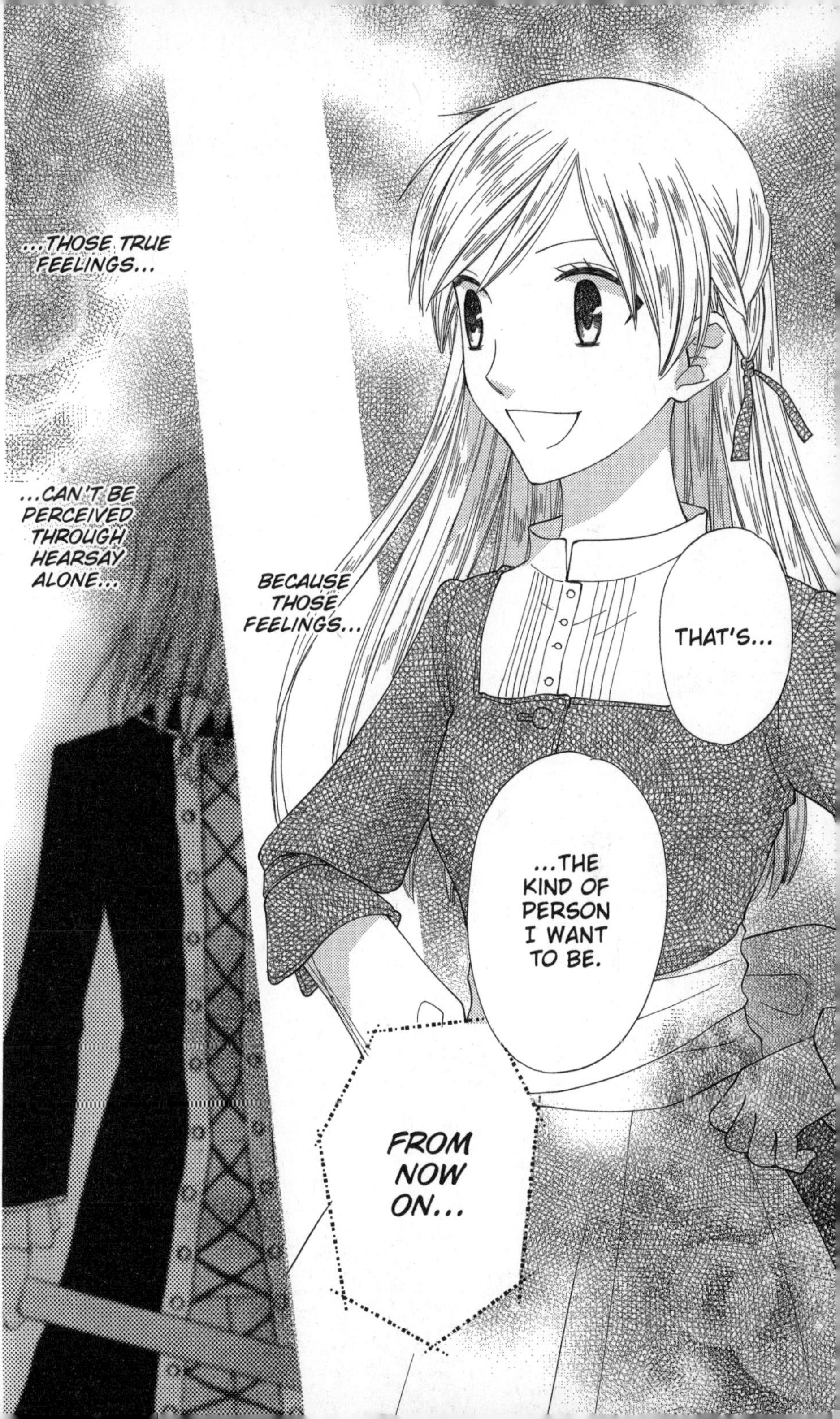
BECAUSE THOSE FEELINGS...
...THOSE TRUE FEELINGS...
...CAN'T BE PERCEIVED THROUGH HEARSAY ALONE...
THAT'S...
...THE KIND OF PERSON I WANT TO BE.
FROM NOW ON...

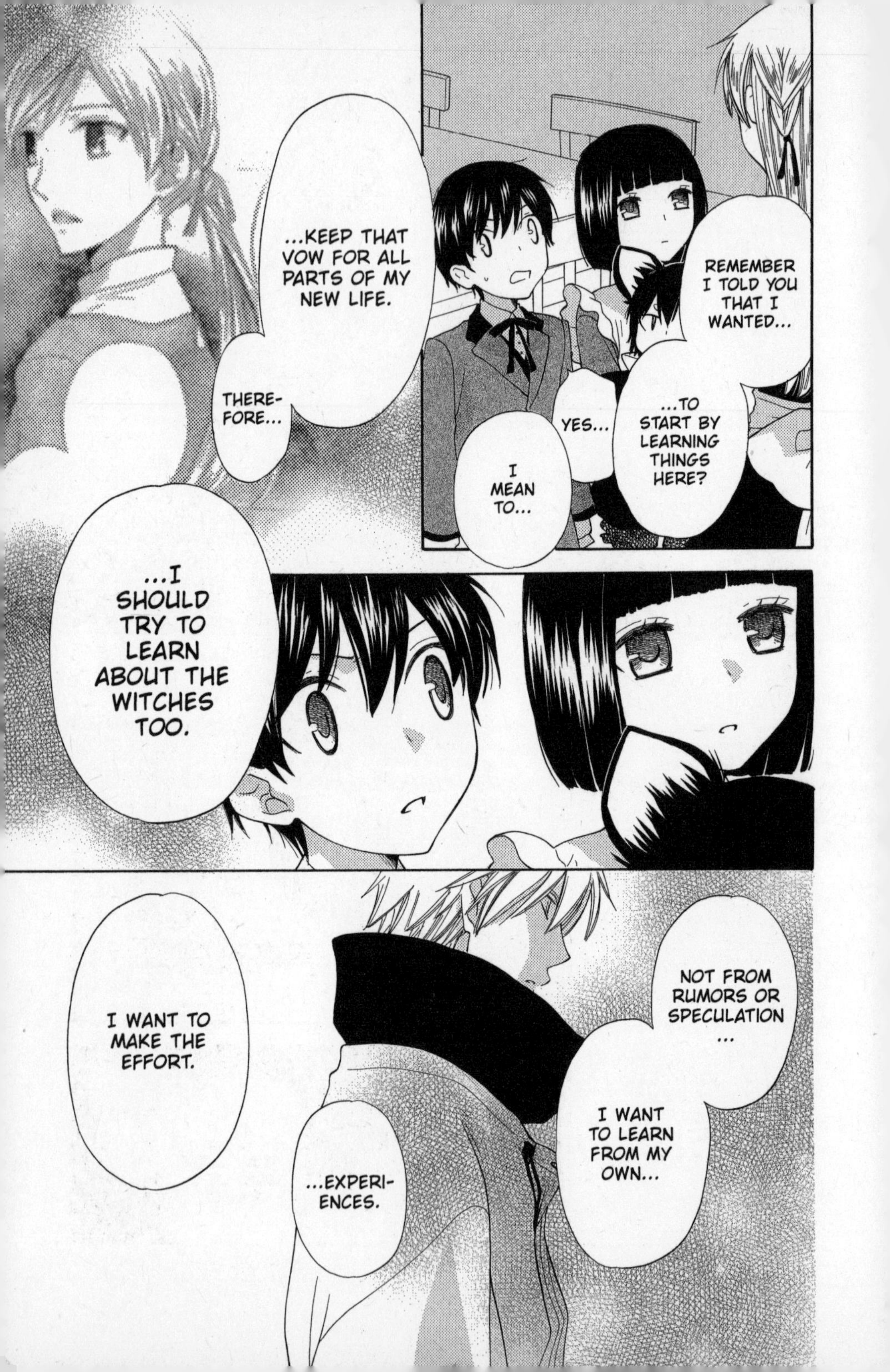

REMEMBER I TOLD YOU THAT I WANTED...
...TO START BY LEARNING THINGS HERE?
YES...
I MEAN TO...
...KEEP THAT VOW FOR ALL PARTS OF MY NEW LIFE.
THERE-FORE...
...I SHOULD TRY TO LEARN ABOUT THE WITCHES TOO.
NOT FROM RUMORS OR SPECULATION ...
I WANT TO LEARN FROM MY OWN...
...EXPERI-ENCES.
I WANT TO MAKE THE EFFORT.

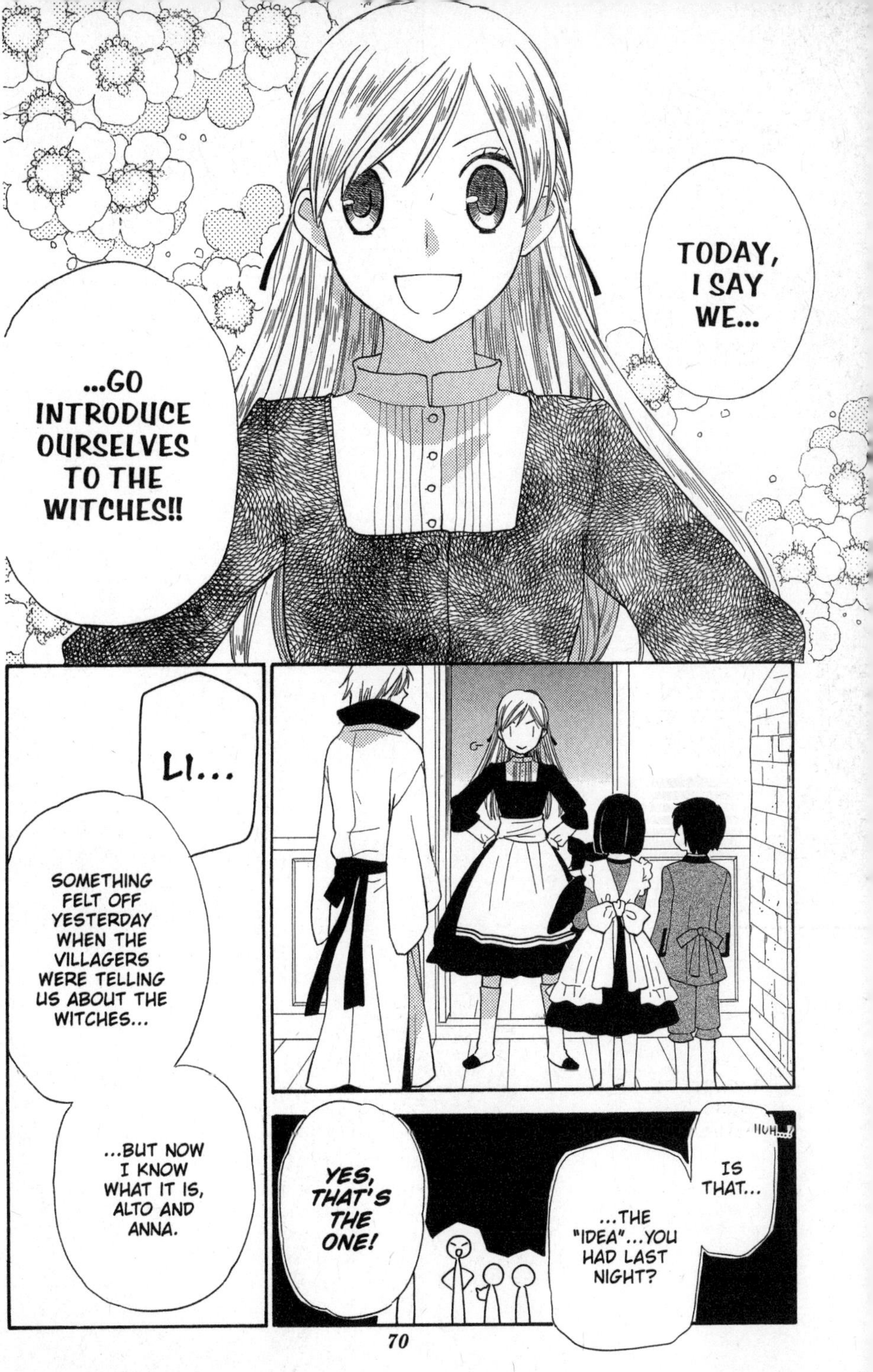

TODAY, I SAY WE...
...GO INTRODUCE OURSELVES TO THE WITCHES!!
HUH...!?
IS THAT...
...THE "IDEA"...YOU HAD LAST NIGHT?
YES, THAT'S THE ONE!
LI...
SOMETHING FELT OFF YESTERDAY WHEN THE VILLAGERS WERE TELLING US ABOUT THE WITCHES...
...BUT NOW I KNOW WHAT IT IS, ALTO AND ANNA.

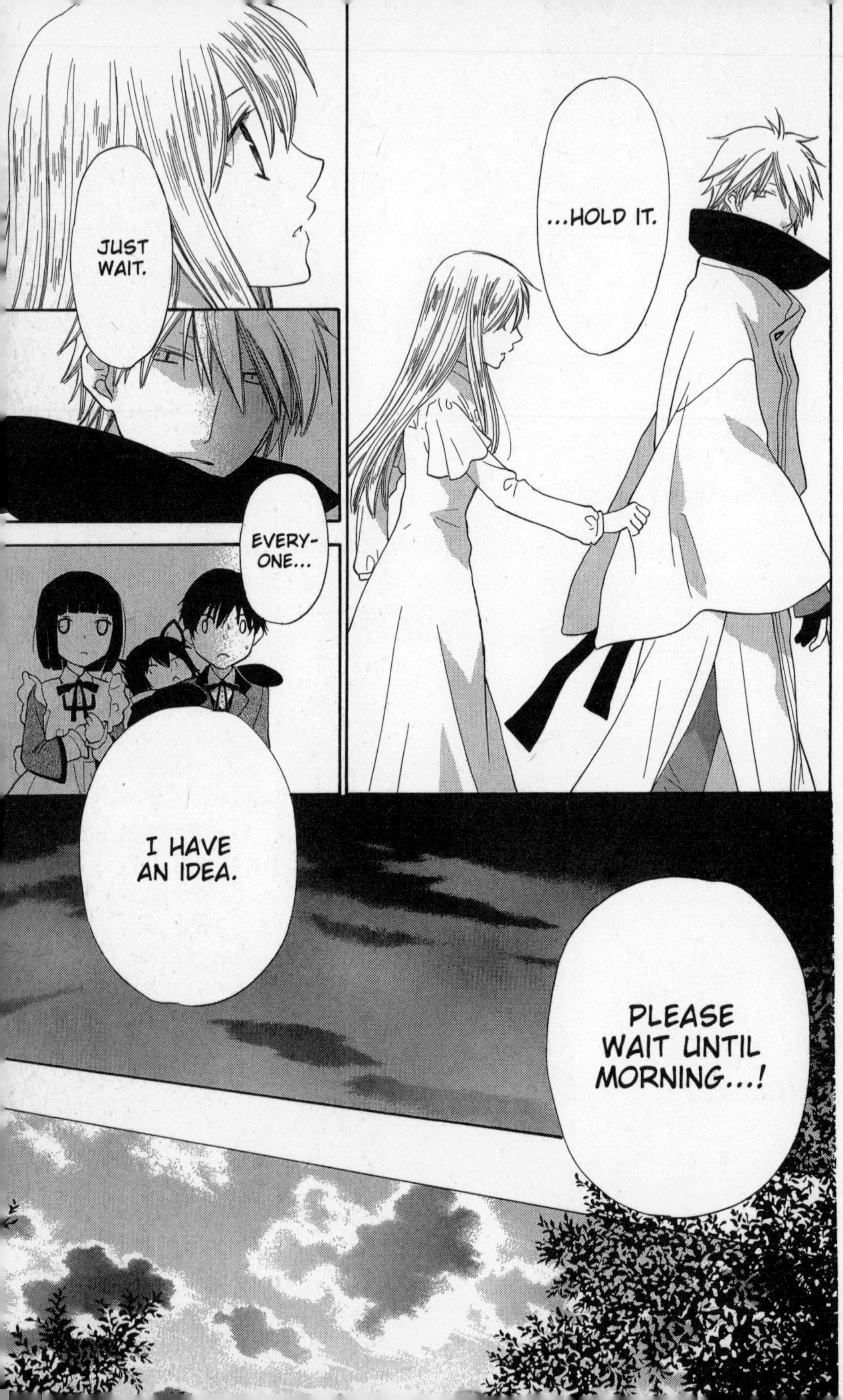
...HOLD IT.
JUST WAIT.
EVERY-ONE...
I HAVE AN IDEA.
PLEASE WAIT UNTIL MORNING...!

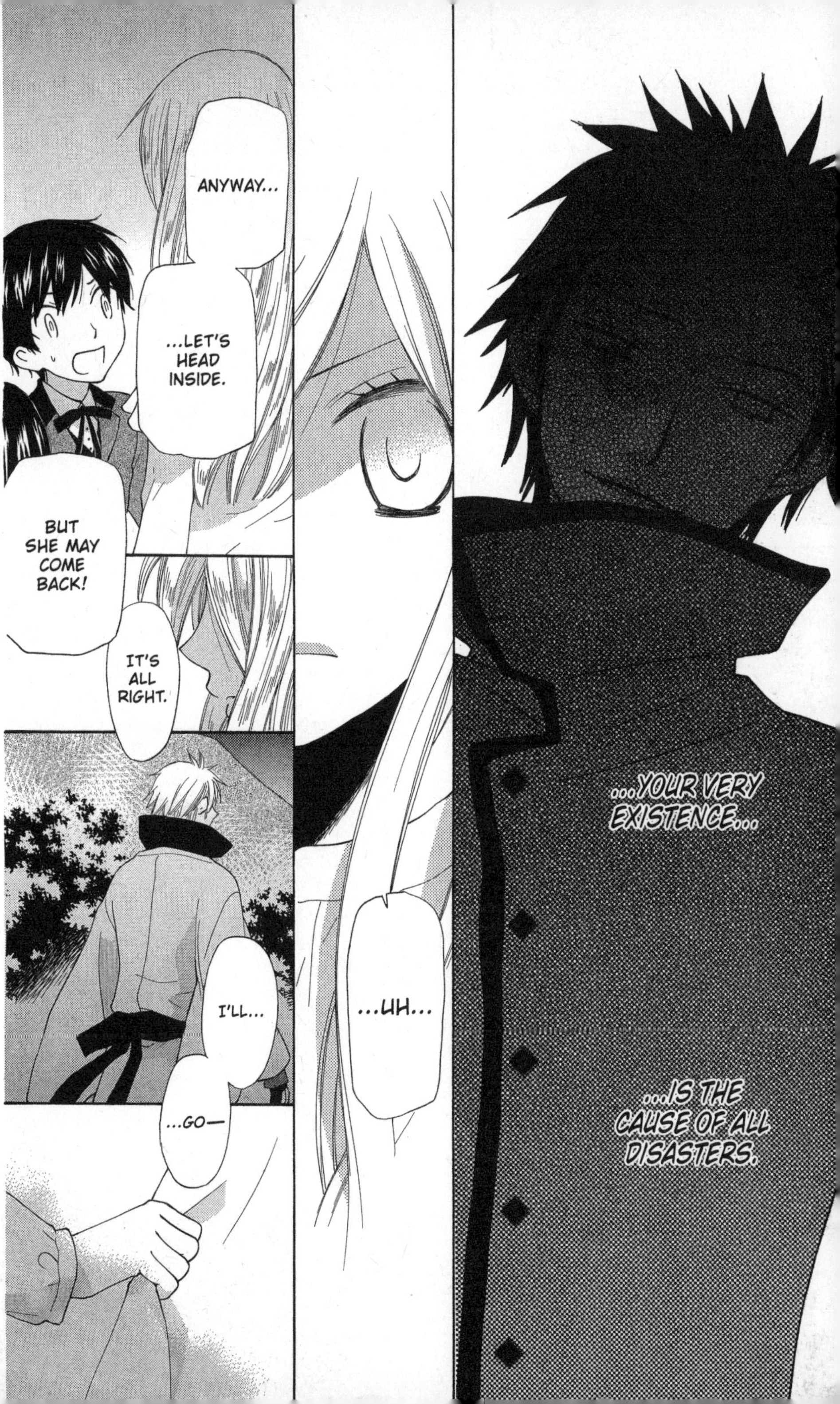
...YOUR VERY EXISTENCE...
...IS THE CAUSE OF ALL DISASTERS.
...UH...
ANYWAY...
...LET'S HEAD INSIDE.
BUT SHE MAY COME BACK!
IT'S ALL RIGHT.
I'LL...
...GO—

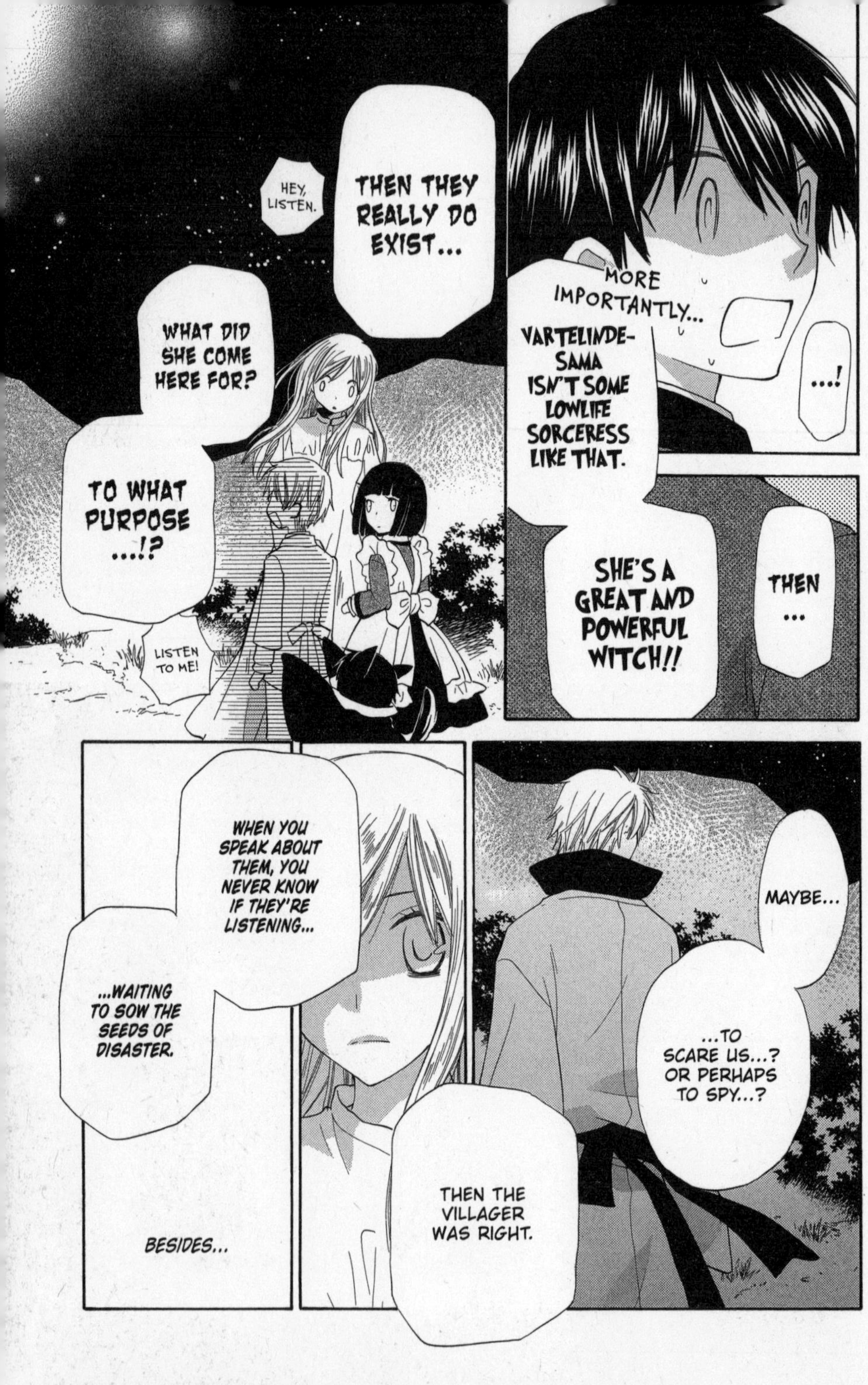

...!
MORE IMPORTANTLY... VARTELINDE-SAMA ISN'T SOME LOWLIFE SORCERESS LIKE THAT.
THEN...
SHE'S A GREAT AND POWERFUL WITCH!!
THEN THEY REALLY DO EXIST...
HEY, LISTEN.
WHAT DID SHE COME HERE FOR?
TO WHAT PURPOSE ...!?
LISTEN TO ME!
MAYBE...
...TO SCARE US...? OR PERHAPS TO SPY...?
THEN THE VILLAGER WAS RIGHT.
WHEN YOU SPEAK ABOUT THEM, YOU NEVER KNOW IF THEY'RE LISTENING...
...WAITING TO SOW THE SEEDS OF DISASTER.
BESIDES...

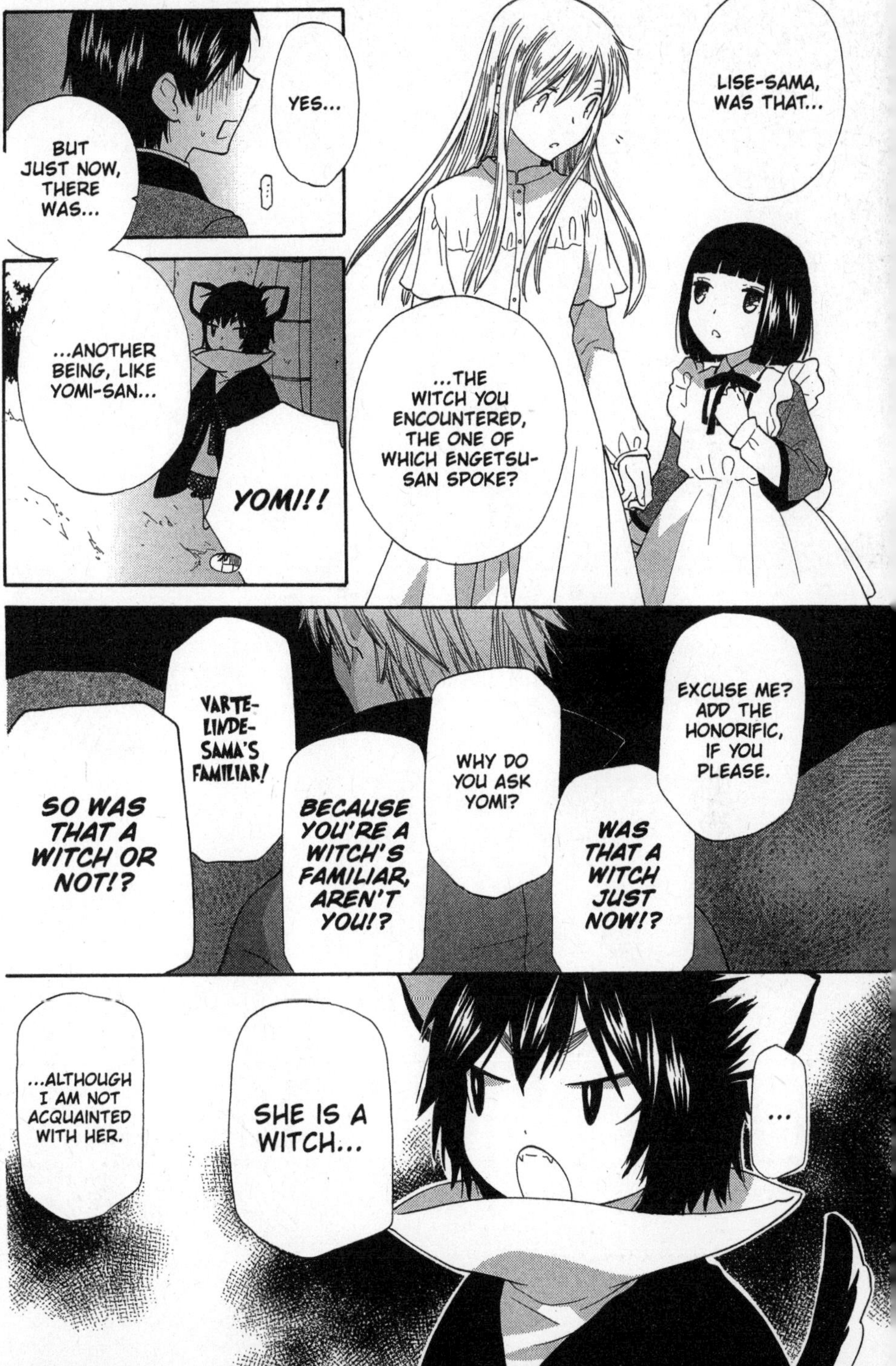
LISE-SAMA, WAS THAT...
...THE WITCH YOU ENCOUNTERED, THE ONE OF WHICH ENGETSU-SAN SPOKE?
YES...
BUT JUST NOW, THERE WAS...
...ANOTHER BEING, LIKE YOMI-SAN...
YOMI!!
EXCUSE ME? ADD THE HONORIFIC, IF YOU PLEASE.
WAS THAT A WITCH JUST NOW!?
WHY DO YOU ASK YOMI?
BECAUSE YOU'RE A WITCH'S FAMILIAR, AREN'T YOU!?
VARTE-LINDE-SAMA'S FAMILIAR!
SO WAS THAT A WITCH OR NOT!?
...
SHE IS A WITCH...
...ALTHOUGH I AM NOT ACQUAINTED WITH HER.

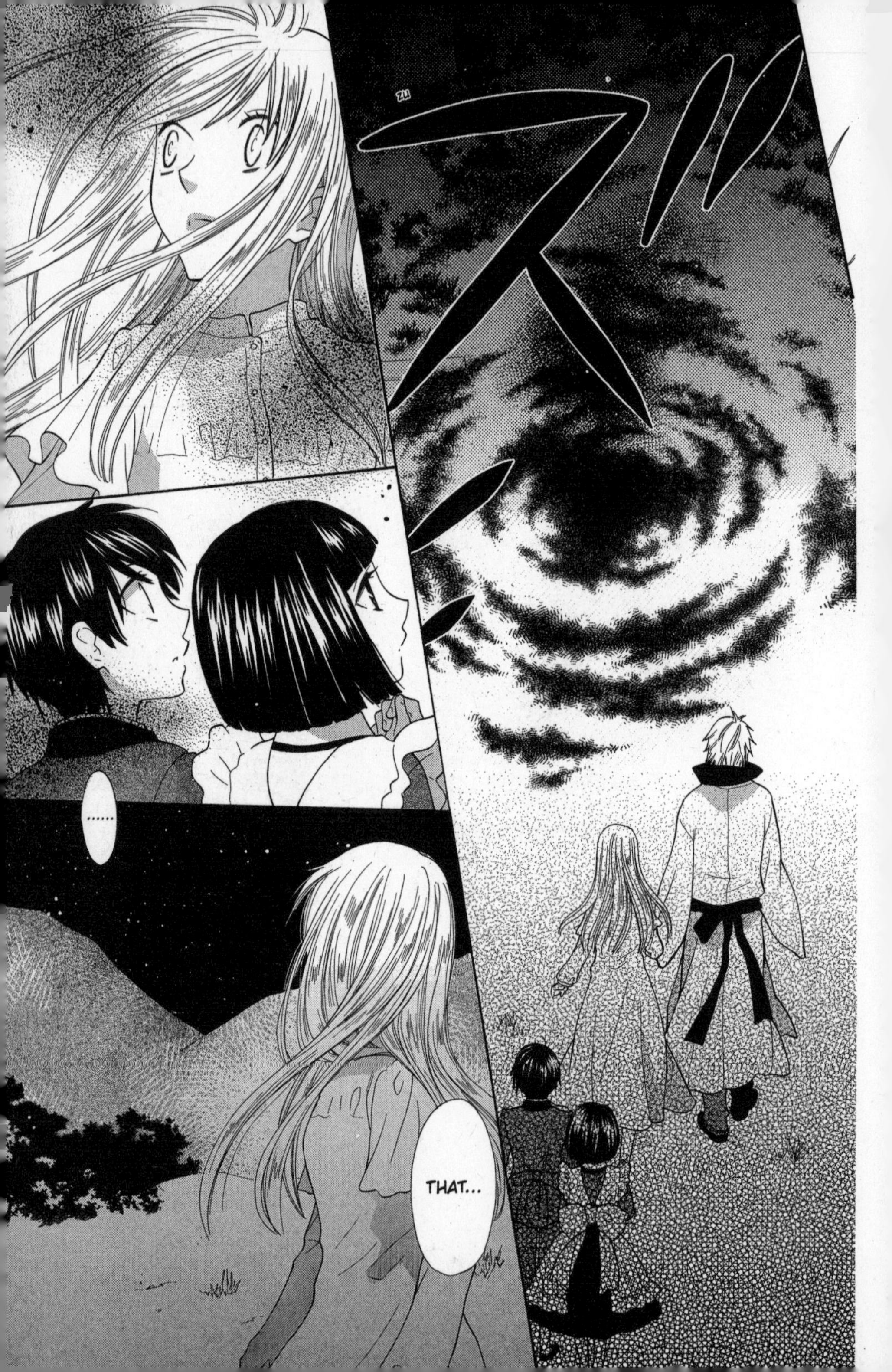
ZU
......
THAT...

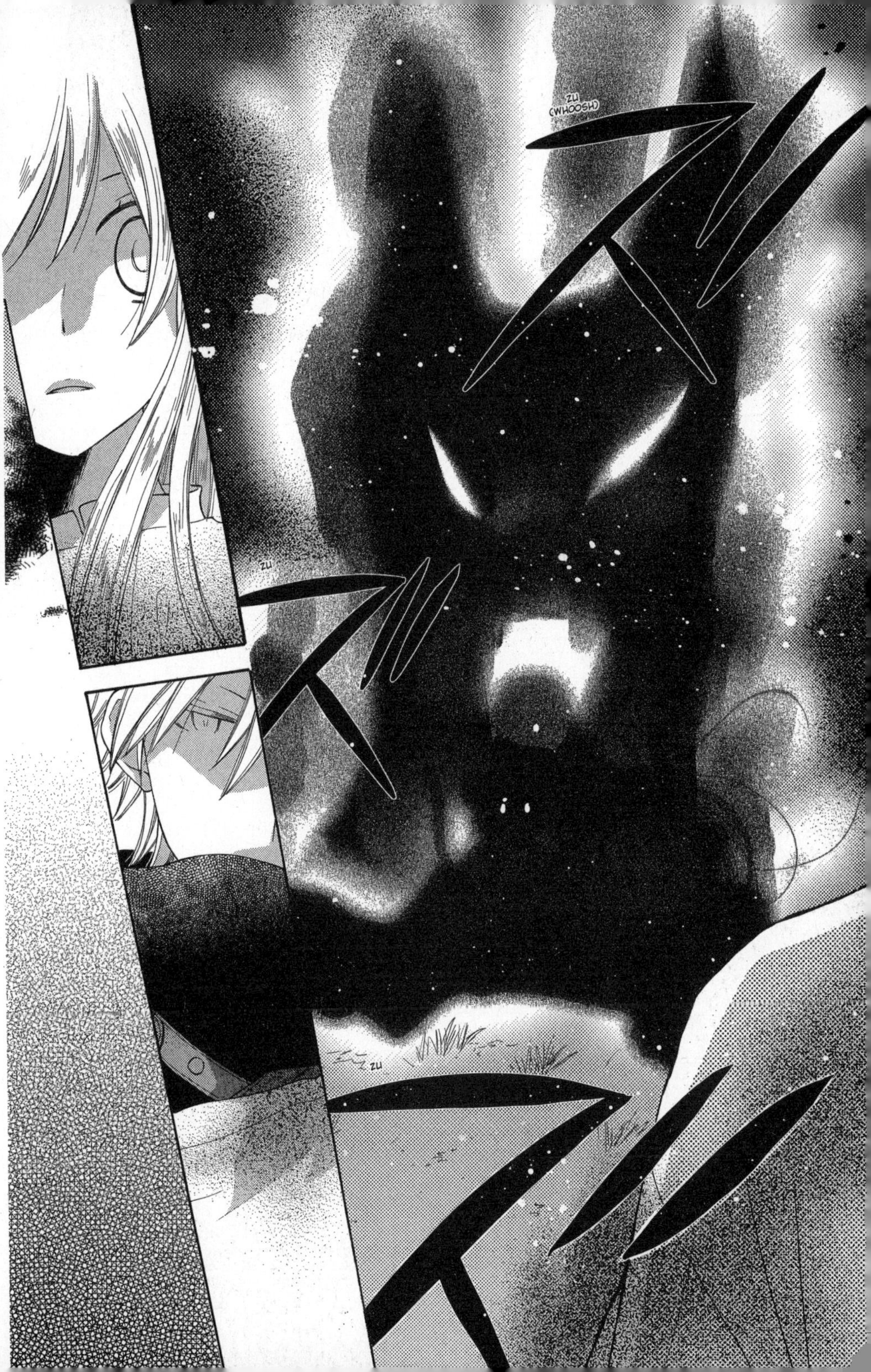
ZU
(WHOOSH)
ZU
ZU

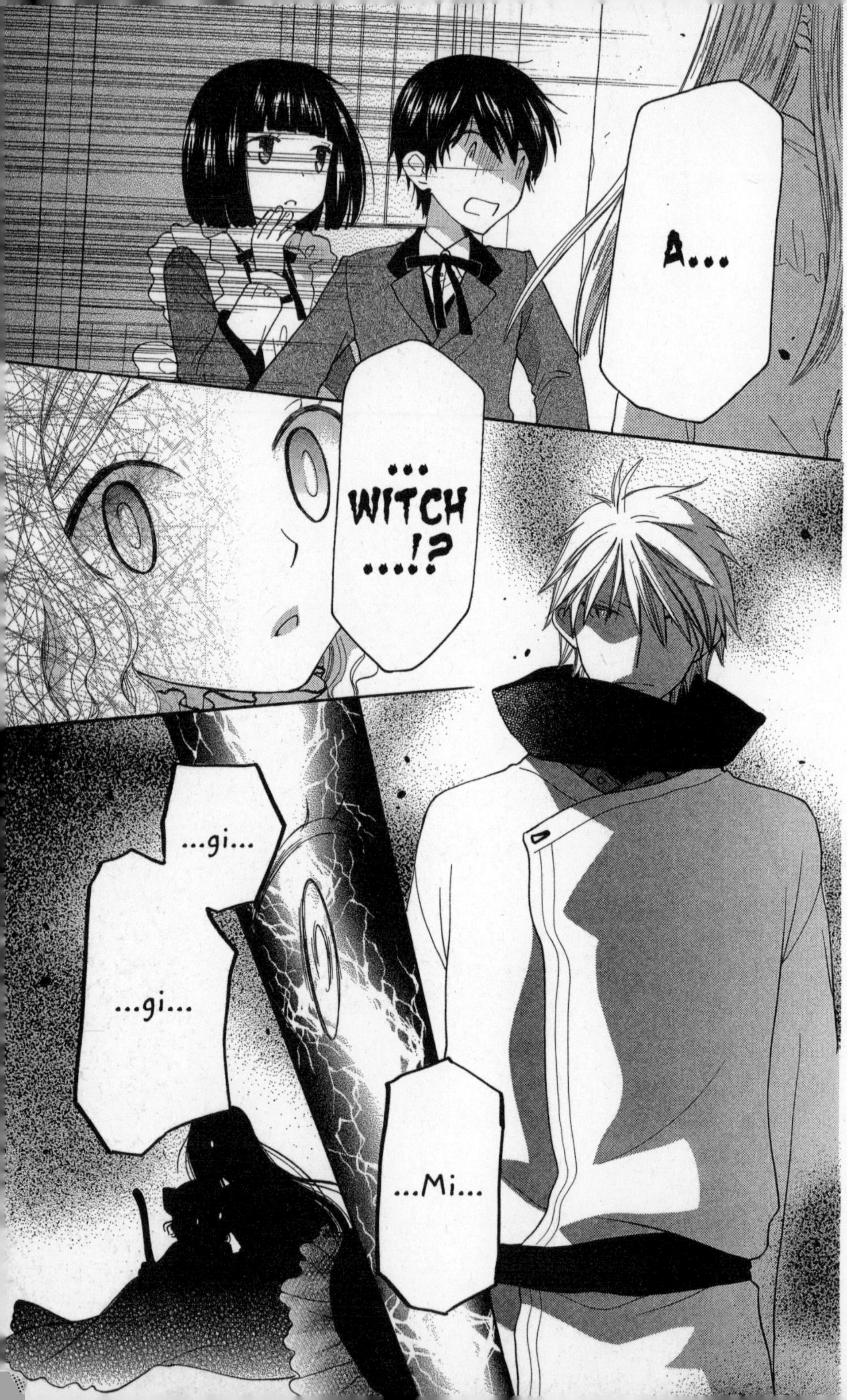
A...
...WITCH ...!?
...
...Mi...
...gi...
...gi...

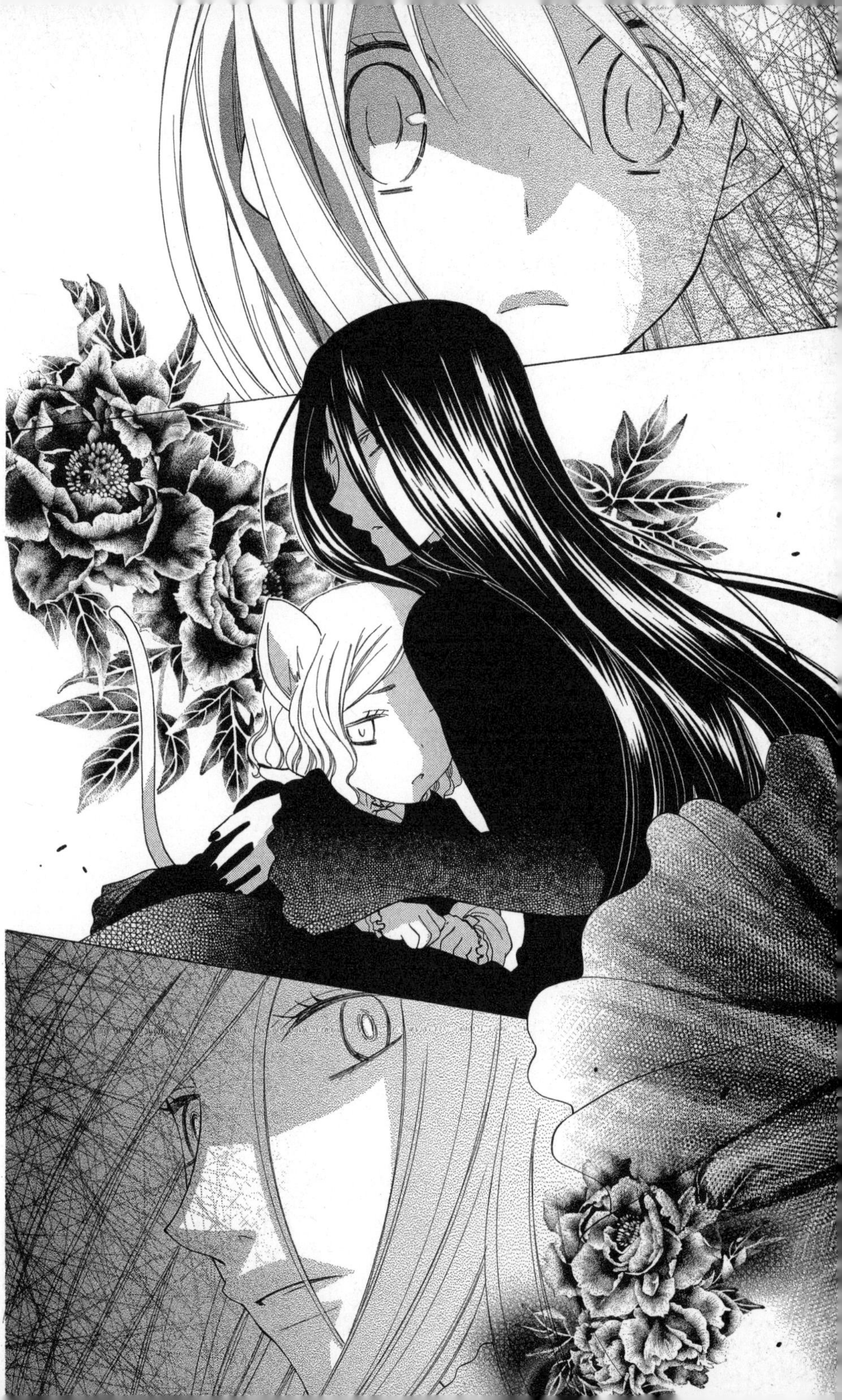

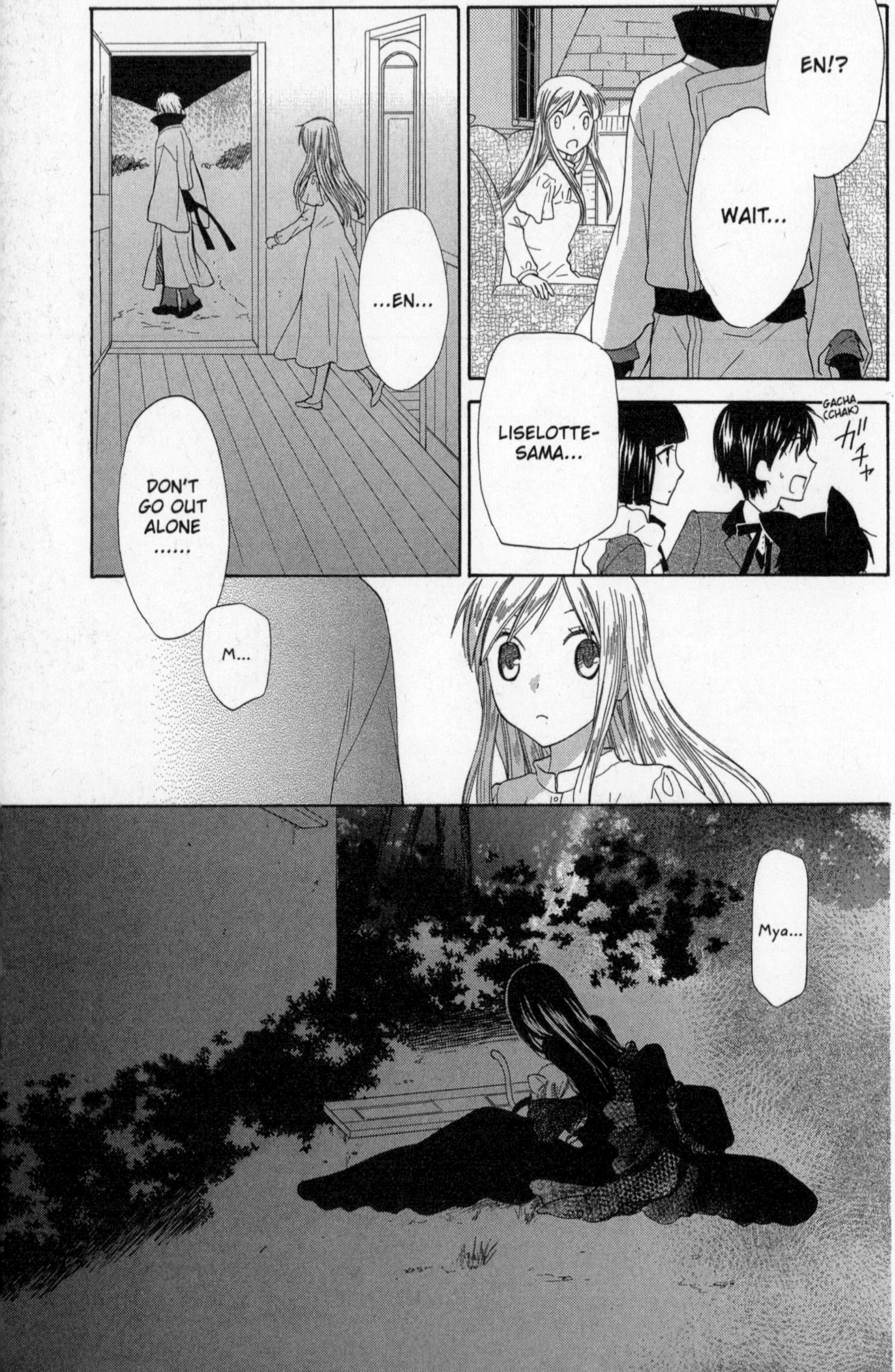
EN!?
WAIT...
LISELOTTE-SAMA...
GACHA (CHAK)
ガチャ
...EN...
DON'T GO OUT ALONE ......
M...
Mya...

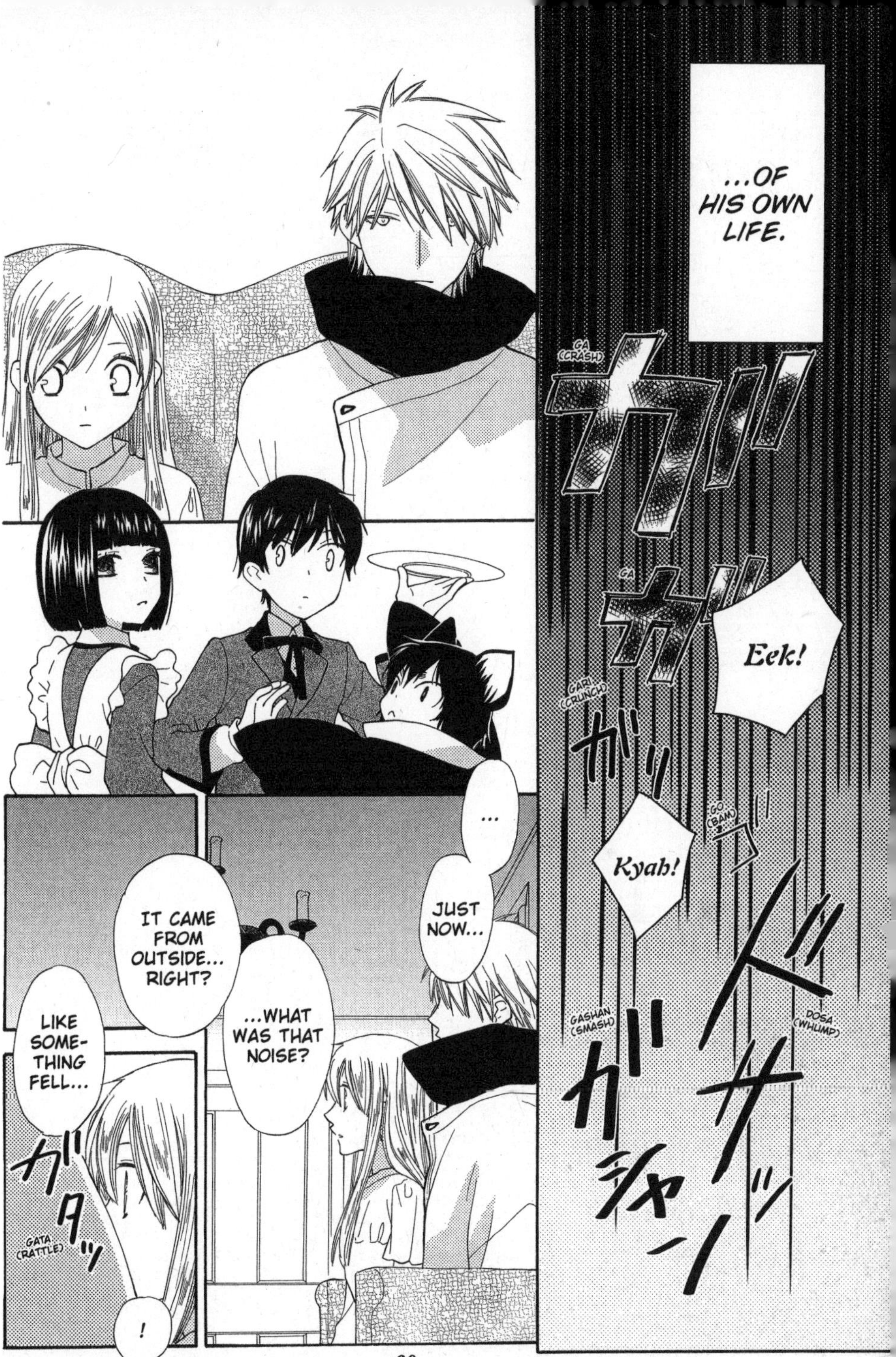
...OF HIS OWN LIFE.
GA (CRASH)
GA
Eek!
GARI (CRUNCH)
GO (BAN)
Kyah!
DOSA (WHUMP)
GASHAN (SMASH)
...
JUST NOW...
IT CAME FROM OUTSIDE... RIGHT?
...WHAT WAS THAT NOISE?
LIKE SOME-THING FELL...
GATA (RATTLE)
!

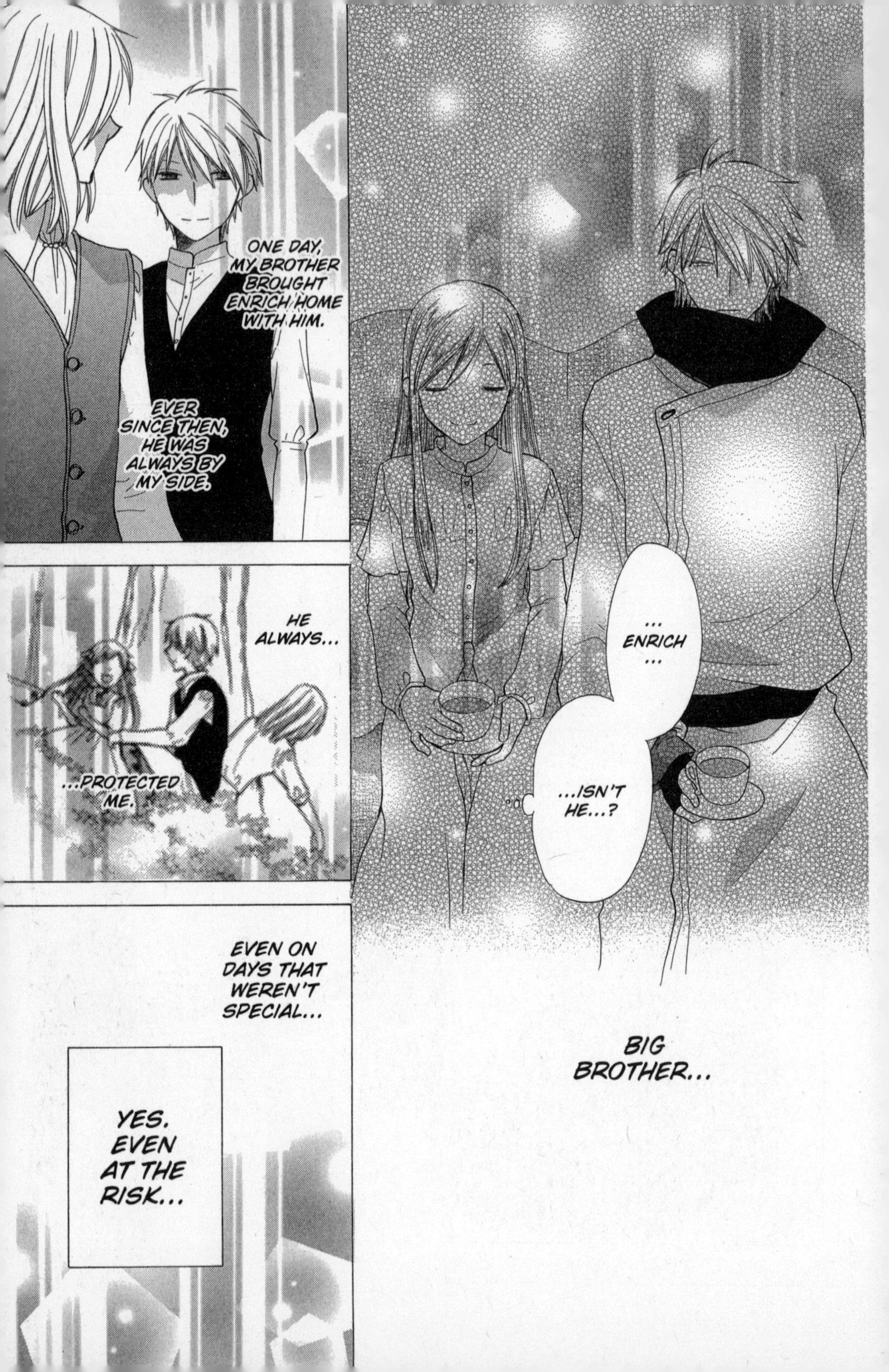

... ENRICH ...
...ISN'T HE...?
BIG BROTHER...
ONE DAY, MY BROTHER BROUGHT ENRICH HOME WITH HIM.
EVER SINCE THEN, HE WAS ALWAYS BY MY SIDE.
HE ALWAYS...
...PROTECTED ME.
EVEN ON DAYS THAT WEREN'T SPECIAL...
YES. EVEN AT THE RISK...

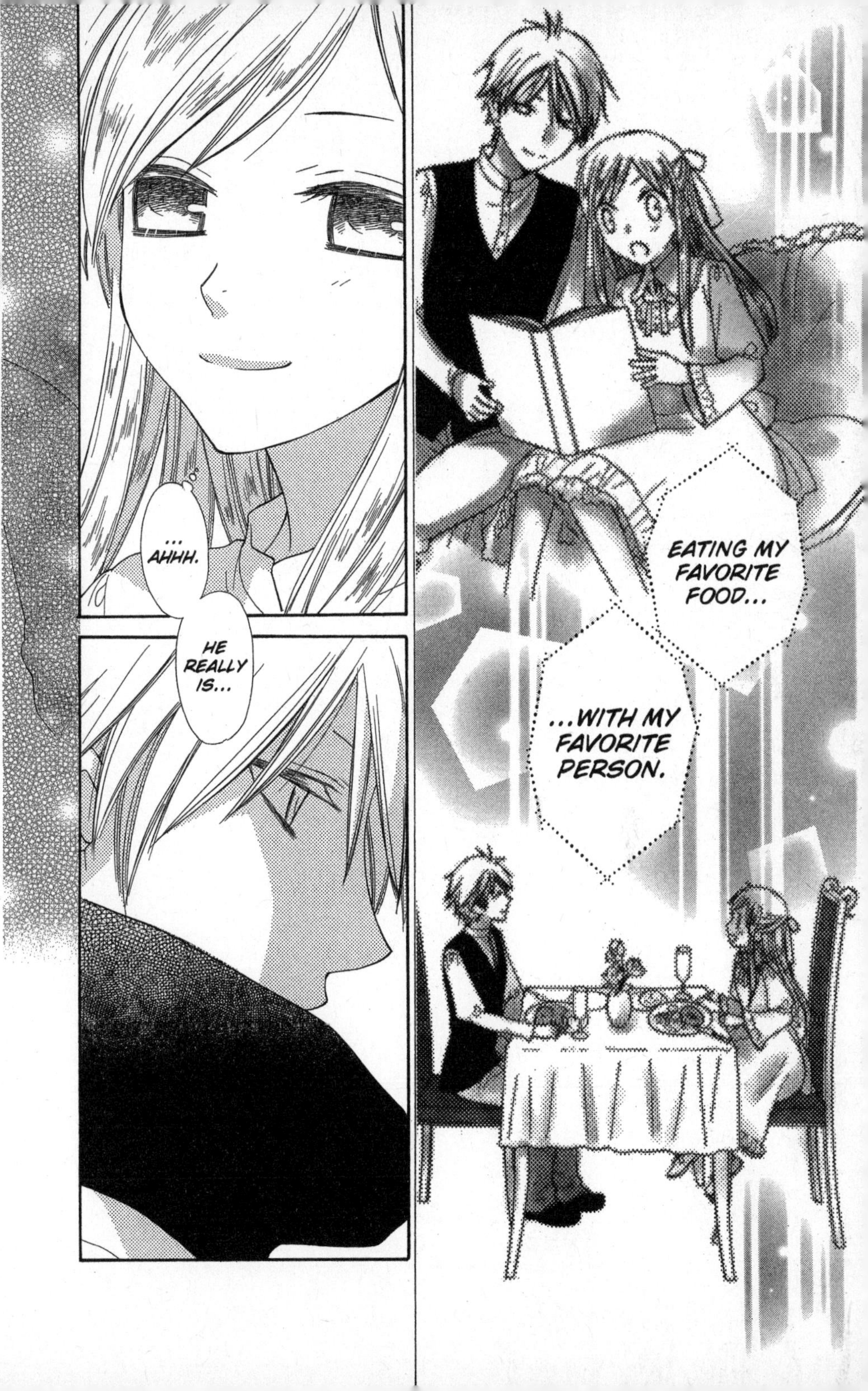
EATING MY FAVORITE FOOD...
...WITH MY FAVORITE PERSON.
...AHHH.
HE REALLY IS...

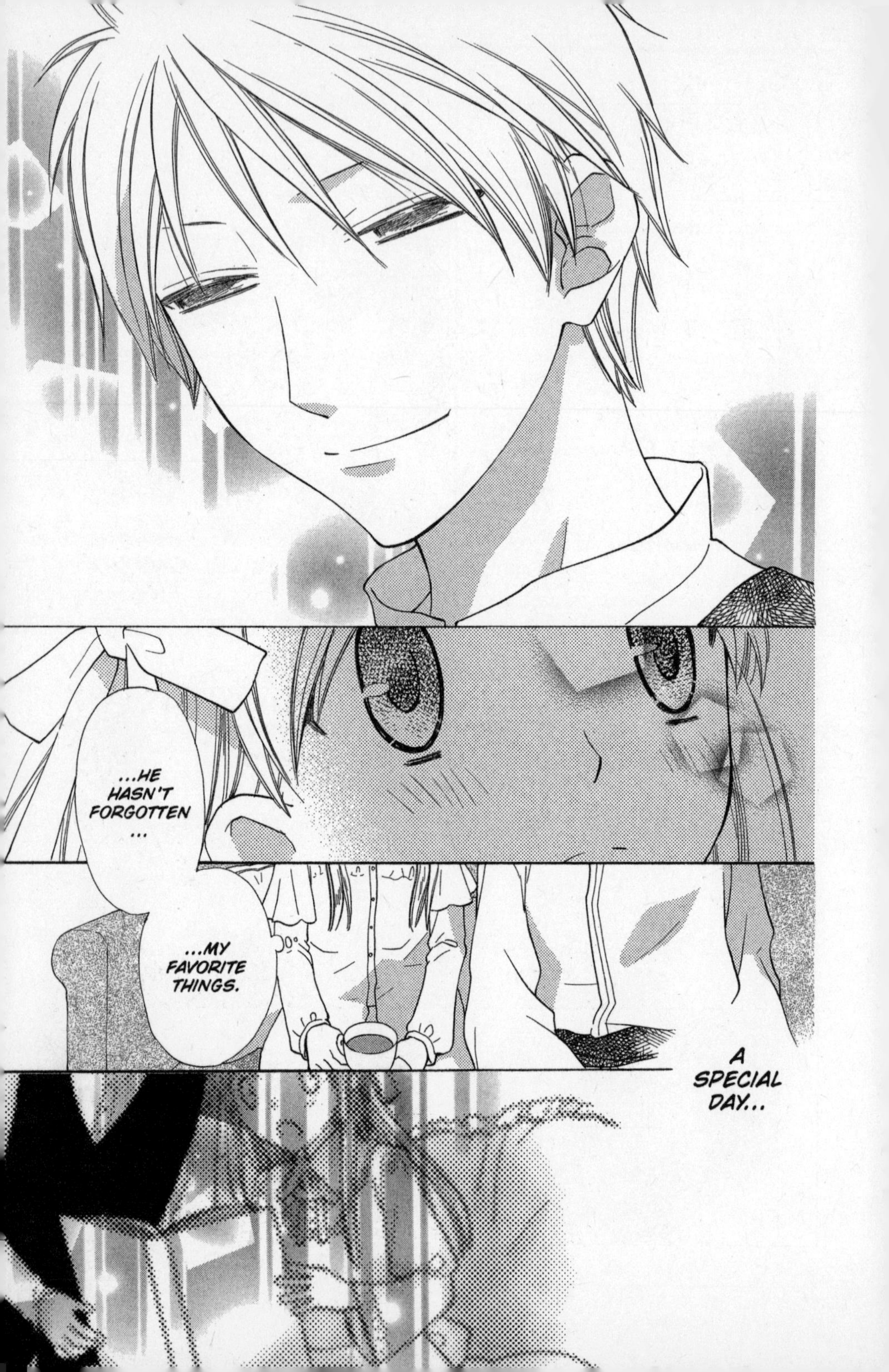
...HE HASN'T FORGOTTEN ...
...MY FAVORITE THINGS.
A SPECIAL DAY...

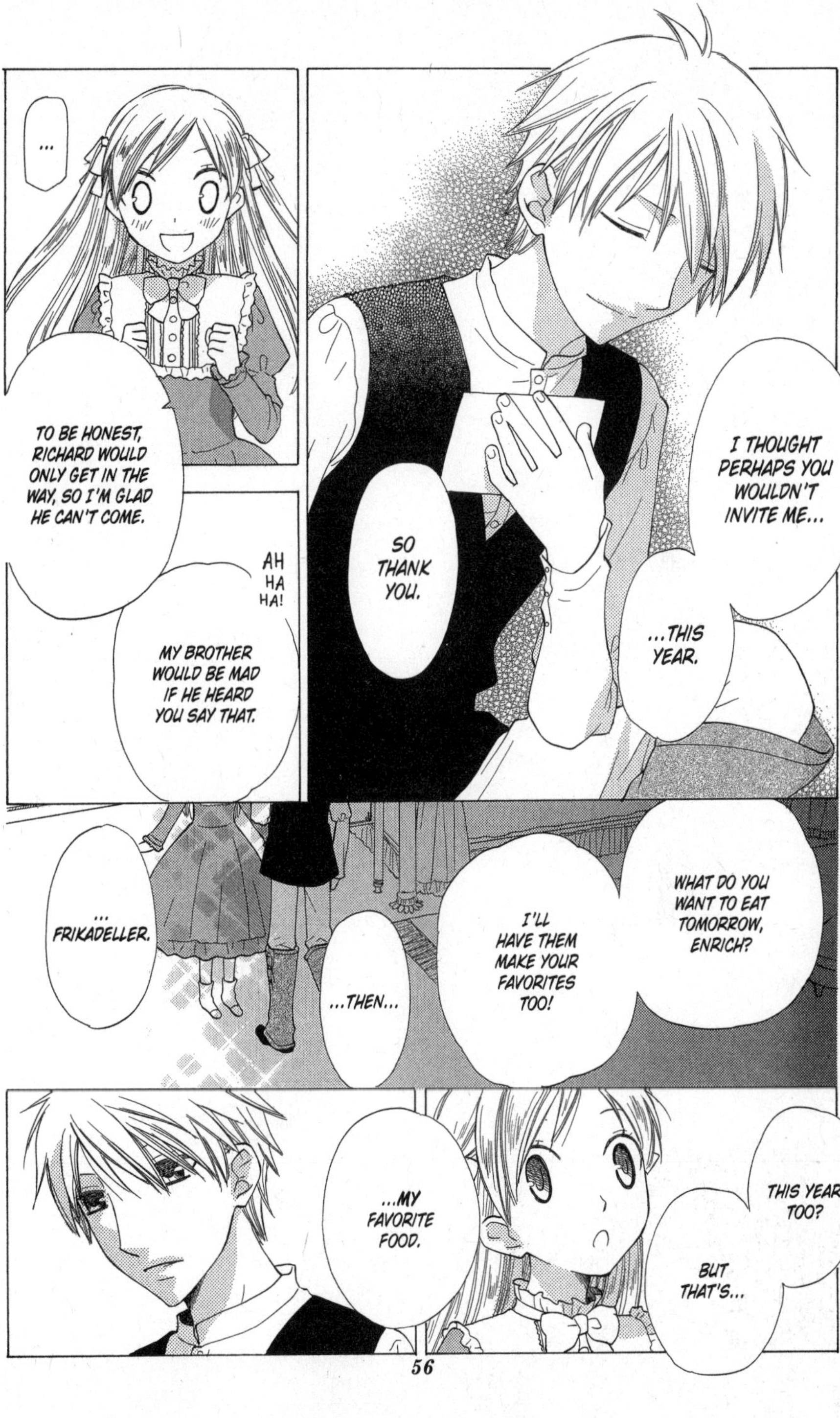
I THOUGHT PERHAPS YOU WOULDN'T INVITE ME...
...THIS YEAR.
SO THANK YOU.
...
TO BE HONEST, RICHARD WOULD ONLY GET IN THE WAY, SO I'M GLAD HE CAN'T COME.
AH HA HA!
MY BROTHER WOULD BE MAD IF HE HEARD YOU SAY THAT.
WHAT DO YOU WANT TO EAT TOMORROW, ENRICH?
I'LL HAVE THEM MAKE YOUR FAVORITES TOO!
...THEN...
... FRIKADELLER.
THIS YEAR TOO?
BUT THAT'S...
...MY FAVORITE FOOD.

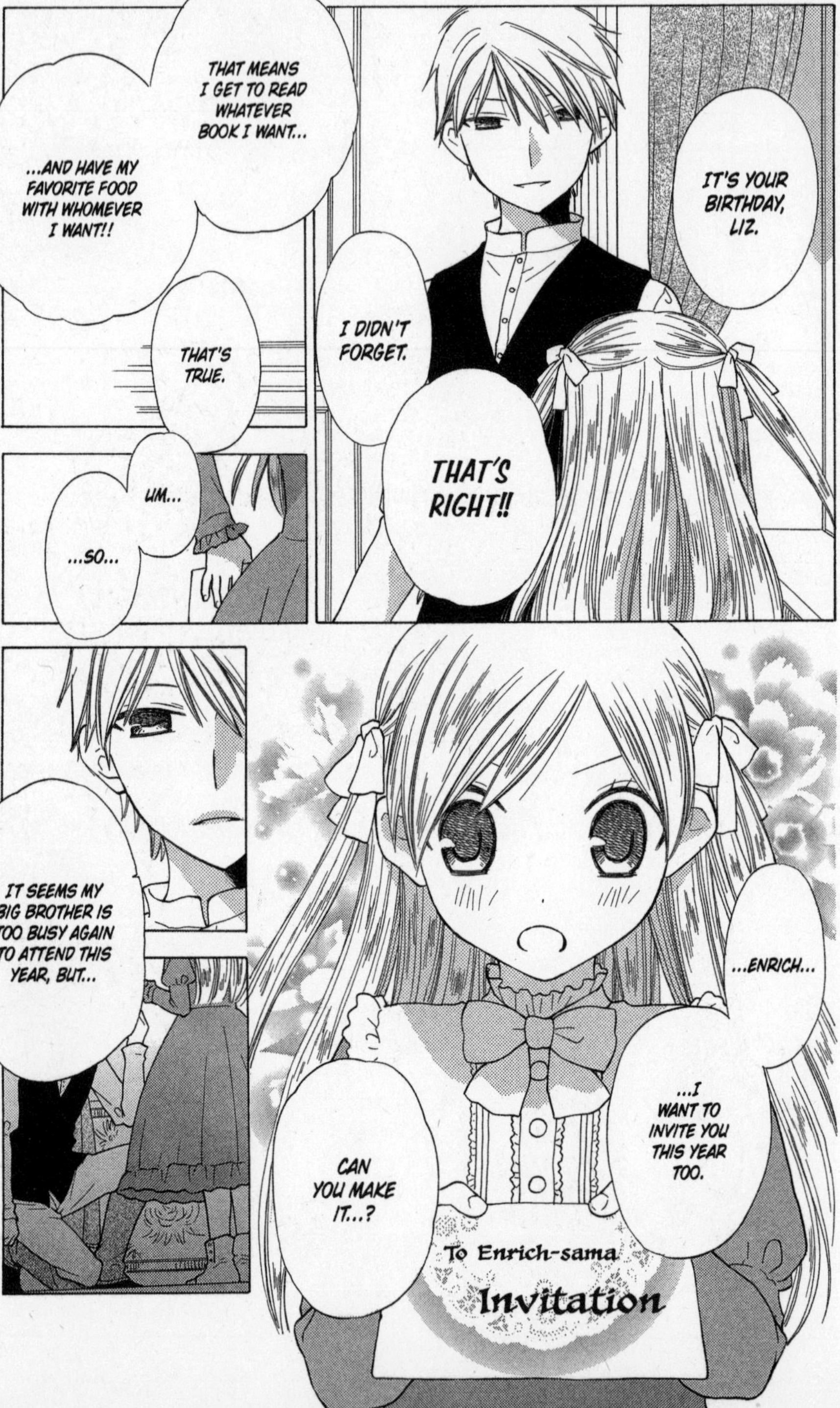
IT'S YOUR BIRTHDAY, LIZ.
I DIDN'T FORGET.
THAT'S RIGHT!!
THAT MEANS I GET TO READ WHATEVER BOOK I WANT...
...AND HAVE MY FAVORITE FOOD WITH WHOMEVER I WANT!!
THAT'S TRUE.
UM...
...SO...
...ENRICH...
...I WANT TO INVITE YOU THIS YEAR TOO.
CAN YOU MAKE IT...?
To Enrich-sama
Invitation
IT SEEMS MY BIG BROTHER IS TOO BUSY AGAIN TO ATTEND THIS YEAR, BUT...

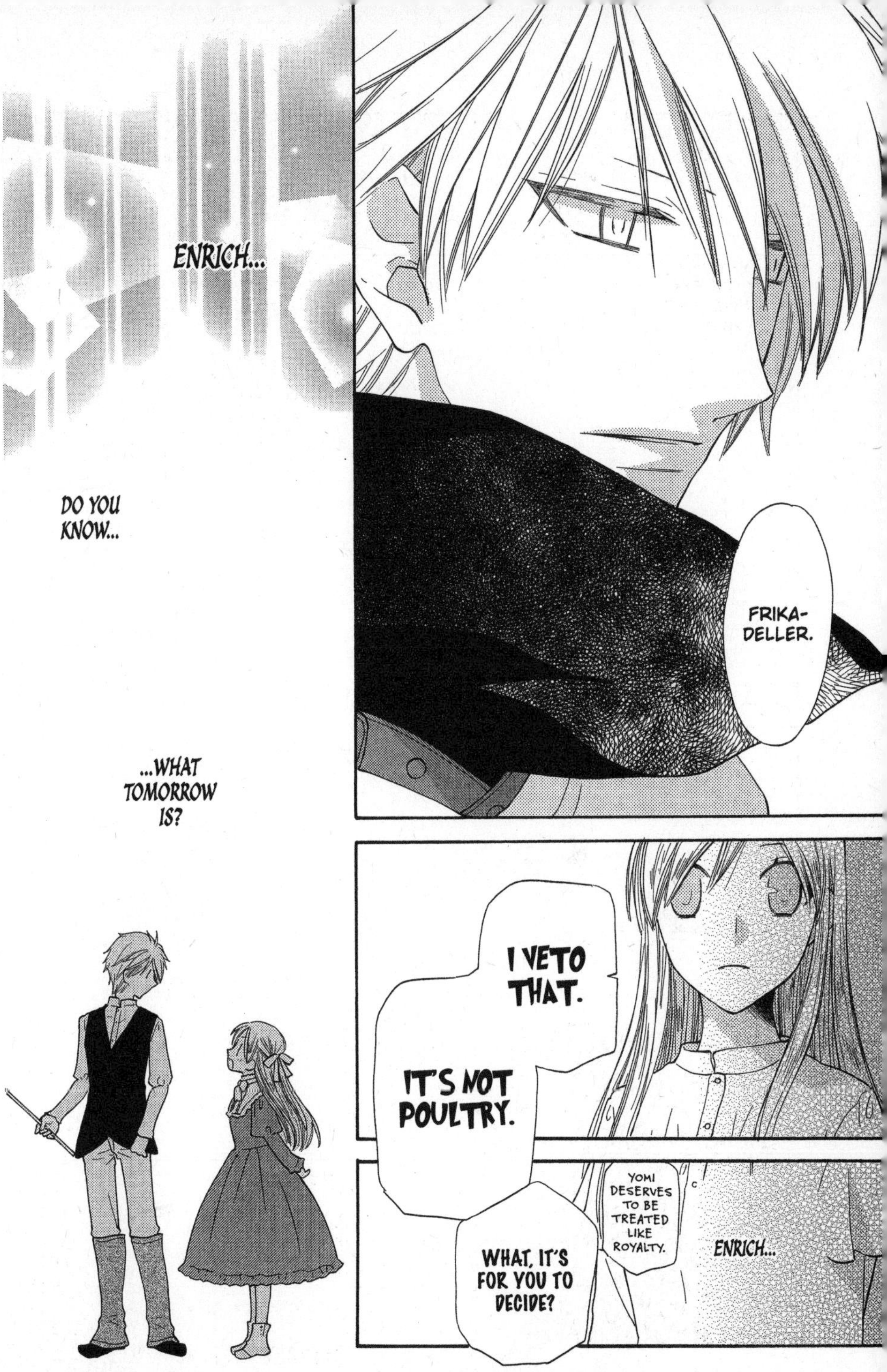
FRIKA-DELLER.
I VETO THAT.
IT'S NOT POULTRY.
ENRICH...
YOMI DESERVES TO BE TREATED LIKE ROYALTY.
WHAT, IT'S FOR YOU TO DECIDE?
ENRICH...
DO YOU KNOW...
...WHAT TOMORROW IS?

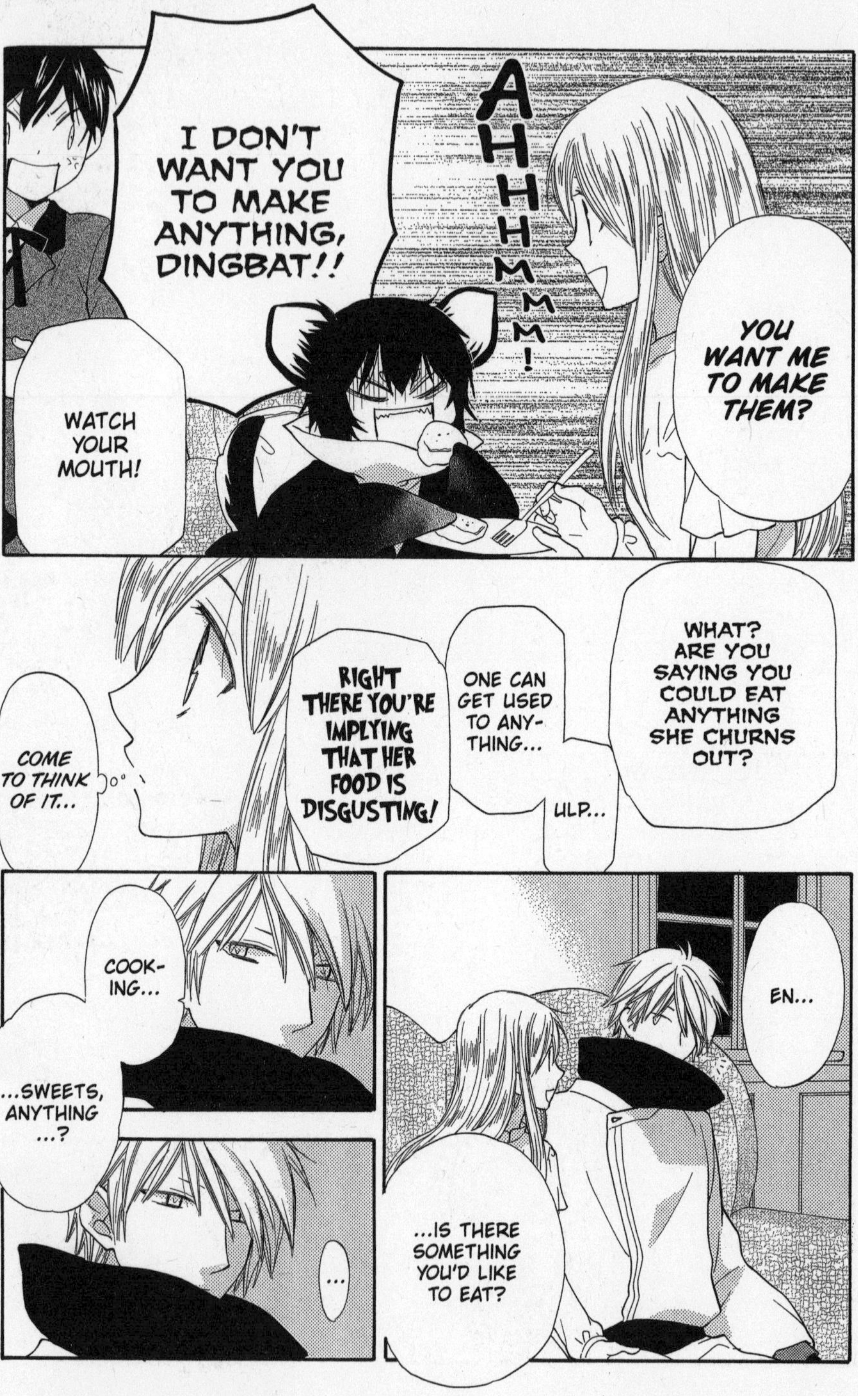
YOU WANT ME TO MAKE THEM?
AHHHHMMM!
I DON'T WANT YOU TO MAKE ANYTHING, DINGBAT!!
WATCH YOUR MOUTH!
WHAT? ARE YOU SAYING YOU COULD EAT ANYTHING SHE CHURNS OUT?
ULP...
ONE CAN GET USED TO ANY-THING...
RIGHT THERE YOU'RE IMPLYING THAT HER FOOD IS DISGUSTING!
COME TO THINK OF IT...
EN...
...IS THERE SOMETHING YOU'D LIKE TO EAT?
COOK-ING...
...SWEETS, ANYTHING ...?
...

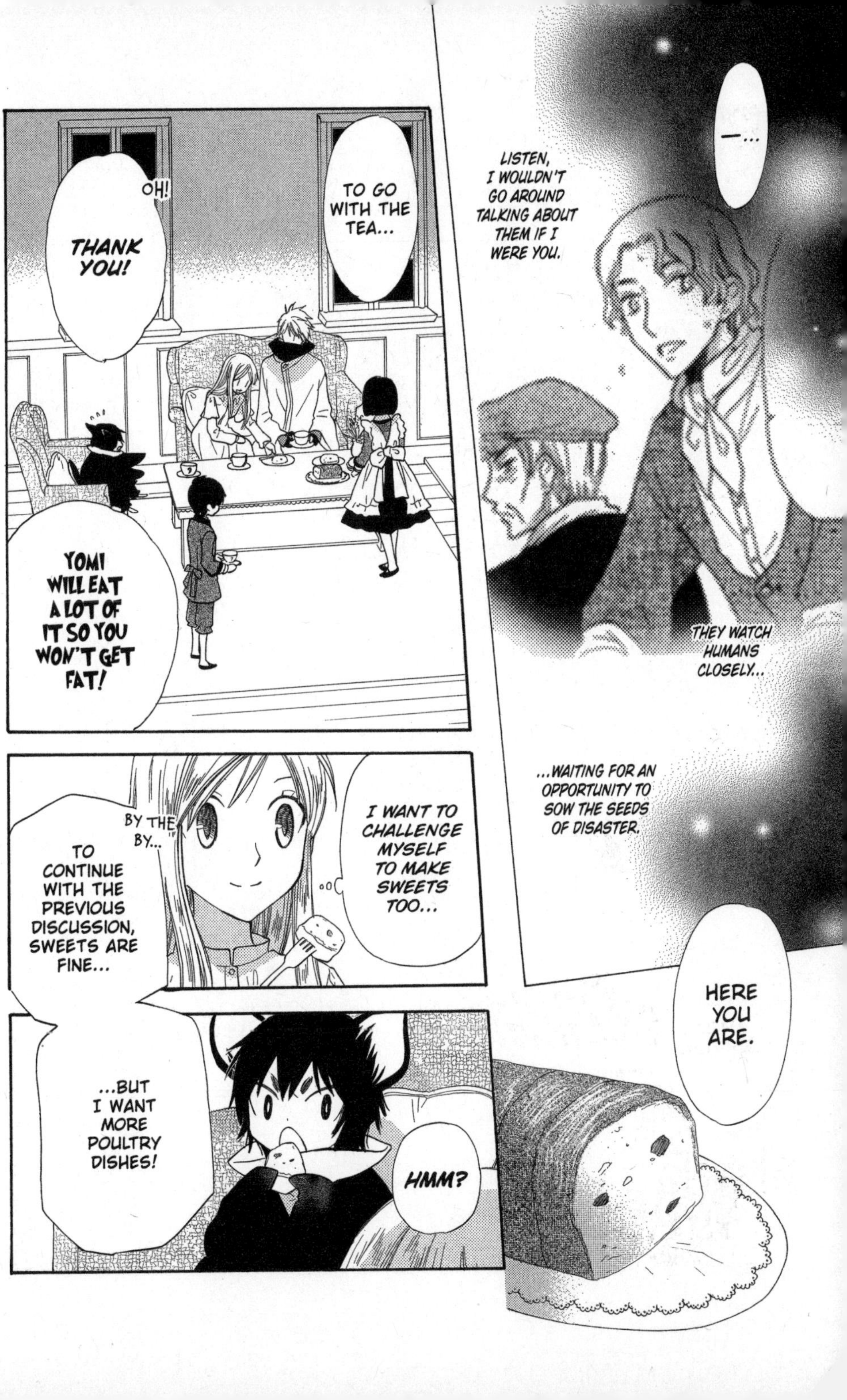

—…
LISTEN, I WOULDN'T GO AROUND TALKING ABOUT THEM IF I WERE YOU.
THEY WATCH HUMANS CLOSELY…
…WAITING FOR AN OPPORTUNITY TO SOW THE SEEDS OF DISASTER.
TO GO WITH THE TEA…
OH!
THANK YOU!
YOMI WILL EAT A LOT OF IT SO YOU WON'T GET FAT!
I WANT TO CHALLENGE MYSELF TO MAKE SWEETS TOO…
BY THE BY…
TO CONTINUE WITH THE PREVIOUS DISCUSSION, SWEETS ARE FINE…
HERE YOU ARE.
HMM?
…BUT I WANT MORE POULTRY DISHES!

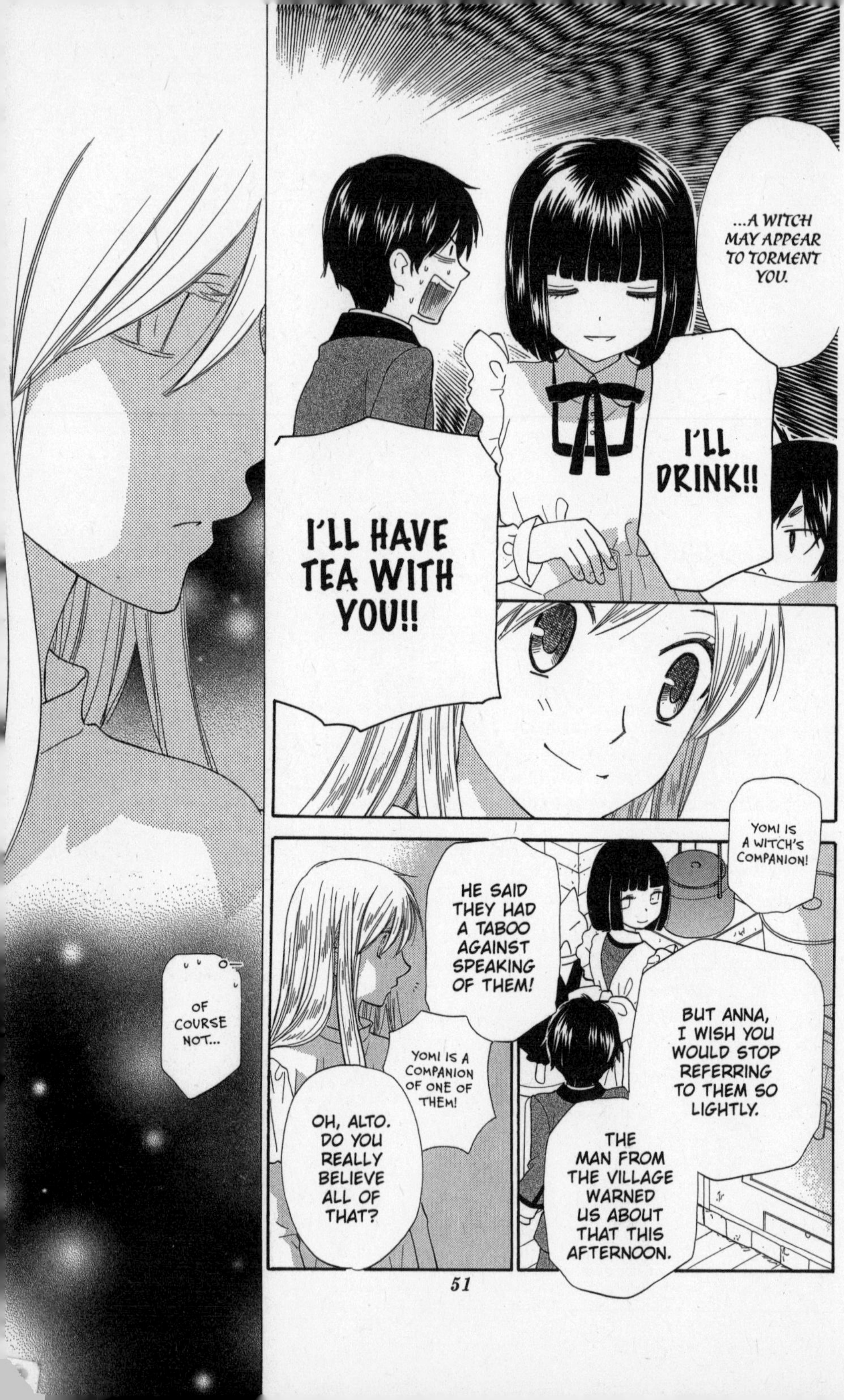
...A WITCH MAY APPEAR TO TORMENT YOU.
I'LL DRINK!!
I'LL HAVE TEA WITH YOU!!
YOMI IS A WITCH'S COMPANION!
HE SAID THEY HAD A TABOO AGAINST SPEAKING OF THEM!
BUT ANNA, I WISH YOU WOULD STOP REFERRING TO THEM SO LIGHTLY.
THE MAN FROM THE VILLAGE WARNED US ABOUT THAT THIS AFTERNOON.
YOMI IS A COMPANION OF ONE OF THEM!
OH, ALTO. DO YOU REALLY BELIEVE ALL OF THAT?
OF COURSE NOT...

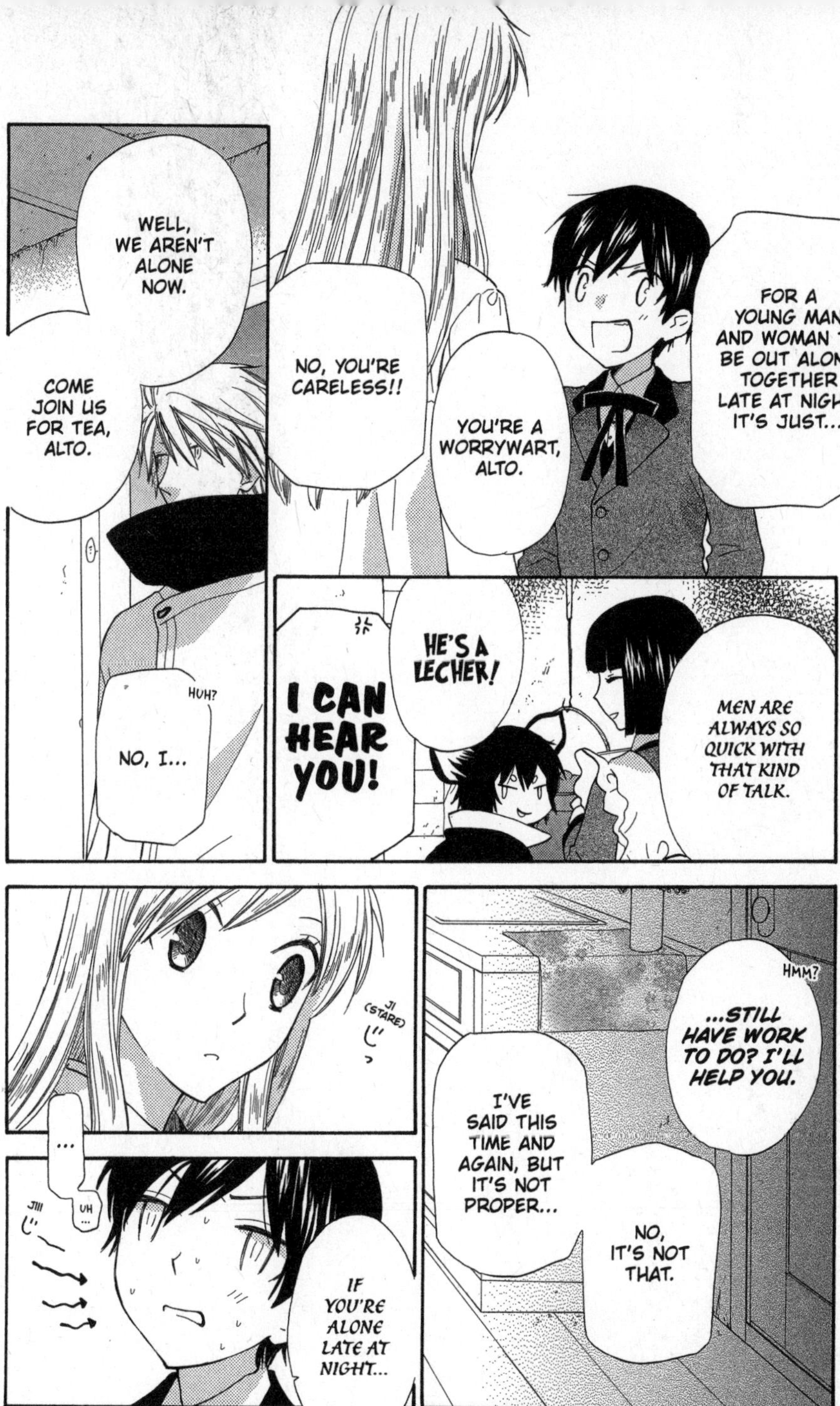
FOR A YOUNG MAN AND WOMAN TO BE OUT ALONE TOGETHER LATE AT NIGHT, IT'S JUST...
YOU'RE A WORRYWART, ALTO.
NO, YOU'RE CARELESS!!
MEN ARE ALWAYS SO QUICK WITH THAT KIND OF TALK.
HE'S A LECHER!
I CAN HEAR YOU!
WELL, WE AREN'T ALONE NOW.
COME JOIN US FOR TEA, ALTO.
HUH?
NO, I...
HMM?
...STILL HAVE WORK TO DO? I'LL HELP YOU.
I'VE SAID THIS TIME AND AGAIN, BUT IT'S NOT PROPER...
NO, IT'S NOT THAT.
JI (STARE)
...
UH...
JIII
IF YOU'RE ALONE LATE AT NIGHT...

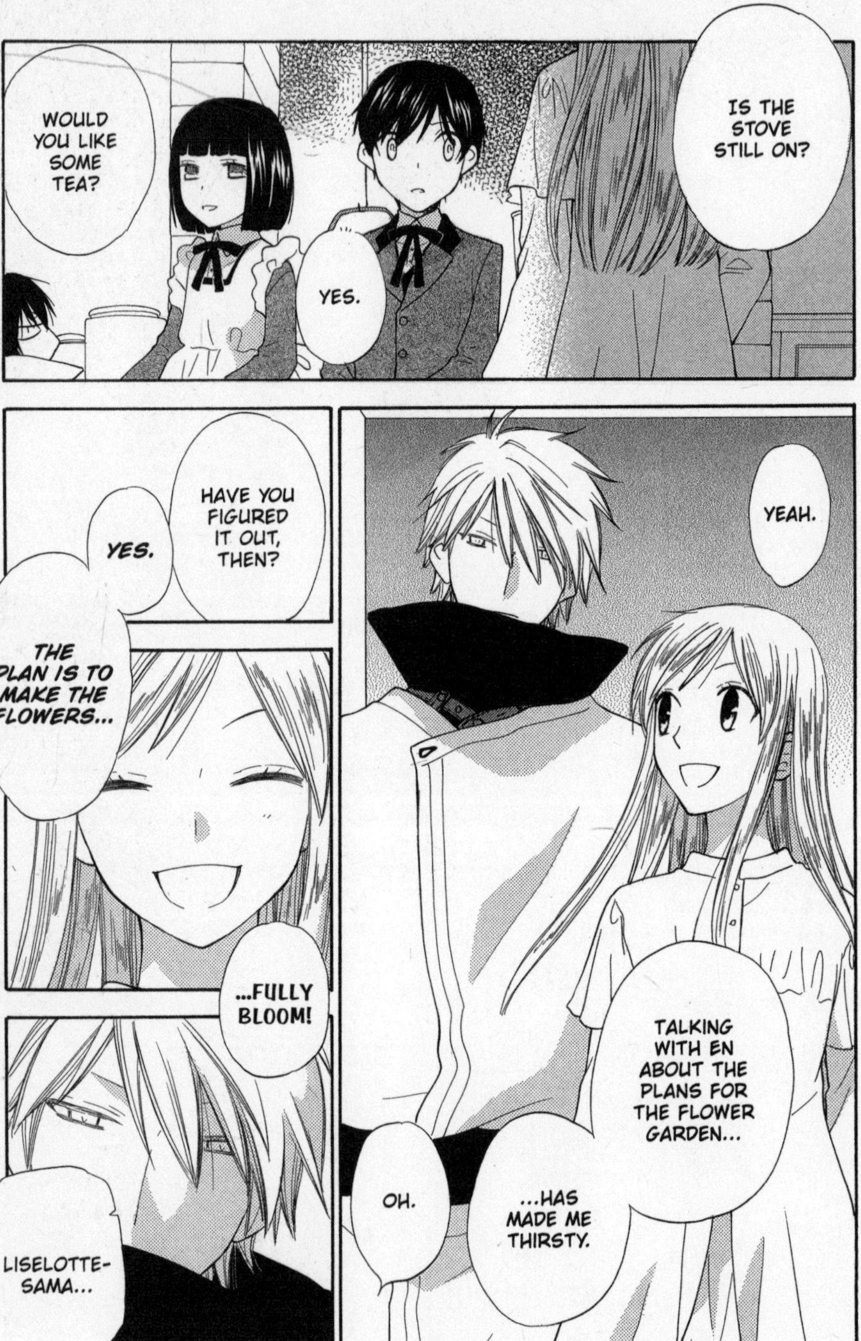
IS THE STOVE STILL ON?
YES.
WOULD YOU LIKE SOME TEA?
YEAH.
TALKING WITH EN ABOUT THE PLANS FOR THE FLOWER GARDEN...
...HAS MADE ME THIRSTY.
OH.
HAVE YOU FIGURED IT OUT, THEN?
YES.
THE PLAN IS TO MAKE THE FLOWERS...
...FULLY BLOOM!
LISELOTTE-SAMA...

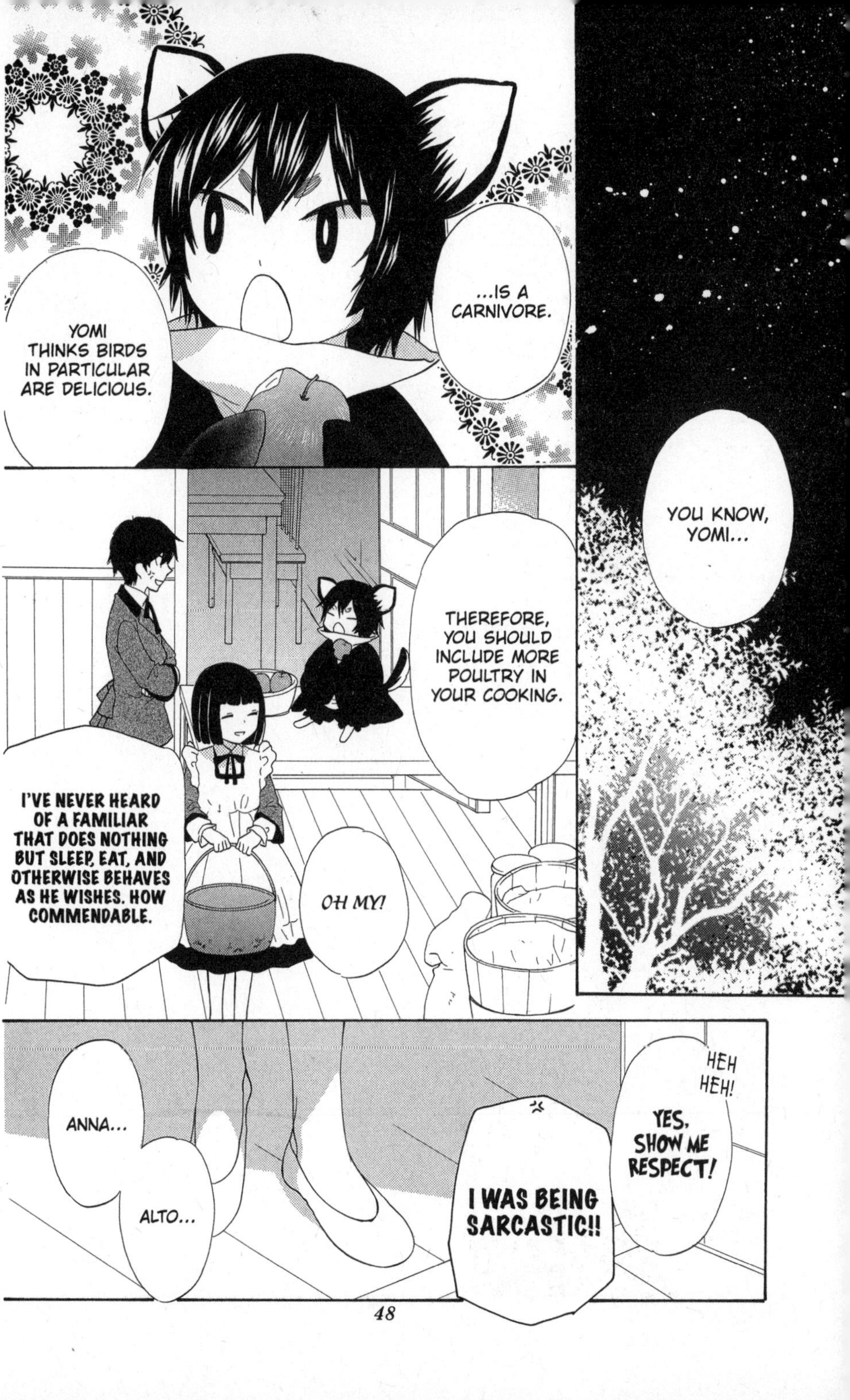
YOU KNOW, YOMI...
...IS A CARNIVORE.
YOMI THINKS BIRDS IN PARTICULAR ARE DELICIOUS.
THEREFORE, YOU SHOULD INCLUDE MORE POULTRY IN YOUR COOKING.
OH MY!
I'VE NEVER HEARD OF A FAMILIAR THAT DOES NOTHING BUT SLEEP, EAT, AND OTHERWISE BEHAVES AS HE WISHES. HOW COMMENDABLE.
HEH HEH!
YES, SHOW ME RESPECT!
I WAS BEING SARCASTIC!!
ANNA...
ALTO...

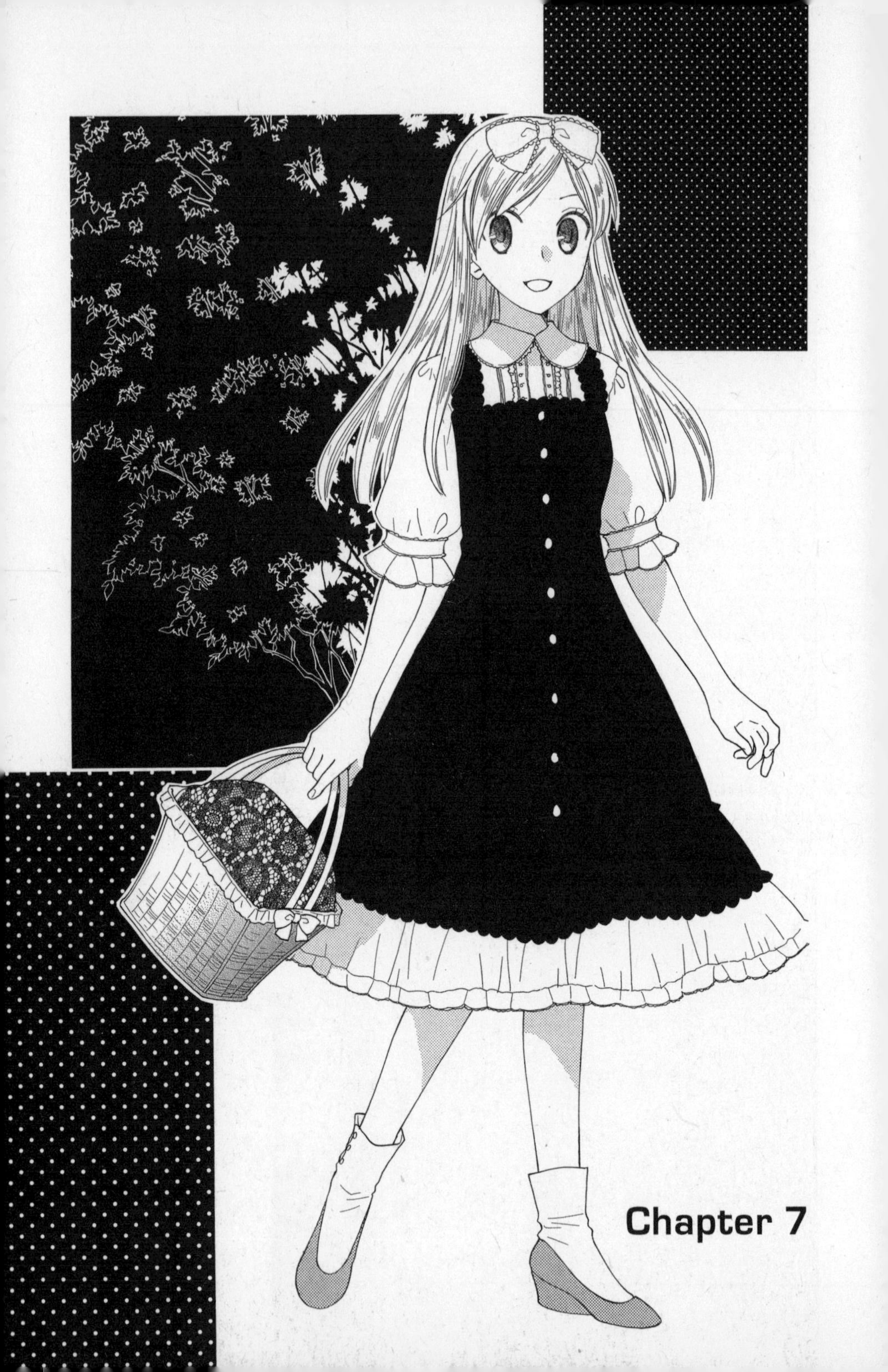
Chapter 7

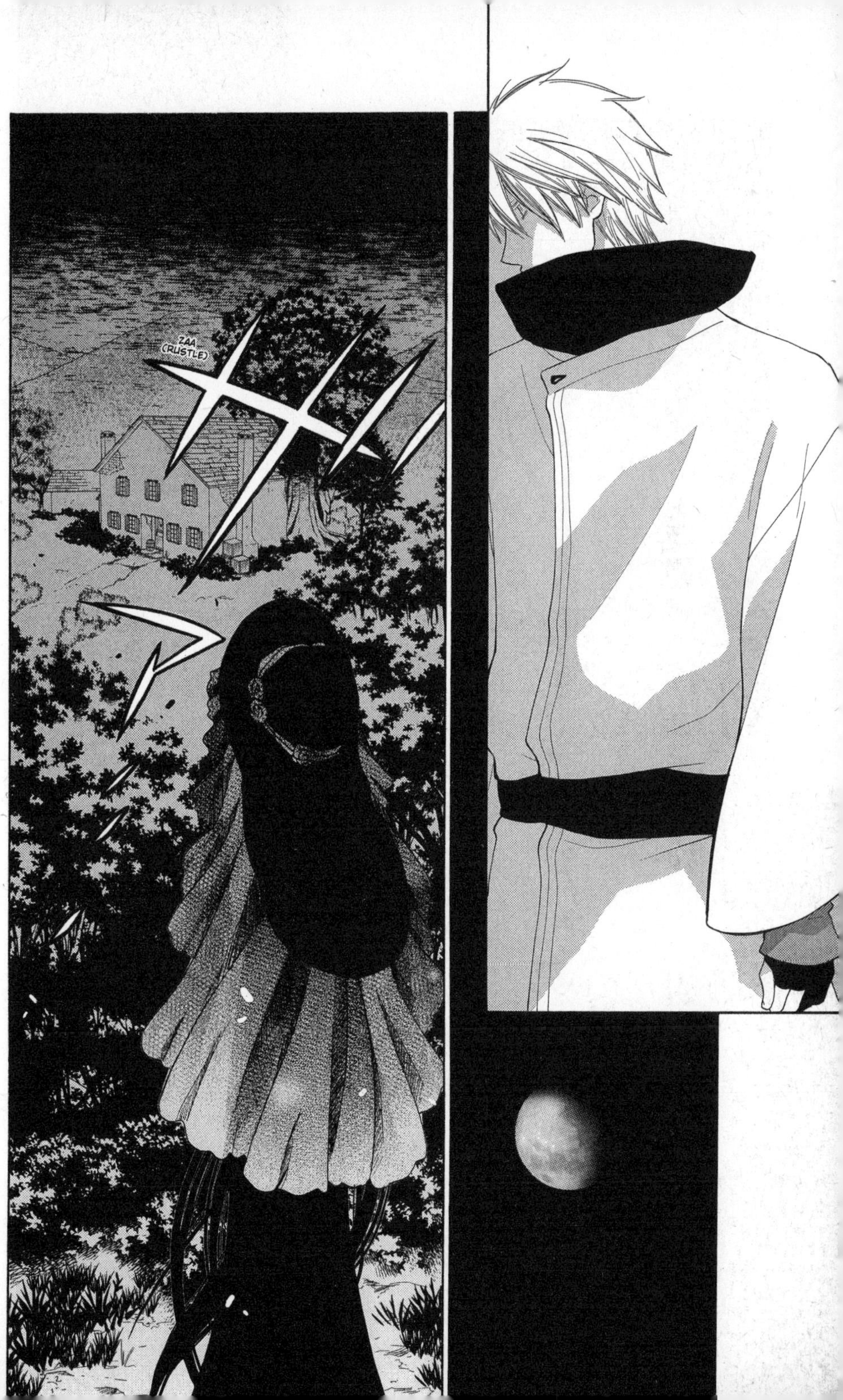
ZAA (RUSTLE)

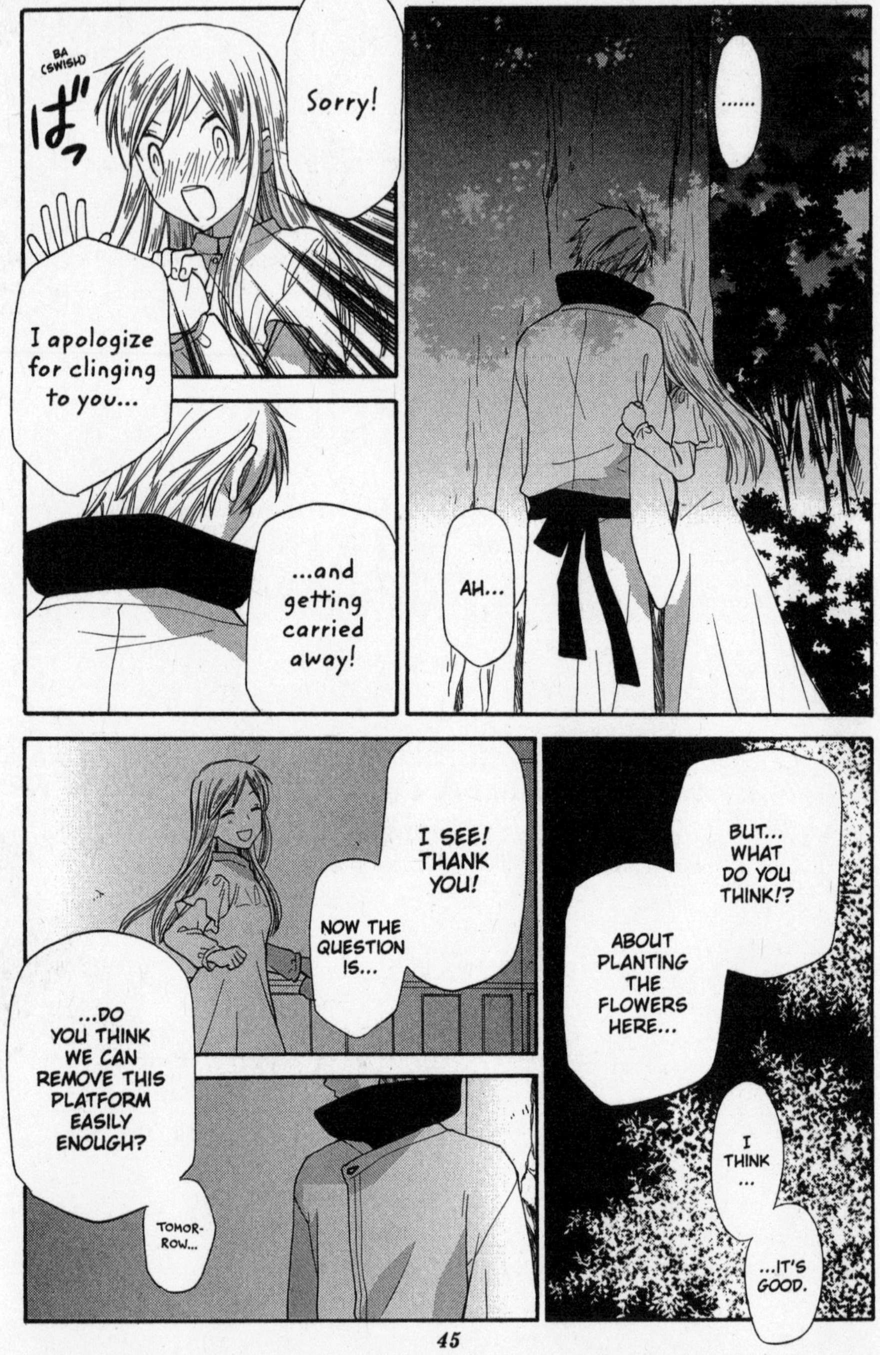
......
AH...
Sorry!
BA (SWISH)
ばっ
I apologize for clinging to you...
...and getting carried away!
BUT... WHAT DO YOU THINK!?
ABOUT PLANTING THE FLOWERS HERE...
I THINK...
...IT'S GOOD.
I SEE! THANK YOU!
NOW THE QUESTION IS...
...DO YOU THINK WE CAN REMOVE THIS PLATFORM EASILY ENOUGH?
TOMORROW...

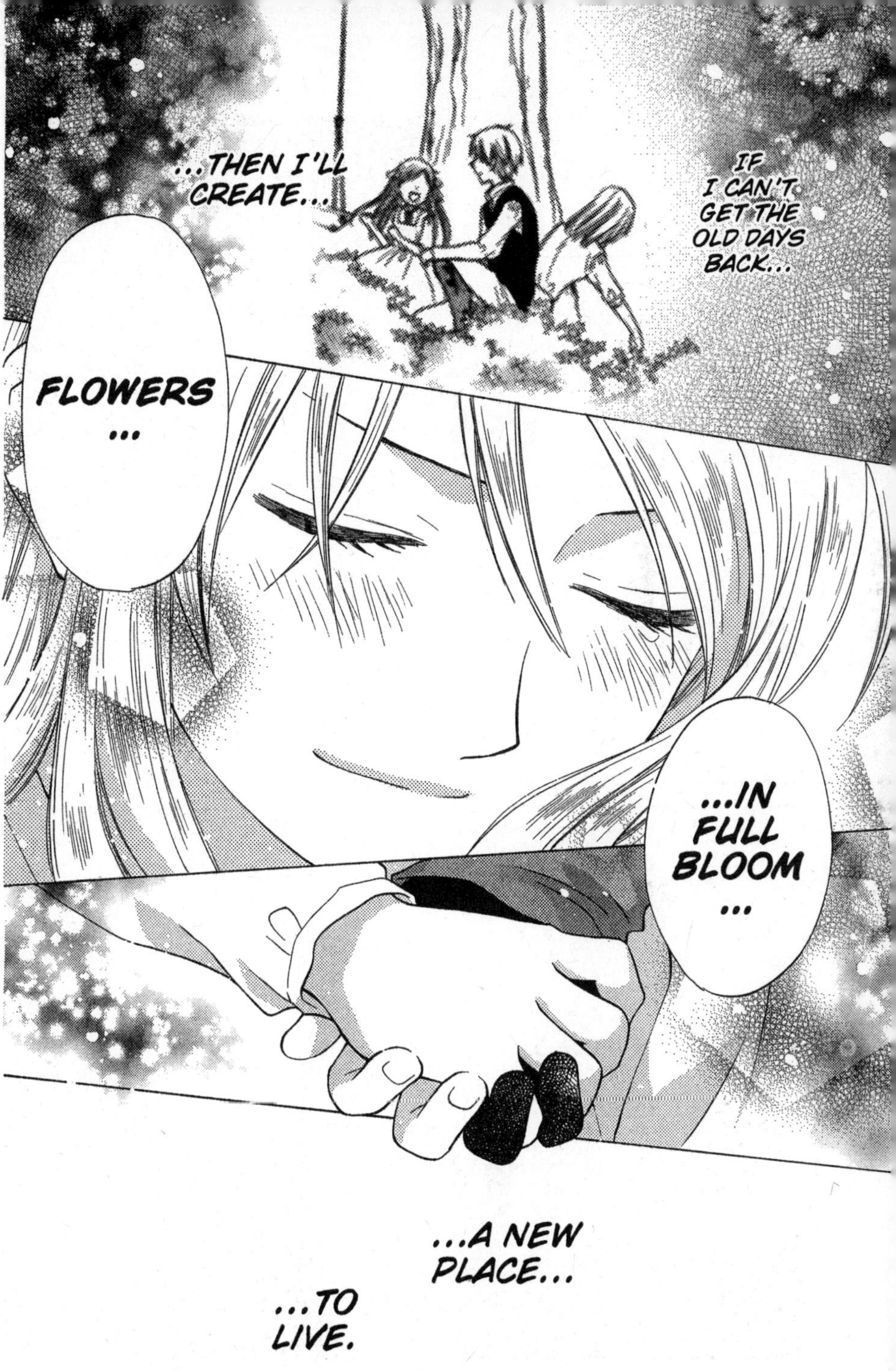
IF I CAN'T GET THE OLD DAYS BACK...
...THEN I'LL CREATE...
FLOWERS ...
...IN FULL BLOOM ...
...A NEW PLACE...
...TO LIVE.

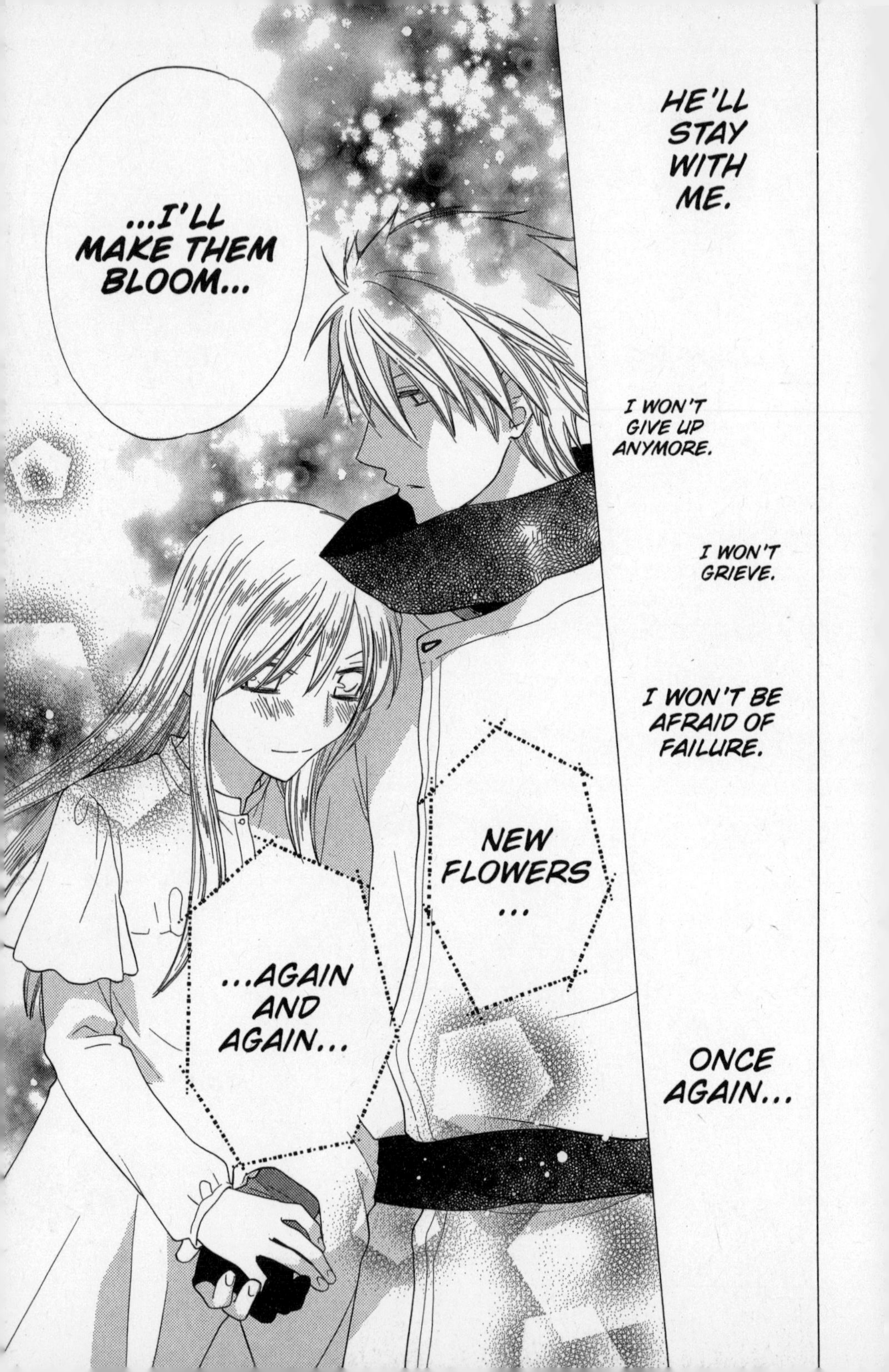
HE'LL STAY WITH ME.
I WON'T GIVE UP ANYMORE.
I WON'T GRIEVE.
I WON'T BE AFRAID OF FAILURE.
ONCE AGAIN...
NEW FLOWERS ...
...AGAIN AND AGAIN...
...I'LL MAKE THEM BLOOM...

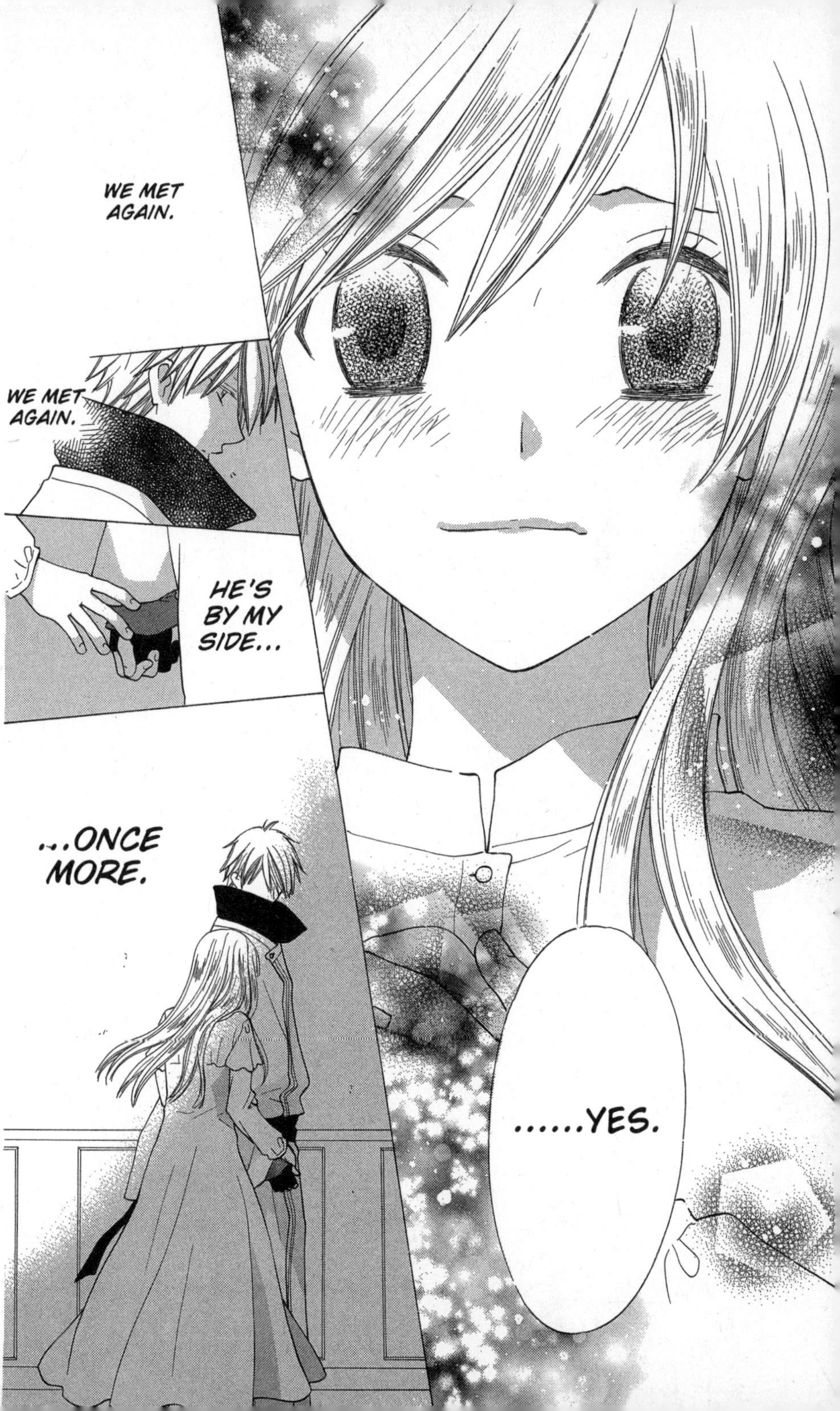
......YES.
WE MET AGAIN.
WE MET AGAIN.
HE'S BY MY SIDE...
...ONCE MORE.

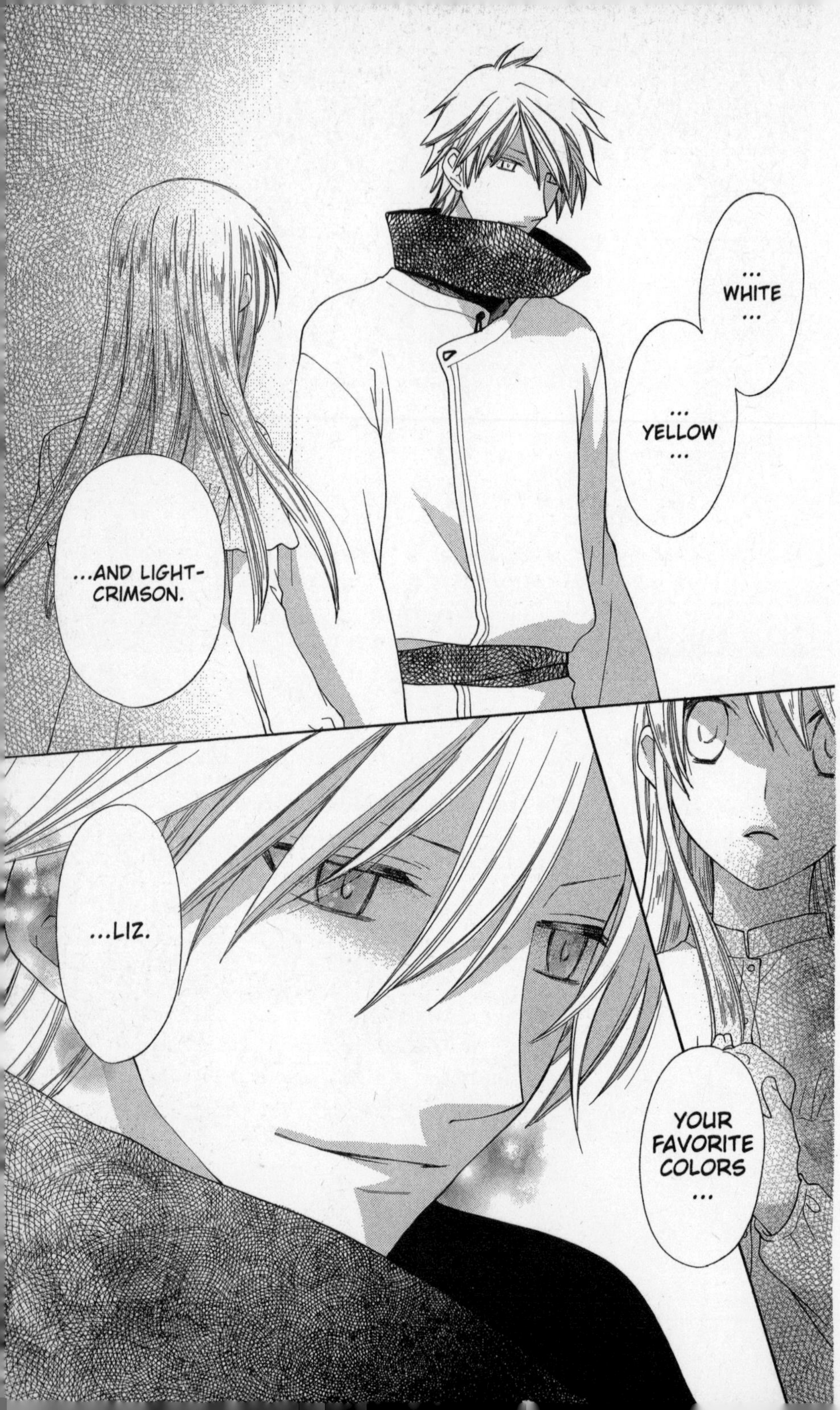
... WHITE ...
... YELLOW ...
...AND LIGHT-CRIMSON.
YOUR FAVORITE COLORS ...
...LIZ.

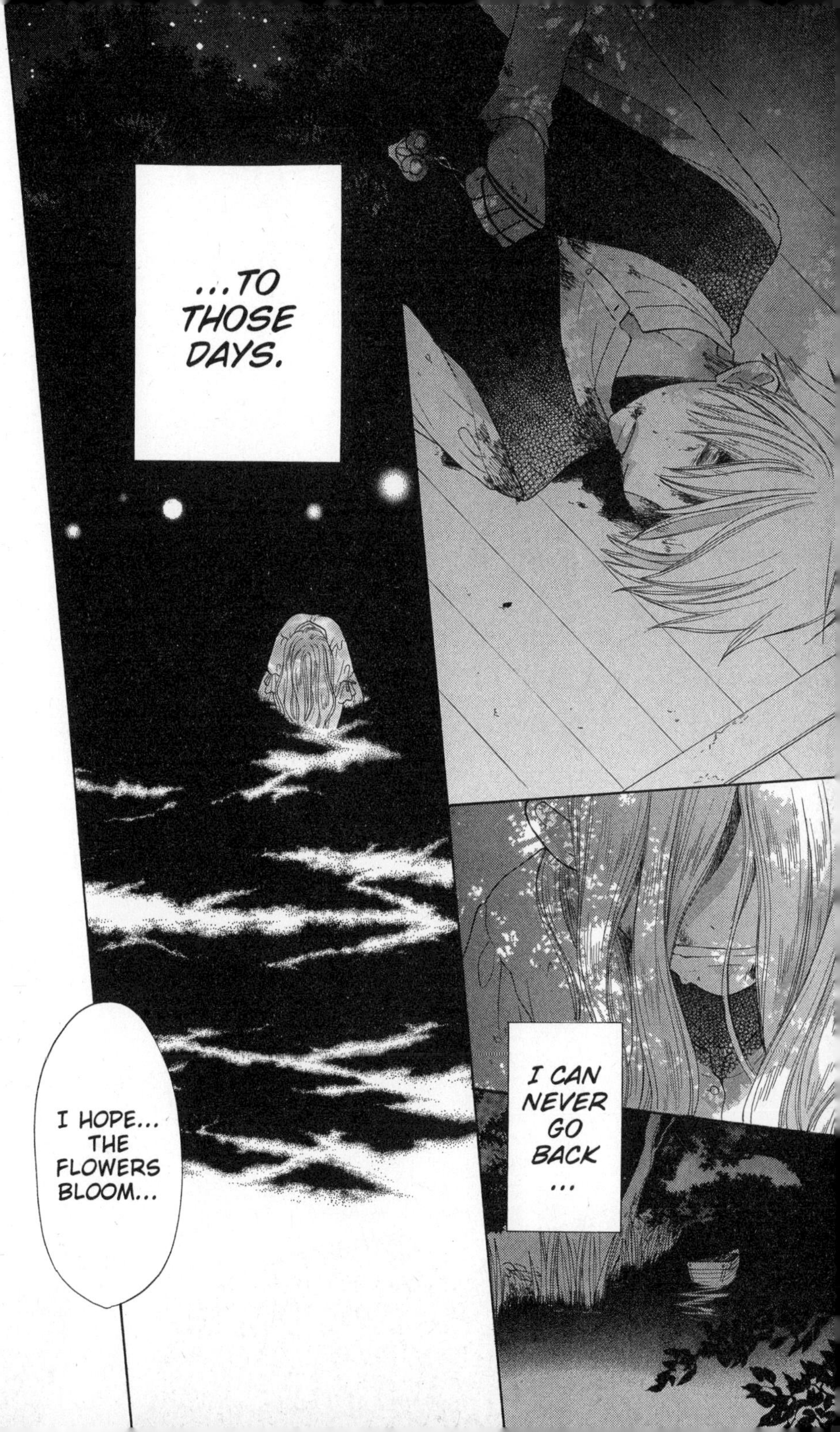
I CAN NEVER GO BACK...
...TO THOSE DAYS.
I HOPE... THE FLOWERS BLOOM...

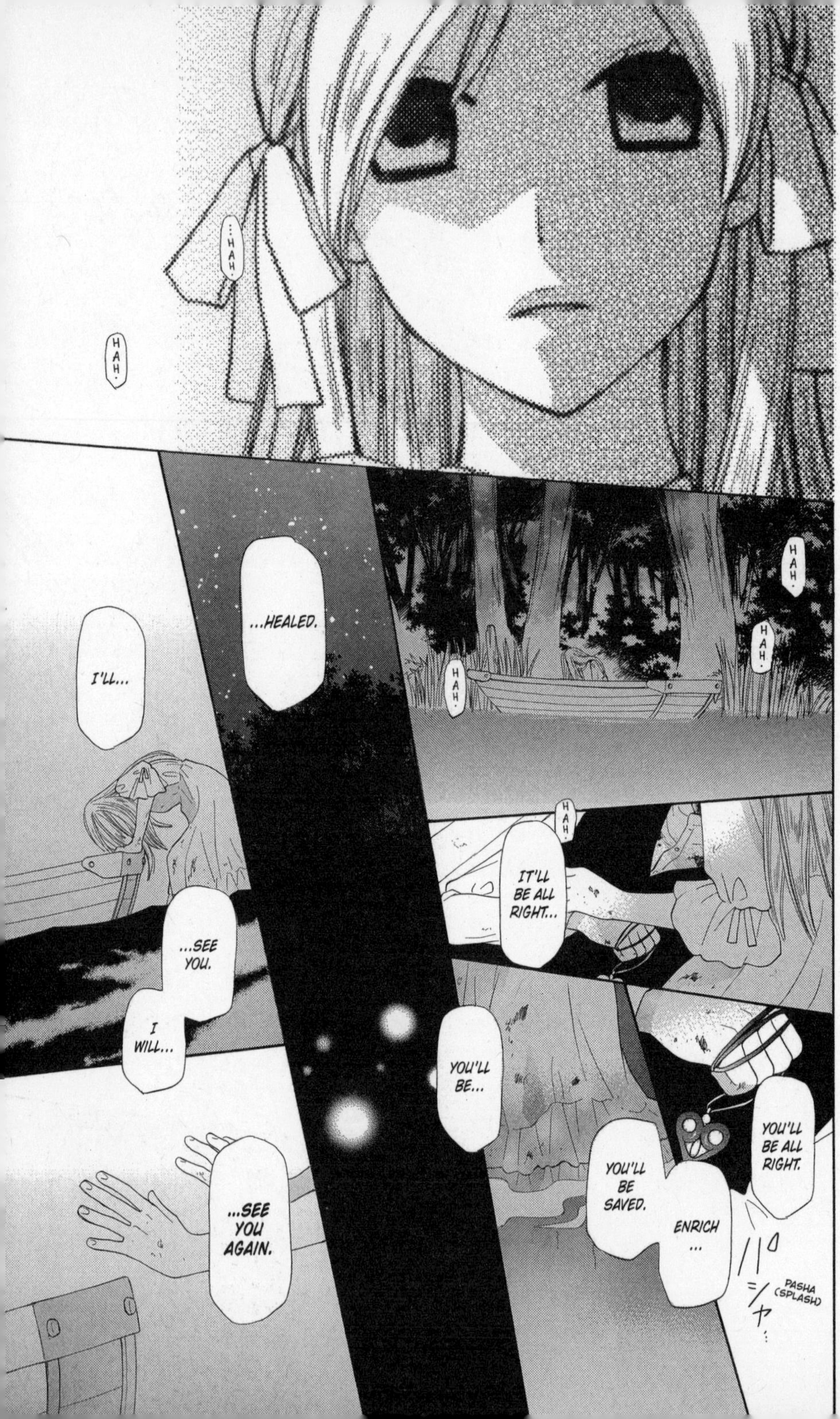

...HAH.
HAH.
HAH.
HAH.
HAH.
HAH.
IT'LL BE ALL RIGHT...
YOU'LL BE ALL RIGHT.
YOU'LL BE SAVED.
ENRICH...
PASHA (SPLASH)
YOU'LL BE...
...HEALED.
I'LL...
...SEE YOU.
I WILL...
...SEE YOU AGAIN.

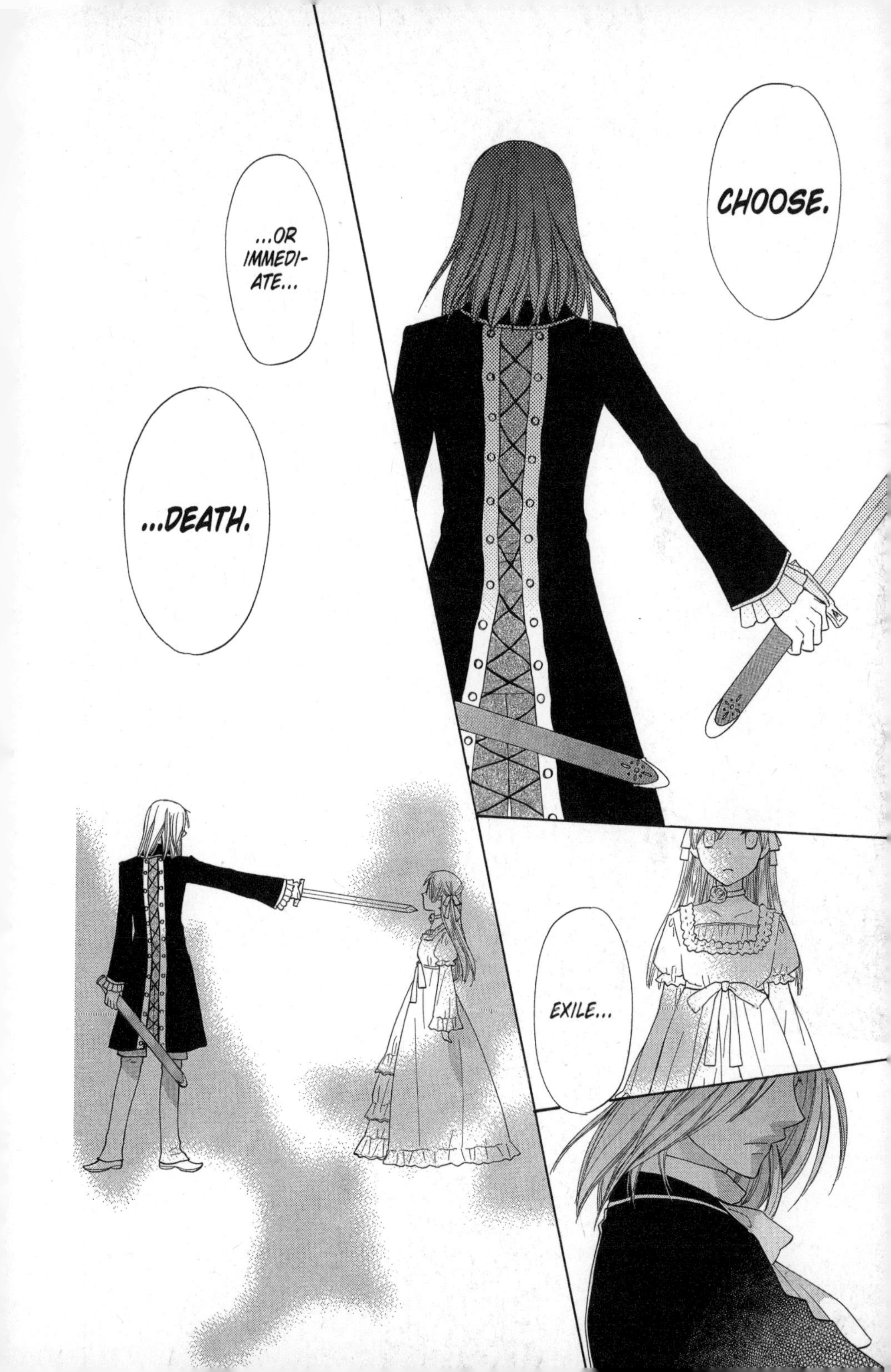

CHOOSE.
EXILE...
...OR IMMEDI-ATE...
...DEATH.

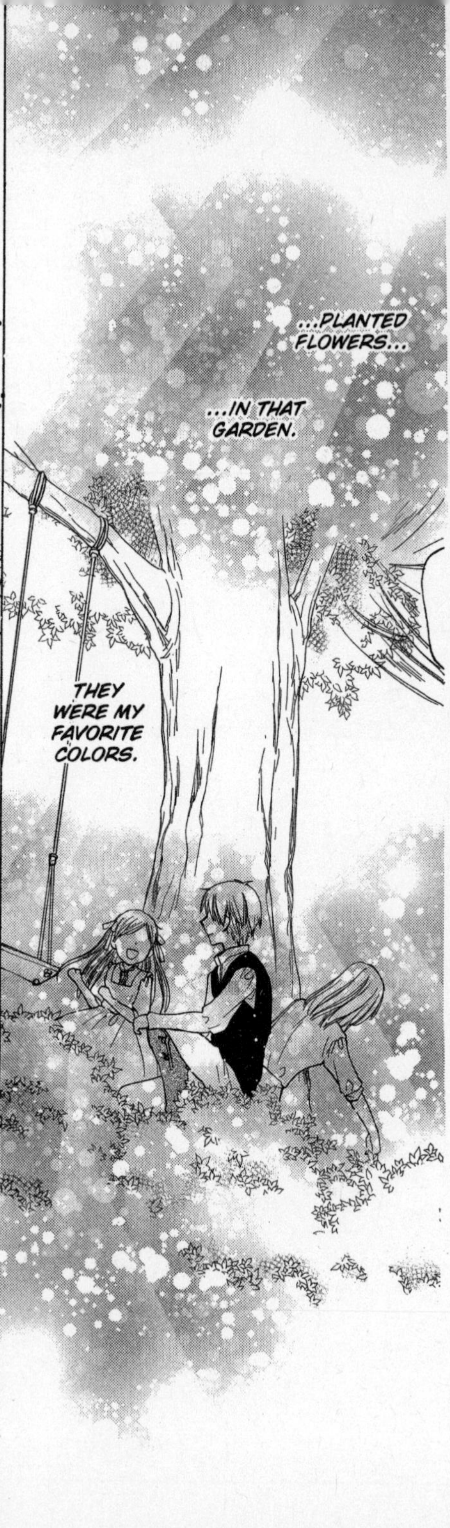
...PLANTED FLOWERS...
...IN THAT GARDEN.
THEY WERE MY FAVORITE COLORS.
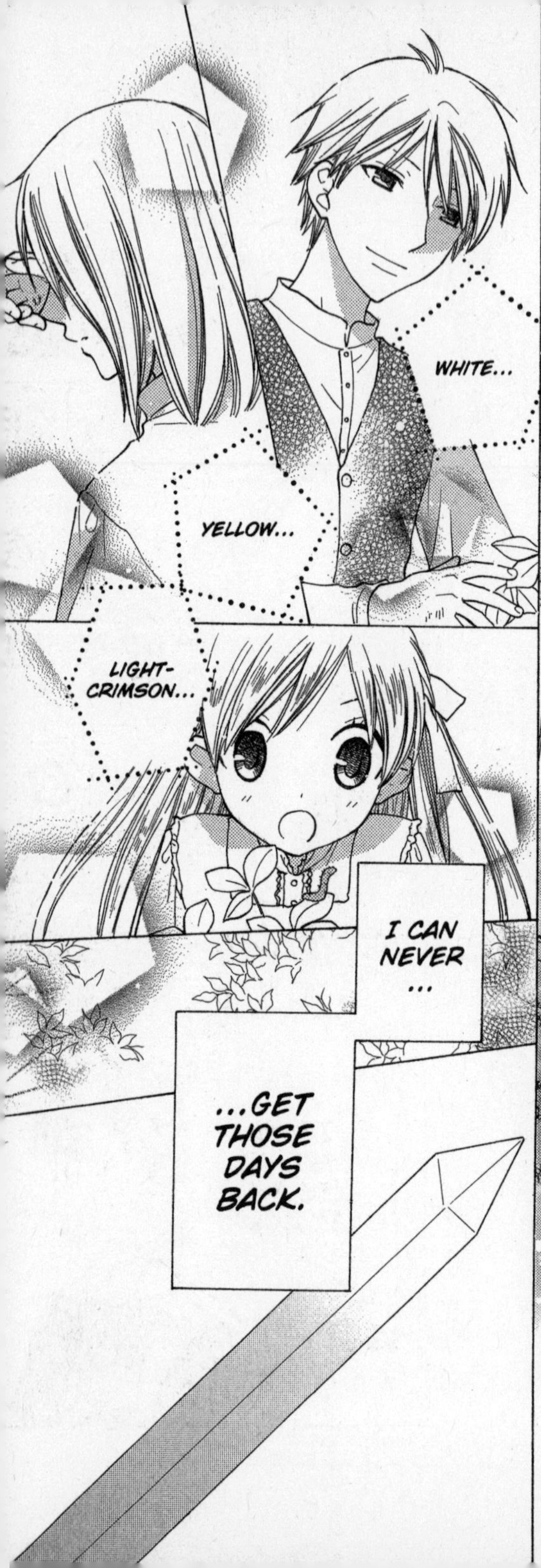
WHITE...
YELLOW...
LIGHT-CRIMSON...
I CAN NEVER ...
...GET THOSE DAYS BACK.

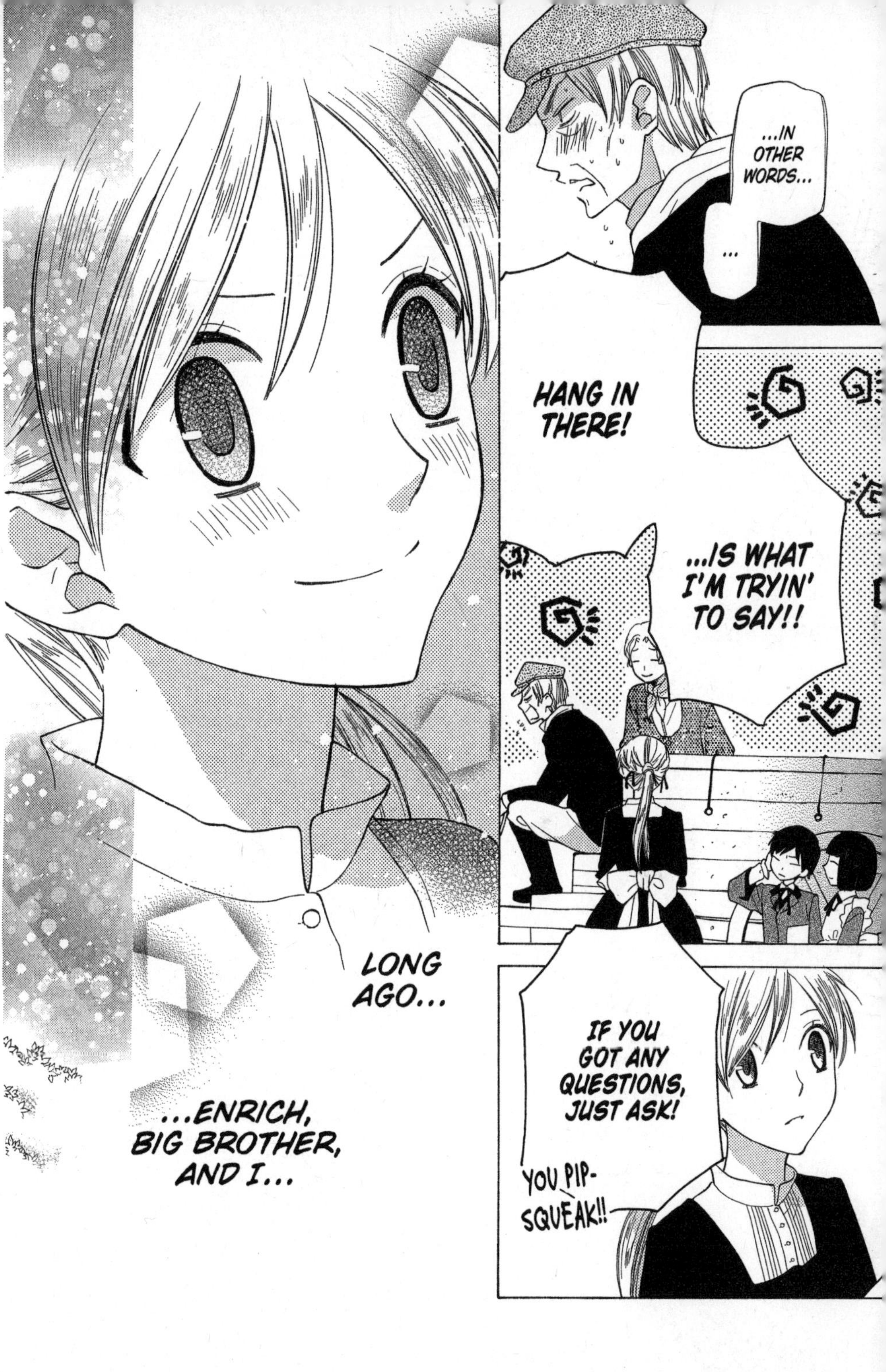
...IN OTHER WORDS...
...
HANG IN THERE!
...IS WHAT I'M TRYIN' TO SAY!!
IF YOU GOT ANY QUESTIONS, JUST ASK!
YOU PIP-SQUEAK!!
LONG AGO...
...ENRICH, BIG BROTHER, AND I...

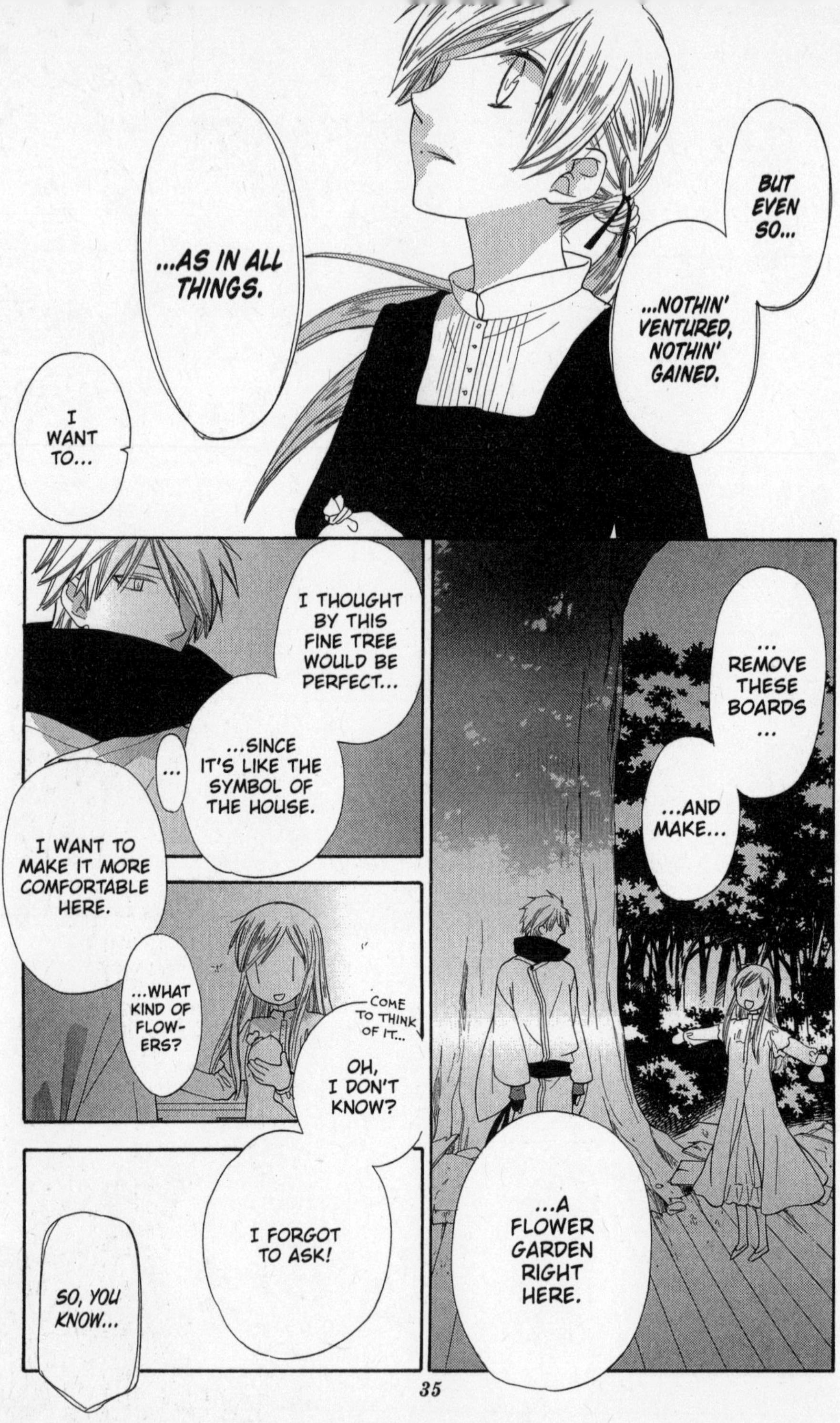
BUT EVEN SO...
...NOTHIN' VENTURED, NOTHIN' GAINED.
...AS IN ALL THINGS.
I WANT TO...
... REMOVE THESE BOARDS ...
...AND MAKE...
...A FLOWER GARDEN RIGHT HERE.
I THOUGHT BY THIS FINE TREE WOULD BE PERFECT...
...SINCE IT'S LIKE THE SYMBOL OF THE HOUSE.
...
I WANT TO MAKE IT MORE COMFORTABLE HERE.
...WHAT KIND OF FLOWERS?
COME TO THINK OF IT...
OH, I DON'T KNOW?
I FORGOT TO ASK!
SO, YOU KNOW...

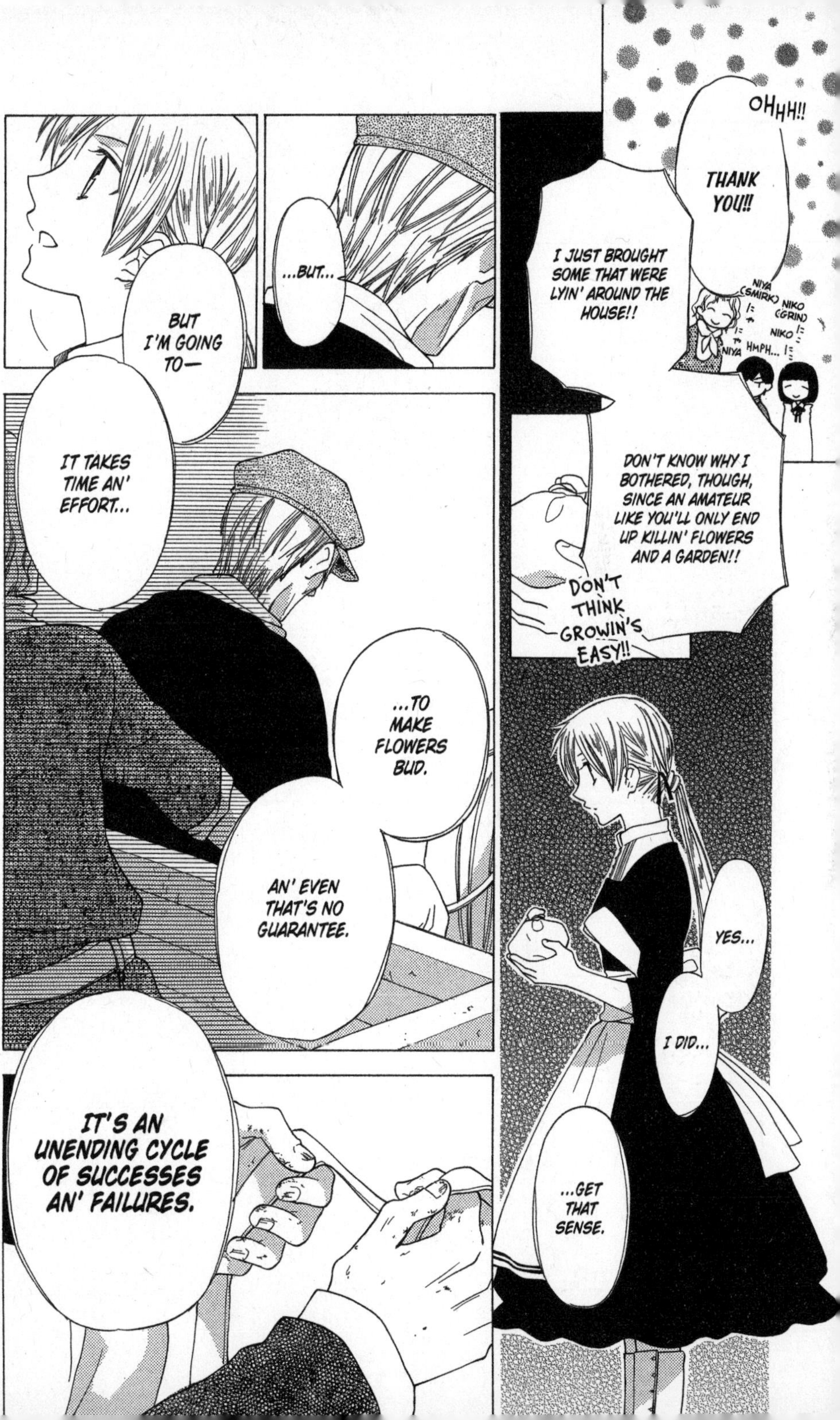
OHHH!!
THANK YOU!!
I JUST BROUGHT SOME THAT WERE LYIN' AROUND THE HOUSE!!
NIYA (SMIRK)
NIKO (GRIN)
NIKO
NIYA
HMPH...
DON'T KNOW WHY I BOTHERED, THOUGH, SINCE AN AMATEUR LIKE YOU'LL ONLY END UP KILLIN' FLOWERS AND A GARDEN!!
DON'T THINK GROWIN'S EASY!!
YES...
I DID...
...GET THAT SENSE.
...BUT...
BUT I'M GOING TO—
IT TAKES TIME AN' EFFORT...
...TO MAKE FLOWERS BUD.
AN' EVEN THAT'S NO GUARANTEE.
IT'S AN UNENDING CYCLE OF SUCCESSES AN' FAILURES.

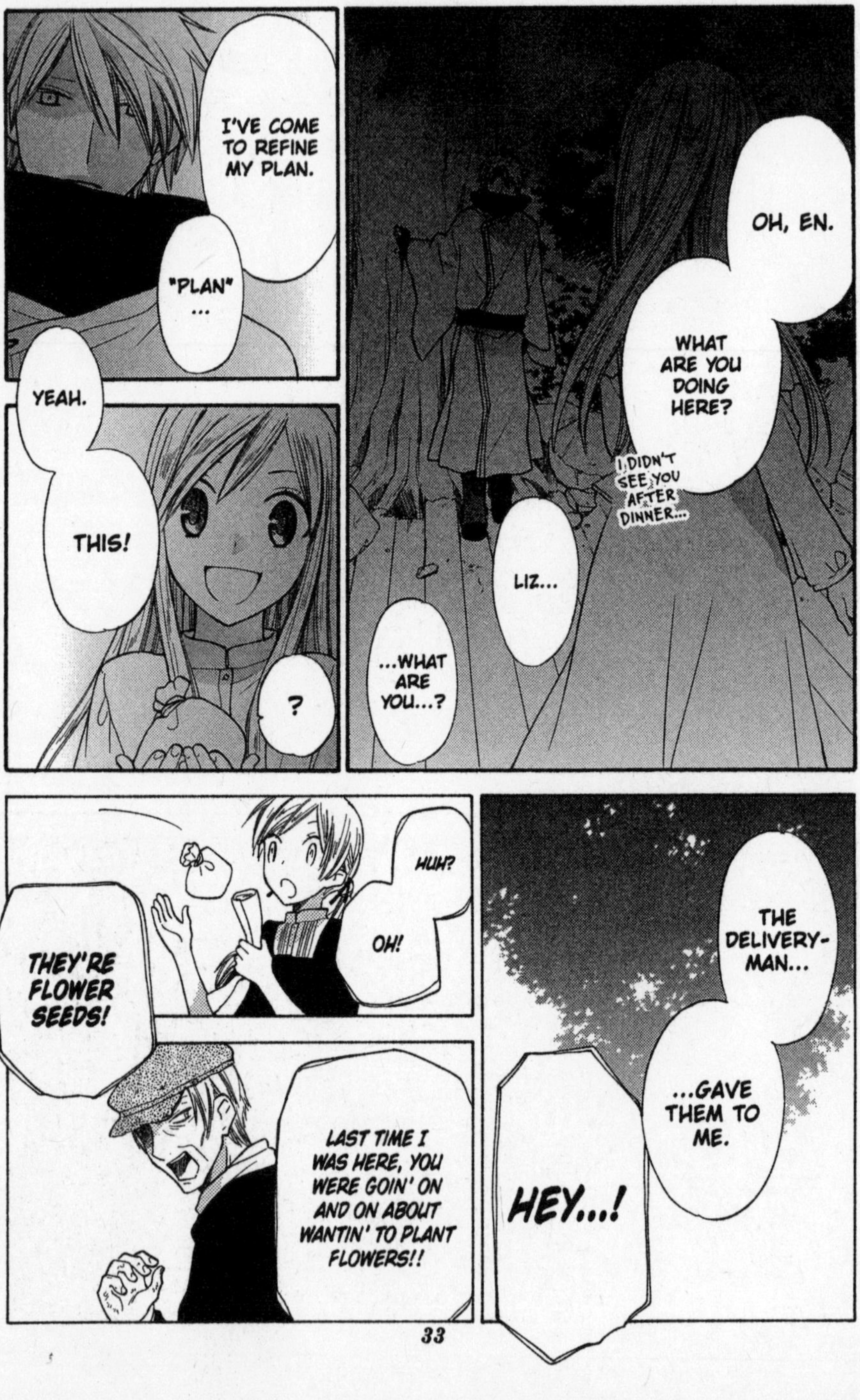
OH, EN.
WHAT ARE YOU DOING HERE?
I DIDN'T SEE YOU AFTER DINNER...
LIZ...
...WHAT ARE YOU...?
I'VE COME TO REFINE MY PLAN.
"PLAN"...
YEAH.
THIS!
?
THE DELIVERY-MAN...
...GAVE THEM TO ME.
HEY...!
HUH?
OH!
THEY'RE FLOWER SEEDS!
LAST TIME I WAS HERE, YOU WERE GOIN' ON AND ON ABOUT WANTIN' TO PLANT FLOWERS!!

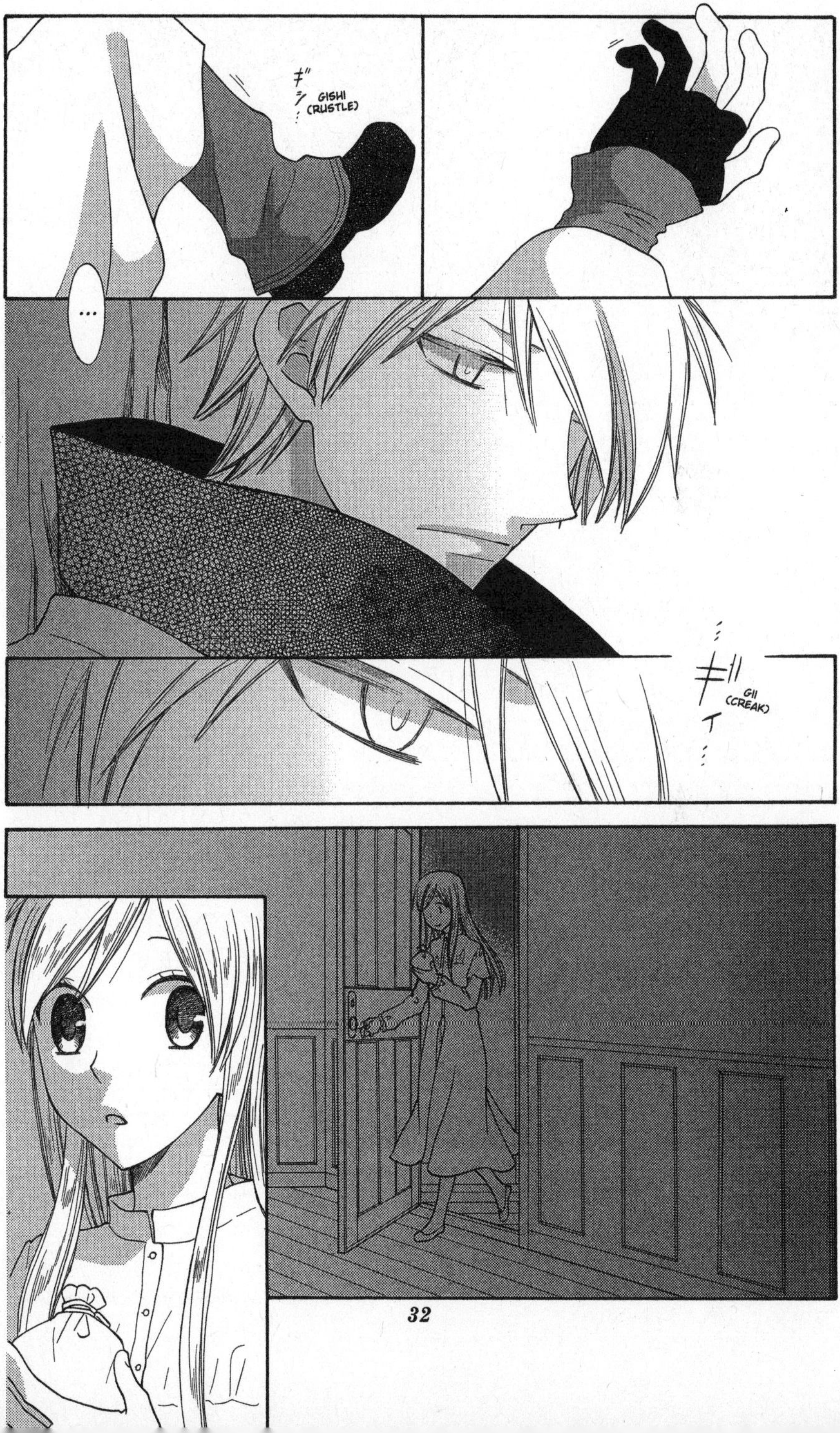
ギシ
GISHI (RUSTLE)
...
ギイ
GII (CREAK)

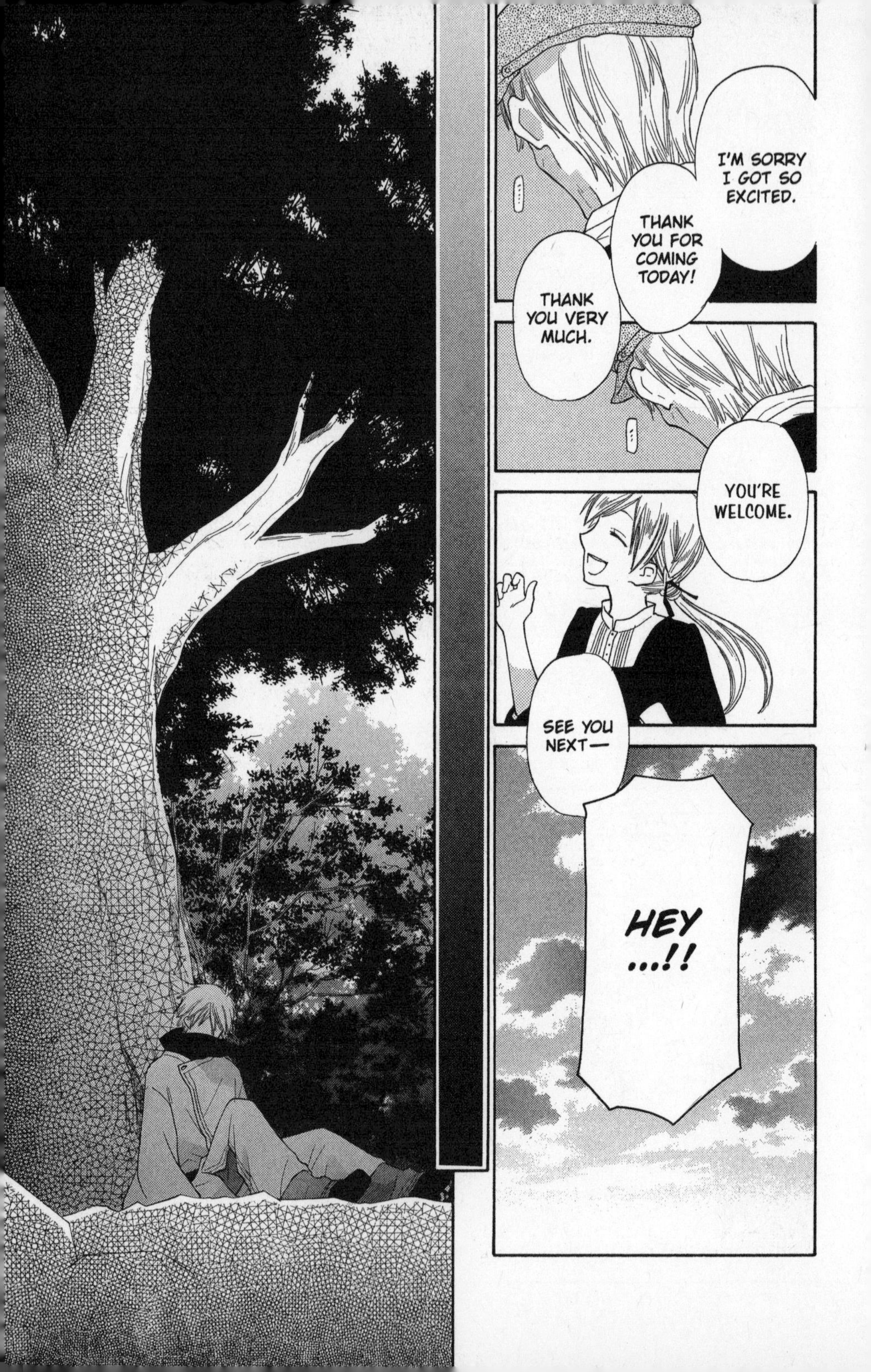
I'M SORRY I GOT SO EXCITED.
THANK YOU FOR COMING TODAY!
THANK YOU VERY MUCH.
YOU'RE WELCOME.
SEE YOU NEXT—
HEY ...!!

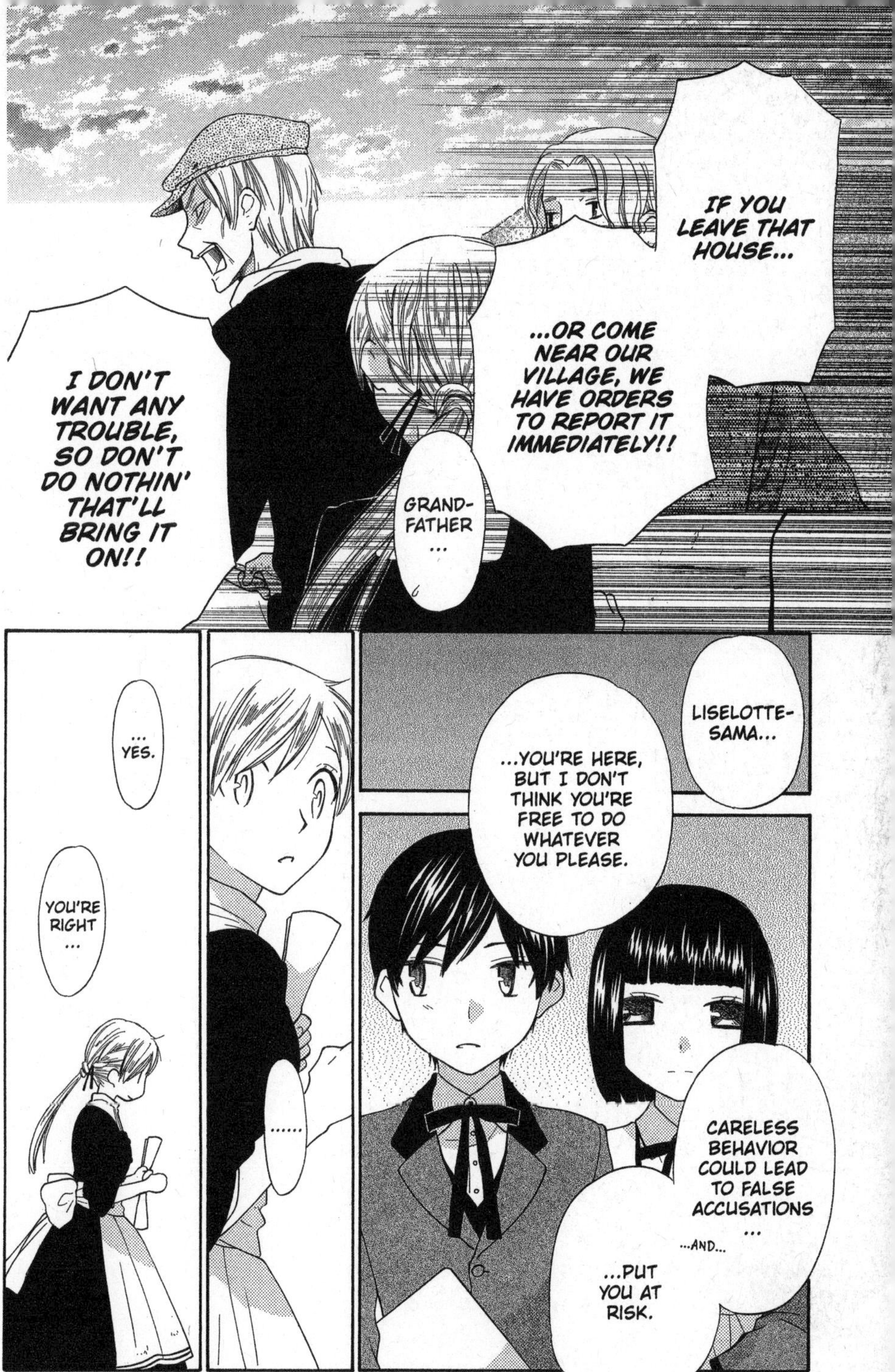
IF YOU LEAVE THAT HOUSE...
...OR COME NEAR OUR VILLAGE, WE HAVE ORDERS TO REPORT IT IMMEDIATELY!!
I DON'T WANT ANY TROUBLE, SO DON'T DO NOTHIN' THAT'LL BRING IT ON!!
GRAND-FATHER...
LISELOTTE-SAMA...
...YOU'RE HERE, BUT I DON'T THINK YOU'RE FREE TO DO WHATEVER YOU PLEASE.
CARELESS BEHAVIOR COULD LEAD TO FALSE ACCUSATIONS...
...AND...
...PUT YOU AT RISK.
......
...YES.
YOU'RE RIGHT...

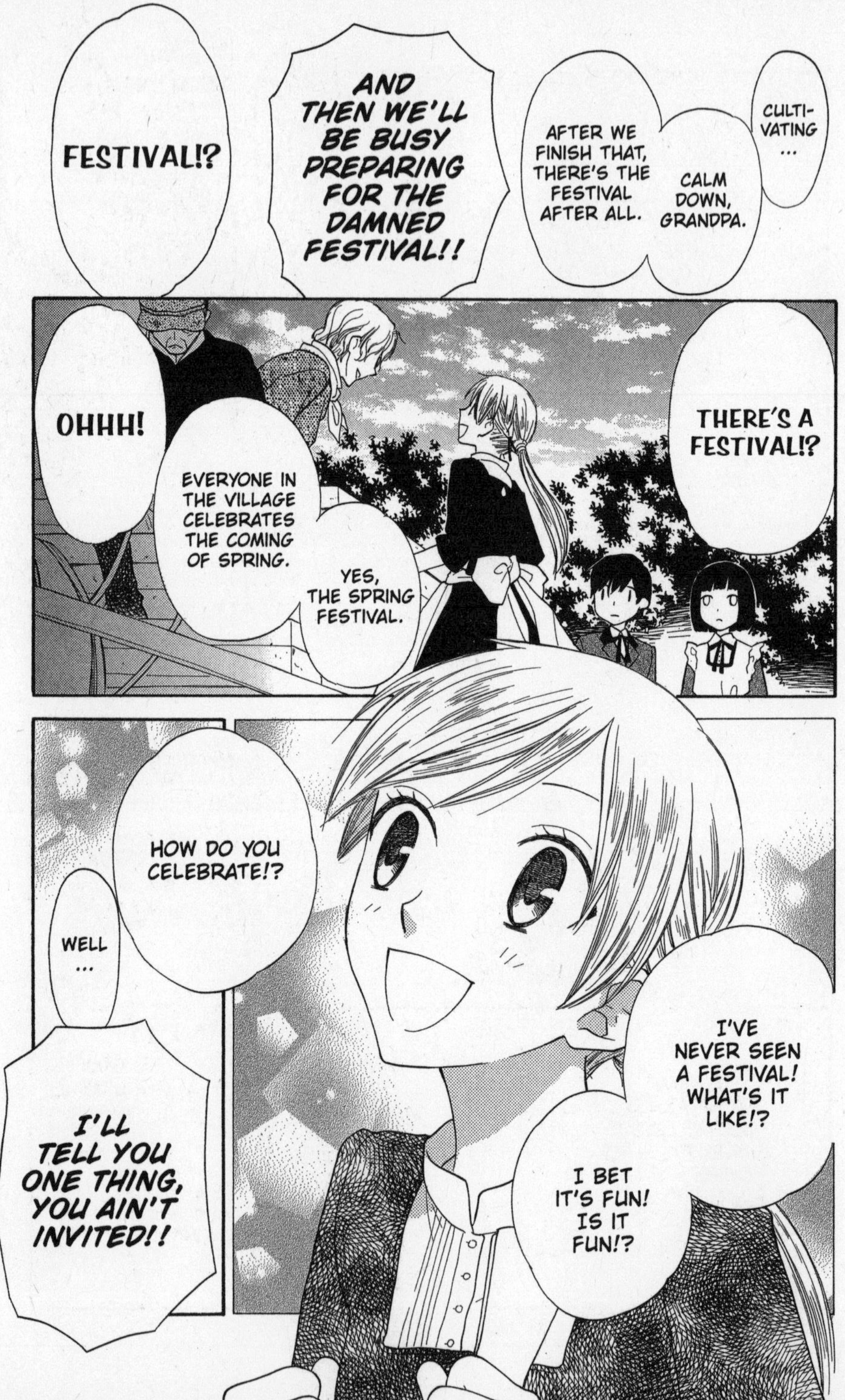
CULTI-VATING ...
CALM DOWN, GRANDPA.
AFTER WE FINISH THAT, THERE'S THE FESTIVAL AFTER ALL.
AND THEN WE'LL BE BUSY PREPARING FOR THE DAMNED FESTIVAL!!
FESTIVAL!?
THERE'S A FESTIVAL!?
YES, THE SPRING FESTIVAL.
EVERYONE IN THE VILLAGE CELEBRATES THE COMING OF SPRING.
OHHH!
I'VE NEVER SEEN A FESTIVAL! WHAT'S IT LIKE!?
I BET IT'S FUN! IS IT FUN!?
HOW DO YOU CELEBRATE!?
WELL ...
I'LL TELL YOU ONE THING, YOU AIN'T INVITED!!

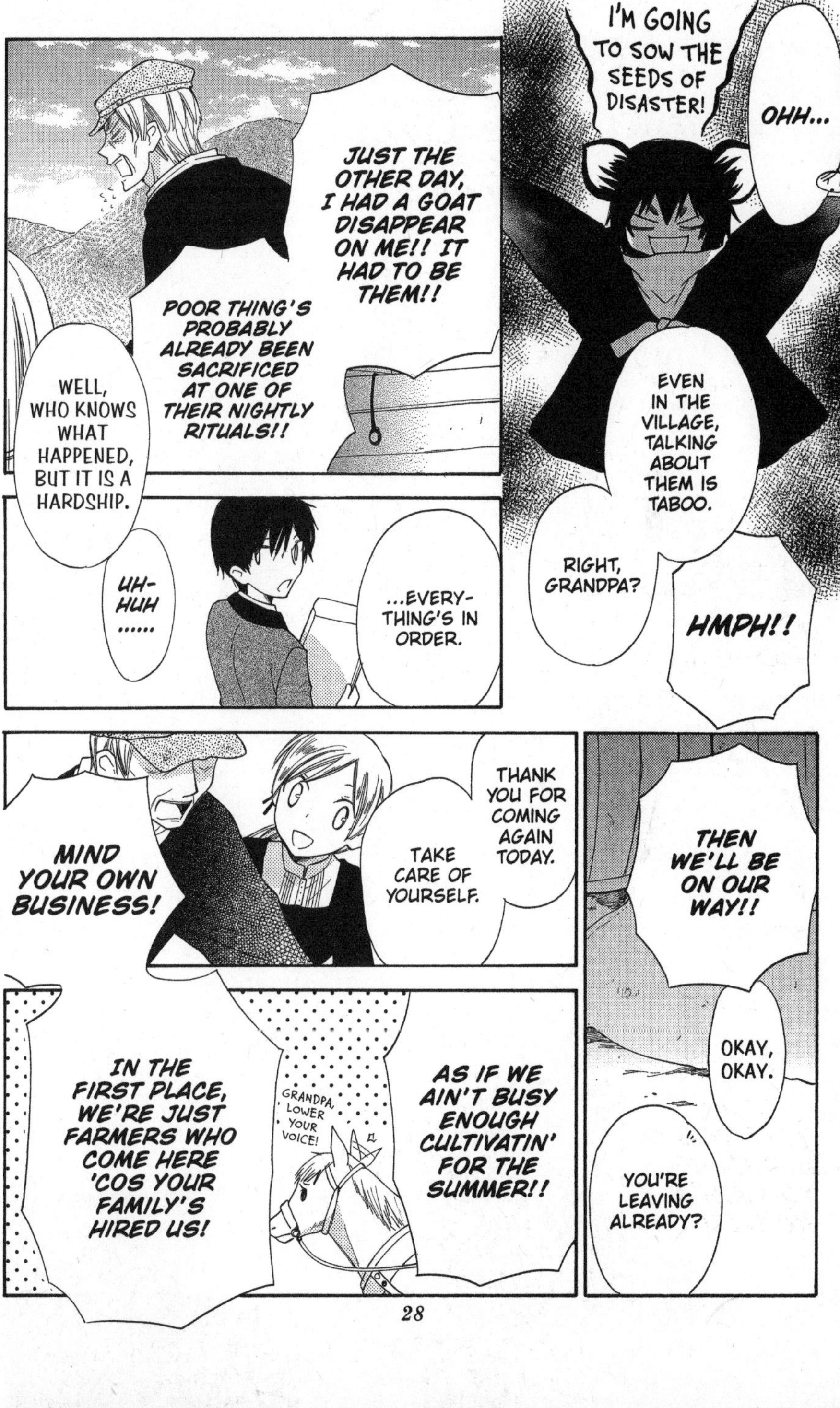
I'M GOING TO SOW THE SEEDS OF DISASTER!
OHH...
EVEN IN THE VILLAGE, TALKING ABOUT THEM IS TABOO.
RIGHT, GRANDPA?
HMPH!!
JUST THE OTHER DAY, I HAD A GOAT DISAPPEAR ON ME!! IT HAD TO BE THEM!!
POOR THING'S PROBABLY ALREADY BEEN SACRIFICED AT ONE OF THEIR NIGHTLY RITUALS!!
WELL, WHO KNOWS WHAT HAPPENED, BUT IT IS A HARDSHIP.
...EVERY-THING'S IN ORDER.
UH-HUH......
THEN WE'LL BE ON OUR WAY!!
OKAY, OKAY.
YOU'RE LEAVING ALREADY?
THANK YOU FOR COMING AGAIN TODAY.
TAKE CARE OF YOURSELF.
MIND YOUR OWN BUSINESS!
AS IF WE AIN'T BUSY ENOUGH CULTIVATIN' FOR THE SUMMER!!
GRANDPA, LOWER YOUR VOICE!
IN THE FIRST PLACE, WE'RE JUST FARMERS WHO COME HERE 'COS YOUR FAMILY'S HIRED US!

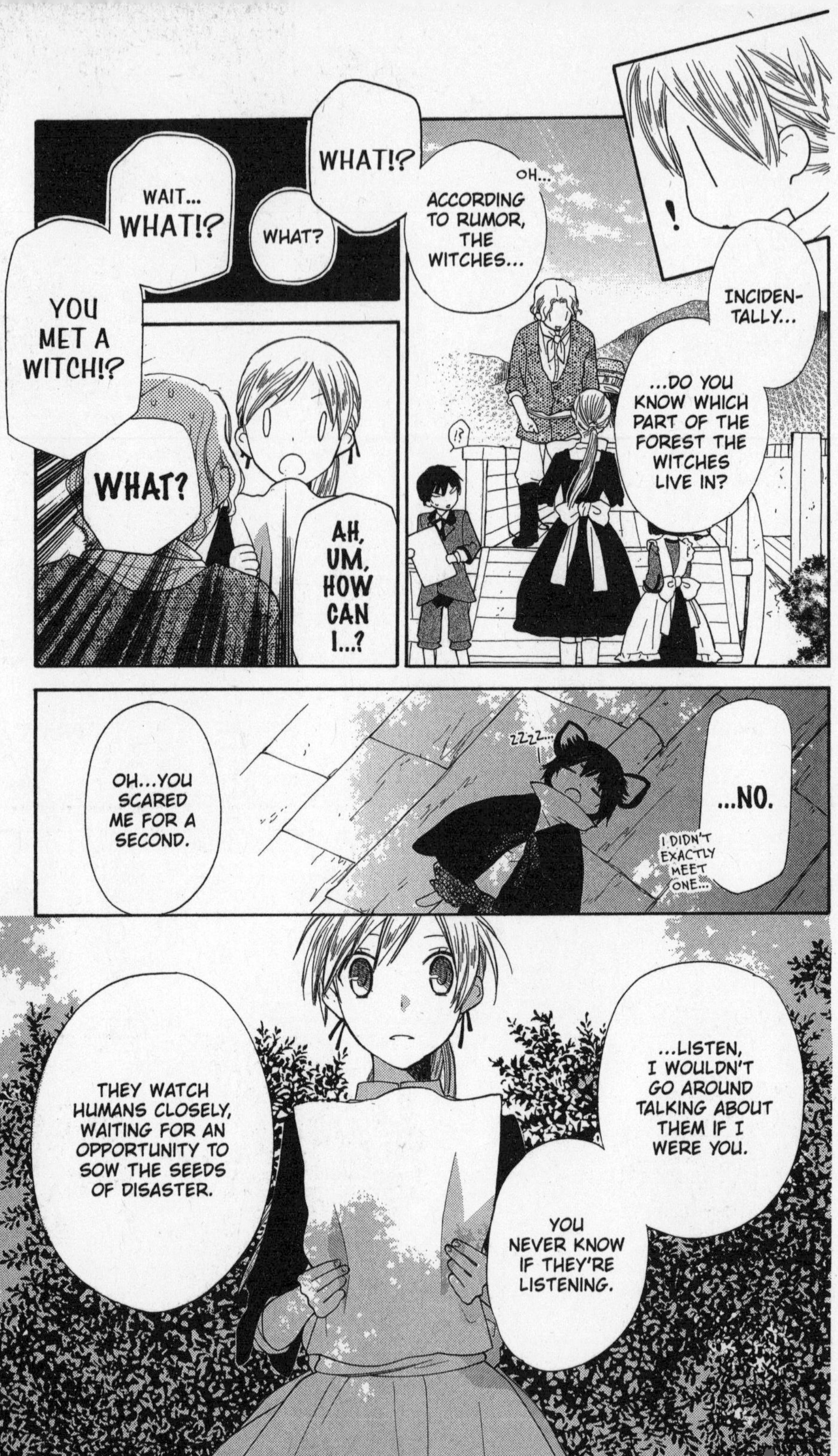
!
INCIDENTALLY...
...DO YOU KNOW WHICH PART OF THE FOREST THE WITCHES LIVE IN?
!?
OH...
ACCORDING TO RUMOR, THE WITCHES...
WHAT!?
WAIT... WHAT!?
WHAT?
YOU MET A WITCH!?
AH, UM, HOW CAN I...?
WHAT?
...NO.
I DIDN'T EXACTLY MEET ONE...
ZZZZ...
OH...YOU SCARED ME FOR A SECOND.
...LISTEN, I WOULDN'T GO AROUND TALKING ABOUT THEM IF I WERE YOU.
YOU NEVER KNOW IF THEY'RE LISTENING.
THEY WATCH HUMANS CLOSELY, WAITING FOR AN OPPORTUNITY TO SOW THE SEEDS OF DISASTER.

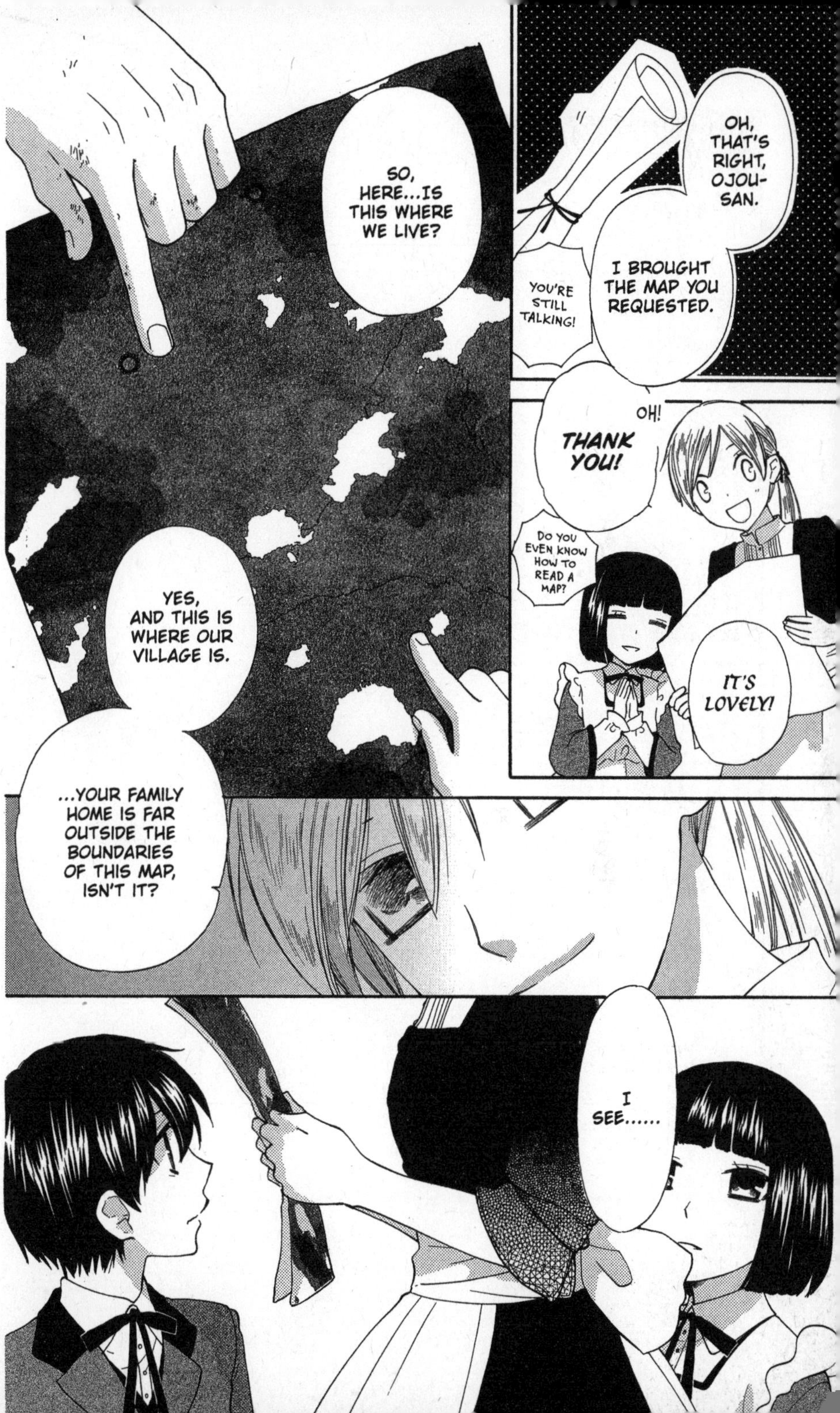
OH, THAT'S RIGHT, OJOU-SAN.
I BROUGHT THE MAP YOU REQUESTED.
YOU'RE STILL TALKING!
OH! THANK YOU!
DO YOU EVEN KNOW HOW TO READ A MAP?
IT'S LOVELY!
SO, HERE...IS THIS WHERE WE LIVE?
YES, AND THIS IS WHERE OUR VILLAGE IS.
...YOUR FAMILY HOME IS FAR OUTSIDE THE BOUNDARIES OF THIS MAP, ISN'T IT?
I SEE......

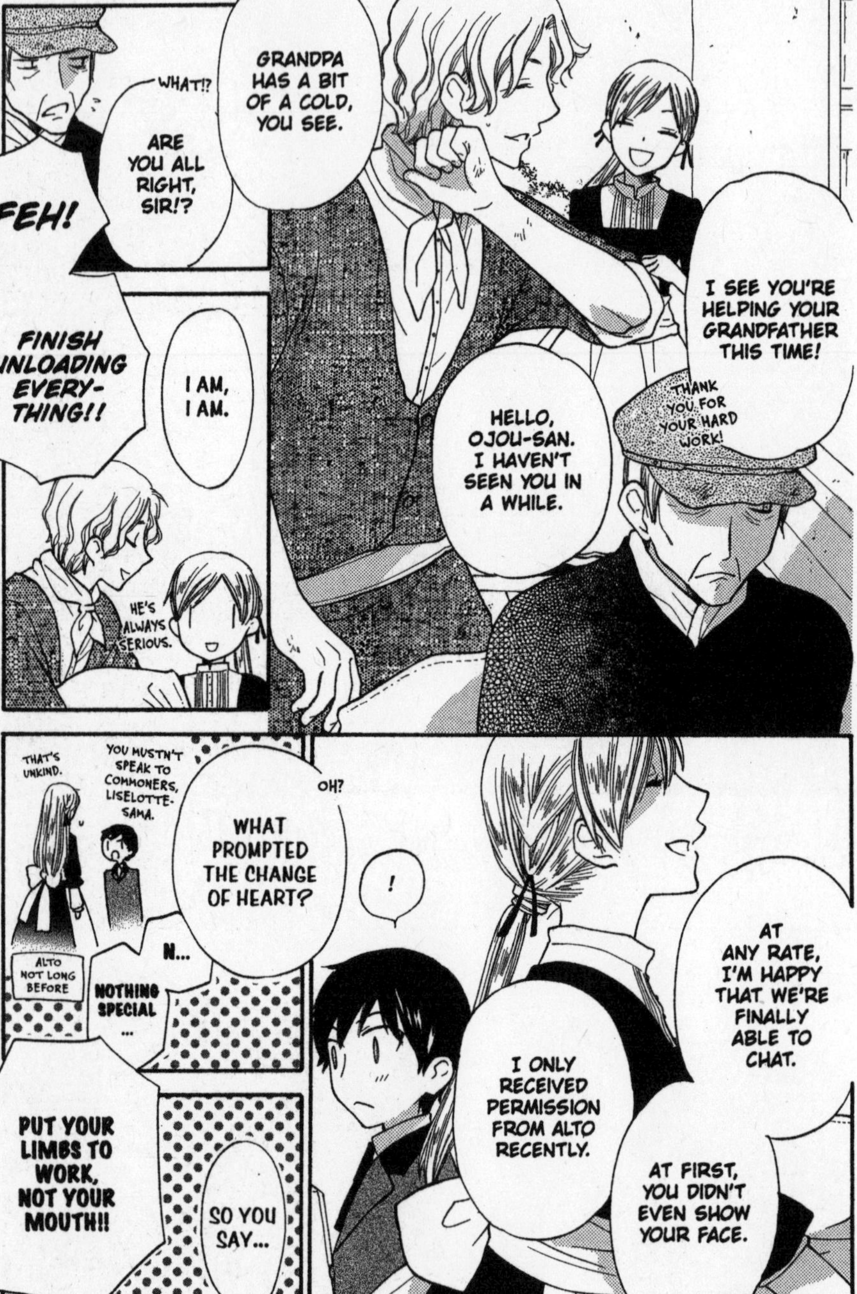
HELLO, OJOU-SAN. I HAVEN'T SEEN YOU IN A WHILE.
I SEE YOU'RE HELPING YOUR GRANDFATHER THIS TIME!
THANK YOU FOR YOUR HARD WORK!
GRANDPA HAS A BIT OF A COLD, YOU SEE.
WHAT!?
ARE YOU ALL RIGHT, SIR!?
FEH!
FINISH UNLOADING EVERY-THING!!
I AM, I AM.
HE'S ALWAYS SERIOUS.
AT ANY RATE, I'M HAPPY THAT WE'RE FINALLY ABLE TO CHAT.
AT FIRST, YOU DIDN'T EVEN SHOW YOUR FACE.
I ONLY RECEIVED PERMISSION FROM ALTO RECENTLY.
!
OH?
WHAT PROMPTED THE CHANGE OF HEART?
YOU MUSTN'T SPEAK TO COMMONERS, LISELOTTE-SAMA.
THAT'S UNKIND.
ALTO NOT LONG BEFORE
N...
NOTHING SPECIAL ...
PUT YOUR LIMBS TO WORK, NOT YOUR MOUTH!!
SO YOU SAY...

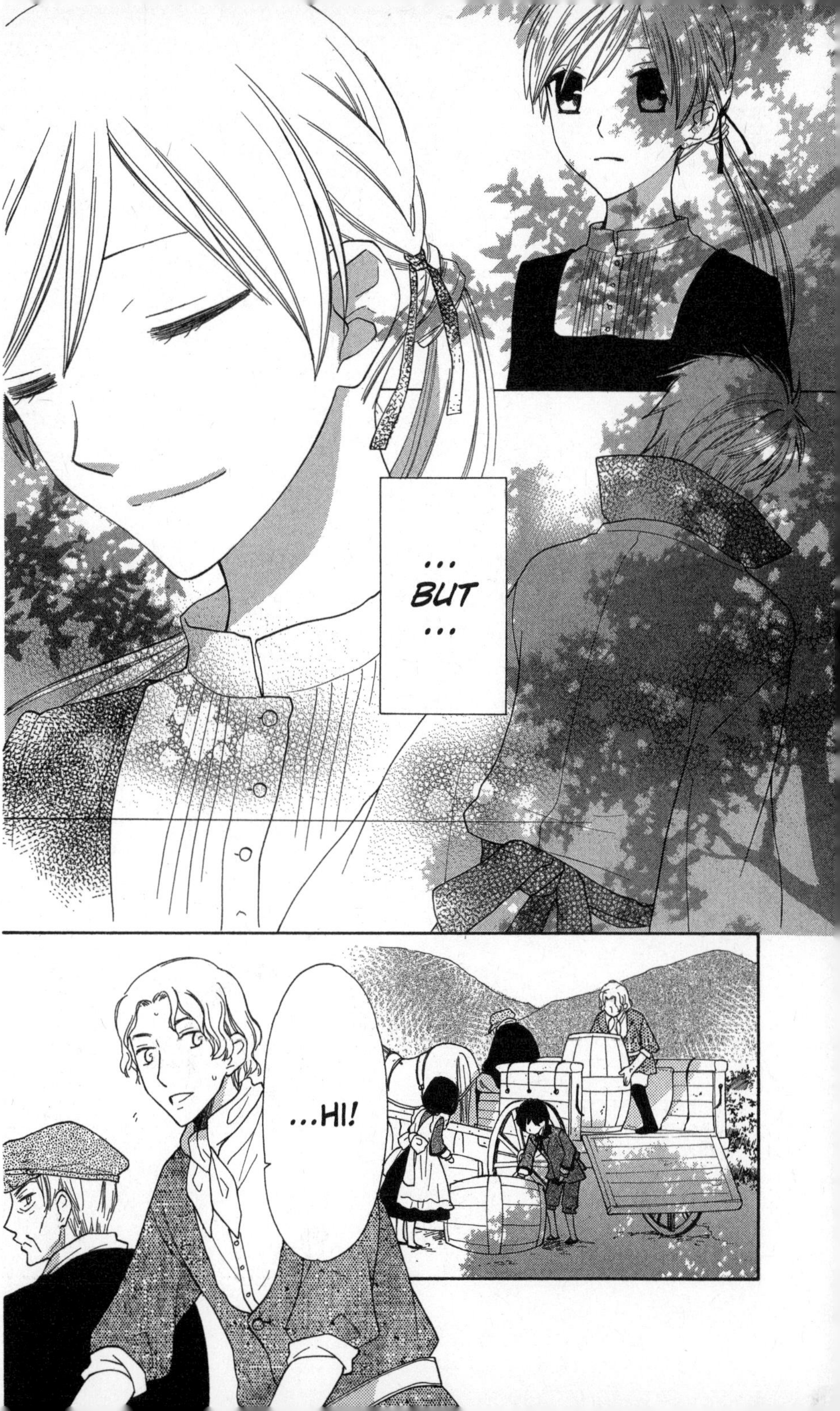
...BUT...
...HI!

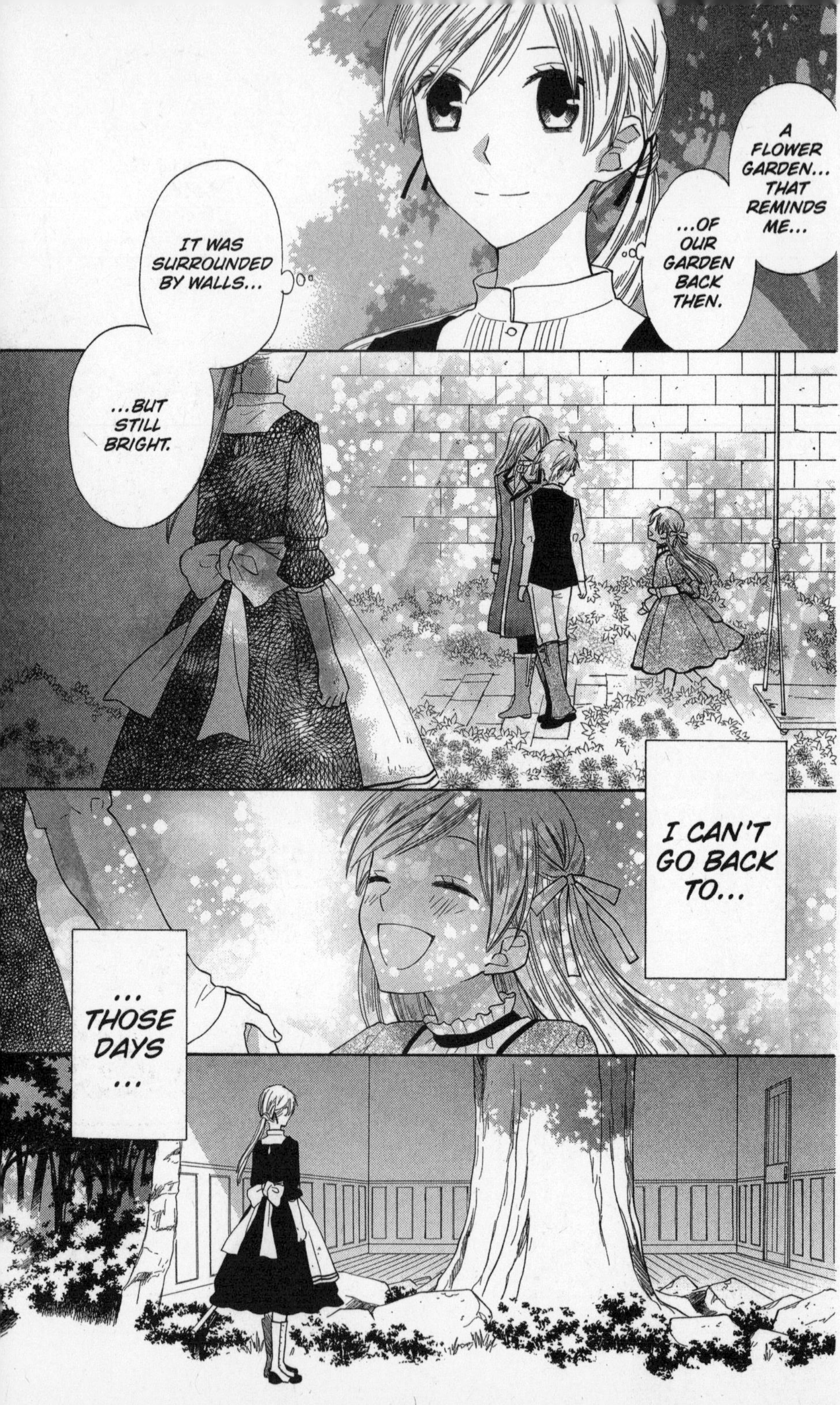
A FLOWER GARDEN... THAT REMINDS ME...
...OF OUR GARDEN BACK THEN.
IT WAS SURROUNDED BY WALLS...
...BUT STILL BRIGHT.
I CAN'T GO BACK TO...
...THOSE DAYS...

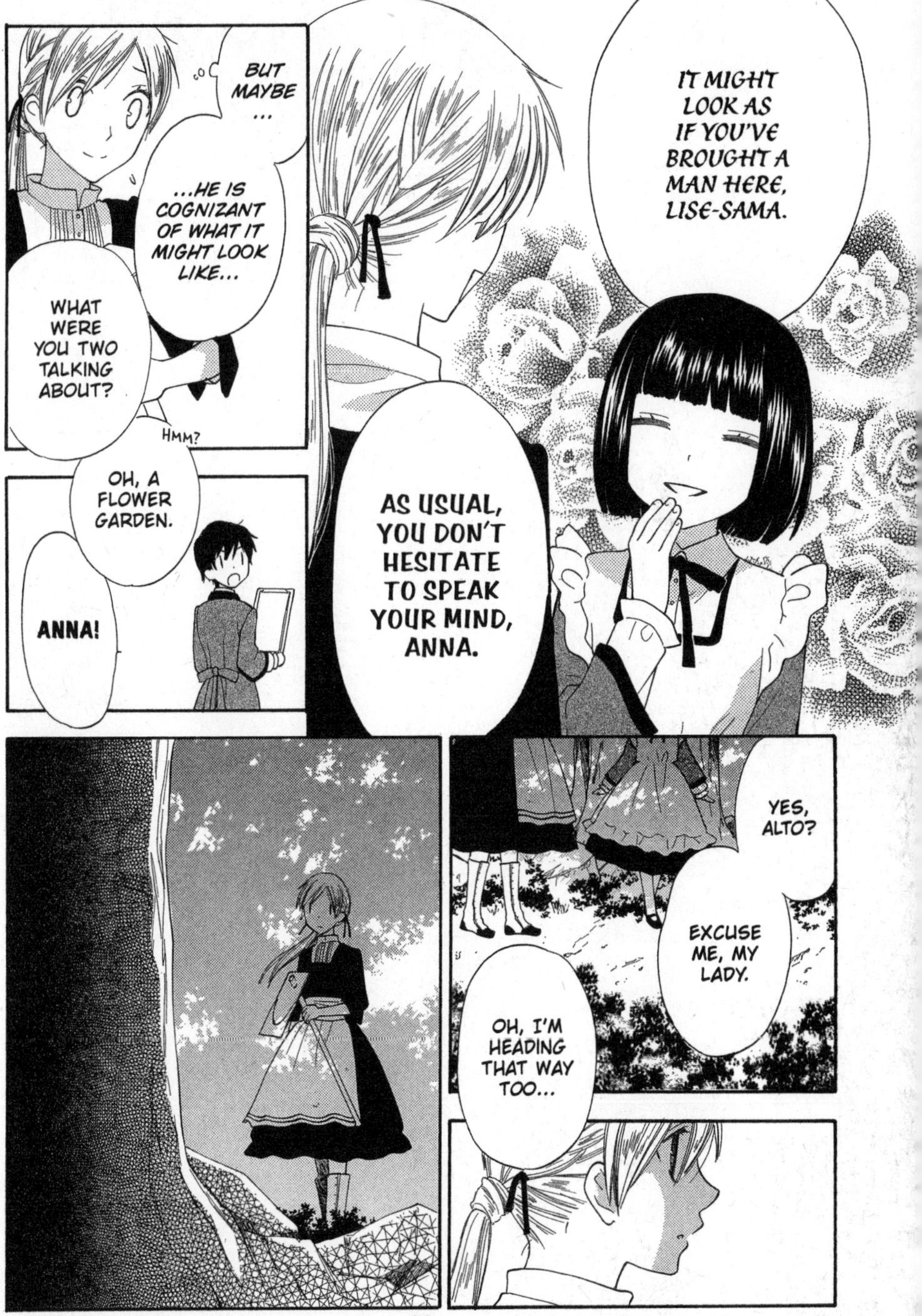
IT MIGHT LOOK AS IF YOU'VE BROUGHT A MAN HERE, LISE-SAMA.
AS USUAL, YOU DON'T HESITATE TO SPEAK YOUR MIND, ANNA.
BUT MAYBE ...
...HE IS COGNIZANT OF WHAT IT MIGHT LOOK LIKE...
WHAT WERE YOU TWO TALKING ABOUT?
HMM?
OH, A FLOWER GARDEN.
ANNA!
YES, ALTO?
EXCUSE ME, MY LADY.
OH, I'M HEADING THAT WAY TOO...

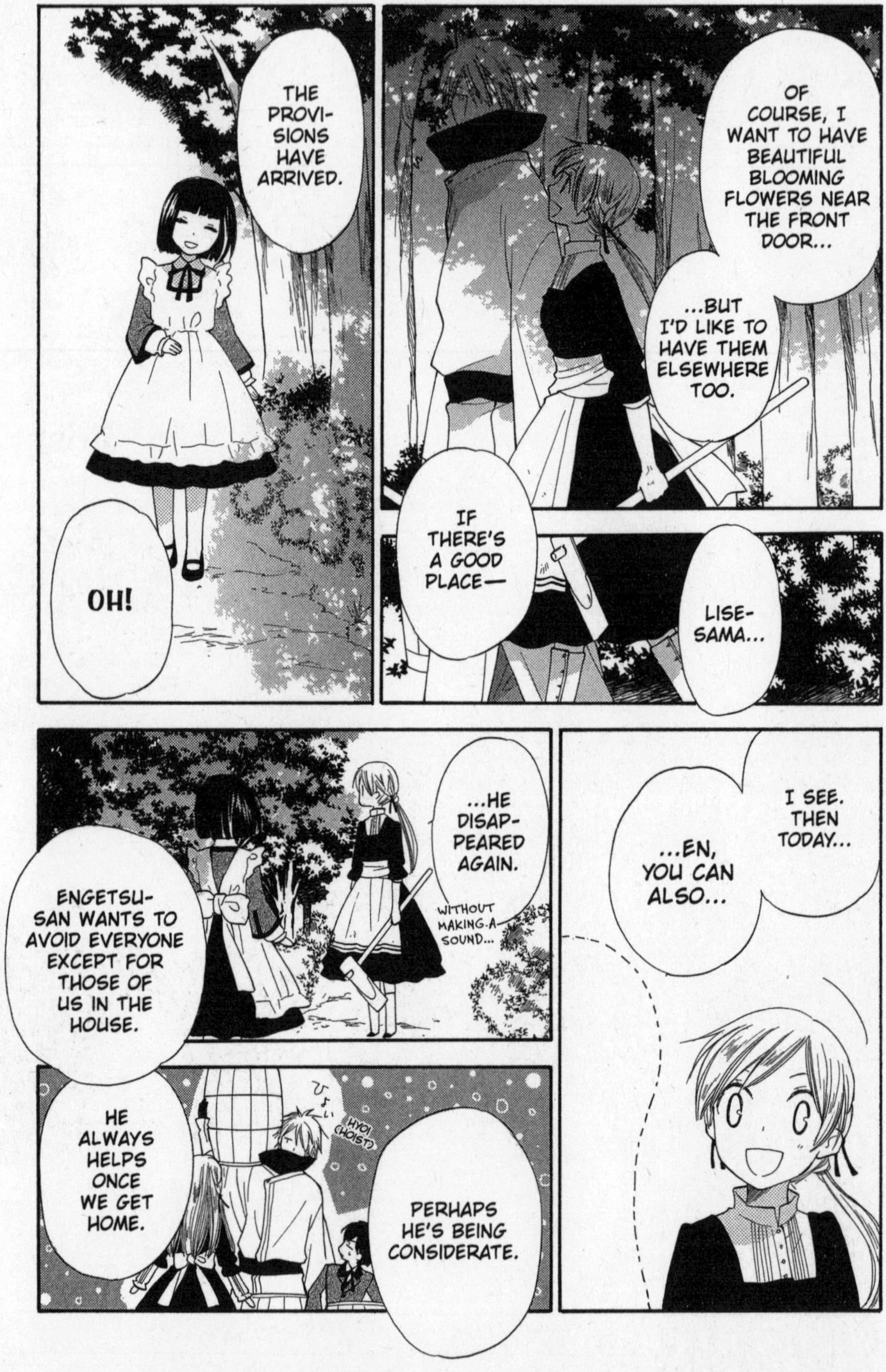
OF COURSE, I WANT TO HAVE BEAUTIFUL BLOOMING FLOWERS NEAR THE FRONT DOOR...
...BUT I'D LIKE TO HAVE THEM ELSEWHERE TOO.
IF THERE'S A GOOD PLACE—
LISE-SAMA...
THE PROVISIONS HAVE ARRIVED.
OH!
I SEE. THEN TODAY...
...EN, YOU CAN ALSO...
...HE DISAPPEARED AGAIN.
WITHOUT MAKING A SOUND...
ENGETSU-SAN WANTS TO AVOID EVERYONE EXCEPT FOR THOSE OF US IN THE HOUSE.
ひょい
HYOI (HOIST)
HE ALWAYS HELPS ONCE WE GET HOME.
PERHAPS HE'S BEING CONSIDERATE.

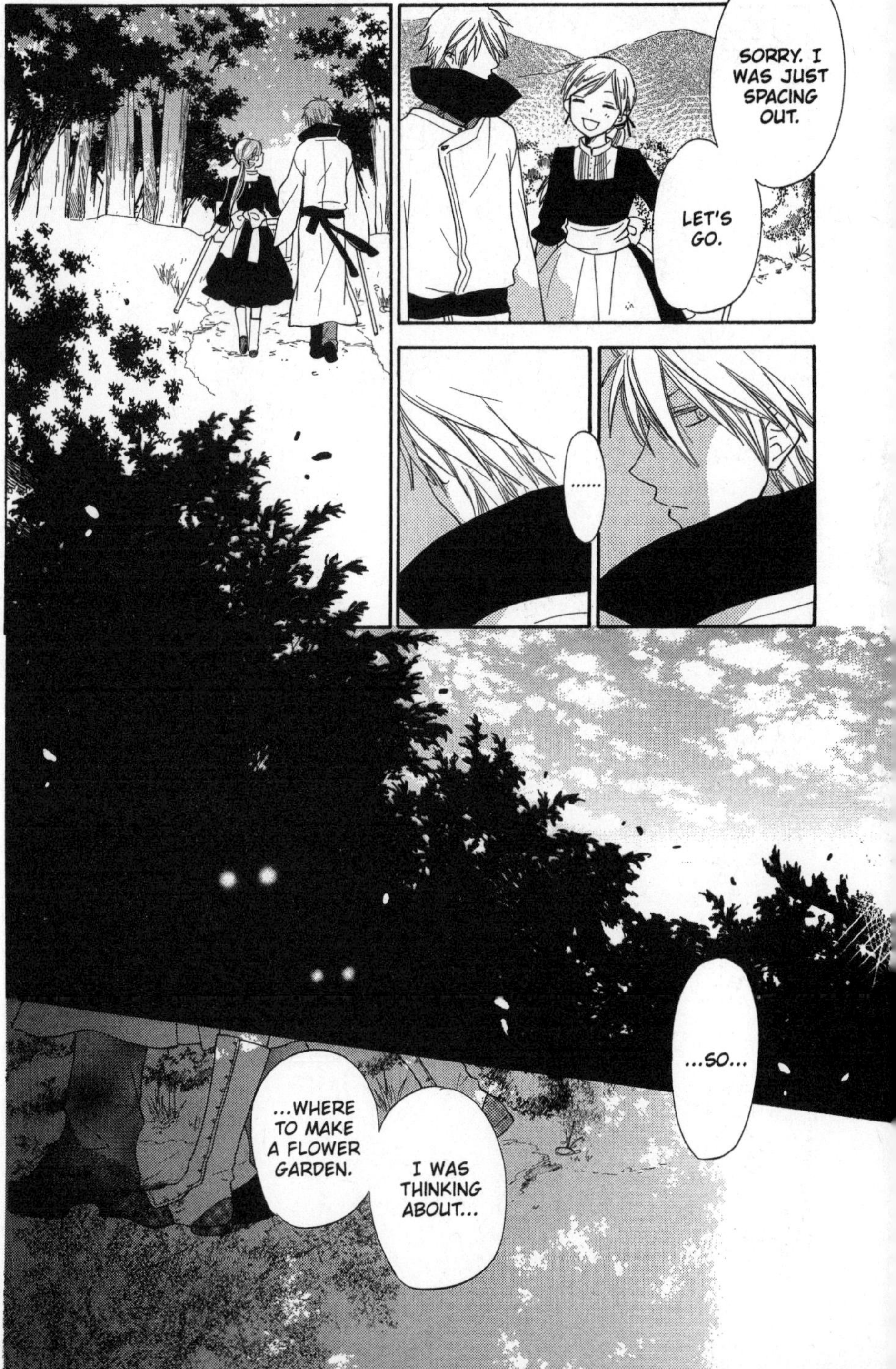
SORRY. I WAS JUST SPACING OUT.
LET'S GO.
......
...SO...
I WAS THINKING ABOUT...
...WHERE TO MAKE A FLOWER GARDEN.

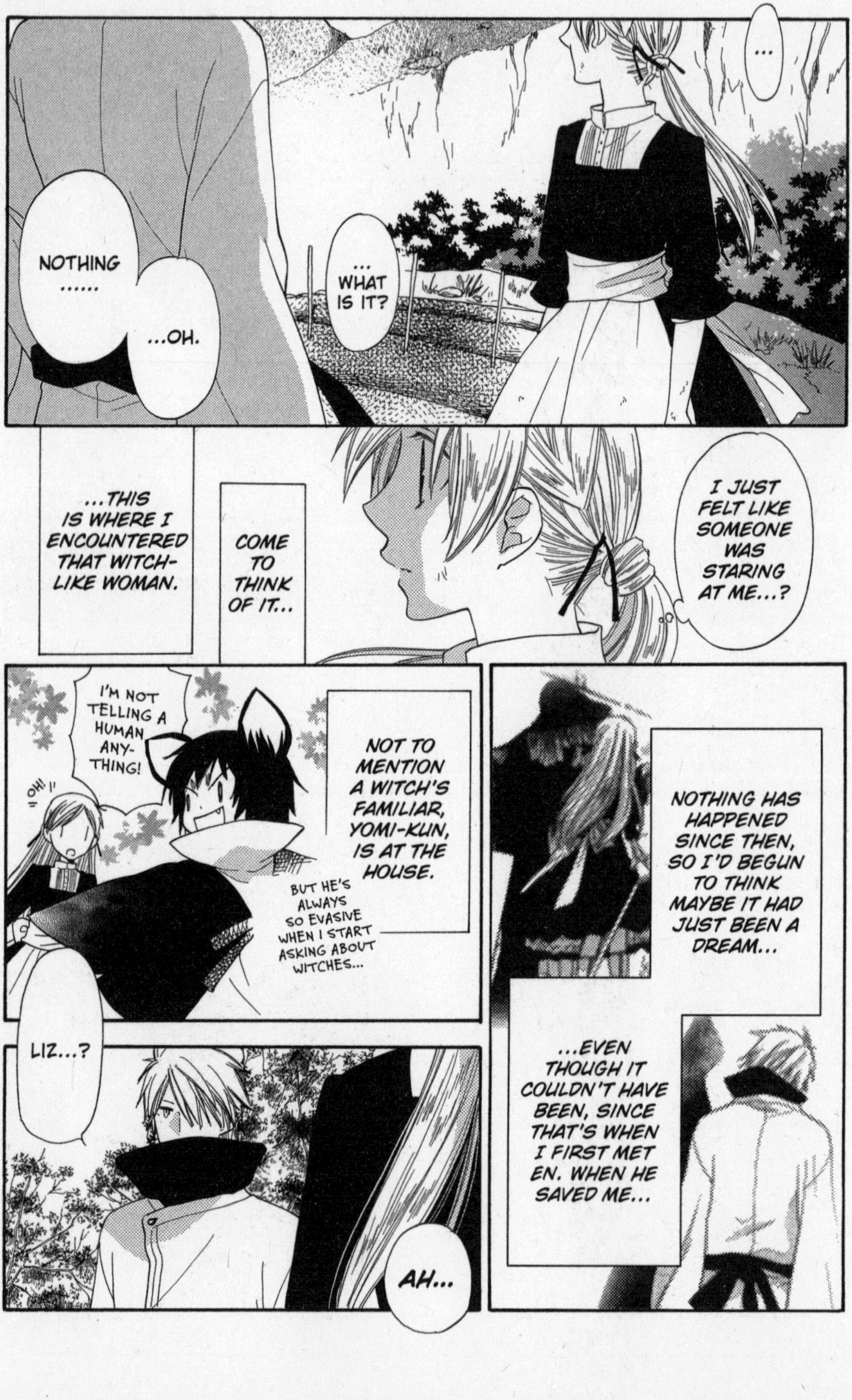
...
... WHAT IS IT?
...OH.
NOTHING ......
I JUST FELT LIKE SOMEONE WAS STARING AT ME...?
COME TO THINK OF IT...
...THIS IS WHERE I ENCOUNTERED THAT WITCH-LIKE WOMAN.
NOTHING HAS HAPPENED SINCE THEN, SO I'D BEGUN TO THINK MAYBE IT HAD JUST BEEN A DREAM...
...EVEN THOUGH IT COULDN'T HAVE BEEN, SINCE THAT'S WHEN I FIRST MET EN. WHEN HE SAVED ME...
NOT TO MENTION A WITCH'S FAMILIAR, YOMI-KUN, IS AT THE HOUSE.
I'M NOT TELLING A HUMAN ANYTHING!
OH!
BUT HE'S ALWAYS SO EVASIVE WHEN I START ASKING ABOUT WITCHES...
LIZ...?
AH...

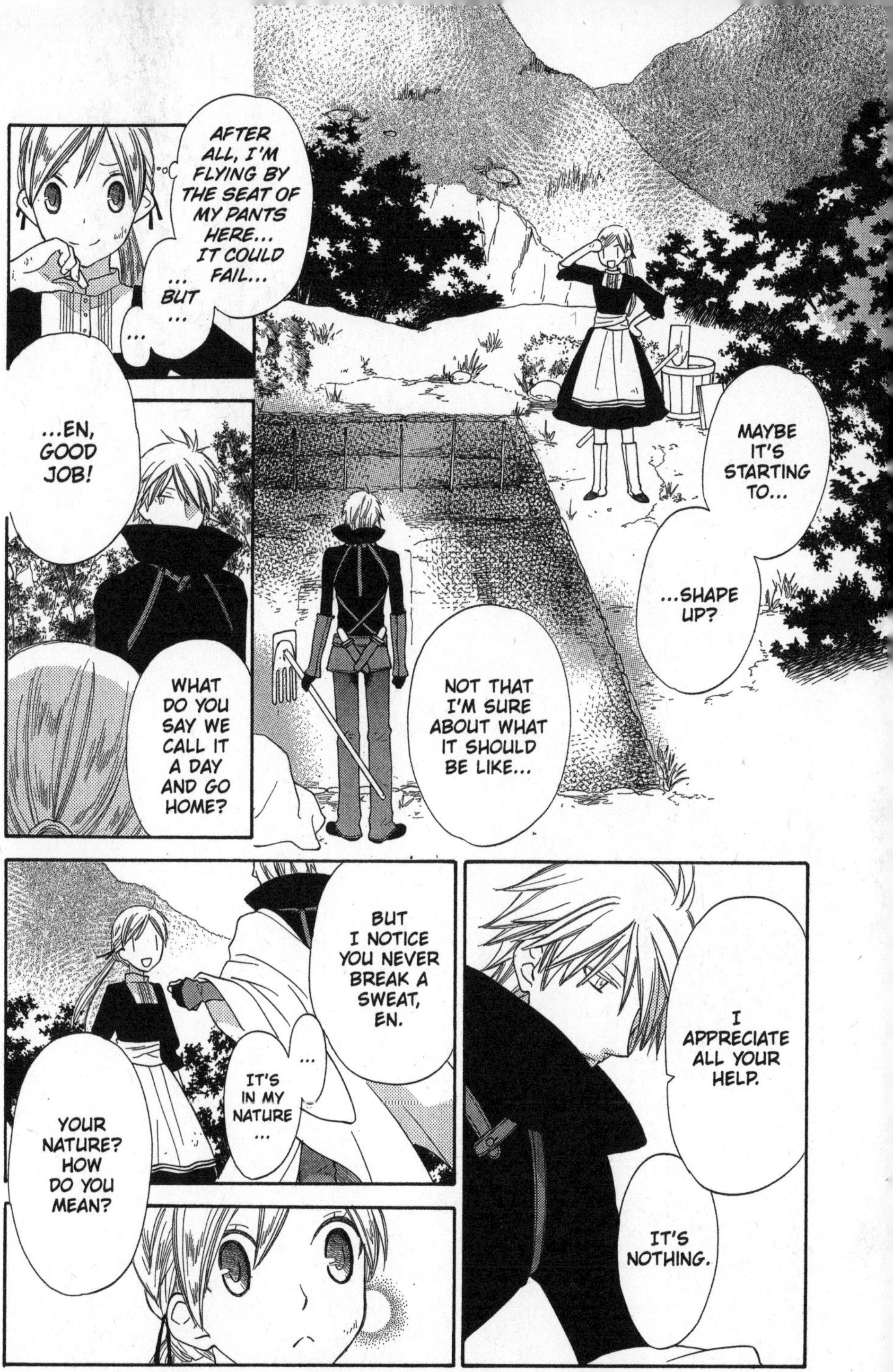
MAYBE IT'S STARTING TO...
...SHAPE UP?
NOT THAT I'M SURE ABOUT WHAT IT SHOULD BE LIKE...
AFTER ALL, I'M FLYING BY THE SEAT OF MY PANTS HERE... IT COULD FAIL...
...BUT...
...
...EN, GOOD JOB!
WHAT DO YOU SAY WE CALL IT A DAY AND GO HOME?
I APPRECIATE ALL YOUR HELP.
IT'S NOTHING.
BUT I NOTICE YOU NEVER BREAK A SWEAT, EN.
...
IT'S IN MY NATURE...
YOUR NATURE? HOW DO YOU MEAN?

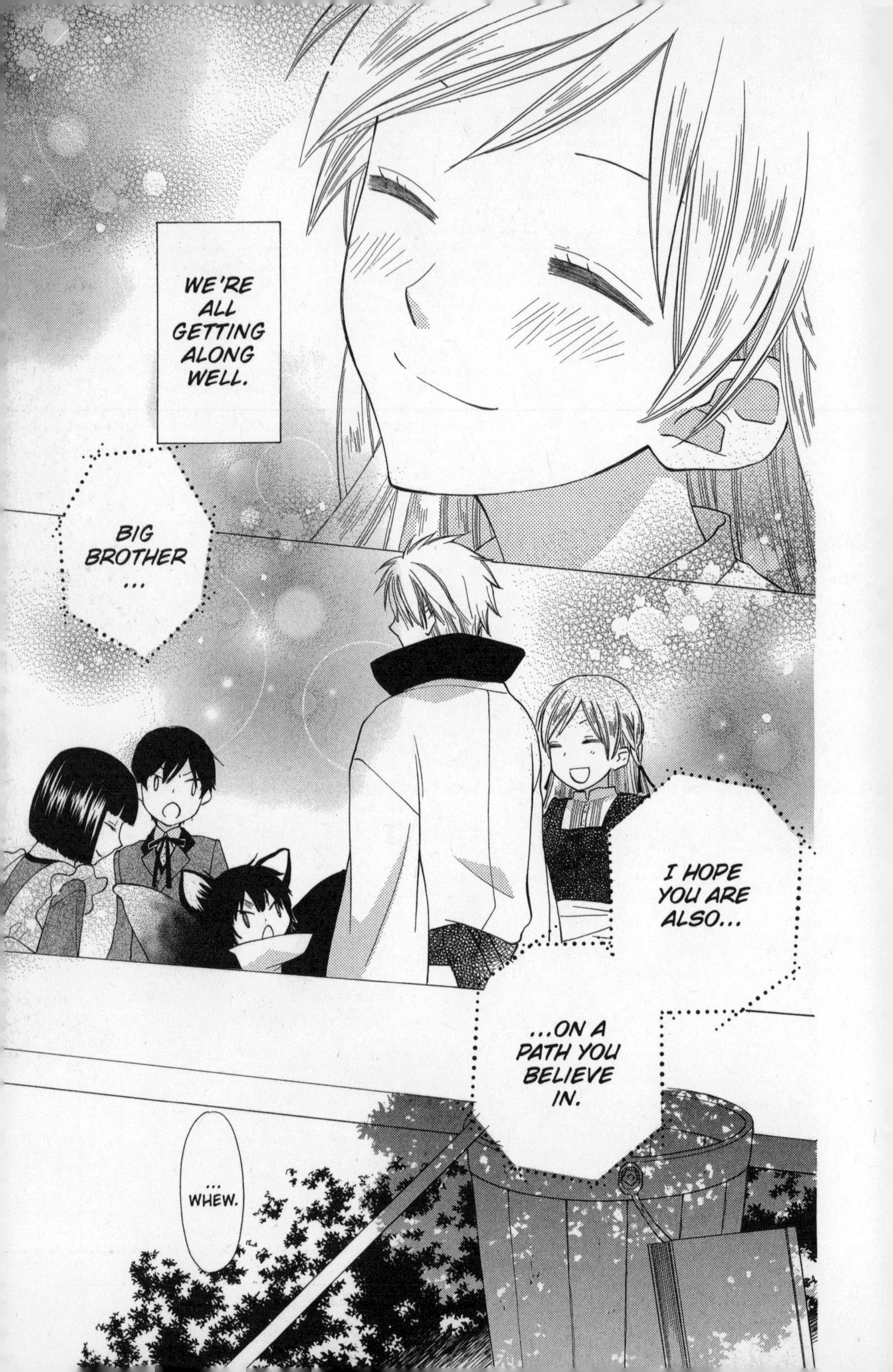
WE'RE ALL GETTING ALONG WELL.
BIG BROTHER ...
I HOPE YOU ARE ALSO...
...ON A PATH YOU BELIEVE IN.
... WHEW.

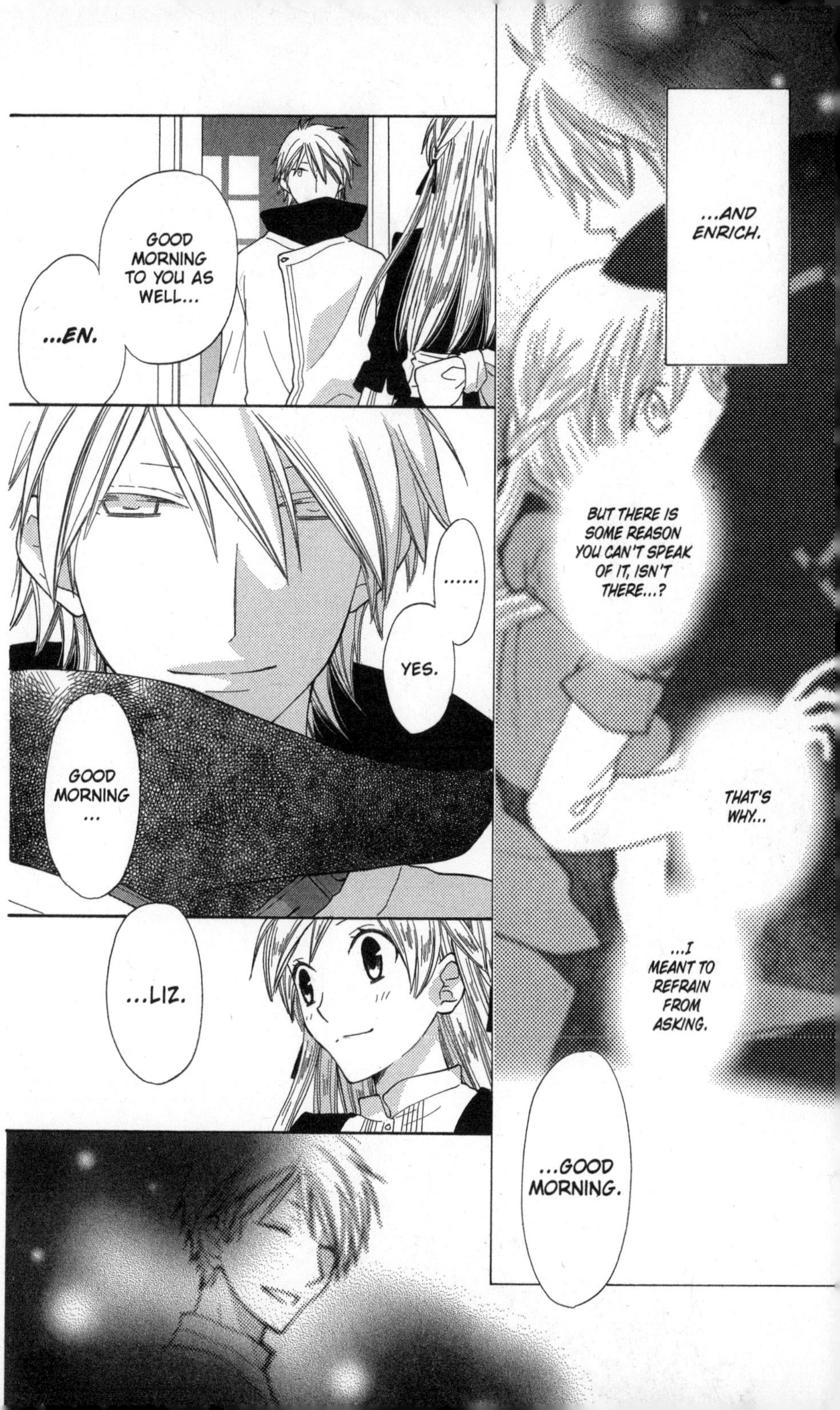
...AND ENRICH.
BUT THERE IS SOME REASON YOU CAN'T SPEAK OF IT, ISN'T THERE...?
THAT'S WHY...
...I MEANT TO REFRAIN FROM ASKING.
GOOD MORNING TO YOU AS WELL...
...EN.
......
YES.
GOOD MORNING...
...LIZ.
...GOOD MORNING.

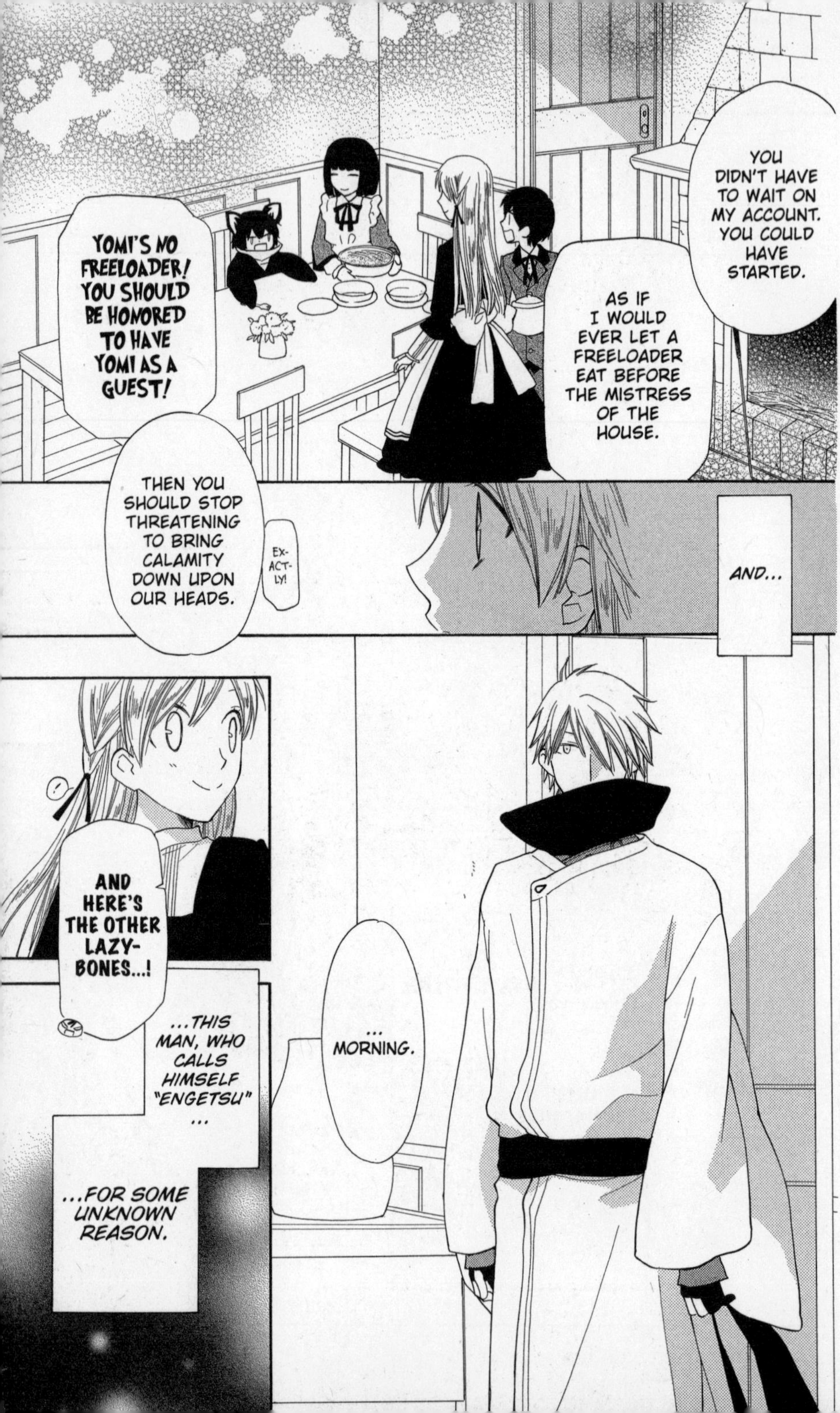
YOU DIDN'T HAVE TO WAIT ON MY ACCOUNT. YOU COULD HAVE STARTED.
AS IF I WOULD EVER LET A FREELOADER EAT BEFORE THE MISTRESS OF THE HOUSE.
YOMI'S NO FREELOADER! YOU SHOULD BE HONORED TO HAVE YOMI AS A GUEST!
AND...
THEN YOU SHOULD STOP THREATENING TO BRING CALAMITY DOWN UPON OUR HEADS.
EX-ACT-LY!
...MORNING.
AND HERE'S THE OTHER LAZY-BONES...!
...THIS MAN, WHO CALLS HIMSELF "ENGETSU"...
...FOR SOME UNKNOWN REASON.

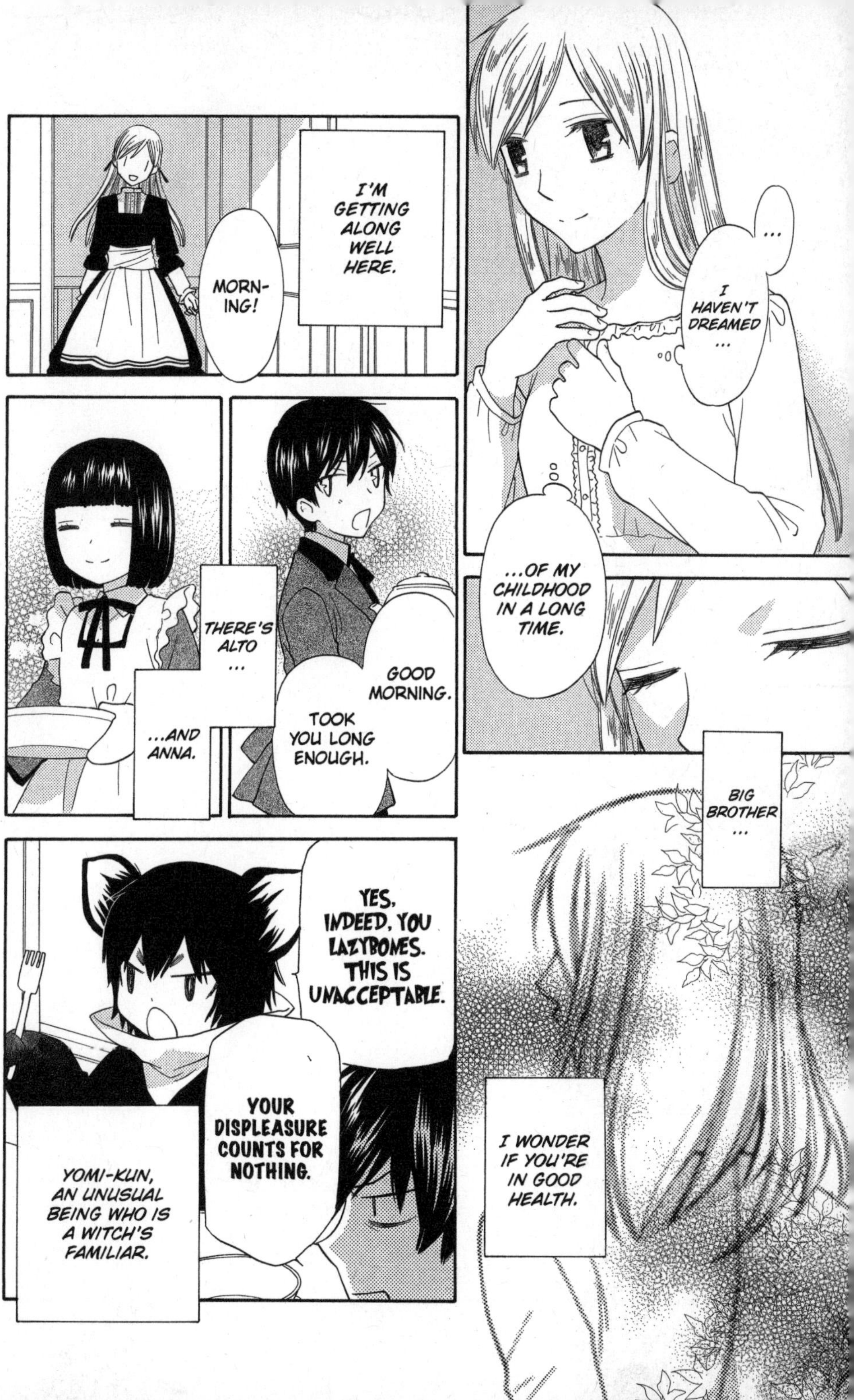
...
I HAVEN'T DREAMED ...
...OF MY CHILDHOOD IN A LONG TIME.
BIG BROTHER ...
I WONDER IF YOU'RE IN GOOD HEALTH.
I'M GETTING ALONG WELL HERE.
MORNING!
GOOD MORNING.
TOOK YOU LONG ENOUGH.
THERE'S ALTO ...
...AND ANNA.
YES, INDEED, YOU LAZYBONES. THIS IS UNACCEPTABLE.
YOUR DISPLEASURE COUNTS FOR NOTHING.
YOMI-KUN, AN UNUSUAL BEING WHO IS A WITCH'S FAMILIAR.

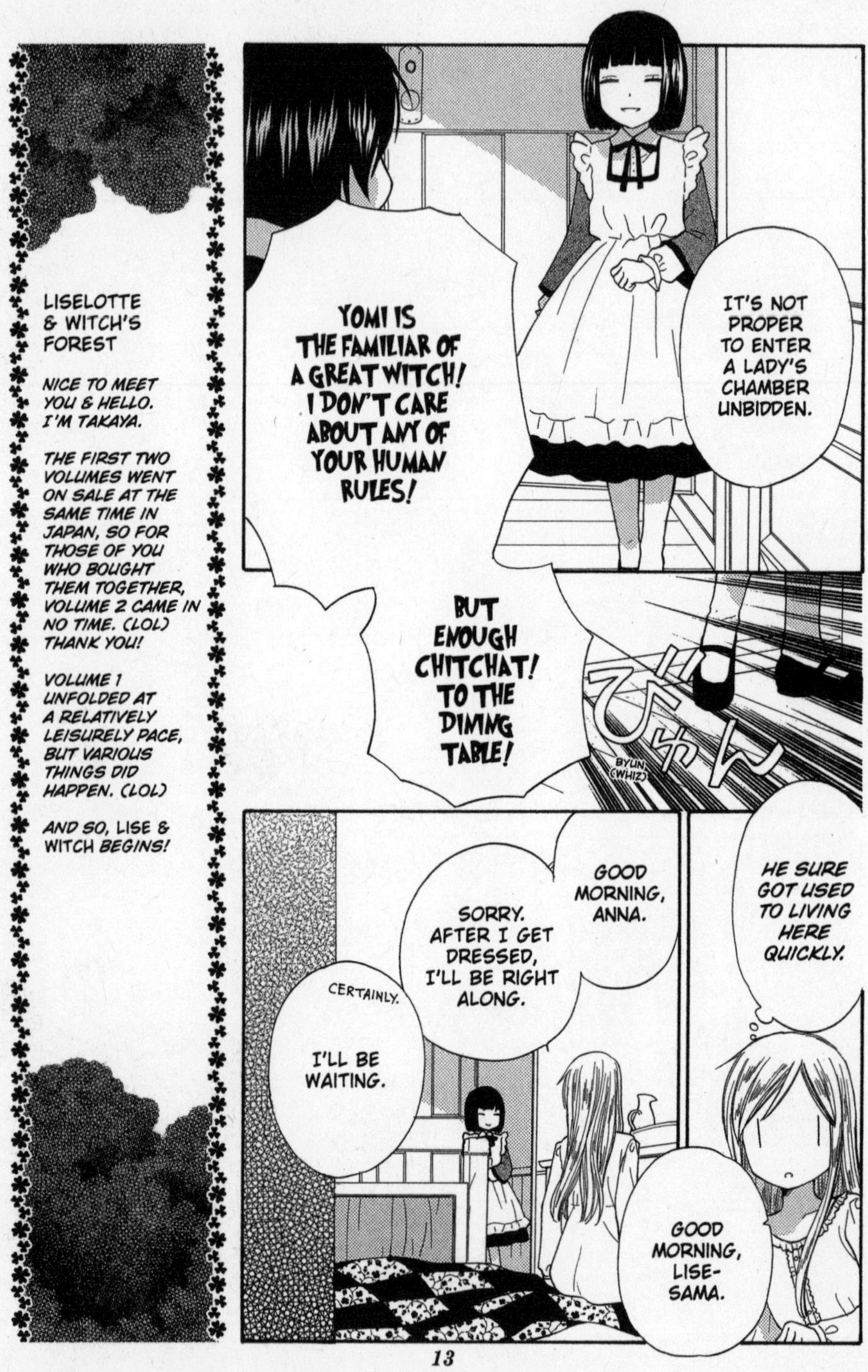
IT'S NOT PROPER TO ENTER A LADY'S CHAMBER UNBIDDEN.
YOMI IS THE FAMILIAR OF A GREAT WITCH! I DON'T CARE ABOUT ANY OF YOUR HUMAN RULES!
BUT ENOUGH CHITCHAT! TO THE DIMING TABLE!
びゅん
BYUN (WHIZ)
HE SURE GOT USED TO LIVING HERE QUICKLY.
GOOD MORNING, LISE-SAMA.
GOOD MORNING, ANNA.
SORRY. AFTER I GET DRESSED, I'LL BE RIGHT ALONG.
CERTAINLY.
I'LL BE WAITING.

LISELOTTE & WITCH'S FOREST

NICE TO MEET YOU & HELLO. I'M TAKAYA.

THE FIRST TWO VOLUMES WENT ON SALE AT THE SAME TIME IN JAPAN, SO FOR THOSE OF YOU WHO BOUGHT THEM TOGETHER, VOLUME 2 CAME IN NO TIME. (LOL) THANK YOU!

VOLUME 1 UNFOLDED AT A RELATIVELY LEISURELY PACE, BUT VARIOUS THINGS DID HAPPEN. (LOL)

AND SO, LISE & WITCH BEGINS!

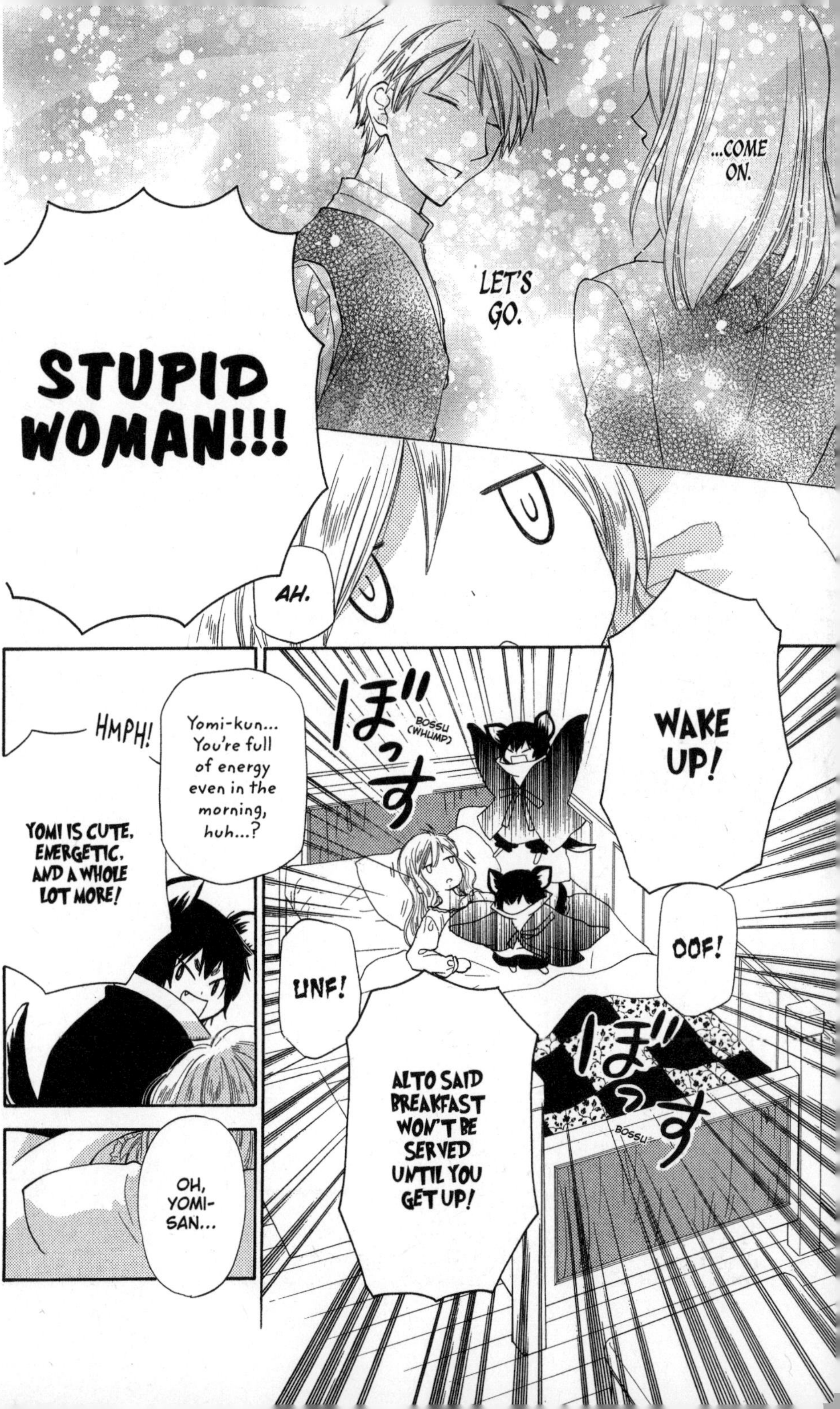
...COME ON.
LET'S GO.
STUPID WOMAN!!!
AH.
WAKE UP!
ぼっす
BOSSU (WHUMP)
OOF!
UNF!
ぼっす
BOSSU
ALTO SAID BREAKFAST WON'T BE SERVED UNTIL YOU GET UP!
HMPH!
Yomi-kun... You're full of energy even in the morning, huh...?
YOMI IS CUTE, ENERGETIC, AND A WHOLE LOT MORE!
OH, YOMI-SAN...

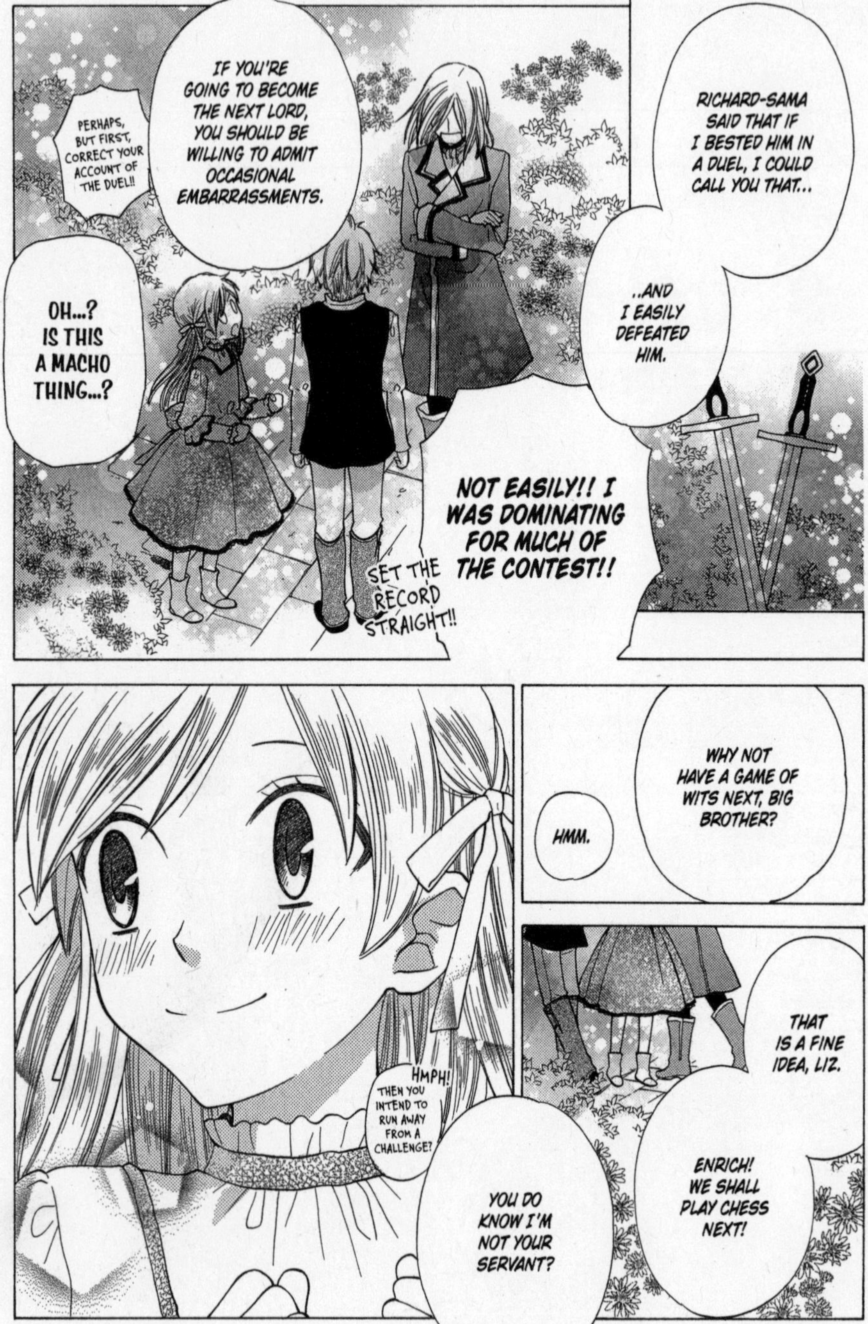
RICHARD-SAMA SAID THAT IF I BESTED HIM IN A DUEL, I COULD CALL YOU THAT...
..AND I EASILY DEFEATED HIM.
NOT EASILY!! I WAS DOMINATING FOR MUCH OF THE CONTEST!!
SET THE RECORD STRAIGHT!!
IF YOU'RE GOING TO BECOME THE NEXT LORD, YOU SHOULD BE WILLING TO ADMIT OCCASIONAL EMBARRASSMENTS.
PERHAPS, BUT FIRST, CORRECT YOUR ACCOUNT OF THE DUEL!!
OH...? IS THIS A MACHO THING...?
WHY NOT HAVE A GAME OF WITS NEXT, BIG BROTHER?
HMM.
THAT IS A FINE IDEA, LIZ.
ENRICH! WE SHALL PLAY CHESS NEXT!
YOU DO KNOW I'M NOT YOUR SERVANT?
HMPH! THEN YOU INTEND TO RUN AWAY FROM A CHALLENGE?

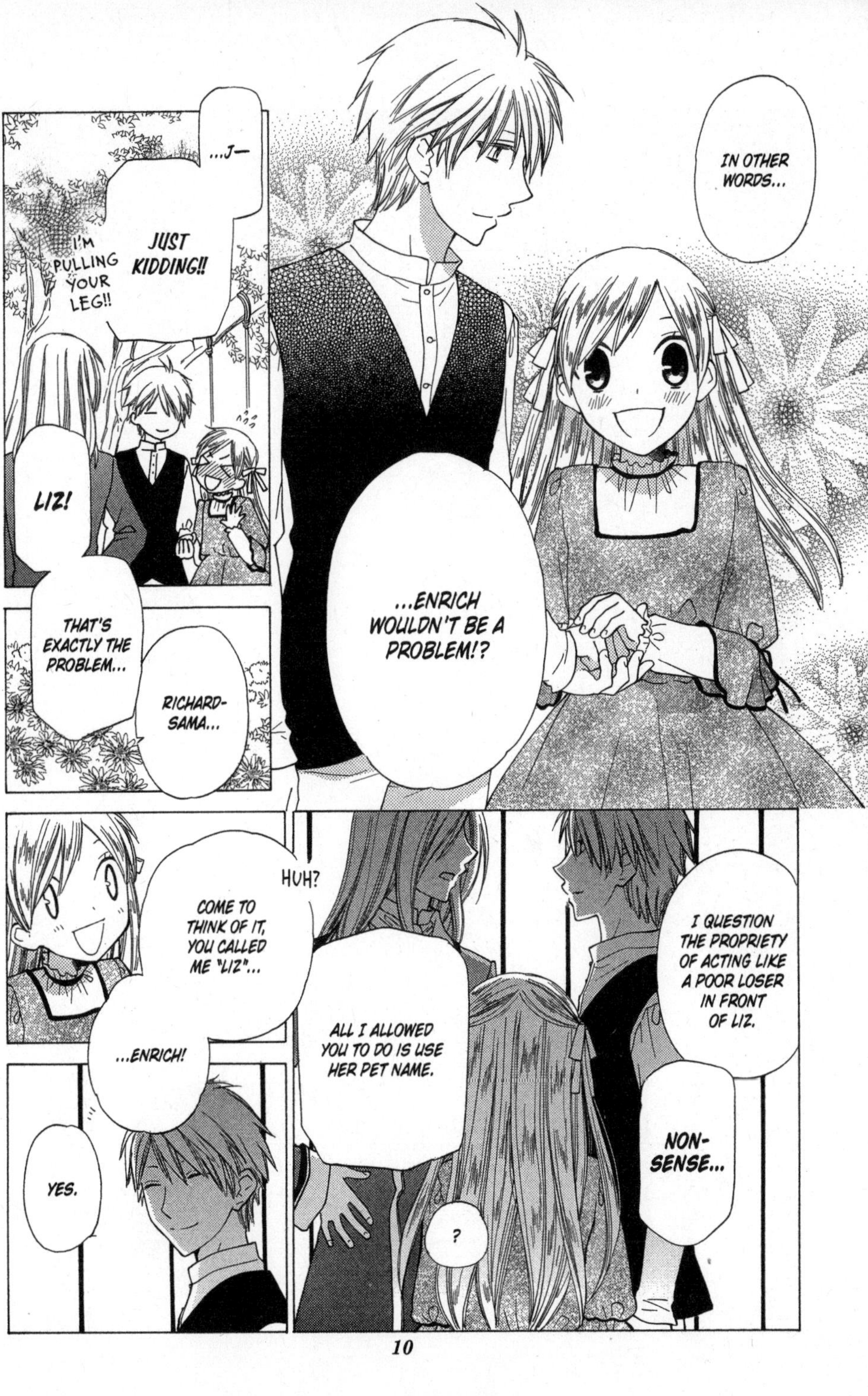
IN OTHER WORDS...
...ENRICH WOULDN'T BE A PROBLEM!?
...J—
JUST KIDDING!!
I'M PULLING YOUR LEG!!
LIZ!
THAT'S EXACTLY THE PROBLEM...
RICHARD-SAMA...
I QUESTION THE PROPRIETY OF ACTING LIKE A POOR LOSER IN FRONT OF LIZ.
HUH?
ALL I ALLOWED YOU TO DO IS USE HER PET NAME.
NON-SENSE...
?
COME TO THINK OF IT, YOU CALLED ME "LIZ"...
...ENRICH!
YES.

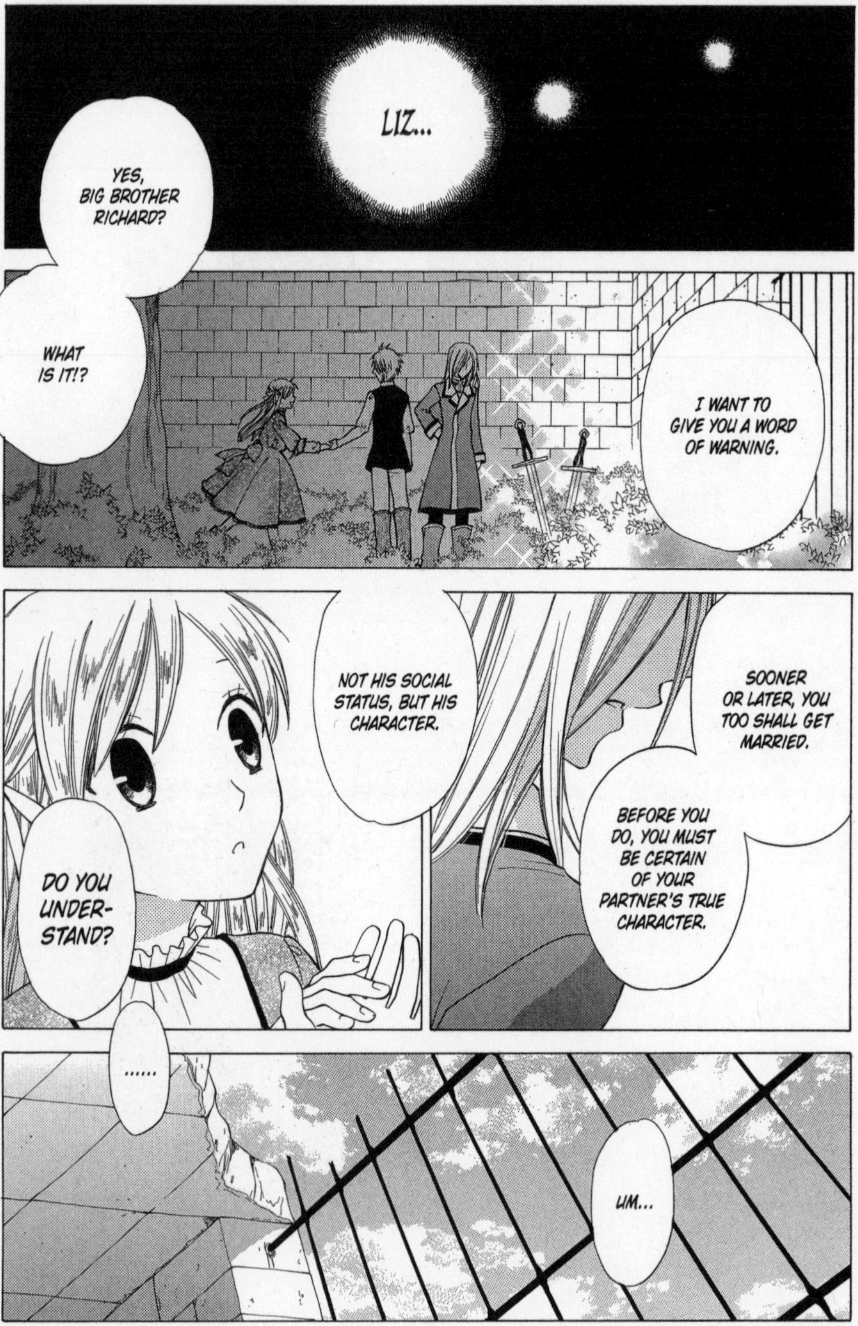
LIZ...
YES, BIG BROTHER RICHARD?
WHAT IS IT!?
I WANT TO GIVE YOU A WORD OF WARNING.
SOONER OR LATER, YOU TOO SHALL GET MARRIED.
BEFORE YOU DO, YOU MUST BE CERTAIN OF YOUR PARTNER'S TRUE CHARACTER.
NOT HIS SOCIAL STATUS, BUT HIS CHARACTER.
DO YOU UNDER-STAND?
......
UM...

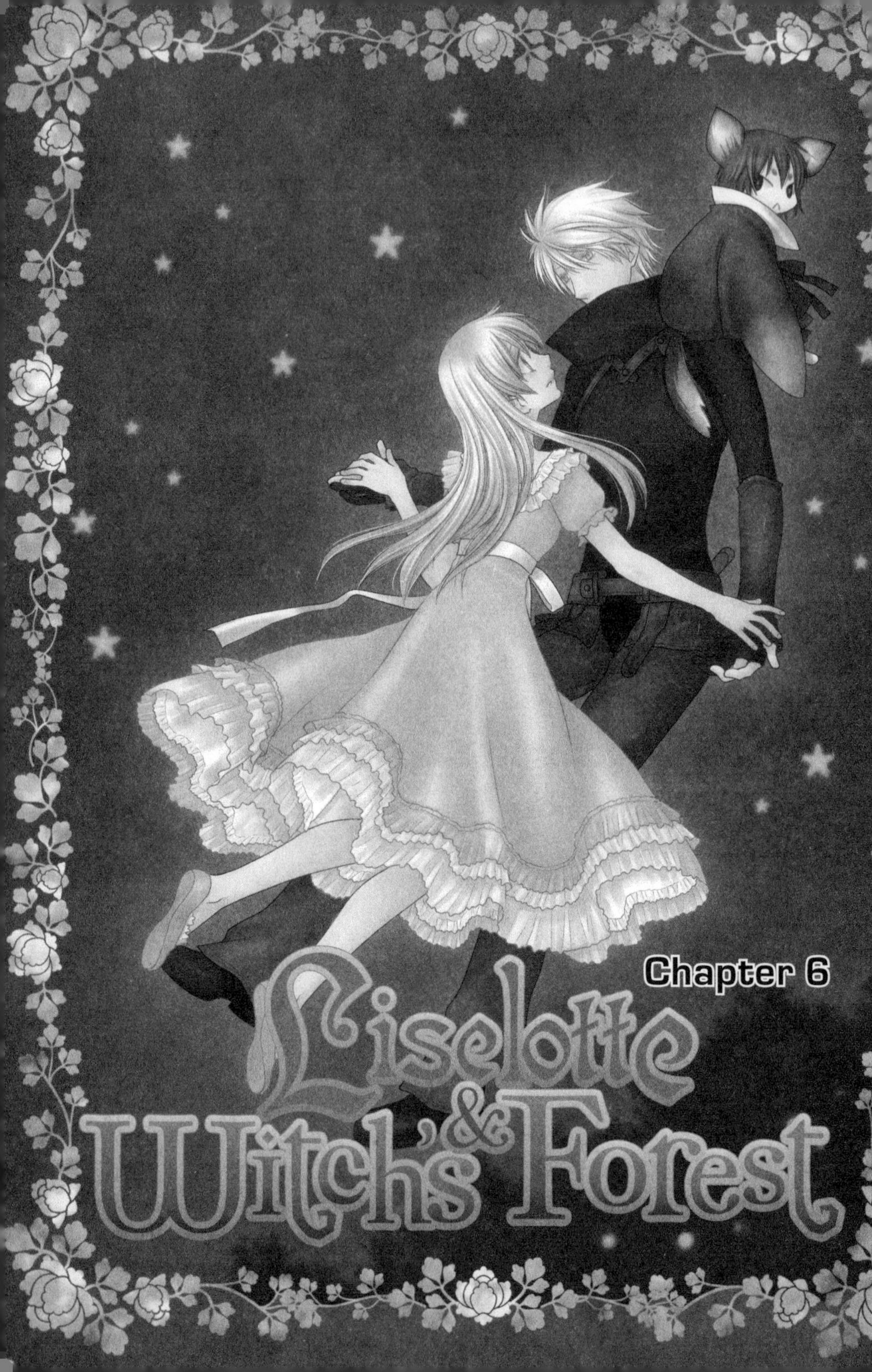
Chapter 6
Liselotte & Witch's Forest

Liselotte & Witch's Forest

VOLUME 2

YOMI

The witch Vartelinde's familiar.
Acquainted with Engetsu?

ENGETSU

A strange young man who saved
Lise-sama. Looks like Enrich,
but has light-crimson eyes.

WITCHES OF THE FOREST

The rumors say they live on their
own deep in the forest but that they
occasionally emerge to use their power
on humans——sometimes to help,
sometimes to harm.

ENRICH

A boy from Lise-sama's past.
Has sky-blue eyes.
Calls Lise-sama "Liz."

SUMMARY

Liselotte, the daughter of a feudal lord, is exiled by her older
brother to the east of the east of the east. Starting her new
life near the witches' forest, she begins finding new reasons
to live. Liselotte's days become livelier with the addition
of two companions, Engetsu and Yomi...

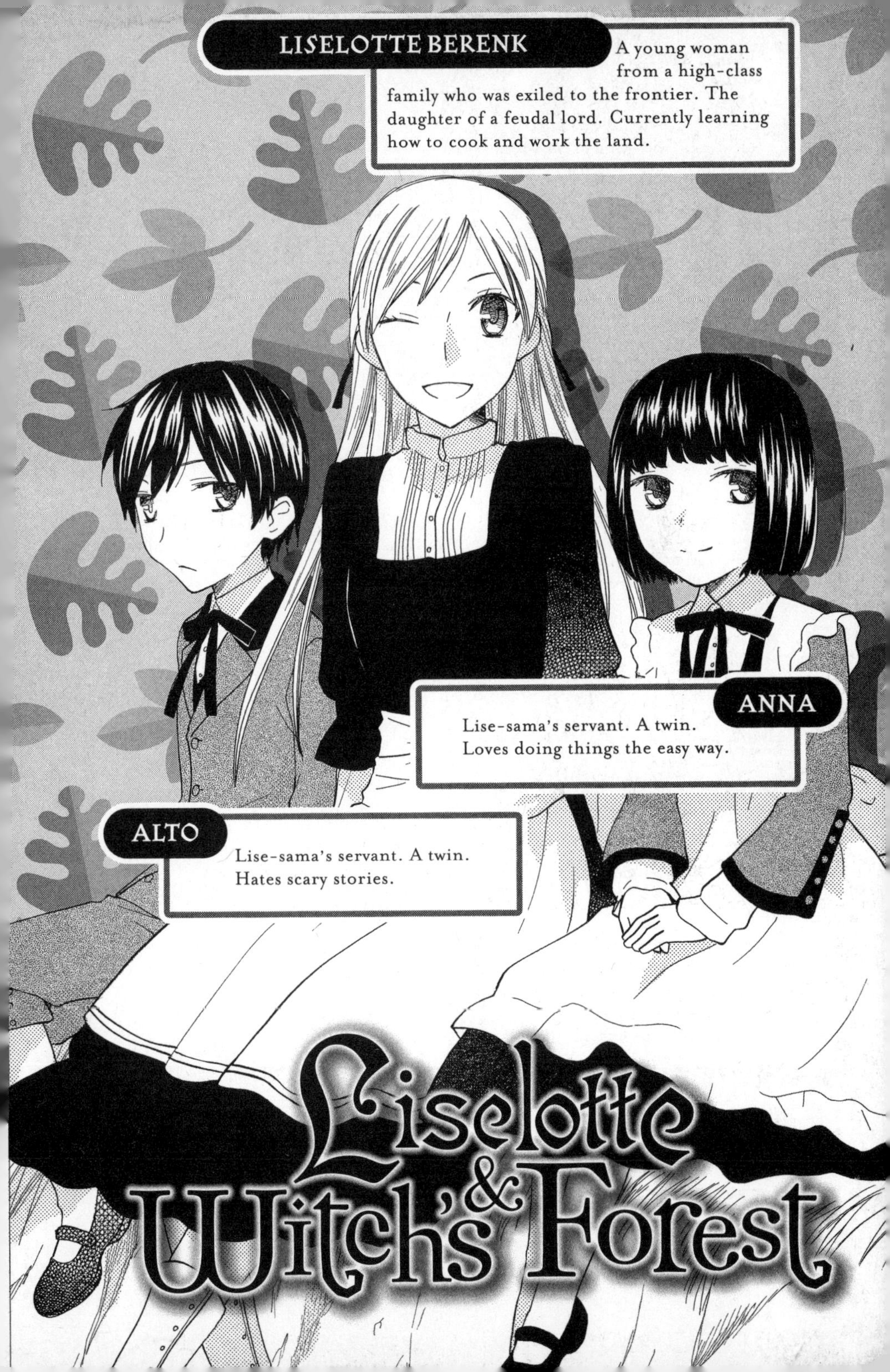
LISELOTTE BERENK
A young woman from a high-class family who was exiled to the frontier. The daughter of a feudal lord. Currently learning how to cook and work the land.
ANNA
Lise-sama's servant. A twin. Loves doing things the easy way.
ALTO
Lise-sama's servant. A twin. Hates scary stories.
Liselotte & Witch's Forest

Liselotte & Witch's Forest

2

NATSUKI TAKAYA

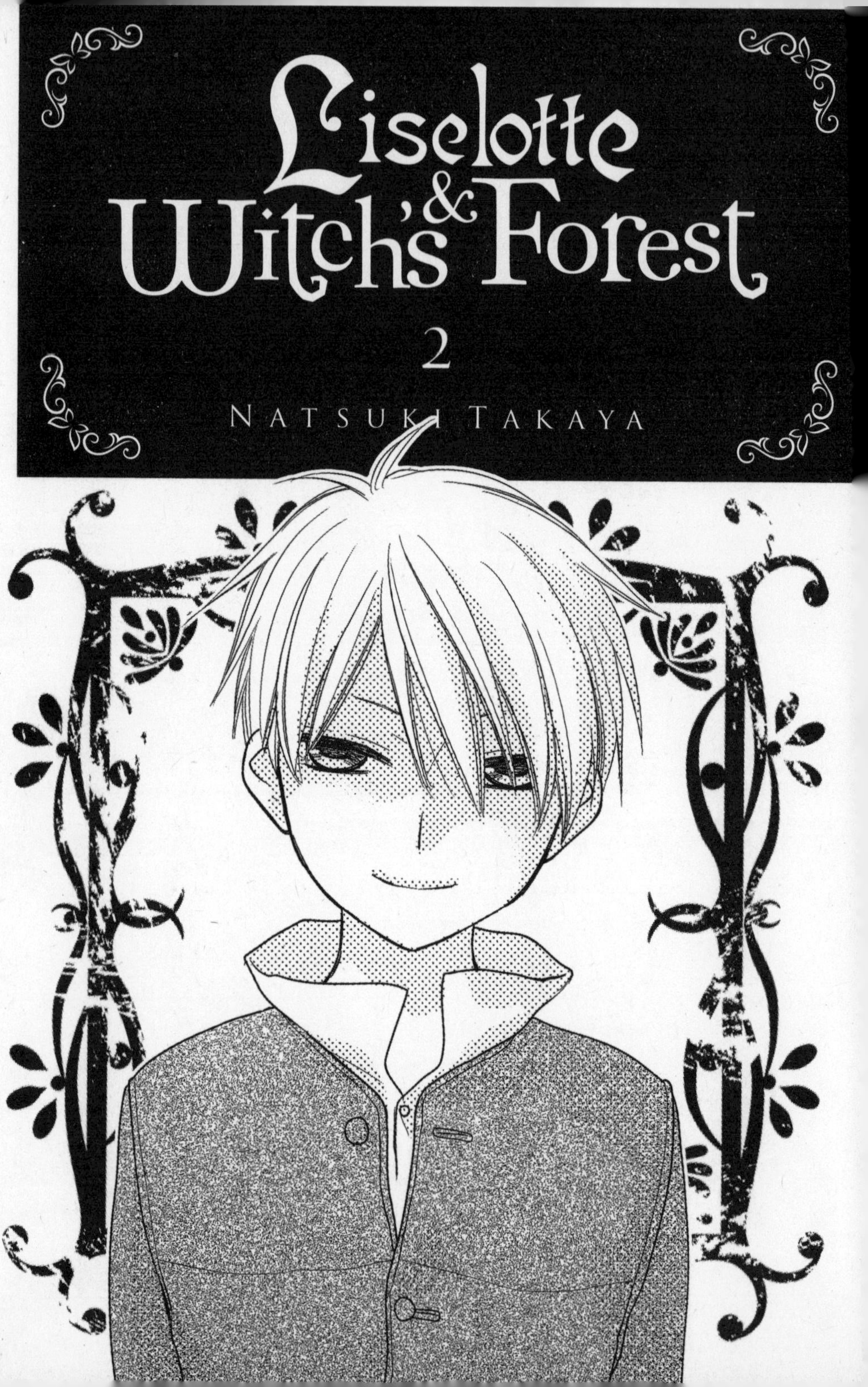

Liselotte & Witch's Forest

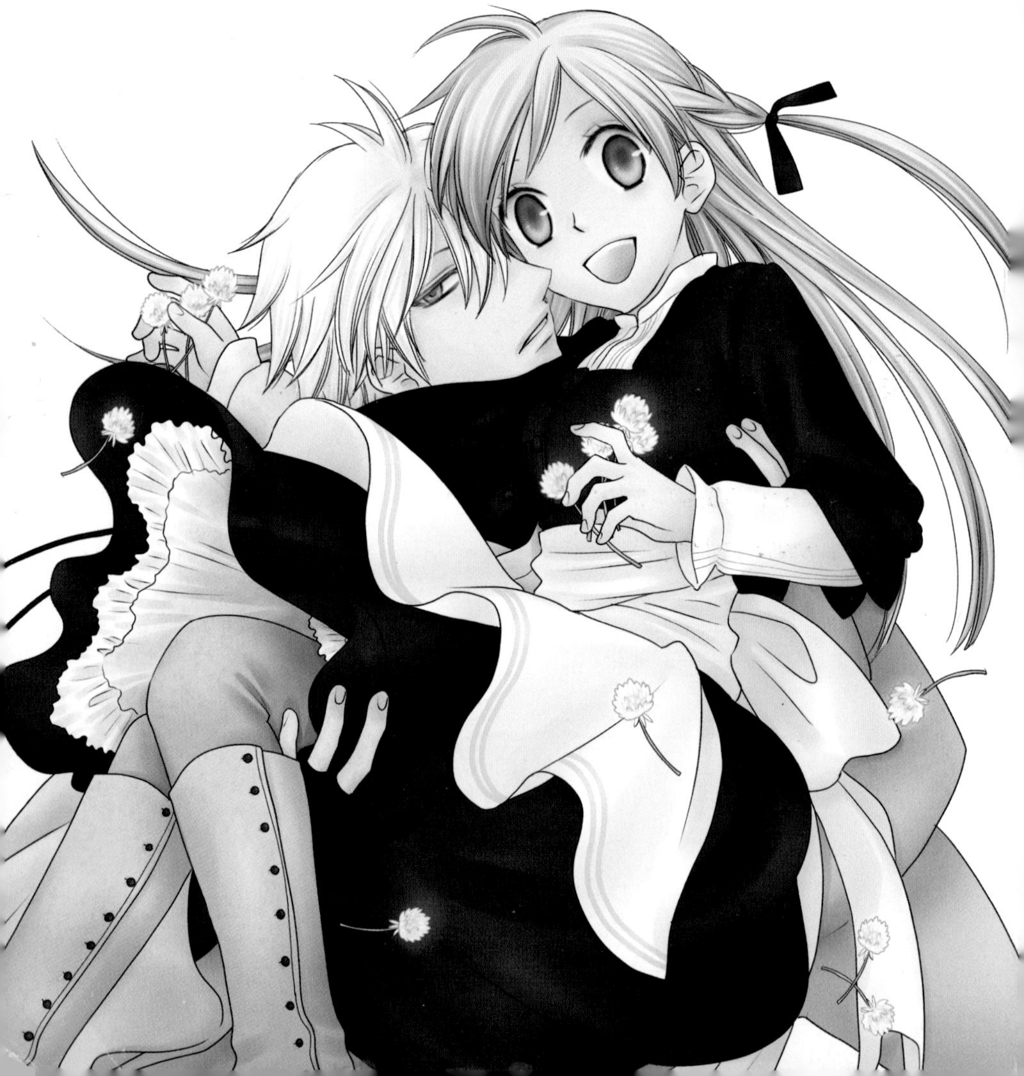